On the Battlefield of Memory

The First World War and American
Remembrance, 1919–1941

Steven Trout

THE UNIVERSITY OF ALABAMA PRESS
Tuscaloosa

Typeface: Baskerville

∞

The paper on which this book is printed meets the minimum requirements of
American National Standard for Information Sciences—Permanence of Paper
for Printed Library Materials, ANSI Z39.48-1984.

Cover photo: *The Return of Private Davis from the Argonne* (1928–1940) by John
Steuart Curry. Oil on canvas, 38 x 52 inc. Courtesy of the Westervelt-Warner
Museum of American Art.

Library of Congress Cataloging-in-Publication Data

Trout, Steven, 1963–
   On the battlefield of memory : the First World War and American remembrance, 1919–1941 / Steven Trout.
      p. cm.
   Includes bibliographical references and index.
   ISBN 978-0-8173-1705-8 (cloth : alk. paper) — ISBN 978-0-8173-8349-7
(electronic) 1. World War, 1914–1918—Social aspects—United States. 2. Collective memory—United States. 3. Memory—Social aspects—United States.
4. World War, 1914–1918—Influence. I. Title.
   D524.7.U6T78 2010
   940.3'1—dc22

                                                              2010003555

To Conrad Trout,
teacher and bookman

Contents

Illustrations

Acknowledgments

This study of collective memory is, like all monographs, ultimately a collective effort. The book's errors and defects are of my own making; its merits reflect the cooperation and assistance of many different people. Among these individuals, two were of particular importance—namely, the pair of anonymous readers who evaluated this manuscript for The University of Alabama Press. Both of these scholars understood where I was going and helped me get there. For the wise advice contained in their detailed reports, I am deeply grateful. And I must thank the staff at The University of Alabama Press for selecting these readers and for offering such expert guidance at every step of the publication process.

My home institution, Fort Hays State University, supported this project in every way, starting with a sabbatical leave in 2007. Without this block of time, I would never have been able to complete such a dense, interdisciplinary project. For this reason, I am deeply indebted to Provost Lawrence Gould, who has supported my scholarly work for more than fifteen years now, and to the members of the FHSU Sabbatical Committee. Other individuals at my institution helped as well. Paul Faber, dean of the College of Arts and Sciences, granted me a course reduction for one semester so that I could bring this study closer to completion; Cheryl Duffy, my department chair in 2007, and Carl Singleton, my current chair, made helpful adjustments to my teaching schedule; and Sheran Powers, head of the Interlibrary Loan Department at Forsyth Library, tracked down each and every one of the literally hundreds of obscure World War I titles that I ordered during my leave. Sheran also convinced the Archives of American Art at the Smithsonian Institution to send me a major portion of the

John Steuart Curry Papers on microfilm. Ray Nolan, a gifted graduate student (now finishing his PhD in history at Kansas State), served for a semester as my research assistant, scouring period newspapers and periodicals for articles related to war commemoration. Many of the primary sources consulted in this study were his discoveries. Ever helpful, Mitchell Weber of the FHSU Center for Teaching Excellence and Learning Technology created the digital images for most of the illustrations in this book.

An interdisciplinary course on war and memory, which I team-taught with my friend and colleague Steven Kite during the spring 2009 semester, sparked a number of ideas that helped shape the final version of this monograph. For some of the most exciting classroom discussions of my career, I am grateful to Steve, a fine historian, and to the students in that class, especially Jodanna Bitner, Morgan Chalfant, Ian Conkey, Chis Dinkel, Brian Gribbin, and Theresa Kraisinger. These excellent graduate students taught me a great deal and, in the process, changed what I thought I knew about American remembrance and World War I.

Research for this book carried me to many different archives, where, without exception, I encountered generous and considerate individuals. Jonathan Casey provided invaluable assistance as I worked in the archives of the National World War I Museum. Kris McCusker of the Special Collections Department at the University of Colorado not only made the Thomas Fletcher scrapbook, an exceedingly fragile artifact, available for my inspection, but she also made a special effort to locate other items relevant to my study. Likewise, the fine staff at the National Archives (College Park, Maryland) listened patiently to my many questions and suggested many leads (few of which failed to pan out), as did the team of archivists at the Dwight D. Eisenhower Presidential Library and the helpful reference librarians at the Kansas History Center Library.

In some cases, due to finances or scheduling, I was unable to visit the site where specific materials are held. Once again, friendly, enthusiastic professionals made sure I obtained what I needed. Joseph J. Hovich, librarian/curator of the American Legion Headquarters Library in Indianapolis, sent me several invaluable items related to the 1928 War Novel Competition. Sarah Dunbar Hamilton at the Schlesinger Library, Harvard University, kindly processed my photocopying request for relevant files in the Mary Lee Papers.

And when it came time to secure permission for the reproduction of words and images, I again met with courtesy and consideration. Howard

Trace at the American Legion Headquarters Library approved my request to feature pages from the *American Legion Monthly* as illustrations. Kristen Bucher of the Cummer Museum of Art and Gardens provided me with a digital image of John Steuart Curry's *Parade to War.* Pam Overmann, curator of the U.S. Navy Art Collection, sent me a high-quality copy of Kerr Eby's *Down the Net.* Ellen Shea of the Schlesinger Library gave me authorization to quote from the Mary Lee Papers. Timothy Rives of the Dwight D. Eisenhower Presidential Library was most helpful in sorting out the permission details regarding Eisenhower's prepresidential papers and the Thomas North Collection. And my friend Virgil Dean, editor of *Kansas History,* graciously allowed the reprinting of material I had published earlier in that fine journal.

An unexpected and exciting moment in my research came when I interviewed Donald Davis, the nephew of the World War I soldier whose posthumous homecoming John Steuart Curry famously depicted in *The Return of Private Davis from the Argonne.* Donald shared family memories and artifacts that helped make my discussion of Curry's painting, featured in chapter 3, one of the centerpieces of this study. I thank him for his generosity not only to me but also to the National World War I Museum, where the bulk of materials related to William L. Davis (donated by Donald) is now preserved.

A number of scholars interested in World War I and cultural history watched this project unfold and offered encouragement along the way. Keith Gandal, Pearl James, Richard Harris, Janis Stout, Jennifer Haytock, Celia Kingsbury, Milton Cohen, Jennifer Keene, and Janet Sharistanian helped convince me, for better or worse, that what I had to say about World War I and American memory could indeed fill an entire monograph. And Daniel Clayton and Thomas Bowie of the Regis University Center for the Study of War Experience, an outstanding oral history archive, likewise helped boost my confidence when I had doubts.

Finally, I must thank those closest to me for putting up with this project for more than two years. Writing a book of this complexity and length produces a necessary monomania that is hard on one's friends—and harder still on one's family. My closest friends—Greg Farley, Avi Kempinski, Daryl Palmer, Martin Parsons, Patrick Quinn, and Robert Rook—probably all hope they will never hear the words "war" and "memory" combined in a sentence again. As for my wife and daughters, all I can do is promise to make amends—and to wait a few years before starting my next monograph.

Prologue

"Guide-Book Ike"

Ruthlessly he struck out commas; without mercy he slaughtered periods. Sternly he dotted "i's." He strangled sentences, scrambled paragraphs, defied stenographers, and cussed draftsmen and messengers in utter abandon. Without respite, and without regard for his personal danger or infringement of copyright, he wrote, unwrote, half-wrote and rewrote above and beyond the call of beauty until stricken with writer's cramp.

> —From the citation for the "Disgusted Service Medal" presented to Dwight David Eisenhower by his staff at the American Battle Monuments Commission, 1929.

In 1937, two years before Europe descended into the Second World War, the American Battle Monuments Commission (ABMC), the organization responsible for the construction and maintenance of permanent American war memorials and cemeteries located overseas, completed its final commemorative project of the Depression era—a comprehensive guidebook titled *American Armies and Battlefields in Europe*. Published in 1938, this 547-page tome provided a complete narrative of American military involvement in the Great War, ultra-detailed itineraries for battlefield visitors, and descriptions and photographs of every American memorial on the former Western Front, as well as the eight official American war cemeteries in France, Belgium, and England. A decade in the making, the book represented a Herculean effort on the part of a small team of U.S. Army officers, who verified each and every detail pertaining to American troop movements, traced and retraced travel routes through the battlefields, and recorded the precise locations of the more than one hundred American war monuments. And these officers did it all without credit, their names absent from the finished volume. "It is unfortunate," remarked one reviewer, "that the present passion for anonymity does not let us know the authors of this book. They have labored well and deserve equally well."[1]

One of those authors who "labored well" was none other than Dwight David Eisenhower. For two extended periods—six months in 1927 and nearly seventeen months in 1928 and 1929—then-major Eisenhower served as an author, editor, and production manager for the guidebook and its precursor, a slimmer book titled *A Guide to the American Battle Fields in Europe* (1927). In so doing, the future supreme commander of Allied forces in Western Europe became immersed not only in the history of American participation in the First World War, a subject that he came to know inside and out, but also in the processes of remembrance. Indeed, Eisenhower's service with the ABMC constituted a crash course in the often complex political and social dimensions of memory. By the time of his generalship in World War II, he would understand how modern wars are memorialized, and, more important, he would understand the urgencies that drive military commemoration. The story of his involvement with the ABMC underscores the frenetic nature of American war remembrance in the 1920s and 1930s (contrary to the myth that most Americans quickly forgot about the Great War) and illuminates a neglected connection between the two world wars, the first of several such links described in this study.

Ironically, when he joined the ABMC, Eisenhower had no firsthand knowledge of the First World War battlefields that would quickly become his area of formidable expertise. The war ended before his tank corps, stationed at Gettysburg, Pennsylvania, had completed its training. However, the major's lack of combat experience was arguably an advantage. One can imagine the kind of battlefield guidebook that Douglas MacArthur or George S. Patton might have produced. Unlike officers who had served overseas, Eisenhower had no fierce loyalties, no attachment to a particular combat division or regiment (or prejudices against other units), and no heroic reputation to protect. What he did have— political finesse, an aptitude for organization, and above-average writing ability (displayed, for example, in an article that he had published earlier in the *Infantry Journal*[2]) —made him the perfect choice for a project that if not quite on the scale of the D-day landings nevertheless involved a staggering number of details and a broad range of competing political interests. Moreover, according to biographer Stephen E. Ambrose, Eisenhower knew when he signed up to work on the 1927 version of the guidebook that he could count on his younger brother Milton, whose "special talent was journalism," for assistance with the writing.[3] Then the assistant director of the Department of Agriculture, Milton lived, conveniently enough, near Eisenhower's apartment in Washington, DC.

Recommended by Gen. Fox Conner, his commanding officer during the war, Eisenhower was personally appointed to the Historical Section of the ABMC by its chairman, John J. Pershing, in January 1927. For an officer in the funding-starved, promotion-scarce U.S. Army of the interwar decades, it was not, on the face of it, an especially desirable post. However, as biographer Peter Lyon observes, service in an organization devoted to the memory of the nation's fallen could not help but evoke powerful feelings or carry a certain degree of prestige. Work at the AMBC was "a trust, a matter of military honor, like being selected as one of the guards at the bier of a once and future hero, and so appointment to the commission was much prized and reserved for the most promising of officers."[4] In addition, Eisenhower's assignment did not lack challenges, something the ambitious officer craved. Although most of the ABMC's memorials in Europe would not be completed until the 1930s, Pershing ordered the Historical Section to begin work immediately on a guidebook that would provide American visitors to the Western Front with useful, accurate information about American wartime operations and the myriad hills, rivers, valleys, towns, and villages where these operations had occurred. And Pershing wanted the book fast—before the American Legion staged its Second AEF (American Expeditionary Forces) convention in Paris, an event expected to draw nearly twenty thousand veterans, most of whom would tour at least some of the American battlefields. Since the legion's gathering was scheduled for November, the officers assigned to write and to edit the guidebook were given just six months to complete their task.

Eisenhower's job description reflected his superiors' confidence in his abilities. As Maj. Xenophon H. Price, the secretary of the ABMC and Pershing's executive officer, made clear in a memo dated January 26, 1927, the new appointee would essentially run the entire operation: "Major Dwight D. Eisenhower . . . will hereafter have direct supervision over all work connected with the guide book. Officers working on this book will make sure that he is informed of the progress of their work up to the present time and will report to him in the future for instructions."[5] Only Price himself, with whom Eisenhower had a sometimes difficult relationship, would exercise greater authority over the project. In all, Eisenhower coordinated the efforts of five U.S. Army officers and one representative of the U.S. Marine Corps. Responsibilities were carefully divided among them. In addition to his supervisory role, Eisenhower teamed up with his brother to write the "general narratives" for the volume—the accounts of various campaigns, in other words, that provided a necessary context for the battlefield excursions that the book described. Another member of the team, a Captain Cahill, prepared the maps; Captain Fuller prepared the itineraries; and so forth.[6] Eisenhower's biographers disagree about the degree of difficulty attached to the project. Stephen Ambrose, for example, describes the guidebook as a "scissors-and-paste job" that required relatively little effort from Eisenhower.[7] Peter Lyon, on the other hand, stresses the volume of material—"maps, pictures, statistical data, historical data, chronologies and so on, most of it superfluous"—that Eisenhower had to whip into "coherent shape" in just a few months.[8] Add inexperience to the mix (neither Eisenhower nor his subordinates had ever worked on any kind of book before), along with the demand for absolute accuracy in military details (every member of the Second AEF could be expected to look up information on his own unit), and it becomes clear that the project was hardly stress-free. Further complicating the writing process was the fact that Eisenhower and most of his staff worked out of the ABMC headquarters in Washington, DC—an ocean away from the battlefields themselves. Much of the information about French roads and topography had been collected earlier, and as Eisenhower would learn following the book's publication, some of that information was erroneous or already out of date.

Despite these obstacles, copies of *A Guide to the American Battle Fields in Europe* became available for purchase from the U.S. Government Printing Office in August 1927, well ahead of schedule. The book's press release, which Eisenhower probably wrote and then revised in consultation with the ABMC's Press Relations Section, captures well the strengths of the volume (and the expanded edition that would appear twelve years later), especially its careful consideration of audience:

> The publication is in no sense technical in nature. Rather it is a plain, straight forward [*sic*] story told in every day [*sic*] language in which as far as possible purely military terms have been carefully avoided. In addition, for the benefit of persons who have not been in the military service a glossary is included which defines unusual terms and expressions employed in the text.
>
> Altogether, it is a work which will undoubtedly enjoy a wide distribution, and will furnish to the public, at nominal cost, a clear and concise understanding of our part in the World War.[9]

As expected, veterans bound for the legion's Paris convention snatched the book up quickly. According to a later press release, "Twenty thousand copies of 'A Guide to the American Battle Fields' were printed and the supply was completely exhausted within nine months."[10] For his leadership in bringing such a successful government publication to press, Eisenhower received a copy of a letter from Pershing, who wrote to Maj. Gen. Robert H. Allen, Chief of Infantry, that the major had "shown superior ability not only in visualizing his work as a whole but in executing its many details in an efficient and timely manner." (The reference to the book as "his" [Eisenhower's] is telling.) And the ordinarily dour Pershing did not stop there: what Eisenhower had done "was accomplished only by the exercise of unusual intelligence and constant devotion to duty."[11] Eisenhower's own quiet pride in the volume is suggested by his inscription in the copy that he presented to his older brother Arthur, a bank executive in Kansas City: "I hope that in this book, which I helped prepare, you will find something of interest."[12]

On August 15, his assignment completed, Eisenhower left the ABMC to attend the Army War College, little suspecting that his entanglement with what he later called "a sort of Baedeker to the actions of Americans in the war" was far from over.[13] After graduating in June 1928, he learned that Pershing wanted him back. Not surprisingly, given the guidebook's popularity, the ABMC had already drawn up plans for a revised, expanded edition, and if Eisenhower would agree to resume his duties as writer and editor, he would be assigned to an especially attractive post: the ABMC office in Paris. Although Eisenhower's other option at this point—a general staff position—made the most sense career-wise, his family had never been to Europe before, and the prospect of living in Paris proved, in the end, irresistible. His wife, Mamie, insisted upon it.

Shortly before leaving for France, however, Eisenhower discovered that his reputation as a wordsmith could be a curse as well as a blessing. Indeed, his well-known facility with prose now landed him in an awkward situation faced sooner or later by all writers—namely, that of being asked, by an individual who cannot be refused, to give editorial advice that is likely to offend. In this case the person desirous of Eisenhower's opinion was none other than John J. Pershing. By 1928 Pershing had completed a considerable portion of his lengthy war memoir (published in 1931 as *My Experiences in the World War*), having worked steadily on "the evolving manuscript" during his many trips to France on commission business.[14] But distilling the complex Saint Mihiel and Meuse-Argonne campaigns into an account that made sense to a general readership proved difficult, and Pershing was dissatisfied with what he had written so far. Would Eisenhower look over the manuscript? Probably with reluctance, Eisenhower did so and suggested that in the chapters devoted to the AEF's climactic operations Pershing should abandon "diary form" in favor of a seamless narrative. The former commander in chief took the criticism well—so well, in fact, that he asked Eisenhower to rewrite the chapters for him. With "considerable effort," Eisenhower completed this assignment in just a few days and to Pershing's satisfaction. The Iron Commander, he noted with pride, was actually "happy" with the rewritten chapters.[15]

However, the major's efforts received a quite different response from Pershing's primary editorial consultant—Col. George Marshall. As Eisenhower later recalled in *At Ease: Stories I Tell to Friends* (1967), within days of submitting the revised chapters, he received a less-than-friendly visit from Marshall (the two men had never met before), who explained that he had advised Pershing to restore the sections on the Saint Mihiel and Meuse-Argonne battles to their original form.[16] Eisenhower stood his ground before the senior officer, but to no avail. It was a unique moment in history: two future commanders, among the most powerful men of World War II, arguing over the best way to present the personal recollections of the top American general of World War I. Ultimately, Pershing deferred to Marshall, and in *At Ease* Eisenhower could not resist pointing out that many readers of the published memoir, which won the Pulitzer Prize for History in 1932 (a tribute more to Pershing's generalship than to his writing ability), found its account of the AEF's largest battles all but impossible to follow.[17]

In late July 1928, the Eisenhowers (Dwight, Mamie, and their son John) sailed for France, where they would live for more than a year. All three would remember the sojourn fondly. Comfortably ensconced on the Quai d'Auteuil in Paris, within walking distance of the ABMC office, the family entertained frequently—so much so that their apartment became known as "Club Eisenhower." However, the assignment meant considerably more to Eisenhower than, as Ambrose puts it, "a restful, pleasant fifteen months, spent pretty much doing nothing of any importance in a charming setting."[18] Equipped with a motor car and a French driver who doubled as a translator, Eisenhower traveled up and down the former Western Front, studying the terrain and making corrections to the itineraries originally presented in the 1927 guidebook. In the process, it is fair to say, he became one of the U.S. Army's foremost (if unofficial) experts on the topography of the American battlefields, able at a moment's notice to describe the villages, woods, and hills that any given unit in the AEF encountered as it advanced.

His biographers have typically seen little of importance in these excursions, or in the terrain-related minutiae that Eisenhower absorbed, perhaps because his tours sometimes took on the character of pleasure outings.[19] In *At Ease* he nostalgically recalled his encounters amid the battlefields with the "sound and friendly people" of rural France. "Whenever possible," he wrote, "I stopped along the road to join groups of road workers who were eating their noonday lunch." Sometimes accompanied by his son, the gregarious officer would carry groceries and "an extra bottle of *vin rouge*" in the trunk of his car and share them with the workers.[20] Compared with the stresses and strains of his later life, these were undoubtedly happy times. However, travels in such blood-soaked regions as the Aisne-Marne and the Meuse-Argonne must have been sobering as well as cathartic for a soldier so immersed in the memory of a conflict that he had narrowly missed. Everywhere along the former front line, Eisenhower encountered (perhaps with an understandable feeling of guilt) reminders of the more than fifty thousand Americans who perished there, most in less than six months of ferocious fighting. It was a landscape of ghosts, and in more ways than one. Phantoms of the past and of the future—of the AEF and of the forces that Eisenhower would later move over the same countryside—passed the major's motorcar.

Eisenhower's duties in Paris and subsequently back in Washington, DC (he would spend nearly a month and a half with the ABMC after his return from Europe), were likewise more taxing and more important to his education as a future commander than most scholars have granted. Although most of the records in the ABMC's Paris office were lost after the German declaration of war in 1941, circumstantial evidence suggests that Eisenhower's second stint with the commission demanded as much, if not more, from him as the first. Since the revised guidebook would be nearly double the length of its predecessor and would "meet the need for a concise reference book and a brief history of the American Expeditionary Forces," the amount of research and fact-checking required went well beyond what Eisenhower and his staff had been able to handle so expeditiously in 1927.[21] Expanded accounts of major battles and smaller operations in specific sectors were required, along with more reliable maps. In addition, Pershing wanted new chapters on the Vosges Front, American military operations in Italy and northern Russia, and "Interesting Facts and General Information Concerning the American Expeditionary Forces." These had to be started from scratch. And, finally, the steady completion of the ABMC's battlefield monuments (few of which had existed except as architect's plans in 1927) and permanent cemeteries added yet another dimension to the project. Each monument and cemetery would have to be photographed, situated within an up-to-date itinerary, and described with perfect accuracy. Combined, these requirements postponed the book's publication until 1938.

Thus, when not studying the actual ground where American troops had fought and died, Eisenhower found himself once again at the center of an editorial maelstrom, surrounded by an ever growing number of historical prose narratives (some of which he wrote, some of which he delegated to other officers), thousands of official war photos and images of memorials (the final volume would contain a total of 520 photographs, many with captions penned by Eisenhower), and dozens upon dozens of travel itineraries and maps (perhaps the most tiresome part of the project), which required almost constant correction due to the postwar rebuilding of devastated areas and the construction of new French roads. Eisenhower's sensitivity to language and his necessary ruthlessness as an editor come through in the rather spotty correspondence that has survived from this period of his career. For example, in a letter to Price dated October 28, 1929, near the end of his time with the commission, Eisenhower took two of his subordinates to task for "looseness of expression," and he stressed the importance of writing *outside* a professional soldier's vocabulary and mind-set.[22] As it turned out, Eisenhower's editorial philosophy left its mark. The prose in the published guidebook, much of it revamped years after his departure from the ABMC, reflects his emphasis on exactitude *and* accessibility.

The kinds of micro-level military details tracked down by Eisenhower and his colleagues—along with the rarified, scholarly title of their office, the Historical Section—suggests a team of researchers whose sole purpose was to dispel the fog of war through the disciplined pursuit of pure fact and linguistic precision. However, in this instance the writing of history could not be so easily disentangled from memory. (Definitions of terms such as "memory" and "remembrance" appear in the introduction to this study.) After all, the federal organization that produced *American Armies and Battlefields in Europe* was, if you will, in the memory business—and on a grand scale. As massive as any European monument at the Somme or Verdun, killing fields that saw far greater suffering and loss of life than the AEF's hallowed grounds, the ABMC's memorials in the Aisne-Marne, Saint Mihiel, and Meuse-Argonne regions are, in part, Pershing's personal rebuke to the Allied generals who had belittled America's military contribution—and who had had repeatedly pressured the AEF's commander to parcel his troops out to French and British units. These colossal monuments, visible from miles away and dominating the surrounding landscape, leave little question, at least for American visitors, that the AEF won the war for the Allies. Likewise, the generous spacing between grave markers in the ABMC's eight permanent cemeteries leaves a misleading impression, making American combat losses (terrible though they were) seem comparable to those of France and Great Britain. Although supposedly compiled by objective historians, who (as Eisenhower put it) "knew the facts of the case," *American Armies and Battlefields* could not help but share in this triumphal agenda.[23] The book points the way—it is a guidebook, after all—to monuments that are, in turn, signifiers of a governmentally sanctioned version of memory. And in its language the published text often contradicts its supposedly objective, "historical" intentions. Consider, for example, the following passage, which appears in the very section (an account of the 28th and 32nd Divisions' attacks along the Ourq River) that Eisenhower earlier highlighted in his letter to Price: "The fighting was of a most severe character and although most of the American divisions were participating in an offensive for the first time *the natural courage and fighting spirit of the American soldiers* carried them forward to accomplishments which could not have been excelled by veteran assault divisions" (my emphasis).[24] Given the poor performance of so many novice divisions in the later Meuse-Argonne battle, this nod to official commemorative discourse ("natural courage," "fighting spirit") is more propaganda than history.

While the urgencies of memory inevitably shaped the historical details over which Eisenhower and his colleagues agonized, the issue of *whose* memory the ABMC served affected the guidebook project as well. Predictably, as the Historical Section made its revisions, calls came in from various branches of the armed forces for more attention and coverage, along with implicit allegations that the ABMC favored the army over the Marine Corps and the navy. For example, among the ABMC documents housed at the Eisenhower Library is a letter to Eisenhower from Capt. Clifton B. Cates, USMC, which includes a list of more than a dozen recommended corrections. Not surprisingly, most of the errors detected by the captain in the 1927 edition related to his own wartime unit, the Marine

Brigade of the Second Division; for example: "On page 194, paragraph #7, it states that St. Etienne was cleared of Germans on October 8th, by the 142nd Infantry, assisted by the Marines. This is not the case as the town was captured by the 1st Battalion, 6th Marines."[25] Cates assured Eisenhower that he had no "axe to grind" nor any wish to "usurp [the major's] authority," but the partisan nature of his requested changes was clear.[26] For Eisenhower, such situations provided valuable training in diplomacy, and in this instance he responded, sensibly enough, by investigating each of the officer's claims. A duplicate copy of Cates's letter, with Eisenhower's handwritten marginalia, shows that the Historical Section made some of the recommended revisions but deemed others "insignificant" or "unnecessary."[27]

Another example of Eisenhower's initiation into the politics of memory is amusing—although he probably found little to laugh about at the time. On July 19, 1928, Pershing received from Rear Adm. Andrew T. Long a list of errors detected in the naval chapter of the 1927 edition. In his cover letter the admiral indicated that he had recently met with Eisenhower, who had assured him "that when the book is later revised, a fuller and more comprehensive chapter on the Navy will be included."[28] Nothing, it would seem, was further from Pershing's intentions, and two days later he fired off a response to Long, in which he claimed (somewhat disingenuously) that the "general revision of the book" was by no means certain, but that "Navy authorities" would "be freely consulted regarding any material affecting that department which *may* be included" (my emphasis).[29] Obviously in hot water, Eisenhower wrote to Pershing with his side of the story the same day. Under an emphatic heading, which reads "*The facts of the case are:*" Eisenhower explained that he had made no promises whatsoever to Long, and he bluntly described the admiral's recalcitrance: "Admiral Long stated emphatically that the Navy view had been, and still is, that the chapter [on the navy] should either be a fuller account of naval operations, or omitted entirely. He said the Naval authorities could under no conditions give their consent to regarding a mere correction of existing errors as an adequate revision of the narrative as a whole."[30] In other words, Long wanted a lengthier, more substantial treatment of the U.S. Navy in the revised guidebook—or nothing at all. Perhaps because of the admiral's inflexibility and apparent prevarication, Pershing opted for neither. The wartime operations of the U.S. Navy received exactly eight pages in the 1938 revised edition, the same amount of space allotted in the original guidebook.

Because the ABMC's real purpose was not to record history but to shape memory (always a magnet for controversy), service in the organization did not lack drama or even, as we have seen, warfare of a sort, waged primarily between competing branches of the armed forces. However, by the summer of 1929 Eisenhower had had enough. Now nearing age forty, he craved the opportunity to command troops or, short of that, to participate in war planning (as opposed to historical research). Despite the prestige attached to service with the commission, he had come to feel that his career was going nowhere. In late August, after discussions with Major Price, Eisenhower received what he wanted—transfer orders. Following a three-week leave, just enough time for a grand tour of the Continent, he would depart for Washington, DC, aboard the USS *Leviathan*. Then, once in Washington, he would continue to work for the ABMC until, it was tacitly understood, a new assignment could be provided for him by the War Department.

In many respects the European vacation that Eisenhower took during his leave was the most memorable—and revealing—portion of his fifteen months overseas. Accompanied by friends, Maj. William Gruber and his wife, Helen, the Eisenhowers drove an incredible eighteen hundred miles (often on roads that would today be considered primitive) in seventeen days, taking in sights in France, Belgium, Germany, and Switzerland. It was the kind of trip that just a few decades earlier had been within the reach of only the wealthiest, most cosmopolitan of Americans, the kind portrayed in Henry James novels, and its impact on Eisenhower, who had grown up in rural Kansas, comes across in the detailed journal that he coauthored with Gruber (Eisenhower wrote entries for the first half of the trip; Gruber, the second). In a way, the vacation was a surrogate form of the Great War, which Eisenhower had missed out on in 1918, and like many a doughboy before him, he enthusiastically, sometimes floridly, recorded his impressions of the Old World. In Germany, for example, Eisenhower noted the friendliness and courtesy of the people (referred to by most Americans as "Huns" just a decade earlier), as well as the stunning beauty of the Black Forest, where "[l]ittle villages nestle along the rushing streams, and everywhere the countryside seems cool, fresh and clean."[31] No stranger to travel writing, the guidebook author sometimes jotted down his impressions in a self-consciously literary fashion, as when describing an alpine lake: "Brilliant morning sun. Tiny craft skimming the sparkling surface. Boatmen's bodies tanned to a nut-brown. Glistening green slopes. Exhilarating air."[32]

Gruber's section of the diary, which covers the journey from Geneva back to Paris via the battlefields of the Western Front, is far more prosaic; however, it contains one of the most illuminating descriptions of Eisenhower's immersion in the memory of the First World War. For both men (Gruber saw action as an artillery officer in the Second Division), the final days of this European vacation became a trip into the American military past. All roads, in a sense, led back to the AEF's sites of memory. On the morning of Wednesday, September 11, 1929, the party reached the Saint Mihiel sector, where Gruber pointed out, among other things, "a hole in the side of a steam bank" that he had once used as a command post.[33] He showed where "mines & tank traps had barely been avoided."[34] While Gruber related his firsthand experiences to the group, Eisenhower explained the battle in a way that left even the combat veteran Gruber in awe: "He had studied the operations so thoroughly & could provide us with so much information. My information," Gruber conceded, "was limited to the restricted areas in which my battalion had fought."[35] From Thiacourt, the party drove to Verdun, "a monument of human courage and sacrifice," then stopped at the summit of Montfaucon, the intimidating peak where the crown prince of Germany had once had his headquarters (and where the ABMC's enormous Meuse-Argonne Memorial would soon be completed).[36] In the late afternoon the motorists pulled into the American war cemetery at Romagne, which "Ike and Mamie" had visited "many times before," and located the grave of Helen Gruber's cousin, a second lieutenant killed in the Argonne fighting just three days before the armistice.[37]

The next day, Mamie and Helen, who probably felt they had seen enough battlefields, stayed behind at the village of Romagne to rest while Eisenhower and Gruber made a solo expedition to war sites in the Meuse-Argonne and Champagne regions. "Ike," Gruber wrote, "was a grand battlefield guide for he had been over these areas time & again & had written the excellent American Battle Monuments Commission guide book of the battlefields."[38] However, for Eisenhower, this final pilgrimage to the Western Front (he would not see France again until World War II) must have been bittersweet. No one knew more about the battlefields, but traveling with Gruber probably reminded him, again and again, of the intensity of war experience—something that Eisenhower could only imagine. For example, when the two men drove into the village of Exermont, where Gruber had put his regiment of field artillery into position on October 31, 1918, the veteran related incidents that "were as vivid as if they had occurred the day before."[39] Gruber recalled a forced march through the Argonne Forest, at the end of which German planes, with the Americans at their mercy, dropped propaganda leaflets on them. And when the pair of officers reached Blanc Mont, the site of one of the Second Division's costliest battles, Gruber revisited a position from which his regiment had laid down "a tremendous amount of firing in supporting attacks on St. Etienne and in repulsing counterattacks."[40] In all, the two men covered 140 miles of memory-rich territory, hitting virtually every point of military interest on both sides of the Argonne Forest—an apt farewell, on Eisenhower's part, to the Western Front (of the *First* World War, that is) and to his service with the commission.

But shaking free of the ABMC again proved difficult. By September 26, 1929, Eisenhower was back at the ABMC office in Washington, DC, eagerly anticipating a new assignment outside the commission. Price had charged him with several tasks, none of which seemed likely to keep him busy for long. For example, the Paris office needed accurate lists of the missing for the ABMC's cemetery chapels, where the names of soldiers who had no known graves would be honored on bronze plaques. Eisenhower was to "do everything possible to expedite this work."[41] In addition, Price ordered Eisenhower to find two more officers for the European branch of the Historical Section and to secure the appropriate orders from the War Department. On September 30, confident that these assignments and others were nearing completion, Eisenhower formalized his request to leave the commission.

Price approved the major's request, but, as it turned out, Eisenhower's departure was delayed for several weeks. Even so simple a matter as obtaining the officers that Price needed proved challenging, thanks to War Department red tape, and before his service with the ABMC was over, Eisenhower would complain of the "many conferences, arguments, useless talks, and irritated delays" that he endured while completing this task.[42]

Things went better but just as slowly with the lists of the missing. Now an experienced editor, accustomed to the vagaries of information, Eisenhower wisely concluded that the parents or siblings of missing soldiers should be given the chance to check names; otherwise, errors would inevitably find their way onto the plaques. Thus, soon after his arrival in Washington, he introduced a timetable for correspondence with relatives, one that would give them reasonable time to mail in corrections. On October 18 Eisenhower proudly reported the results of his efforts to

Price: "Day by day we are getting additional proof of the wisdom of sending the lists of missing to relatives. The Veterans Bureau also has uncovered many mistakes. In two cases in the Navy, the parents have reported that men carried as missing have actually been brought home and buried in family plots."[43] The sensitive task of eliminating errors in the lists of servicemen whose bodies had been blown to pieces, or lost in the mud of the Western Front, or swallowed by the Atlantic Ocean rounded out Eisenhower's service with the commission. It was a poignant coda. In France the future general had surveyed the battlefields with the dispassionate eye of the professional soldier, noting the military dimensions of the landscape and reconstructing the movements not of individuals, but of regiments and brigades. In contrast, ensuring that the missing, who numbered more than four thousand, received suitable—and accurate—commemoration involved a direct confrontation with war's human cost, with its myriad personal tragedies. Not a bad form of training, one could say, for an officer who would later make decisions that directly affected thousands of American lives.

In late October Eisenhower's service with the commission finally came to a end. As a parting gift, his friends in the Historical Section (the "Second American Unexpurgated Editionary Farce") presented him with "The Disgusted Service Medal," a decoration whose accompanying citation, a delightful parody of military discourse, presented editing as mock combat.

> Refusing to be evacuated or to have his ink eradicated, and continuing his gory singlehanded assault [on the revised edition], he whipped pages into shape, deleted plates, revised chapters, and, with the help of God and a handful of erasers, pushed on at the point of pen and pencil until he fell dripping with ink within the first revision, thereby assuring the success of his mission.
>
> For these meritorious acts he received many decorations, gained the admiration of his fellow citizens and won the immortal title of GUIDE-BOOK IKE.[44]

"Guide-Book Ike" did not stick as a nickname. If it had, scholars today would perhaps think differently about Eisenhower's life before 1941 and its often overlooked intersection with the memory of the First World War. During the decade that followed his release from the Historical Section, Eisenhower obtained assignments that, without question, did far more for his career. For example, while attached to the office of the assistant secretary of war (his first post-ABMC position), the former historian helped draft mobilization plans for "American industry and manpower in the event of world war."[45] The *next* conflict, as opposed to the one that ended in 1918, became Eisenhower's focus; with his new assignment, he was, as the editors of his selected prewar papers write, finally where he wanted to be—"*on the inside*, observing the maneuvers necessary to match the army's growing needs with the politicians' demands for austerity" (my emphasis).[46]

And then there was Eisenhower's critical six-year connection (1932–1938) with Douglas MacArthur, first as MacArthur's Washington assistant (a three-year assignment that coincided with the general's tenure as army chief of staff) and later as one of his most trusted staff officers in the Philippines. By this point it seemed that "Guide-Book Ike" had at last shaken free from the war that he had missed. However, during the first year of Eisenhower's service with the general, World War I once again cast its shadow across his career—and this time in a particularly disturbing way. In July 1932 Eisenhower stood at MacArthur's side as the "American Caesar" ordered approximately one thousand U.S. Army troops, including members of the Third Cavalry led by George S. Patton, to drive World War I veterans known as the Bonus Marchers from Washington, DC.[47] Ironically, the former guidebook author now found himself in the grotesque position of having to take up arms against men whose battles he had earlier celebrated and whose footsteps he had followed while traveling up and down the Western Front. And a very different kind of war memorial from those that he had seen erected by the ABMC in France now confronted him: spread across the Anacostia Flats, the Bonus Army's Camp Marks, a bustling Hooverville where nearly five thousand veterans at a time lived in shacks constructed of plywood and tin, presented a grim monument to the federal government's failure to provide for its former citizen soldiers.

For Eisenhower, who recognized the Bonus Marchers for what they were—down-and-out veterans with nowhere to go (rather than "Reds" bent on a reign of terror)—military action against them was, as he later wrote in his official report, "a disagreeable task" undertaken partly with the interests of the marchers themselves in mind.[48] Thousands of men crowded into makeshift quarters invited disease, thereby posing a danger to themselves and others. However, for MacArthur, who subscribed to the paranoid notion that Communists had orchestrated the Bonus March, the breakup of the veterans' camp represented an opportunity for glory.

As biographer Merle Miller comments, a photograph taken of the two men just before the Bonus Marchers' eviction says it all: "Eisenhower looks as if he wished he were anywhere else, while MacArthur looks delighted."[49] During the mayhem that ensued, MacArthur displayed characteristic flamboyance and an equally characteristic disregard for orders. And Eisenhower, his subordinate, covered for him. Indeed, Eisenhower's report for the secretary of war, written in MacArthur's name, failed to mention that the general had deliberately disobeyed President Hoover by clearing the Anacostia Flats. Hoover's directive called for the removal of the Bonus Marchers from some abandoned warehouses and from the capital's business district, not their expulsion from the entire city. MacArthur had charged forward anyway. Eisenhower also held his tongue when it came to the excessive violence directed at the ragged veterans and their families. It was the Bonus Marchers, he less-than-plausibly asserted, who started the fires that consumed Camp Marks.[50] Press photographs and newsreels of MacArthur's soldiers in action showed otherwise.[51]

As we will see in chapter 1 of this study, the Bonus Army represented an especially dramatic mobilization, driven from the bottom up, of memory in the service of politics. On the streets of Washington, DC, in 1932, Eisenhower encountered remembrance at its most violent and divisive. Nothing could have been further removed from the sequestered operations of the ABMC's Historical Section. Thus, not surprisingly, most biographers devote more pages to Eisenhower's participation in the "disagreeable" events of a single day than to his entire period of "disgusted service" with the ABMC. However, when placed within the wider cultural history of America between the wars, Eisenhower's nearly two years as a historical researcher, editor, and author take on greater significance. For example, his tenure as a war historian in the late 1920s coincides with an especially important phase in the ongoing debate, much of it conducted via literature and film, over the meaning of American participation in the Great War. While Eisenhower and his colleagues in the Historical Section tracked down military facts that would eventually be situated within the federal government's official version of memory, powerful alternative visions became common cultural currency.

Nineteen twenty-nine, a year of turbulent memory conflicts of various kinds, saw Erich Maria Remarque's *All Quiet on the Western Front*, the most popular war novel ever written, become a mega–best seller in the United

States—but not without strong criticism from veterans who were skeptical of the German writer's version of war experience.[52] Triggered in part by Remarque's success, novels and memoirs that were focused on the Great War (collectively known simply as "war books") flooded the American market. In all, no fewer than thirteen major American war books came out in 1929 (including Ernest Hemingway's *A Farewell to Arms* and William Faulkner's *Sartoris*),[53] and still more would appear in 1930, along with important cinematic spectacles such as Howard Hughes's *Hell's Angels* and Lewis Milestone's Academy Award–winning version of *All Quiet*.[54] While Eisenhower roamed the battlefields in France, the American Legion and Houghton-Mifflin teamed up to offer a twenty-five-thousand-dollar prize—approximately three hundred thousand dollars in today's currency—for the best American novel of the Great War. The controversy over the contest's outcome, addressed later in this study, received considerable press coverage. And in New York's theater district, where Maxwell Anderson and Laurence Stalling's smash hit *What Price Glory?* (1924) had earlier established the First World War as a dependable draw for theatergoing audiences, R. C. Sherriff's British war play, *Journey's End* (1928), began its successful American run.[55] Nineteen twenty-nine was also the year when the United States Congress, in an unprecedented move, voted to give so-called Gold Star Mothers, women who had lost sons or daughters in the war, the chance to visit the ABMC's cemeteries at government expense. President Calvin Coolidge signed the legislation into law shortly before leaving office, and in 1930, within a few months of Eisenhower's return to Washington, DC, members of the first Gold Star Mothers' Pilgrimage set off for the former Western Front.

Contrary to the assertions of some historians, widespread fascination with the First World War remained relatively constant in America between 1919 and 1941. However, the tail end of the first postwar decade stands out as a period of especially frenetic activity related to memory. And Eisenhower was, if you will, "on the inside" of this activity, just as he would later be "on the inside" when it came to war planning and politics. Moreover, the text that "Guide-Book Ike" helped author later became an important cultural touchstone on the eve of World War II. In other words, through his work in the Historical Section, Eisenhower both received an education in the dynamics of memory *and* made his own direct (if anonymous) contribution to the culturally pervasive debate and ongoing reinterpretation that the First World War inspired.

Given the atmosphere of international crisis at the time, reviewers of *American Armies and Battlefields in Europe* (1938) tended to read the revised guidebook through the lens of contemporary events. And, for many, the book's facts and figures added up to a cautionary tale with an isolationist message. For instance, the unsigned review in the *Roanoke World News*, titled "Two Million an Hour," opened as follows: "Americans who are glibly discussing our possible participation in another World War may be interested in some figures on the last war."[56] Perhaps not surprisingly, since the late 1930s and early 1940s were hardly the best times for Americans to visit the AEF's battlefields (in this respect, the book's timing could not have been more ironic), the review ignored entirely the guidebook's detailed itineraries and maps and focused instead on the statistics contained in the "Interesting Facts and General Information" section. For example, by the time of the armistice, the reviewer noted, the Great War had cost the United States an average of two million dollars per hour and consumed an unimaginable amount of industrial materiel: "Ammunition expended by the A.E.F. in combat included 302,292,443 rifle cartridges, 21,385,163 pistol cartridges, [and] 2,274,229 one-pounder shells."[57] Although never stated outright, the reviewer's main point was difficult to miss: the ABMC's guidebook documented a colossal waste of lives and resources.

But not everyone read the text in this fashion. Published in 1940, just after the German blitzkrieg in Western Europe, Leslie E. Edmonds's review in the *Topeka Capital Journal* angrily imagined the AEF's monuments defiled by Hitler's armies:

> As the Nazi of today, who is the Boche of yesterday, sweeps over the fields of "World War I," retaking in reverse order the cities and towns, the hills and valleys, and crossing the rivers whose names loom so large in the annals of American fighting forces, one may well wonder how sleep our dead. For nearly twenty-two years America, Canada and other friends of France . . . have consecrated monuments and memorials to those who fell in the first great war to save democracy.
>
> Now all that is beauty, all that is sacred, all that has been contributed by the United States in the name of "memory" has been engulfed by the malevolence engendered by the mad leader with a fanatical following.[58]

For Edmonds, the sad juxtaposition between memorials to the "War to End All Wars" and Nazi violence constituted not a lesson in war's futility and waste but a new call to arms. The fallen Americans commemorated at the ABMC's monuments, chapels, and cemeteries in Europe demanded no less. Little did Edmonds know that one of the authors of the First World War guidebook that inspired his reflections would soon lead a new crusade in Europe and take his own place in American memory. Here, as elsewhere, remembrance of World War I carried unforeseen connections to World War II.

On the Battlefield of Memory

Introduction

Memory, History, and America's First World War

> No less than war itself, the memory of war is a complex and messy phenomenon. . . . On the battlefield of memory are an infinite number of paths and trajectories, entry and exit points, psychic wounds and traumas.
> —Philip West, Steven I. Levine, and Jackie Hiltz, *America's Wars in Asia: A Cultural Approach to History and Memory* (1998)

Dwight D. Eisenhower was just one of the millions of individuals in the 1920s and 1930s who contributed to what historian Jay Winter has called the "memory boom," an international wave of public involvement in war remembrance triggered by the cataclysm of the First World War.[1] Yet for the most part, historians have ignored or misunderstood the American manifestation of this phenomenon. Although the study of collective memory in connection with other American conflicts—particularly the Civil War, World War II, and Vietnam—has become a cottage industry, only a handful of studies have examined remembrance of World War I (and seldom for more than one chapter). With some notable exceptions, those works that do address this neglected subject tend to imply that the First World War became America's forgotten war almost as soon as it ended or that collective memory of the conflict was significant only insofar as it inspired pacifism and isolationist sentiment.[2] This study offers a more complex picture. By examining a wide array of cultural artifacts—including war memorials, paintings, magazines, and works of literature—it contends, first of all, that the First World War was hardly a forgotten conflict in the America of the interwar period. Neither Prohibition-era excess nor Depression-era hardship dulled the nation's fascination with its first global conflict. Indeed, what stands out most vividly during the 1920s and 1930s is the intensity with which Americans memorialized their war dead (through some of the most grandiose remembrance projects in American history), revisited wartime experience through literature and the newly introduced medium of film, and argued over the meaning—

the "true" memory as each side saw it—of a conflict shrouded in ambiguity and contradiction. If anything, these responses to the First World War reveal the processes of American war remembrance at their most supercharged.

Secondly, this study argues that from its beginning American memory of the war was fractured and unsettled, more a matter of competing versions of memory—each with its own spokespeople—than a single, culturally pervasive construction of the past. For example, the American Legion, the largest veterans organization in American history and the dominant force in postwar memorial building and commemoration ritual, remembered the war as a time of accelerated cultural assimilation (or "Americanization") and national harmony. For most legionnaires, participation in World War I remained drenched in a nostalgia that grew only more intense with the passage of time. However, African Americans and radicalized whites, both of whom were excluded from the legion's patriotic embrace, recalled a quite different war. And so did many of the nation's writers, especially those whose works we continue to read and revere in the early twenty-first century.

Indeed, it is worth pointing out that the present-day canon of classic American literature from the 1920s and 1930s reflects, with just a few notable exceptions, one version of America's First World War and its aftermath—just one strand in the frayed remembrance discourse of the interwar period.[3] Too often we mistake this piece for the entire puzzle. Through works of high modernism such as Ernest Hemingway's *The Sun Also Rises* (1926), William Faulkner's *Soldiers' Pay* (1926), E. E. Cummings's *The Enormous Room* (1922), John Dos Passos's *Three Soldiers* (1921), and F. Scott Fitzgerald's *Tender Is the Night* (1934), literature students continue to learn that the horrors of World War I produced a "Lost Generation" of Americans whose members wandered aimlessly through a postwar wasteland or (to shift clichés) through the decadent hedonism of the Jazz Age.[4] Considerable artistic talent gave shape to this mythos; however, when it comes to understanding the dynamics of American collective memory in the 1920s and 1930s, the well-worn notion of the Lost Generation has serious limitations. Millions of Americans who had contributed to the war effort felt anything but lost during this period (at least in terms of their patriotic identity), and the artifacts inscribed with *their* variety of collective memory deserve—in the interest of historical understanding—the same scrutiny afforded modernist novels and poems.[5]

Moreover, as literary critic Keith Gandal has recently shown, the version of war memory expressed by the three most prominent modernist writers of the period—Hemingway, Faulkner, and Fitzgerald—is perhaps not the one that we remember from our literature classes. Such writers, he asserts, were traumatized not by wartime violence, which Hemingway alone experienced directly (albeit as a noncombatant who subsequently made a self-promotional spectacle of his wounds), but by their inability to achieve war records worthy of "real men." Indeed, the American mobilization of 1917–1918 brought emasculating embarrassment to all three. Unable to serve in the U.S. Army, because of vision problems, Hemingway reached the war via the American Red Cross, whose insignia (the ignominious badge of a quasi–military aid worker) he removed from his tunic whenever photographed. As for 2nd Lt. F. Scott Fitzgerald, military authorities generally agreed that the Princeton dropout was an incompetent junior officer. He never made it to France. And in the cruelest cut of all, Faulkner was judged too dwarfish to serve in the U.S. Army Air Service. The diminutive Mississippian subsequently dissembled his way into a Royal Air Force camp in Toronto, where he remained until the armistice, and then hobbled back to Oxford with several fake wounds, an RAF uniform complete with pilot's wings (which he never earned), and stories of imaginary dogfights over the Western Front. As Gandal demonstrates, beneath these writers' fashionable antiwar rhetoric—a rhetoric at complete variance with their actual wartime experiences—lurks a kind of war envy as well as a deep-seated resentment of so-called hyphenated Americans who successfully answered the call. The Lost Generation, Gandal quips, might more accurately be titled the "generation that lost out."[6]

Once we set the Lost Generation mythology to the side—or, rather, in its appropriate place as one version of the past among many—and look beyond the narrow segment of interwar texts now deemed "classic," the literature of the 1920s and 1930s emerges not as a unifying force in collective memory but as a source of cultural disruption and splintering. Flashpoints, moments when the schism between two or more versions of the Great War suddenly came into stark relief, abounded during the interwar decades, and books often served as the catalyst. In 1921 John Dos Passos's controversial novel *Three Soldiers* inspired testimonials—one actually signed by "three soldiers"—in numerous magazines and newspapers.[7] Many veterans wrote that Dos Passos's sour recollections of life in the American Expeditionary Forces (AEF), albeit camouflaged as fiction, were consistent with their own. Others denounced the novel as an aberrant product of faulty memory. Two years later, when Willa Cather's

One of Ours received the Pulitzer Prize for Fiction, the same fault line appeared, but with the two sides now reversed: critics of Cather's novel found her depiction of the AEF too cheerful; defenders, many of them former soldiers, praised the same portrayal as an antidote to *Three Soldiers.* Even as late as 1933, literary controversies continued to reveal fissures in the landscape of memory. That year, Laurence Stallings's book of sardonically captioned war photographs, grimly (if prophetically) titled *The First World War,* inspired Malcolm Cowley and Archibald MacLeish, both respected men of letters and former soldiers, to square off in two consecutive issues of the *New Republic.*[8] Their debate quickly moved beyond the specific strengths and weaknesses of Stallings's text to address the ultimate meaning of the war, a subject upon which, revealingly, these two American veterans could find no common ground. Fittingly, historian David Kennedy refers to a "hole in the fabric of American culture" created by such discordant memories of World War I.[9] Instead of speaking uniformly for a Lost Generation, interwar literature, through its contradictions and divisions, documents a lost consensus over the meaning of America's first overseas crusade.

As the examples of *Three Soldiers* and *One of Ours* indicate, prominent works of literature, and the controversies surrounding them, offer a useful starting point for understanding collective memory, especially during a turbulent twenty-two-year period when multiple versions of the same historical event vied for public acceptance. However, less familiar cultural artifacts are often even more revealing. Thus, this study will examine a host of forgotten venues for contemplation and discussion of the war.

Each chapter offers a different cross-section of the memory culture(s) active at the time. Chapter 1 outlines the version of the Great War contained in the pages of the *American Legion Weekly* and *American Legion Monthly,* publications that reached far more readers than the war-related works of Dos Passos and Cather combined (by 1921, circulation of the *American Legion Weekly* stood at nearly three-quarters of a million readers) and thus arguably had a far greater impact on collective memory. Likewise focused on a relatively obscure form of remembrance, chapter 2 sets an iconic public shrine, the Tomb of the Unknown Soldier, alongside *Spirit of the American Doughboy,* a mass-produced monument purchased by more than 140 communities in the 1920s and 1930s. War paintings stand at the center of chapter 3, which explores the careers of three very different visual artists—Harvey Dunn, Horace Pippin, and John Steuart Curry—all of them haunted by the war. And, finally, chapter 4 traces the evolution of meanings attached to Quentin Roosevelt's original burial site in France, once one of the most famous graves in the world, and then focuses on the recent wave of remembrance activities—and flood of new World War I books, both academic and popular—that has attended the passage of America's last doughboys.

Strikingly different constructions of America's First World War emerge from this intentionally eclectic assortment of cultural artifacts. And in this regard, the "memory boom" in the United States contrasts sharply with that of Great Britain. Although certain war-related images—such as trenches, troopships, and the Statue of Liberty—retained iconic stature between 1919 and 1941, no single version of the war dominated American imagination. Thus, while British culture saw the arrival in the late 1920s of what Samuel Hynes has called "The Myth of the War," a nearly ubiquitous expression of collective memory that stressed waste and futility as the central themes of World War I, ambivalence continued to characterize American responses, even as the nation drifted ever more deeply into isolationism.[10]

Examples of this ambivalence abound in American interwar cinema, war literature, and the internal culture of the nation's largest veterans' organization. Not surprisingly, Hollywood offered perhaps the most explicitly schizophrenic variety of remembrance as ostensibly "antiwar" films simultaneously emphasized go-it-alone heroics, the very thing that the First World War's industrialized carnage seemed to have rendered obsolete, and played up the excitement and spectacle of battle. Indeed, as historian Michael T. Isenberg demonstrates in a shrewd analysis of director King Vidor's 1925 blockbuster *The Big Parade,* even a film featuring radical breakthroughs in cinematic realism (such as the truly harrowing battle scenes that Vidor staged with the assistance of military advisers) and graphic depictions of physical trauma (the protagonist of the *The Big Parade,* played by John Gilbert, loses a leg), ultimately depicts "war as a worthy arena for heroic adventure and romance."[11] While Vidor believed he had unequivocally denounced military violence, the film's script, written by Laurence Stallings, complicates the movie's message: though maimed, Gilbert's playboy turned enlistee becomes a wiser, better man by virtue of his combat experience and suffering, and his postwar reunion with his French love interest in the final frames seems a just compensation for his disfiguring wound. Individual action and fulfillment occupy the foreground in *The Big Parade* despite the film's groundbreaking images of mass industrialized warfare.

For a true antiwar movie, audiences had to wait until 1930 when director Lewis Milestone's uncompromising adaptation of *All Quiet on the Western Front* reached theaters. One of the first explicitly pacifist films in Hollywood history, *All Quiet* received rave reviews and swept the Oscars; however, it cornered only one segment of the memory market. Nineteen thirty also saw the release of Howard Hughes's aviation spectacle, *Hell's Angels,* a far more ambivalent presentation of modern warfare that nevertheless racked up its own impressive share of critical accolades and box-office revenue. Focused, like most military aviation films of the period, on a love triangle (with Jean Harlow in the middle), Hughes's epic combined romance with state-of-the-art aerial spectacle. Nothing could be further removed from the claustrophobic trench world of *All Quiet*. The extravagant premier of *Hell's Angels* at Grauman's Chinese Theater said it all: while aircraft "buzzed Hollywood Boulevard" and "parachutists floated to earth," lucky ticket holders passed "ersatz illuminated airplanes" and other props bankrolled by the movie's billionaire producer.[12] If *All Quiet* presented the faceless fighting conditions produced on the ground by twentieth-century military technology, then *Hell's Angels* exploited the public's fascination with the one arena of modern warfare where heroism and machinery seemed to coexist (as least for those who had never experienced actual air combat). Unlike *Wings* (1927), which launched the World War I aviation craze, Hughes's movie sometimes infused the air war with a dark surrealism, especially in its famous zeppelin sequence, a depiction of mass suicide analogous to the senseless wave of attacks across no-man's-land so vividly captured in *All Quiet*. However, as in *The Big Parade,* melodrama, combined with crowd-pleasing thrills and chills, kept the antiwar message muted. Aces and flying machines gave lift, as it were, to a version of war memory far different from the images of impersonal slaughter, unrelieved by romance or heroism, presented by Milestone and Remarque.

As for American war novels of the 1920s and 1930s, so often seen as an ideologically unified collection of texts, it is important to remember that works that today may seem straightforwardly antiheroic and expressive of Lost Generation disillusionment were not necessarily read that way when they first appeared. Again, a closer look reveals uncertainty and contradiction, not consensus. The curious history of Thomas Boyd's *Through the Wheat* (1923), among the bleakest of all American First World War narratives, is a case in point. Boyd's novel tells a brutally simple and, one would think, relatively unambiguous story: focused on a nondescript Marine

Corps private named William Hicks (about whose civilian background we learn almost nothing), the book chronicles the sights and sounds of three major battles—Belleau Wood, Soissons, and Blanc Mont—as registered by the protagonist's increasingly shell-shocked consciousness. Indeed, as in Stephen Crane's *The Red Badge of Courage* (to which reviewers frequently compared *Through the Wheat*), the world of combat, with its alternating rhythm of adrenaline and fear, dominates the narrative from beginning to end.[13] The only plot, per se, resides in Hicks's harrowing descent, after one firefight too many, from gung-ho warrior to battle-fatigued zombie, his condition in the novel's final sentence, which reads, "The soul of Hicks was numb."[14]

This work of apparent neo-realism, unsparingly drawn from Boyd's own traumatic war experience, might never have been published without the behind-the-scenes intervention of F. Scott Fitzgerald, who convinced his editor at Scribner's, Maxwell Perkins, to give the manuscript a second look. Fitzgerald's personal connection with Boyd partly explained this lobbying effort. Two years before the publication of *Through the Wheat*, the two men met and became friends in St. Paul, Minnesota, where Boyd ran the literary page of a local newspaper and managed the Kilmarnock Bookstore, a popular gathering spot for Midwestern writers, including the likes of Sinclair Lewis and Theodore Dreiser. Each writer found something in the other to admire. Fitzgerald respected and envied Boyd's combat experience; Boyd could not help being dazzled by Fitzgerald's literary gifts. However, Fitzgerald's endorsement of *Through the Wheat* reflected more than the warmth of his feelings toward the former marine. Here, as elsewhere in his career, he displayed considerable critical acumen. The reception of *Through the Wheat* proved as much. More than twelve thousand copies of Boyd's novel sold in 1923 and 1924, not a bad showing for a first-time author, and positive notices poured in from, among others, the *Nation, Dial,* the *Book Man,* the *New York Times,* and the *Times Literary Supplement.*[15]

Yet no one could agree on what Boyd had accomplished. What exactly was *Through the Wheat* about? What kind of memory did it present? To John W. Crawford of the *Nation,* the answer was simple enough: the novel offered a "panorama of 'grim comic imbecility.'"[16] Placing the book squarely in the camp of antiwar fiction, Crawford emphasized the many avoidable blunders made by Hicks's inexperienced and arrogant superiors (the worst of these, not surprisingly, is a former English professor) and interpreted the protagonist's collapse into torpor as a chilling "spiritual disintegration."[17] In his review for *Dial,* Edmund Wilson agreed, identifying the "tone" of *Through the Wheat* as one that "if persisted in, should ultimately discourage humanity with war altogether."[18] For both critics, the novel contrasted war's "actualities," as Crawford put it, with the seductive lies of the "recruiting poster."[19]

Surprisingly, however, Scribner's did not market *Through the Wheat* as an antiwar narrative. In fact, the dust jacket for the first edition, which featured a lengthy endorsement (presumably written by Maxwell Perkins) on the front cover, claimed the following: "The author has not been content with the surface indications of war; he has plunged through the nightmare of fear, horror, and privation to bring up into the light the beaten gold of the spirit which has passed through the test by fire."[20] *The beaten gold of the spirit.* The blurb's idealistic language—used, ironically enough, to describe a protagonist who is nearly comatose by the end of the narrative—was jarringly out of sync with the novel it promoted. But Boyd's publisher was not alone in asserting that *Through the Wheat* described triumph as well as horror. Fitzgerald's own review of the novel, published in the *New York Evening Post,* maintained that Boyd "strikes one clear and unmistakable note of heroism, of tenuous and tough-minded exaltation, and with this note vibrating sharply in the reader's consciousness the book ends."[21] That Fitzgerald, a central player in the construction of the Lost Generation myth, read *Through the Wheat* in this fashion is ironic—and revealing. Instead of rejecting traditional constructions of war experience, as major writers of his generation were supposed to do (according to our reigning critical assumptions), Fitzgerald was, in this case, unable to look past such constructions. Although his critical instincts told him that Boyd's novel was thematically important and commercially viable, he nevertheless resisted its stark depiction of combat fatigue. For Fitzgerald, who longed for the very war experience that haunted Boyd, nobility *had* to survive on the modern battlefield. Thus, in this instance at least, the gap between the modernist vision of the Great War and the competing vision upheld by patriotic organizations such as the American Legion was narrower than one might expect.

Boyd's sad and nearly stillborn career (after a string of literary flops, he died at age thirty-seven) likewise defies our conventional understanding of American World War I literature. Although claimed by his biographer as a member of the Lost Generation, Boyd swung back and forth between modernism and lesser-brow literary activities, including popular biographies and historical fiction.[22] And his attitudes toward war varied from text to text. In 1925, seeking to build on the success of *Through the Wheat,* Boyd published *Points of Honor,* a collection of war stories that significantly expanded the range of military experiences treated in his novel.[23] For the most part, the stories are brutally sardonic in the way we have come to expect of American World War I literature: a compassionate lieutenant turns martinet after eavesdropping on his men (a grim parody of the camp scene in Shakespeare's *Henry V*); a shell-shocked veteran shoots his wife's lover and is placed on death row; a French peasant hides the location of a wartime cemetery from Graves Registration officers so that she may nourish her vegetables with American remains, and so on. However, the final piece in the collection, titled *"Semper Fidelis,"* pays tribute, without any discernable irony, to the frontline heroics of Marine Corps Sgt. Maj. John H. Quick, an exemplar (decorated in the Spanish-American War and in World War I) of the Corps' legendary Old Breed. As this story indicates, the repugnance and loathing expressed in *Through the Wheat* represented just one facet of Boyd's complex reaction to modern warfare. Esprit de corps, comradeship, and even valor remained part of the writer's vision—so much so, in fact, that he was even able to publish short stories in the *American Legion Monthly,* the last place where one would expect the author of *Through the Wheat* to surface.[24]

However, as we will see more fully in chapter 1 of this study, a close reading of American Legion magazines from the interwar period reveals many such surprises. Boyd's appearance in such a staunchly nationalistic, nostalgia-drenched venue is just one revelation among many. Indeed, much of what we may think we know about the legion in the 1920s and 1930s falls apart—not unlike the myth of the Lost Generation or the notion of thematic consistency in American World War I literature—once we consult the material culture of the period. Consider, for example, the ideological strange brew, soaked into the pages of the *American Legion Monthly,* that resulted as the legion drifted closer to the America First movement. By 1939, mirroring the nation's growing contempt for European militarism, the legion's slogan had unofficially become "Let's Keep America Out of War" (or "Absolute Neutrality"), and even the organization's ordinarily hawkish founder, Theodore Roosevelt Jr., had become an isolationist. Given this political turn, one would assume that the legion's collective memory of the Great War, so warmly nostalgic in the 1920s, had darkened by the late 1930s. But such, curiously enough, was not the case. As it turned out, the *American Legion Monthly* continued, even on the eve of World War II, to focus on the courage, patriotic self-sacrifice, and military manliness displayed by American soldiers in World War I. While editorials in the magazine warned with ever-increasing fervor against the horrors of another world war, the material that surrounded these editorials and that made up the bulk of each issue—that is, short fiction, cartoon strips, and other forms of narrative—depicted the American military as a desirable melting pot and defined combat as the ultimate initiation into manhood. An outsider reading these magazines might well have asked the following question: If the Great War had been so great for the United States, in the sense that it offered positive experiences for millions of American soldiers, then why deny the virtues of war to another generation?

In surveying artifacts such as *The Big Parade, Hell's Angels, Through the Wheat, Points of Honor,* and the interwar issues of the *American Legion Monthly,* one is struck not so much by the antiwar sentiment that frequently emerged (one expects to see that), but by the resilience of ideologies that valorize military violence. In *The Big Parade* and *Hell's Angels,* crowd-pleasing spectacle (combined with sex, war's partner since antiquity) overshadowed any protest or condemnation, and combat remained a test of masculinity and an opportunity for self-growth, albeit painfully purchased. In Boyd's surprisingly varied World War I writings, heroism and pride remained fortified against Lost Generation angst, even though *Through the Wheat* stands as perhaps the most starkly antiheroic text of its time (a distinction that, ironically, F. Scott Fitzgerald could not discern even after lobbying on the novel's behalf). And in the *American Legion Monthly,* even the growing specter of another world war failed to drain the Great War of its romance. In short, these examples suggest that ideological continuities, of various kinds, linked pre- and postwar America— despite Willa Cather's conviction, shared by many of her fellow modernists, that with World War I the world "broke in two."[25]

A newspaper cartoon from 1921, the year of French general Ferdinand Foch's triumphant American tour, conveys conflicting impulses that surfaced in the United States throughout the interwar decades, even at the height of isolationist sentiment (see fig. 1). The cartoon depicts Foch seated next to Uncle Sam with a map of the Western Front spread out before them. One grinning figure says to the other, "Never again! But wasn't it great, eh!"[26] With this revealing cartoon in mind, the following chapters will maintain that although the themes of disenchantment and horror characterized much of the war-related literature, film, and

1. "Never Again! But Wasn't It Great, Eh!" (1921).

visual art produced in the United States between the world wars—just as the subjects of disarmament, pacifism, and isolationism often dominated political discourse during the same era—collective memories of World War I never swung completely to the negative. Although events like the Veterans Bureau scandal and the dispersal of the Bonus Marchers soured many veterans, particularly those of the working class, a significant number of former soldiers continued to see their military service as an enriching, formative experience, an attitude reflected in the American Legion's periodicals (even on the eve of World War II) and in more war novels and films than one might expect. Even more important, a set of popular heroic narratives—the story of the Lost Battalion, Alvin York's heroic escapade, Eddie Rickenbacker's epic dogfights, and so forth—connected American combat experience in the First World War to grand, overarching themes in American military history. Such narratives added not to a "Myth of the War" but to cherished traditions of American soldiering, and so they enabled many Americans to feel a sense of martial pride that was conveniently separated from the specific causes—and dubious international benefits—of the Great War.

Thus, this study will argue that American memory of World War I was not only ambivalent and contradictory during the 1920s and 1930s, but also was ambivalent and contradictory in ways that accommodated— sometimes openly, sometimes covertly—affirmative interpretations of modern warfare and military service. In other words, it will contend, somewhat in the face of conventional wisdom (and reigning literary stereotypes), that World War I did not destroy the glamour of armed conflict for all, or even most, Americans, a conclusion that carries implications for our understanding of American responses to World War II. The United States may not have wanted war in 1941, but when war came, the ideological apparatus that justifies and celebrates military action proved robust—and not simply because of outrage felt toward the Japanese attackers at Pearl Harbor. Despite the disillusionment that followed the Versailles Treaty talks and the League of Nations debacle (less widely felt than some historians have assumed), and despite the mistreatment of some veterans (most infamously, at the Bonus Army camp), positive images of the *previous* World War endured. Such images remained wedged in the personal memories of those, such as Eisenhower, who would lead in this new crusade and in the collective imaginations of young men and women who "remembered" the First World War through books and films—or the stories told by their parents.

However, before turning to the primary artifacts upon which this argument rests, two issues must be addressed: First, what does this study mean by "collective memory" and "remembrance"? Notoriously imprecise, these terms have become a minefield for unwary scholars. The section offered below will provide some working definitions and attempt to render the theoretical assumptions underlying this study (such as they are) as transparent as possible. Second, what was it about the American experience of World War I that led to such unsettled interpretation during the two decades that followed? How did this experience compare with that of other Allied nations, whose losses far exceeded those of the United States? And how did World War I stack up against earlier American wars? What kinds of ambiguities were peculiar to America's First World War, and what kinds of interpretive challenges did these ambiguities pose for Americans between 1919 and 1941?

"Collective Memory" and "Remembrance"

No less a scholar than Samuel Hynes, the preeminent cultural historian of Great Britain and the First World War, has objected to the concept of collective memory. Human beings, he insists, cannot remember what they have not experienced. Thus, in his view, "myth" would serve as a more accurate term than "collective memory" for the shared narratives and images that members of various social groups come to accept as the truth about their past.[27] However, in a very real sense, people *do* remember what they have not experienced personally, and the term "collective memory," as opposed to "myth," suggests the complexity and power of that phenomenon.

The benefits of the former term over the latter become clear if we briefly consider both titles in relation to an eccentric but revealing sample: present-day American Civil War reenactors. No less than the American Legion of the 1920s and 1930s, or any of the other commemorative organizations that this study will explore, reenactors form a distinct culture held together by a particular construction of the past (what this study will refer to as "collective memory") and a set of practices and processes through which that vision is assembled, communicated, and perpetuated (henceforth termed "remembrance"). To say that cultural myths about the Civil War inspire otherwise ordinary men and women to dress up in period costumes and to perform "living history" is a true statement as far as it goes. However, attributing the reenactment phenomenon to myth alone does not do justice to the complicated dynamics at work. Consider, for example, the role of historical research in Civil War reenactment. We typically conceive of myth as an interpretive mode that is separate from the disciplined study of history—not an inferior mode but one that offers its own variety of truth, a truth that may or may not have a basis in the archival materials that historians must use to support their arguments. Like myth, collective memory is not bound by the rules of historical evidence, but, importantly, it can be—and often is—informed by historical scholarship, both popular (as displayed on the History Channel, for example) and arcane.

Indeed, it would be hard to imagine more intense scholars of military micro-history than the elite cadre of Civil War reenactors who take their hobby to an extreme. In his often hilarious passage through reenactment culture, chronicled in *Confederates in the Attic,* Tony Horwitz describes the goal of this ascetic, scholarly fringe as "absolute fidelity to the 1860s:

its homespun clothing, antique speech patterns, sparse diet and simple utensils."[28] These are reenactors who are willing to suffer for the sake of memory, as Horwitz learns when he spends a frigid night outdoors with a group of self-described "hardcores," who huddle together under authentically inadequate blankets and "spoon," rolling over en masse every few minutes to avoid freezing.[29] Underlying this particularly demanding form of remembrance—ritual, performance, masochism, call it what you will—is extensive research into the day-to-day lives of Civil War soldiers. Most of the hardcores, one suspects, have digested entire libraries of Civil War firsthand accounts. Good historians, they have done their homework. And one could even argue that the value of reenactment as *a form of research,* as a kind of field laboratory experiment (How did Civil War soldiers get any sleep? How did the aches and pains produced by a night of "spooning" affect their physical mobility in battle?), has perhaps been overlooked by more conventional historians who prefer book-lined studies over tents with dirt floors.

Of course, in the case of hardcore reenactors, as with all groups that practice remembrance, "absolute fidelity" to the past is an illusory goal, however frequently such a phrase may be invoked. Collective memory does not contain absolute truths about the past, any more than the works of professional historians do (as theorists such as Hayden White have shown).[30] However, the people doing the collective remembering will always disagree with this statement. Horwitz's hardcores, for example, report feeling a "period rush," an almost narcotic high that kicks in once their reenactment has achieved such perceived perfection that all reminders of the present day have disappeared.[31] At such moments, reenactors feel that they are no longer reenacting, that they have literally traveled through time, coming face to face with the real Civil War. As eccentric as it sounds, this notion of the period rush, the sensation produced when remembrance seems in perfect alignment with the past event that it commemorates, when the signifier appears to point directly to the signified, is not unique to reenactment culture. Collective memory thrives on such powerful feeling—and ceases to exist when emotion is absent. "Period rush" summarizes the sensations of American Legionnaires when they returned to France in 1927 as part of the so-called Second AEF and toured the battlefields of their youth. The phrase also fits, as we will see, the cathartic overflow of impressions recorded on the canvases of Harvey Dunn and Horace Pippin, both of whom suddenly began to produce war paintings in the late 1920s, following a decade-long hiatus. The "period rush," in various forms, will appear throughout this study.

And it is in regard to this crucial emotional element, so frequently expressed through acts of remembrance, that "collective memory" again serves as a more useful label than "myth." Whether thought of narrowly as falsehood or more broadly as, in Samuel Hynes's words, "simplified, dramatized story," myth can be revealed, dispelled, debunked.[32] Collective memory, on the other hand, is *memory*. It, too, can be studied and challenged. However, as the words themselves suggest, collective memory is far more intractable than myth and far less easy to see (especially from within). Indeed, just as an individual will nearly always object to the suggestion that what he or she remembers wasn't so, groups that are formed around conceptions of the past respond defensively, sometimes violently, when those conceptions, which carry the emotional force and conviction of personal memories, are threatened. Far more than "myth," the term "memory" expresses the formidable defenses that we all build around our shared conceptions of the past, the thickness of the armor encasing these conceptions and depth of their purchase in our psyches. What gives memory in its collective form this often frightening power of resistance is, of course, its role as a foundational component of identity. Our constructions of the past tell us who we are by telling us who we have been. Thus, memory wars such as the recent clash over the Smithsonian Institution's *Enola Gay* exhibit or the ongoing dispute over monuments on the Little Big Horn battlefield involve more than competing myths about the past; they involve individuals who, as members of groups joined together by memory, refuse to revise their very sense of self.[33] The acrimony and inflexibility displayed in these confrontations is understandable. Wounds that touch upon identity, whether personal or collective, go as deep as wounds can go.

As used in this study, then, "collective memory" refers to the version of past events that any given group—say, a veterans organization, a literary movement, the citizens of a specific community, or a nation—expresses through "remembrance," the set of cultural usages by which that version is constructed and presented. Two points should be made about this definition: First, neither "collective memory," understood here essentially as a product, nor "remembrance," a process, is stable or unchanging. Though groups that engage in remembrance may believe that their view of the past is "timeless," these groups are, of course, mistaken. Memory, as the epigraph to this introduction notes, is "a complex and messy business."[34] Bodies of collective memory change as the culture around them changes, and they are always contested. Over time, such bodies invariably collide with other equally committed sets of truths, sometimes absorbing new impressions of the past as a result, sometimes pulling even tighter into their ideological centers. And technological developments—such as the refinement of portable personal cameras, which caused something of a memory revolution during World War I, or the arrival of modern motion pictures—can transform ways of remembering, on both an individual and a collective level, virtually overnight. For example, throughout the 1920s and 1930s, the meeting halls of American Legionnaires, sites of memory resonant with Civil War associations (as latter-day versions of Grand Army of the Republic [GAR] or United Confederate Veterans [UCV] posts), were popular venues for the presentation of war films. The relatively new medium of cinema quickly became a part of the legion's sacred spaces. Likewise, plans for the Victory Highway, the most grandiose commemoration scheme in American history, called for the construction of a paved transcontinental highway (the nation's first) lined with statues of eagles and doughboys. Supported by seven states and then aborted in the late 1920s, the project represented a remarkable fusion of the traditional and the contemporary—commemorative statuary, a form of remembrance regarded by many Americans as obsolete in the post–World War I era, to be viewed from passing automobiles, the symbol of the new.[35] Paradoxically, memory often embraces modernity.

Second, the inclusion of "nation" in this definition requires some justification. In *Remembering War* (2006) Jay Winter summarizes the resistance, now shared by many historians, to scholarship that approaches memory on a national level. "Multi-vocality," he rightly asserts, "is the order of the day," noting that the "[t]he thrust in much recent work in social and cultural studies has been away from an earlier top-down approach, which emphasized the capacity of dominant groups to act in effect as puppeteers, pulling the strings of cultural activity."[36] Like Winter's work, this study will emphasize the plurality of memory, and it will contend that many, if not most, acts of American war remembrance between 1919 and 1941 came from the bottom up—a conclusion that may surprise readers whose understanding of World War I memory comes chiefly from naturalistic works of literature such as John Dos Passos's *1919* (1932) and William March's *Company K* (1933). Indeed, the two chief examples of war remembrance conducted by the American government

during the interwar period—the construction of permanent war cemeteries in Europe and the enshrinement of the Unknown Soldier—both
reveal the limits of federal control over memory. Military officials, almost
to a man, shared Pershing's conviction that America's war dead should
remain in Europe. However, when the War Department tried to emulate
the policies of Great Britain's Imperial War Graves Commission, which
forbade the repatriation of bodies, public pressure originating at the
grassroots level (albeit combined with effective professional lobbying in
Washington) led to compromise. As a result, between 1920 and 1923, tens
of thousands of dead American soldiers defied the military elite, slipped
free of the grasp of federal commemoration, and returned home. In a
sense, these bodies went AWOL. They would no longer take orders from
above. Likewise, the ceremonial entombment of the Unknown Soldier
produced responses that Congressman Hamilton Fish Jr. and other early
proponents of the scheme could hardly have anticipated. The mystery of
the Unknown Soldier's identity was supposed to generate his power as
a symbol of patriotic sacrifice. However, for many Americans, the symbolism was dubious, even offensive. Literary artists, ranging from John
Dos Passos to Carl Sandburg, presented the Unknown Soldier not as an
anonymous hero, but as a pathetic figure whom the nation had victim-
ized twice—first, by sending him off to war and, second, by manipulating
his remains into a false icon. Both of these memory conflicts involve a
collision between what John Bodnar has termed "official culture," with
its emphasis on the ideal, and "vernacular culture," which is formed not
by abstractions but by a particular group's sense of experiential truth.[37]
Bodnar's dichotomy of the "official" versus the "vernacular" will appear
throughout this study as we see remembrance projects launched in a top-
down manner meet with resistance and, more often than not, failure.

However, we lose more than we gain by shying away entirely from generalizations, however qualified, that describe collective memory as a national phenomenon. Remembrance activities can have significance at the
national level, even—perhaps especially—if they do not reflect a governmental agenda, and the reader of this study will encounter many illustrations of this dynamic. Consider, for instance, the American Legion's
impact on America between the two world wars, a subject considered in
greater detail in chapter 1. In addition to cultivating a specific collective memory among its members and within its meeting halls—halls that
within three years of the armistice appeared in virtually every town and
neighborhood in the United States—the legion aggressively promoted its

vision of World War I and of American war veterans (to say nothing of its politically reactionary, anti-Leftist themes) within the larger culture that surrounded each individual legion post. Through shooting competitions, war relic displays, school awards, fund-raisers, film viewings, monument dedications, and honor guard ceremonies, activities local in nature but replicated in thousands of communities, the legion wove its commemorative tendrils into the very fabric of day-to-day life during the interwar period. Thus, it is not an exaggeration to say that *America* in the 1930s and 1940s would have been a very different place without the version of collective memory that the American Legion promoted.

History and America's Missing War

Although generalizations about national memory are, as we have just seen, increasingly regarded with suspicion, it is hard not to read the current configuration of war memorials on the National Mall in Washington, DC, as a reflection of how Americans in the early twenty-first century feel about the armed conflicts of the past one hundred years. A quick tour is in order. So integral to the mall's overall aesthetic effect that it seems decades older than it is, the National World War II Memorial, a circular array of elegant fountains and arches with little text and no statues—except for wreath-bearing American eagles—sits at the very center of the open expanse separating the Washington Monument and the Lincoln Memorial and in perfect alignment with both structures. As befits America's triumphant role in the Allied war effort, the memorial is unavoidable to anyone traversing the mall on its east-west axis. Thus, if the scenic center of Washington, DC, is national memory communicated through the medium of space and architecture, then this tribute to the soldiers of the Second World War stands at the very heart of that memory, in a position of pride that is unmatched by any other war memorial in the capital.

In contrast, the National Vietnam War Veterans Memorial, located to the northeast of the Lincoln Memorial, is a shadowy place, veiled by trees and invisible as one looks in its direction from the steps of the Lincoln Memorial—or from the National World War II Memorial. As a structure, this monument to the veterans of a still-controversial conflict doesn't beckon. It is, in fact, literally sidelined. To find it, one follows the crowds, or the line of souvenir trailers, some flying the black MIA-POW flag, parked near its entrance. While the World War II Memorial's splashing fountains, Romanesque arches, and hovering bronze wreaths quietly celebrate, the wall of the Vietnam Veterans Memorial confounds. The differences between the two monuments could not be more pronounced. For example, no names appear on the World War II Memorial for reasons both practical (a list of four hundred thousand dead would require an impossibly colossal structure) *and* culturally revealing. The array of gold stars at the center of the monument, one per every ten thousand Americans killed, asserts itself as a meaningful abstraction, because World War II has, for most Americans, retained a coherent identity as the "Good War" fought by the "Greatest Generation." On the Vietnam Memorial wall, on the other hand, the names of the dead are all there is—with no commemorative apparatus to explain or justify their sacrifice. Symbolic stars would be completely out of place on the memorial's cryptic black surface, which refuses to interpret or editorialize.[38] Even the nearby statue of dazed-looking infantrymen, added to the memorial site as a concession to its critics, is metaphorically, as well as literally, mute.

More expressive statues dominate the mall's other monument to a problematic war—the National Korean War Veterans Memorial. Situated opposite the Vietnam Veterans Memorial, on the southwest corner of the mall (and likewise invisible from the World War II Memorial), the Korean War Veterans Memorial features the sculpted lifelike figures of nineteen infantryman fanned out over a gentle incline as if on permanent patrol. Their faces are tense and wary, and their vulnerability is poignantly conveyed by their rain ponchos, which conceal their backpacks and ammunition belts and ominously suggest burial shrouds. As one crosses the mall to reach the memorial, the soldiers rise up like hunchbacked phantoms. If Maya Lin's design for the Vietnam Veterans Memorial takes its cue from Hemingway's Frederic Henry, who contends that words like "glorious" and "sacrifice" have become debased through misusage and that only concrete proper nouns signify, then this very moving memorial to Korean War veterans goes beyond language.[39] Here, it isn't words that matter (not even names), but bodies—and the details of the things they carried, the rifles that stick out from their ponchos, the slender antenna that rises from the radioman, and so forth. An anti-memorial of sorts, like its cousin to the north, the Korean War Veterans Memorial pays tribute not through graceful architecture or even through naming, but through the detailed presentation of soldiers themselves.

Ironically, absent among the twentieth-century conflicts represented prominently on the mall is the most memorialized conflict of them all—

the First World War. Washington, DC, does not, of course, lack World War I monuments. Dedicated in 1924, the elegant First Division Monument, a classical column mounted by the female figure of Victory and inscribed with the names of the division's more than five thousand fatalities, stands south of the Dwight D. Eisenhower Executive Building (formerly the State, War, and Navy Building) in President's Park. In 1919, when reviewing plans for this structure, the federal Fine Arts Commission recommended expanding its focus to commemorate every fallen member of the AEF, thereby creating a true national monument to American forces in the First World War; however, Maj. Gen. C. P. Summerall, the division's former commander (and one of Pershing's favorites), successfully defeated the scheme.[40] At Seventeenth Street and Constitution Avenue stands the far more bellicose Second Division Memorial, a huge bronze fist clutching a flaming sword. Completed in 1936, the monument's image of strength and defiance evokes the Second Division's critical role in the defense of Paris during the summer of 1918. And then there is the bronze statue of "Black Jack" Pershing, surrounded by markers that describe the deeds of the AEF, located in Pershing Park, not far from the White House. Although claimed by some as a national World War I memorial, the monument's central focus is the AEF's Iron Commander. Dedicated in 1981, at a time when World War I inspired little interest among most Americans, Pershing's statue attracts few visitors. Most tourists do not even know of its existence.

Indeed, none of the monuments mentioned above enjoys anything like the cultural prominence of the National World War II Memorial or Maya Lin's inscrutable wall. The capital's scattered shrines to the American doughboy don't even come close. Americans who served in World War I and who witnessed the wave of memorializing that came afterward would find this situation surprising. Serious talk of constructing a national memorial to the veterans and the fallen of America's first overseas crusade abounded in 1919, and grandiose proposals were multitudinous. For example, by February of that year the *New York Times* reported that plans were under way for the construction of the George Washington Memorial Hall, a colossal "temple" that would commemorate both the patriots of 1776 and "the men of 1917."[41] Estimates put the cost of this structure at ten million dollars.[42] However, nothing ever came of this scheme (or any other)—in part because of the subsequent popularity of the Tomb of the Unknown Soldier, dedicated on Armistice Day 1921. According to the American Legion, in the year 1937 alone, "1,586,086 visitors viewed the Tomb of the Unknown Soldier," while various domestic organizations and foreign representatives left 339 "wreaths, sprays, and medals" at the site, "an average of nearly one a day."[43] Throughout the interwar decades, the tomb served as a de facto national monument to the Great War, a function not without irony, since this site of memory was not, after all, a conventional public war monument but a sepulcher housing an unrecognizable corpse (presumably rendered so by that most horrific and impersonal of modern weapons—high explosives).

The notion of entombing an arbitrarily selected unidentified soldier with ritualistic honors was new to Americans in 1921 and a foreign import at that. The United States borrowed the idea from France and Great Britain, both of which performed their own Unknown Soldier ceremonies in 1920, and one could argue that only a war as strange and terrible as the First World War could have produced such a strange and terrible form of commemoration. More ironic still is the fact that the tomb lost its specific connection to the First World War in 1958, when it became, through the addition of three more corpses (one from each theater of the Second World War, the third from Korea), the Tomb of the Unknowns.[44] So many wars have passed since 1921 that one doubts whether many of the tourists who flock to the tomb today, drawn primarily by the spectacle of the changing of the guard, still remember its once exclusive connection to World War I.

However, even though it is largely invisible on the mall, the First World War does not lack a federally designated center of national remembrance. Since 2006 that center has been the Liberty Memorial (otherwise known as the National World War I Museum) in Kansas City, Missouri, located half a continent away from Washington, DC. Completed in 1926, the Liberty Memorial was never intended as a national site. Instead, its twin museum halls, observation tower, and wooded grounds commemorate the more than four hundred Kansas City citizens lost in the war. Yet in size Kansas City's tribute to its fallen actually dwarfs all three of the national war memorials on the mall, and if this gargantuan structure were somehow moved to the heart of Washington, DC, the First World War, not the Second, would stand out as the central American conflict of the twentieth century. It is also interesting to note that the three memorializing modes displayed on the mall—architectural (the World War II Memorial), name-based (the Vietnam Veterans Memorial), and statuary-focused (the Korean War Memorial)—come together in the Liberty Memorial, an expression of an earlier time when overtly celebratory and idealistic commemoration, achieved through a combination of artistic elements, had not yet gone out of fashion. Indeed, the memorial proclaims the heroic and the sacred at every turn through its massive scale and through an allegorical idiom that seems almost quaint nearly a century later. Four sword-bearing guardian spirits ("Honor," "Sacrifice," "Patriotism," and "Courage") gaze down from the observation tower while twin stone sphinxes (one representing the Past, the other the Future) crouch before each of the cavernous museum halls, where the names of the dead are inscribed.[45] This is an iconographic language that most visitors no longer speak—hence, perhaps, the facility's inevitable shift in focus from remembrance to education. In 2006, after its designation as a national museum, the Liberty Memorial opened a vast new exhibit area, located underground, where its collection of First World War artifacts—probably the largest in North America—combines with interactive, multimedia displays to tell the story of 1914 to 1918. And in terms of historical narrative artfully presented through physical objects and explanatory text and moving images, it is one of the finest museums in the world. On weekends visitors pack the underground space, and eavesdropping on conversations, one hears frequent references to grandparents and to great-aunts and -uncles—proof that this supposedly forgotten war is actually well remembered in many American families.

Thus, it would seem that the First World War is oddly situated in present-day American memory. Not only does the conflict lack a national memorial in Washington, DC, but also its current center of commemoration, located in a Midwestern city, was created by local desires and needs and has only recently received federal recognition. How, then, do we explain the First World War's decentered and unsettled position in American culture? A large part of the answer resides in the ambiguities of the war itself—ambiguities that perhaps made commemorative efforts during the 1920s and 1930s that much more urgent.

Consider, first, the situation stateside. As historian Robert Zieger has observed, American participation in the First World War violently upended cultural and political norms.[46] Among other things, the nation's commitment to total war necessitated a reappraisal of long-standing assumptions about gender and the workforce, the reliability of African Americans and so-called hyphenated Americans during a time of national emergency, and the boundaries and proper uses of federal power. Yet the brief duration of the American war effort—less than nineteen months—meant that sudden changes in outlook never became as transformative as they could have. However progressive their results, policies born of wartime urgency usually faded fast. Within weeks of the armistice, manufacturers jettisoned women workers from their assembly lines and labor unions closed their doors to female members. And in the American South, Jim Crow returned with a vengeance as 1919 became a record-setting year for lynchings. Moreover, as historian Richard Slotkin demonstrates in his study of Lower East Side New Yorkers who became part of the famous Lost Battalion, first-generation Jewish immigrants quickly lost the positive press and WASP approval that they briefly enjoyed during the war.[47] (The tightening of federal control on dissent, on the other hand, endured the transition to peacetime, thanks to the Red Scare.)

Thus, the war's legacy at home was mixed and unclear. So, too, was the meaning of the overseas crusade. Did the American troops who fought in France and Belgium in any sense win the war for the Allies? Or was it the vast reservoir of manpower in the United States, most of it still untapped by the time of the armistice, that had made the difference, crushing the Germans' will to fight? Still revisited by historians in the early twenty-first century, these questions had no clear-cut answers in the 1920s and 1930s. Nor was the military performance of the American Expeditionary Forces free from mystery and debate. It remains uncertain today whether the central narrative of the AEF in combat was one of success or failure. Although Pershing believed that his tactical emphasis on movement (usually mass frontal assaults) and small-arms marksmanship had borne fruit in the AEF's major battles, considerable evidence suggests that his anything-but-modern approach to modern warfare worked best, as David Kennedy observes, not when applied to determined German resistance (as happened in the early phases of the Meuse-Argonne offensive), but "when directed at the backs of a retreating foe."[48] Many veterans of the costly Meuse-Argonne offensive, the biggest and deadliest battle in American history (with more than 26,777 Americans killed[49]), interpreted the experience as a brutal but triumphant affair, a forty-seven-day punching match, fought amid terrain favoring the German defenders, that ultimately demonstrated the superiority of the American fighting man. After all, the battle ended with German forces retreating so quickly that some American units could barely keep up. Yet other eyewitnesses offered a less flattering picture, citing inadequate logistics (many troops went hungry), lack of artillery support, poorly prepared field hospitals, and senseless charges straight into machine-gun fire. Thomas M. Johnson later described some of the AEF's logistical and tactical shortcomings in a book suggestively titled *Without Censor* (1928).[50]

Further adding to the interpretive fog that enveloped the war and complicated its memory were profound experiential differences among its military participants. Not surprisingly, postwar literature and cinema tended to focus on the excitement of combat, as if direct participation in armed violence defined the collective experience of American soldiers. In actuality, however, nothing could be further from the truth. Of the more than four million men who served in the U.S. Army during the First World War, just half made the journey to France, and of these, approximately one million saw action. The intensity of that action varied enormously. For example, soldiers in the 88th Division, a unit comprised primarily of draftees from Iowa and Minnesota, spent most of their war in a quiet "live and let live" trench sector in Alsace. In November 1918 the 88th moved north to join the Meuse-Argonne battle, but the war ended just hours before the division entered the front line. In all, this "combat division" lost just ninety men.[51] Outfits like the 88th Division offer ample support for David Kennedy's characterization of AEF members as "summer soldiers"—tourists, that is, rather than combatants.[52]

However, units whose initiation into open warfare came earlier in the Meuse-Argonne offensive, when German defenses effectively brought the American army to a standstill, had a quite different experience. Most tragic, perhaps, of the many tragic stories produced by Pershing's inordinate belief in the power of American infantry was the ordeal of the 35th Division, a unit of initially gung-ho National Guardsmen from Kansas and Missouri.[53] One of nineteen inexperienced divisions that went "over the top" on September 26, 1918, the first day of the battle, the 35th made impressive gains initially but then became hopelessly bogged down. Everything went wrong. Units collided with one another, became mixed up, and wandered the battlefield lost. German depth defensive—machine-gun nests and pillboxes laid out on a grid (as opposed to recognizable lines)—caught the advancing Americans in cross fires, while German artillery, notoriously accurate, zeroed in wherever the inexperienced soldiers bunched together. The 35th Division's own artillery proved largely useless, since the cratered battlefield made it difficult to move the guns forward. And all of this occurred during near-constant rain and drizzle with temperatures nearly below freezing at night—so much for "summer soldiers." Given such conditions, it is little wonder that many troops in the 35th simply slipped away, forming bands of stragglers in the rear. After just five days the division was relieved, having suffered more casualties in less time than any other unit in the battle—a staggering 7,074 (more than twice the total losses suffered by *all* units at Omaha Beach in 1944).[54]

Yet even within this particular division, experiences—and thus subsequent personal memories—were far from uniform. Future president Harry S. Truman, a battery commander in the 35th, regarded his participation in the Meuse-Argonne offensive as positive and personally enriching. As David McCullough writes, through Truman's war experience, he "discovered he could lead men and that he liked that better than anything he had ever done before. . . . He found he had courage."[55] Yet Truman's sense of having triumphed in his trial by fire was, comparatively speaking, inexpensively purchased. Though sometimes subject to counter battery fire, AEF artillery units were, for the most part, safe places to be— even in the unfortunate 35th Division. The casualty figures for Truman's unit prove this. Only three men in his particular battery were wounded.[56] And the roll of honor for his regiment, the 129th Field Artillery, lists just twenty-three men killed in action.[57] In contrast, the ranks of infantry regiments in the 35th Division, which operated a few miles in advance of Truman's unit, were thinned by 50 to 70 percent during the five days of fighting. Many of the men in these hard-hit regiments came from the Kansas City area, which explains in part the passions that led to the Liberty Memorial.

Such comparisons can sound heartless—as if five minutes in the inferno of a World War I battle would not have been more than enough for anyone, whether infantryman or battery commander. Yet Truman's experience *was* fundamentally different from that of the infantry officers in his division. He lost no friends during the fighting. No one near him was shot, blown to pieces, or shell-shocked. And he was spared the shattering experience of receiving orders that he knew would result in pointless deaths (a common enough occurrence for infantry officers in the Meuse-Argonne).

By the same token, however, the trauma inflicted on the infantry regiments of the 35th Division, terrible though it was, pales in comparison with that endured by the AEF's most experienced units, some of which spent more than one hundred days in action. If a soldier had the misfortune of being assigned to one of the divisions rushed to the Aisne-Marne sector during the summer of 1918, then his chances of being wounded or killed were grim indeed. Casualty rates during the repulse of the German summer offensives—and during the Allied counterattacks that followed—were as bad as anything seen during the coming fall. And most of the divisions involved in the summer fighting later participated in the Saint Mihiel offensive and took their turn in the Meuse-Argonne. As a result, replacement rates in some of these divisions exceeded 100 percent. The First Division, the longest-serving American unit in France, received 30,206 replacements as it moved from battle to battle.[58] The Second Division, which contained the marine brigade that fought so famously at Belleau Wood, took in 35,343.[59] Since a World War I American division (double the size of its World War II successor) contained at full strength 27,000 men, these figures provide a chilling measure of military carnage that is almost unimaginable today, at least in the United States, where the media keep a close accounting of daily military deaths that can potentially have a direct impact on national policy.

Thus, although the American Legion would aspire during the interwar decades to establish a monolithic image of the American First World War soldier as an experienced, battle-tested *combatant* (painter Harvey Dunn's cover illustrations for the *American Legion Monthly* typically depict doughboys with steel helmets, that unmistakable signifier of overseas service, set against the backdrop of a trench parapet, dug-out entrance, or the ruins of a French village), former soldiers, even those laying claim to the title "combat veteran," shared less common ground than one might assume. Indeed, many legion members wore silver service stripes (denoting domestic service) on their mothballed uniforms, as opposed to the gold variety that symbolized time overseas. Despite its rhetoric and imagery, the legion could not deny the historical reality that for more than half of the U.S. Army in 1917 to 1918, the war had offered not the Great Adventure, but the Great Anticlimax. Some soldiers never even left their own state. Thousands of troops drafted in Kansas, for example, were still at Camp Funston, a huge training facility constructed near Fort Riley, when news of the armistice reached the American Midwest. The greatest wartime threat to their lives came from the Spanish flu, which caused many units that might otherwise have crossed the Atlantic to spend weeks in stateside quarantine.

Another group largely missing from postwar consciousness was the million or so American troops who made the journey to France but arrived too late to participate in the fighting. Northwestern novelist James Stevens, best known for his Paul Bunyan tales, was virtually alone among

postwar writers in exploring the frustrating experiences of these soldiers. And his perspective was fiercely satirical. In his 1927 novel, *Mattock,*
Stevens focused not on the horrors of World War I warfare (a subject already well covered by Thomas Boyd and others) but on the pettiness and
banality—the "chickenshit," to use World War II parlance—that constituted military life for units that remained far from the battlefield.[60] For
the would-be crusaders in Stevens's pitiable outfit, part of a depot division
that is periodically broken up to provide replacements for other units,
"combat" comes solely in the form of café brawls and internal politics,
as American officers wage war with one another by using enlisted men
as pawns—among them, the novel's odiously self-righteous narrator, the
"Christian American Citizen" Pvt. Parvin Mattock.[61]

Yet the most incisive literary treatment of the war's strange blend of ferocity and anticlimax comes from a surprising source: Ernest Hemingway,
whose famous adventure on the Italian front, where he became the youngest wounded American (without ever serving in the military), was anything but typical. In Hemingway's short story "Soldier's Home" (1925),
Harold Krebs, a member of the casualty-ridden Second Division—recall
those 35,343 replacements—and thus an exceptionally seasoned combat
veteran, returns home from the Great War to his small town in Oklahoma, where he invariably meets with either apathy or misunderstanding.
Since the Second Division served in the First World War's Army of Occupation in Germany, Krebs arrives long after the town's other soldiers
have reentered civilian life. Thus, no one has any interest in his experience. Other, less battle-worn veterans have already told the community
all that it wishes to hear about the Western Front, and even when Krebs
substitutes tall tales for authentic anecdotes he is unable to find an audience. Meanwhile, at home, he is infantilized by his mother, who wor-
ries chiefly about the sexual "temptations" that her son must have faced
overseas (we know from the first paragraph of the story that Krebs succumbed to those temptations with little struggle), and patronized by his
father, who allows this veteran of multiple battles to use the family car for
dating—provided he confine his interest to "nice girls."[62] Fed up with his
hellish "soldier's home" (though converted to the singular, Hemingway's
title alludes to nineteenth-century facilities for indigent or crippled veterans[63]), Krebs decides at the end of the story to light out for the com-
parative freedom of Kansas City.

Frequently interpreted as a depiction of war trauma, Hemingway's
story in fact presents a former soldier who is far from shell-shocked. Krebs

derives considerable satisfaction from his wartime performance as an infantryman—even, it is suggested, from his prowess at killing. He recalls with pride the moments "when he had done the one thing, the only thing for a man to do, easily and naturally, when he might have done something else." Thus, his trauma comes not from the war but from a more ironic source—namely, his community's inability to process recent history into a coherent collective memory that carries meaning for both civilians and veterans. In other words, the nuances, paradoxes, and ironies of the war are too much for Krebs's parents and neighbors, who lump all servicemen together and who "think it ridiculous for Krebs to be getting back so late, years after the war was over."[64] No one understands that the most bloodied units in the AEF were among those selected for six months (or more) of additional service in the Rhineland. No one comprehends that going "over there" meant hardship and fierce fighting for some units, but a comparatively nonviolent (but chickenshit-dominated) existence for others.

Thus, Hemingway's "Soldier's Home," a landmark work of American war literature, confronts that "hole in the fabric of American culture" identified by Kennedy as the legacy of World War I and its many ambiguities. At its core the story is about miscommunication, conflicting perspectives, and *failed* memory—about the absence of a stable "Myth of the War" that Krebs and his fellow townspeople can agree upon and share. Further complicating the cultural condition that Hemingway so effectively diagnosed, what we might call the problem of unresolved memory, were two additional issues, neither of which appears in his short story: the Spanish flu epidemic of 1918, which proved more lethal for the AEF than its German adversaries, and racial segregation within the armed forces, a practice that (at least for its more thoughtful observers) called into question the entire rhetorical and ideological basis of the American war effort.

In *Fever of War* (2005), a long-overdue study of the influenza epidemic within the U.S. Army, Carol R. Byerly establishes illness as perhaps *the* defining feature of American military experience in World War I. And she shows how the military impact of the flu, which killed more than fifty-seven thousand soldiers, was moved to the margins of history, first by veterans, then by military historians, and then (ironically enough) by scholars of memory.[65] For our purposes it is important to note that the prevalence of influenza served, like the existence of large numbers of American troops who never reached the front, to prevent the emergence of a satisfying master narrative for the war. The plot structures of conventional American war stories (whether heroic or antiheroic) left little room for these realities. And yet neither could be wished away.

Likewise, racial segregation—mandated by the War Department for African American troops but not (significantly) for Hispanics, Native Americans, or soldiers of Asian descent—created yet another challenge for postwar remembrance. More than 367,700 African Americans served in the U.S. Army in 1918, the largest mobilization of black soldiers since the American Civil War.[66] Yet the performance of these troops remained, like so much else pertaining to the American experience of World War I, subject to debate. Not surprisingly, given the volatility of race relations at the time, completely contradictory images of African American soldiers emerged in the years immediately following the war. Hoping finally to erase the military color line, civil rights advocates highlighted the valor and efficiency of the famous 369th Infantry Regiment, the "Harlem Hellfighters," as well as other highly decorated African American regiments that fought under French command, but to no avail. Officials at the War Department ignored the heroic Hellfighters and focused instead on the embarrassing record of the 368th Colored Infantry, two battalions of which broke and ran during the Meuse-Argonne offensive (a not uncommon occurrence among white outfits).[67] This dubious sample would help keep military segregation in place until the Truman administration. In reality, however, neither the celebrated 369th Infantry nor the much-maligned 368th typified African American units in the AEF. The vast majority of black soldiers under Pershing's command wound up not in combat units but in grotesquely mislabeled Pioneer Regiments, engineer outfits that were in fact hard-labor details—in effect, military chain gangs. The story of these troops—who constructed roads, dug trenches, unloaded supplies at Brest Harbor, or exhumed and reburied American war dead—has never been told. Laborers in uniform were invisible men from the start, at least where most whites were concerned, and they have largely remained so ever since.

Compounding the anguish created by such discriminatory treatment was the fact that African Americans joined the war effort with high expectations, urged forward by W. E. B. Du Bois and other leaders of color who saw the conflict as an opportunity for bartered racial advancement: in exchange for their loyal service at a time of national emergency, African Americans would at last see an end to their treatment as second-class citizens. However, white America reneged on this compact in every way possible. As a result, throughout the 1920s and 1930s many African

Americans responded with silence to the question of just how and where they figured into the memory of the Great War—a numbed silence that speaks volumes about their disappointment and frustration. Significantly, the Harlem Renaissance produced few major works that confronted the war and its hypocrisies directly, and it would be decades before writers such as Ralph Ellison and Toni Morrison explored the war's lasting scars in African American communities.[68] However, if conditions within the Jim Crow army of 1918 proved too painful for many blacks to contemplate, the same could not be said of the nation that America had gone to war to "save." As Mark Whalan has recently demonstrated, the positive cultural interactions experienced by African American soldiers in France, where racial prejudice was far less pervasive than in the United States, became an inspiring and, at the same time, deeply subversive memory. As transformed into a trope by Du Bois and other influential African American writers, who were willing (for the sake of a powerful myth) to overlook the racist underpinnings of French colonialism, France came to stand for genuine democracy—as opposed to the morally compromised American variety. In other words, France became a vision of what could be—of "emancipatory idealism"—and, as such, had a politically energizing effect within African American consciousness.[69]

Predictably enough, commemorative projects overseen by whites relegated African Americans to the sidelines of memory—or erased them altogether. For a brief moment the creation of the American Legion in 1919 held out hope for a genuine commingling of former servicemen, regardless of ethnicity or race. Theodore Roosevelt Jr., the organization's founder, held progressive racial views (just as his father had) and intended the legion as an inclusive, nonsegregated organization. Likewise, Hamilton Fish Jr., who drafted the legion's preamble, believed strongly in racial equality. As an officer in the Harlem Hellfighters, he had served with distinction alongside black troops, and he respected them. Years later he would lead an effort in the U.S. Congress to secure African American veterans their own monument in France.[70] However, the legion could not help but mirror the racial attitudes of its predominantly white membership, and by the early 1920s nearly all American Legion posts were strictly segregated. Meanwhile, in the pages of the *American Legion Weekly* and *American Legion Monthly*, African American soldiers appeared almost exclusively as clownish figures drawn from the minstrel tradition. (Other minorities fared much better, as chapter 1 will illustrate.)

Even commemorative efforts that explicitly aspired to be inclusive wound up highlighting the racial divide. Hundreds, perhaps thousands, of American communities produced memorial volumes shortly after the war—works like *Our Part in the Great War: What the Horton Community Did* (1919), *Honor Roll of Livingston County, Missouri* (1919), and *Reno's Response: History of Reno County's War Work Activities during the World War, 1917–1918* (1920). Consisting primarily of photographs of individual soldiers, accompanied by a listing of military assignments and battles, such works typically contain a separate section, placed last, for African Americans. For example, the *Honor Roll* for Livingston County, Missouri, provides photographs and biographies for "Our Negro Soldiers and Sailors."[71] And *Reno's Response*, which memorializes the veterans of Reno County, Kansas, includes information on "Reno's Colored Scrappers."[72] Yet the men recorded in such sections have a phantomlike quality. The phrase "No photograph available" appears frequently above biographical details that are conspicuously sketchy. And ironies abound. The anonymous authors of the Livingston County volume, for instance, introduce their listing of black veterans with a well-intentioned but ludicrous generalization: "Among our best fighting men in the lines were the colored soldiers. They having once been a vassal people were in a position to understand what it meant to fight for freedom's cause, so when the call came, our Livingston County colored boys responded generously."[73] In the biographies of the thirty-one African American soldiers that follow this statement, the racial realities of the AEF undermine the generous rhetoric: all but a handful of these veterans served in Pioneer Regiments. Thus, they were not, by and large, "fighting men" (however much they may have wanted to be), and their "understanding of what it meant to fight for freedom's cause" would have been a bitter understanding at best.

Racial injustice thus added considerably to the sense of ambiguity and contradiction already generated by the war's violent but abbreviated impact on domestic policies, the dubious performance of the AEF in combat, the lack of shared experiences among veterans, and the military consequences of the Spanish flu. Yet the greatest engine of unsettled memory was the human cost of the conflict—125,500 Americans killed; 205,690 wounded[74]—and the absence of a clear-cut answer to the question, *why?* Faced with the fathomless ocean of blood that is the First World War, scholars have tended, understandably, to minimize the impact of American losses, which were far fewer than those of European powers. The totals for the United States' allies and adversaries in the war defy comprehension. Great Britain and its empire suffered more than a million war deaths; France, nearly a million and a half; and Germany, more than two million.[75] Total casualties—dead *and* wounded, that is—for Austria-Hungary come to almost seven million, the highest such figure.[76] And nearly 600,000 Italians were killed (another million wounded)[77] in a theater of the war almost completely forgotten today—a "joke front," Hemingway's Jake Barnes calls it.[78] Reaching the Italian rate of mortality in the AEF would have meant the total annihilation of twenty-two American combat divisions—more divisions than Pershing ever had deployed at one time. But perhaps the most vivid comparison that can be made concerning American losses versus European losses is the following: the number of French soldiers recorded as "missing" in the First World War ("missing" meaning their bodies were too mutilated for identification or they had simply disappeared into the mud) is, by itself, nearly double the total number of American dead.[79]

The military history of the United States prior to 1917 also contains a terrible statistical peak, set against which losses in World War I seem mercifully small: the American Civil War, which ended fifty-three years before the armistice, claimed *six times* more American lives than the First World War. More than 618,000 combatants perished in the War Between the States—out of a total population of 34 million.[80] By the end of the war, deaths per each 10,000 of the population stood at roughly 181; approximately 13 percent of all the men who fought on both sides were killed.[81] In other words, the carnage produced by America's Civil War was worse in every possible way than that suffered by the nation five decades later. Since the population of the United States in 1861 was only a third of what it became by 1917, and since the military force mobilized during the Civil War was actually *smaller* (by more than 500,000) than the total number of men inducted into all branches of the U.S. military in World War I, death achieved a ubiquity during America's bloodiest conflict that is indeed hair-raising.[82]

Placed within other contexts, however, American casualty figures from the First World War take on greater collective significance and suggest a more traumatic national experience than comparisons with other combatant nations or with the American Civil War allow us to see. Although memory of the Civil War—memory softened by reconciliation rhetoric and a sentimental nostalgia shared by Union and Confederate veterans alike[83]—refused to fade, by 1917 the United States had avoided the ordeal of modern, industrialized warfare for more than a half century. Thus, like Europe, which had not seen a major conflagration since the Franco-Prussian War of 1871 (a short war that overly optimistic strategists mistook for the shape of things to come), the nation was generally unprepared for the scale of bloodshed that awaited it. Going into the war, few Americans were as dispassionate or as realistic as Pershing, who set the size of American combat divisions at twenty-seven thousand apiece, knowing (based on his study of the Western Front) he would need huge operational units that could hemorrhage thousands of casualties and still remain functional on the battlefield. Moreover, once American forces entered battle in the summer of 1918, their losses quickly outstripped those produced by every other war in American history except for the Civil War and World War II. Four times more American soldiers died in the First World War than in the American Revolution; eight times more than in the Mexican-American War; and twenty times more than in the Spanish-American War.[84] In addition, post-1945 conflicts have cost the United States considerably less (in terms of lives lost) than American intervention in the First World War. For example, roughly half as many Americans died in the Vietnam conflict as in World War I.[85] Thus, to visualize American losses in the First World War, imagine a name-covered wall twice the length of Maya Lin's memorial in Washington, DC. And, importantly, the vast majority of American deaths in World War I occurred in a comparatively short period of time—from May through November 1918. Indeed, American soldiers died at a faster rate during the final summer and fall of World War I than during almost any other period of American military history. At the height of the Meuse-Argonne battle, American combat deaths reached nearly a thousand per day, and by November 7, as intense fighting coupled with the flu severely strained the capacity of the U.S. Army Medical Department, the number of patients occupying beds at military base hospitals peaked at nearly two hundred thousand.[86]

The impact of this sudden avalanche of death and suffering on Americans at home can easily be imagined. Or perhaps *not* so easily imagined, since the United States has seen nothing like it for more than sixty years. To gain a sense of that impact, in terms of its statistical and social contours, one must consult sources unfamiliar to most historians of the First World War. Immediately after the war, the widespread passion for documentation manifested in community and county memorial volumes found expression at the state level as well. Several state governments, including those of Wisconsin, Indiana, Vermont, and Kansas, produced detailed book-length studies of their states' military fatalities, studies that reveal the distribution of war-related deaths among various towns, cities, and counties, as well as the cause for each soldier's demise. Since Kansas sits almost exactly in the middle of a high-to-low ranking of states based on manpower contributions (Kansas mobilized 63,428 troops; New York, at the top of the scale, inducted 367,864; Alaska, at the bottom, contributed just 2,102[87]), its study of fatalities is perhaps particularly revealing.

Compiled by the adjutant general of Kansas, *Kansas Casualties in the World War* and its supplement volume (both published in 1921) demonstrate that the Great War spread death across American communities with surprising unevenness. Some towns lost just a handful of men in uniform—or none at all; others, of comparable size, lost dozens. The vagaries of the flu partially explain such anomalies. However, the main explanation resides within the structure of the National Guard, whose companies, unlike those of the more homogenized National Army (the official term for the draft segment of the U.S. Army), each represented a particular town or region within a state. Not surprisingly, population centers that furnished companies of National Guardsmen suffered more keenly once the AEF entered its most intensive phase of operations than those that did not. For example, the town of Horton, Kansas, home to Company B of the Second Kansas Infantry Regiment, mobilized a total of 571 men and women, out of whom 280 served overseas. Of these, 29 were killed and 80 wounded—much higher numbers than those recorded by comparably sized communities that did not have ties to the National Guard.[88] Likewise, Great Bend, the headquarters for Company C in the same regiment, lost 22 men, while Hays and Garden City, towns of roughly the same population in the same region, recorded 4 and 5 deaths respectively.[89] Of course, for Kansas, whose National Guard units became part of the ill-fated 35th Division, the situation was worse than for many other states, including neighboring Nebraska, whose own National Guard division, the 34th, arrived in France too late to see action. But the pattern that emerges from *Kansas Casualties* was far from unique to the Sunflower State. Other National Guard divisions, such as the 28th from Pennsylvania and the 77th from New York, lost even more men, because, unlike the 35th, they participated in the costly summer fighting at the Aisne-Marne before entering the Meuse-Argonne in the fall. As a result, states like Pennsylvania and New York saw the same clustering of war deaths in particular communities—but with larger numbers in each cluster.

To suggest that what happened to National Guard divisions in 1918 is an American version of the British Army's ill-fated deployment of pals battalions, groups of closely associated volunteers whose slaughter at the Battle of the Somme left some British workplaces and villages nearly emptied of all male members, would be misleading. Even at their worst, casualty rates in the AEF and their impact on male populations at home never came close to the British experience, a fact for which Americans can be grateful. However, the same basic phenomenon operated in both cases—deployment of tight-knit bands of citizen soldiers leading to a concentration of death and injury in specific communities. And it is a phenomenon that continues to bedevil the U.S. Army today, as seen in the Iraq War, where roadside bombs have killed or maimed entire squads of American reservists or National Guardsmen, thus raining tragedy on individual towns and neighborhoods. As one might expect, communities that served as headquarters for National Guard companies, and thus experienced the painful dynamic discussed above, became especially energetic centers of commemoration from 1919 onward. Such communities are more likely to have published memorial volumes or to have erected prominent public war monuments, monuments that often highlight local guardsmen specifically through company rosters or lists of campaigns.

Whether textual or constructed of concrete and bronze, and whether focused on National Guardsmen or draftees, stateside memorials completed between 1919 and 1921, the boom period in postwar commemoration, generally retained the grandiloquent rhetoric of wartime. The "fallen" are "heroes" who "gave their all" or "cheerfully and willingly made the great sacrifice" in the "Great Struggle against Autocratic Rule" or the "Great War for Civilization." Yet even as these lofty sentiments were being printed above honor rolls or etched in stone, consolation proved increasingly elusive for many grieving Americans. Although events like the Versailles Treaty negotiations, where Wilson's Fourteen Points stalled amid European vendettas, and the U.S. Senate's refusal to allow American entry into the League of Nations, a stunning reversal of wartime idealism, did not necessarily have the sweeping impact on memory that many scholars have claimed, they did tend to invalidate the particular variety of affirmative rhetoric left over from the war. Thus, Americans who retained a positive vision of World War I into the 1930s generally did so, as we will see in chapters 1 through 3, by embracing alternative versions of memory, versions that celebrated American service and sacrifice but without invoking the vision of international progressivism that originally underwrote the war effort.

The years immediately following the war, a period of frenetic commemoration and simultaneous reappraisal, also saw an event that pressed the question of *why* with special urgency: the return of American war dead from the battlefields of Europe. After intense debate in 1919 (and an aggressive lobbying effort on the part of the American funeral industry), the federal government elected to give American families the option of repatriating their deceased loved ones at governmental expense. As a result, over a period of three years more than forty thousand sets of remains (nearly half of the American soldiers buried in Europe) were disinterred from military cemeteries along the Western Front, carried to the French coast on special trains, loaded onto American ships, and then transported to Pier 4 in Hoboken, New Jersey, where parties of military and political leaders, sometimes including President Warren G. Harding, turned out to receive the flag-draped coffins—more than two thousand of which would sometimes arrive in one shipment.[90]

From Hoboken, the remains made their way by rail to every imaginable corner of the United States. Ostentatious shrines awaited some; modest headstones, others. In either case, a soldier's reburial was an iconic event, one for which entire towns or neighborhoods turned out. In *The Return of Private Davis from the Argonne* (1940), discussed in detail in chapter 3, regionalist painter John Steuart Curry captured one such ceremony, the details of which played out, again and again, in communities across the country. The painting depicts the members of a small Midwestern town (its water tower visible in the distance) clustered together in the local cemetery, heads bowed, as a preacher gesticulates before a flag-draped coffin. To the side of the group, an honor guard of uniformed legionnaires looks on, flags unfurled. And in the background stands the row of identical black Model Ts that the townspeople rode in on—the perfect detail to evoke the early 1920s. In the case of particularly notable casualties, the crowds were larger, the ritual more elaborate. For example, when Willa Cather's cousin Grosvenor P. Cather, the first Nebraskan officer killed overseas (and the inspiration for the protagonist of Cather's novel *One of Ours*), made his posthumous return to the tiny town of Bladen, Nebraska, in May 1921, two thousand mourners showed up to participate in his reburial.[91] Following musical performances and speeches in the Bladen Opera House, eight flower girls dressed as Red Cross nurses marched behind the horse-drawn hearse that carried Cather's body to the Bladen East Lawn Cemetery, where the local American Legion post subsequently erected a granite monument in his honor.[92] And on Armistice Day 1921 the return of America's war dead culminated in the largest spectacle of them all: the interment of the Unknown Soldier in the Memorial Amphitheater at Arlington National Cemetery, a lavish ritual described for the entire nation, as it occurred, through the new technology known as radio.

These posthumous homecomings carried profoundly mixed messages. On the one hand, stateside reburials anchored the memory of the Great War within the very soil of America. Reminders of American participation in the conflict, and the cost of that participation, became as ubiquitous as the nation's cemeteries. Moreover, interring First World War fatalities in graveyards shared by veterans of the Civil War—or, in the eastern part of the country, veterans of still-earlier conflicts—offered a consoling interpretation of the dead: whatever the causes or outcomes of the war, its fallen participants were absorbed, through repatriation, into a long-standing tradition of patriotic service and valor, a tradition whose compelling social virtues trumped any discussion of historical specifics. This explains the virtual disappearance of Wilsonian rhetoric from the nevertheless affirmative speeches and sermons delivered at reburial ceremonies. For example, the chief orator at G. P. Cather's funeral, Capt. Fred O. Kelly, made little mention of the international aims of the war. Instead, Kelly praised the spirit of self-sacrifice that Cather had shown when, in an act that posthumously won him the Distinguished Service Cross, he mounted the parapet of a trench to direct the machine-gun fire of his men: "To die for others, as Lieut. Cather did, was all that he could possibly do."[93] Significantly, the "others" to whom Kelly referred were Cather's fellow soldiers, not French citizens or the members of a Wilsonian brotherhood of civilized nations. However, for observers who were unable or unwilling to connect the dead to stateside tradition and ritual, this mass repatriation suggested a retreat from "over there"—a disavowal, in other words, of everything for which the United States had fought. (Not surprisingly, in European eyes the removal of American dead reflected American arrogance—as if fallen doughboys were too good for French or Belgian earth.) Indeed, in the final chapter of this study, which recounts the posthumous odyssey of Quentin Roosevelt (the most famous American fatality of the war), we will see just how fraught with conflicting visions and agendas the burial of an American soldier could be.

Largely because of repatriation, the mourning of war casualties in the United States became a more public affair than in other Allied nations—an irony given the scale of European losses versus American. In Great Britain the family of a deceased soldier received, along with the usual correspondence from the soldier's friends and superiors, a condolence note from the king, a set of campaign medals appropriate to the deceased's length and place of service, and a commemorative medallion inscribed with his name. The latter took on the lugubrious nickname the "dead man's penny." The Imperial War Graves Commission, the British counterpart to the ABMC, banned the removal of bodies from the battlefields (along with the erection of private memorials in France or Belgium), and because of the relative proximity of the Continent, concluded that it was unnecessary for the British government to subsidize family pilgrimages to British war cemeteries.[94] In contrast, the U.S. government not only repatriated bodies when requested to do so, but also covered the expenses of widows and mothers who wished to visit overseas cemeteries. A stirring confluence of private grief and public policy, the program of Gold Star Mother Pilgrimages approved by the U.S. Congress and by Calvin Coolidge in 1929 pressed ahead despite the onset of the Depression.[95]

Whether taken "home to God's country," as John Dos Passos sardonically put it, or housed in one of the ABMC's elegant neoclassical cemeteries in France, Belgium, or England, the war dead remained omnipresent in American interwar culture.[96] And the dead *spoke*. Indeed, the trope of the fallen soldier addressing the living from beyond the grave became, as we will see throughout this study, a ubiquitous device for expressing various versions of memory. Again and again—in novels, short stories, poems, plays, sermons, essays, cartoons, and films—lips stilled at Belleau Wood or on the slopes of Montfaucon opened once more, their words intended to cut through the tangle of ambiguities that surrounded the war's essential truths. In "The Body of an American," the concluding section of *1919* (1932), Dos Passos provided the most celebrated literary example of this trope by juxtaposing the plaintive voice of the Unknown Soldier—"Say buddy can't you tell me how I can get back to my outfit?"—with the patriotic banalities uttered by Warren G. Harding during the entombment ceremony and the empty newspaper speak used by the press to describe the proceedings.[97]

However, Dos Passos was hardly alone in reanimating the anonymous corpse deposited at Arlington. Simultaneously everyone and no one—and thus open to endless interpretation and rhetorical manipulation—the Unknown Soldier addressed audiences in the first person in numerous venues. For example, lyricist and New York showman Billy Rose restored the dead man's voice in a popular song of the 1920s titled "The Unknown Soldier." Though he would "do it all over again," Rose's lost doughboy spends most of the song's verses condemning the rich and powerful who suckered him into an early grave:

I wonder if the kings, who planned it all
Are really satisfied?
They played their game of checkers
And eleven million died.[98]

An antiwar documentary from the early 1930s, focused largely on the experiences of African American troops, bore the title *The Unknown Soldier Speaks*.[99] And so did a sermon from the same period by the noted Unitarian theologian John Haynes Holmes. In American poetry of the interwar decades, the Unknown Soldier spoke out everywhere and in many tones—from sentimental (as in E. O. Laughlin's "The Unknown" [1927], where the Unknown Soldier watches his sweetheart unknowingly visit his grave) to credibly profane (as in Carl Sandburg's "And So To-Day" [1922], where the "boy" about to be entombed at Arlington sits up, Lazarus-like, and proclaims, "What the hell?"[100]). Examined in more detail in chapter 2, Americans who utilized the Unknown Soldier as a rhetorically forceful symbol of memory form an impressive list, one that includes, in addition to the names already mentioned above, advertising mogul and U.S. congessman Bruce Barton, Jewish cleric Harold I. Saperstein, Christian writer Harry Emerson Fosdick, American Legion spokesman Frederick Palmer, Harlem Renaissance poet James Weldon Johnson, Southern novelist William Faulkner, novelist and playwright Laurence Stallings, and *Company K* author William March (the penname for William Edward March Campbell).

It is fitting, given the array of ambiguities and interpretive challenges outlined in this section, that the Unknown Soldier, himself an ambiguity, became such a protean agent of memory. By enshrining a nameless lost American, a shadowy stand-in for all Americans sacrificed in World War I, the federal government provided the nation with neither a sense of closure nor a renewal of the seemingly uncomplicated patriotism of the war years. Instead, the Unknown Soldier would become a powerful, culturally pervasive icon precisely because his meaning was as indeterminate as his identity. Acting independently of any official agenda, he would speak with a chorus of polyphonic voices, each identified with a different version of memory, as Americans struggled for two decades to make sense of the First World War.

~

The following chapters tease conclusions about memory from a wide variety of cultural sources. At best, however, this study offers only a sampling of the myriad forms of remembrance that became prominent between the wars, and it easily leaves out more than it includes. Any book devoted to such a broad, interdisciplinary topic will reflect hard choices. For example, war-related radio programs, revealing expressions of patriotism and martial nostalgia, receive little attention here. They deserve more. Also slighted are the many veterans organizations that competed with the American Legion for the attention—and membership dues—of former doughboys, organizations such as the Veterans of Foreign Wars (the legion's chief rival), the Order of the Purple Heart (open to all wounded men), and the hundreds of divisional and regimental reunion societies that flourished after the armistice. Nor does this study explore constructions of the Great War within period war comics, patriotic boys' novels (works with titles like *Over There with Pershing's Heroes at Cantigny*[101]), toy soldier sets, military modeling kits, and aviation pulps. The versions of war memory expressed in the male American youth culture of 1919 to 1941 are crying out for a full-blown analysis that, alas, falls beyond the scope of what can be offered here.

In addition, this study offers an intentionally less-than-exhaustive treatment of topics that have already been thoroughly examined elsewhere. For example, the Gold Star Mother Pilgrimages of the 1930s, poignant spectacles of memory and mourning, will surface repeatedly in the following pages; however, for a definitive account of the pilgrimage program, one should consult John Graham's recent monograph on the subject. By the same token, in his excellent *Unknown Soldiers: The Story of the Missing of the First World War* (2006), Neil Hanson tells the story of the American Unknown Soldier—including his selection, transatlantic passage (at the center of an honorary flotilla), and lavish ceremonial interment—as well as it could be told. Thus, this study focuses on a topic that Hansen does not address—the divided commentary that this ambiguous icon produced among literary artists, clerics, and editorialists. So much has been written on the more familiar works of American World War I literature—*Three Soldiers, The Enormous Room, A Farewell to Arms,* among many others—that they appear at the periphery, rather than the center, of this study. And the same applies to the vast host of Hollywood war films from the 1920s and 1930s, including *Wings, Hell's Angels, Dawn Patrol,* and *All Quiet on the Western Front.* These cinematic expressions of memory are already well served by the fine essays in Peter C. Rollins and John E. O'Connor's *Hollywood's World War I* (1997) and by other sources. Thus, in the pages that might have been devoted to the detailed analysis of film, the reader will instead confront far less familiar artifacts from the period, many of which have never been examined before. In short, this study does not purport to speak from a mountaintop of data collected from every relevant corner of American culture between the wars; instead, it offers several (hopefully well-chosen) case studies in the formation of collective memory—and it examines them in detail. Other case studies might have been offered, with perhaps different thematic results; the topic of World War I in American memory is both large and largely neglected, and if the conclusions offered here provoke challenges from other scholars, so much the better.

One final point: throughout, this book will proceed from the assumption that narrative is as important to the discussion of memory as it is to memory itself. What follows, then, is more than a study of artifacts, of things. It is a study of interesting, often admirable individuals who helped shape collective memory of the First World War—people such as the itinerant painter Horace Pippin, who could barely lift his brush because of wounds sustained during his service with the Harlem Hellfighters; the etcher Kerr Eby, a committed pacifist who recorded the horrors of World War I and then went on, ironically enough, to create some of the most memorable combat art of World War II; the sculptor E. M. Viquesney, a businessman first and an artist second, who created the most popular American statue of World War I only to die in obscurity and despair; the former wartime secretary and canteen worker Mary Lee, whose receipt of a war novel prize in 1929 brought overnight fame and bitter controversy; and the poet James Weldon Johnson, whose anger over the discriminatory treatment of African American Gold Star Mothers prompted one of the most scathing attacks ever launched on a supposedly sacred site of memory. If these compelling individuals, along with others described in following chapters, find a lasting place in the reader's memory, then this book will have succeeded in its own modest form of remembrance.

1

Custodians of Memory

The American Legion and Interwar Culture

> From the point of view of the individual member, the contribution of
> the veterans' organization is magical. By its alchemy, the organization
> transforms an experience that would otherwise be most destructive
> into a social asset. The ex-soldier has lost his years, his youth, and he
> brings back the memory of nameless horrors. There is no place for
> him in civilian society. The veterans' organization gives him a place
> of honor. His fellow soldiers understand him. They value his achieve-
> ments. They do not tire of listening to him so long as he is willing to
> listen to them. When, like all heroes of the past, he is in danger of
> becoming a bore, the society of his fellows saves him from this fate
> so much worse than death.
> —Willard Waller, *The Veteran Comes Back* (1944)

When Willard Waller, a history professor at Columbia University, wrote
the passage quoted above, as part of a study designed to help American
civilians understand the millions of strangers soon to return home from
Europe and the Pacific, the conditions of wartime had all but silenced
criticism of the once-controversial American Legion. After noting the immense value that veterans organizations held for their members, Waller
went on to praise the American Legion in particular for its contributions
to local communities and to the nation as a whole. Waller conceded that
"the social intelligence of [legionnaires] has not always kept pace with
their good intentions," but he urged his readers to consider how much
more dangerous the organization might have been if it "did not mean
well."[1] After all, the professor explained, veterans organizations feed on
an "in-group feeling" that naturally produces a conservative outlook, and
he pooh-poohed allegations that the legion's right-wing ideology undermined American democracy. Americans fearful of groups like the legion
would do well, he suggested, to meet them halfway: "If liberals, intellectuals, labor union members and representatives of the less common shades
of opinion wish to influence veterans in the next twenty-five years, their

best chance will lie in joining the veterans' organizations, participating in their activities, compromising with them, and helping to form their policy in free and democratic discussion."[2]

The unfolding realities of the Second World War (many of which confirmed the legion's predictions), combined with wartime patriotism and feelings of national unity during a time of emergency, helped shape Waller's generous and forgiving assessment of an organization that before 1941 tended to produce polarized responses from Americans. Indeed, for the American Legion's pre–World War II detractors, the organization stood for a brand of hypernationalism that was all but synonymous with fascism. Arguments that equated legionnaires with the Italian paramilitary Blackshirts were, of course, simplistic. Comprised of literally thousands of community and neighborhood posts (not all of which towed the party line), the legion seldom maintained a completely monolithic perspective on anything. Nor was the group's political agenda as consistently right-wing as its critics claimed. In the early 1920s the organization examined several of the U.S. government's wartime industrial initiatives— especially the disastrous aircraft production program (which failed to deliver more than a handful of planes to the AEF)—and demanded to know "who got the money?"[3] Hatred of war profiteers (real or imagined) sometimes shifted this predominantly conservative, middle-class organization into a liberal muckraking mode, which even led to attacks on the short-lived World War I version of what we today call the military-industrial complex. And although the legion had to overcome internal divisions before it could maintain a consistent and coherent position on the matter of adjusted compensation (the so-called bonus that many veterans believed they deserved for lost wages during wartime), the organization hardly displayed a conservative political ethos once it started pressuring the federal government to expand veterans' entitlements. At least when it came to benefits for former soldiers, the legion was no enemy to the welfare state. Although broadly middle-class in outlook, the organization included—and frequently spoke for—working men from across the nation, especially as the Great Depression pushed so many of these veterans into the ranks of the indigent.

However, on a number of hot-button issues, located at the very core of its political identity, the American Legion stood firmly and unapologetically to the right. During the 1920s and 1930s, the organization helped expose and all but eliminate political radicalism in America (during the Red Scare, cartoons in the legion's official magazine longingly portrayed anarchists at the end of a rope), and most legionnaires would have liked nothing better than to stomp out their chief legal adversary, the American Civil Liberties Union. At the same time, educators who sought to uphold academic freedom had good reason to fear the legion: mandatory loyalty oaths for teachers and a standardized curriculum purged of any leftist leanings topped the legion's flag-wrapped agenda for the American classroom. And, finally, on the question of national defense, its true raison d'être, the organization maintained a position that was deeply at odds with the optimistic vision of international brotherhood upheld by Wilsonian progressives and pacifists. Anticipating right-wing arguments later made during the Cold War, the legion asserted that only an intimidating military buildup on the part of the United States could rescue civilization from another world war. According to this reasoning, a formidable American defense force, backed by stockpiles of the latest weapons, would cause potential aggressors to think twice, thereby serving the interests of peace. Disarmament, on the other hand, would invite hostilities, since only the United States could be expected to honor the terms of a given agreement. In one of its earliest articulations of this argument, the legion enlisted the support of none other than John J. Pershing, who in a 1922 issue of *American Legion Weekly* asserted that a stronger peacetime army and navy would have kept the United States out of World War I—and might even have prevented the conflict altogether.[4] Throughout the 1920s and 1930s, the American Legion lobbied for preparedness measures that struck many non-legionnaires not as peace-serving deterrents but as evidence of war mongering. For example, the group called for a peacetime draft, increases in defense spending, an end to American participation in arms talks and treaties, and the guarantee of "universal service" in the event of another war (a proposal intended to equalize wartime salaries for soldiers and civilians and to minimize wartime profits, thereby removing any incentive for arms manufacturers to encourage hostilities). For better or worse, no one in Washington, DC, during the interwar period listened to any of these proposals.

Despite the failure of the American Legion's defense initiatives, even the group's most dismissive critics could not deny that it was a force to be reckoned with—the largest, most powerful veterans organization in American history. More than a million World War I veterans, nearly a quarter of the men inducted into the armed forces in 1917 or 1918, donned the legion's blue uniform. And even before World War II veterans flooded its ranks in 1945, the organization contained more veterans than the combined membership of the Grand Army of the Republic and the United Confederate Veterans at the peak of their popularity. Rival organizations never came close to matching the legion's numbers. The Veterans of Foreign Wars, the legion's chief competitor, failed to attract more than three hundred thousand First World War veterans, and when the head chaplain of the AEF attempted, with Pershing's blessing, to found a society for AEF veterans in 1919, he quickly abandoned the attempt.[5] Too many soon-to-be-discharged servicemen had already flocked to the legion. Within months of its founding in Paris by a small group of maverick AEF officers, led principally by Theodore Roosevelt Jr., the organization became a coast-to-coast presence in the United States as returning veterans fanned out across the nation establishing state-level headquarters that in turn handed out charters for community legion posts (each named after a local fatality). By 1941 more than ten thousand of these posts were in place, seemingly one on every Main Street in America.[6]

From the moment of its inception, this political and cultural juggernaut was news. Of the organizations that became prominent in what a contemporary academic called "The Cult of Nationalism," only the Ku Klux Klan inspired more controversy (or attracted more members).[7] And when the legion wasn't making headlines through its politics, it did so through its notoriously raucous national conventions. Cities selected to host these soirees eagerly anticipated the revenue that so many thousands of comfortable, middle-class men would pour into the local economy, but from a law-and-order standpoint they dreaded the legionnaires' arrival. As Dixon Wecter cleverly put it in his 1944 study of veterans' issues, *When Johnny Comes Marching Home,* "every reunion turned into an *auto da fé* of repudiation against the hapless Eighteenth Amendment."[8] At national meetings like the 1921 convention in Kansas City, a full-scale blowout that featured columns of veterans marching from speakeasy to speakeasy while performing a concert on trash cans, or the 1926 convention in Philadelphia, where representatives of the Colorado chapter released "mules, coyotes, and other Western beasts" onto the city streets, legionnaires behaved like soldiers on leave, which in a sense they were.[9] As the responsibilities of family and career closed in on these men, they increasingly turned to conventions as vacations from middle-class propriety. Reunions with wartime buddies represented fleeting opportunities to reconnect with a youthful experience that became only more glamorous with the passage of time, an experience seemingly freer (despite military constraints) than the civilian routine that came afterward.

Perhaps because the American Legion has just as frequently been associated with lampshade hats and water balloons as it has with antiradicalism and veterans benefits, academics have not always grasped the organization's importance. Scholarly interest in the legion intensified during World War II as historians like Waller and Wecter braced the nation for a new round of social and economic challenges posed by demobilization, but then this interest fell into a deep decades-long slump.[10] Over the years, scattered PhD dissertations focused on the American Legion, along with a trickle of now-forgotten academic and popular-press titles.[11] And that was it—until the publication in 1989 of William Pencak's masterful study *For God and Country: The American Legion, 1919–1941*. Pencak not only provides the fullest account to date of the legion's political activities between the wars, but he also offers a still-unsurpassed analysis of the organization's ideology, as embodied in the all but indefinable term "Americanism." Subsequent monographs on the legion have followed Pencak's lead, revealing the political, social, and cultural complexities of an organization once considered largely irrelevant to the larger narratives of twentieth-century American history. For example, Jennifer Keene's treatment of the legion in *Doughboys, the Great War, and the Remaking of America* (2001) underscores the organization's vital role in the passage of the Serviceman's Readjustment Act of 1944, better known as the GI Bill. Another valuable work, Thomas B. Littlewood's *Soldiers Back Home: The American Legion in Illinois, 1919–1939* (2004), offers a case study in the impact of "sectional differences" on the legion's anything but homogenous internal culture(s).[12] Published one year after Pencak's study, Thomas A. Rumer's *The American Legion: An Official History, 1919–1989* (1990), provides a dense but dependable grand narrative of the organization's history, particularly useful for fact-checking, that complements these other, more exploratory works.[13]

One critical topic, however, has remained unaddressed amid this resurgence of scholarly interest in the American Legion—namely, that of memory. The organization's aggressive politics, which suggest an entirely forward-looking agenda, perhaps explain this neglect. However, while working to strengthen the America of the future and to protect the economic interests of World War I veterans, the legion was, at the same time, memory obsessed, its political outlook and overall ideology informed by a specific vision of the First World War. Two goals contained in the organization's statement of purpose, drafted in 1919, reflected its ties to the past: the legion would strive, first, "to preserve the history and incidents of our participation in the war," and, second, "to cement the ties of comradeship formed in the service."[14] The first of these two objectives was, in part, a matter of literal preservation. Concern over the deteriorating condition of official war records in Washington, DC, prompted the legion to spearhead the congressional lobbying campaign that resulted in the establishment of the National Archives, one of the organization's lesser known but most commendable achievements. At the same time, history, as constructed from the documents that the legion so valued, played an important role in the group's internal culture. Throughout the 1920s the American Legion served as a distributor for dozens of fact-filled divisional histories, tedious works that attempted to clear away the fog of war through overly precise descriptions of troop movements and battles. The legion's own publications also reflected this historical bent. As part of a fund-raising drive for disabled veterans, the organization published a multivolume set (again, all but unreadable) titled *Source Records of the Great War* (1931).[15] Containing a variety of documents, this collection purported to offer the raw material of history for the reader then to interpret. Likewise, the hundreds of legion post histories compiled between the wars reflected the group's interest in preserving a reliable body of archival material covering both the war and the legion's ongoing development. The vast holdings of the American Legion Library and Archives in Indianapolis, more material than could be digested by a hundred researchers in a hundred lifetimes, richly attest to this passion for record keeping.

However, most legionnaires were neither historical researchers nor librarians, and what American participation in the First World War *meant* (the territory of memory) played a far more central role in the organization than efforts to pinpoint exactly what had happened at a given moment on a given battlefield. From the start, the goal of "preserv[ing] the history and incidents" of the war took a backseat to activities designed to lend structure and coherence to shared experience. Memory, not history, shaped the nostalgic content of the legion's periodicals, spawned the organization's remembrance rituals (regularly conducted at the Tomb of the Unknown Soldier and at Armistice Day and Memorial Day functions across the country), and propelled legionnaires out of their posts and into their communities, where they pushed for war monuments and other forms of commemoration long after most Americans felt the desire to pay for them. Between 1919 and 1941, no remembrance organization in the United States expended more energy, raised more money, or enjoyed more success when working to maintain the Great War (especially the memory of its fallen) as a living presence in American culture.

Preserving wartime "comradeship" was also, fundamentally, a matter of formulating and perpetuating collective memory. Bonds between former soldiers required a shared vision of the past, a vision that was powerful enough to offset the natural tendency of wartime ties to weaken over time, so narrative, or storytelling, was important within the legion's internal culture. Rather surprisingly for an organization that supposedly maintained tight control of its members' opinions, the legion's official magazine (known as the *American Legion Weekly* until 1926 and then as the *American Legion Monthly* until 1938[16]) seldom focused exclusively on the group's political agenda. Typically, just one or two feature news stories per issue, along with one or two editorials, reflected the legion's four-pronged mission of crushing radicalism, mentoring America's youth, strengthening national defense, and securing veterans' benefits. Narratives of various kinds comprise the rest of the contents, including humorous cartoon strips (some set in wartime France, others focused on the vicissitudes of middle age), brief "human interest" stories recounting the activities of various posts, historical accounts of World War I battles and campaigns, profiles in courage focused on the exploits of highly decorated soldiers, short stories, and serialized novels. War fiction, in particular, was a staple of the periodical. Well-known war writers such as Leonard H. Nason and Thomas Boyd made regular appearances in the magazine, their action-filled narratives complemented by the dramatic war scenes (painted by Harvey Dunn and Howard Chandler Christy, among others) that often decorated the front cover.

But the American Legion's official news organ was hardly its only venue for narratives that evoked and reinforced collective memory of the war. As Waller understood when asserting that veterans organizations saved their members from becoming bores, "a fate so much worse than death," the legion facilitated oral (as well as written) history.[17] Typically well stocked with alcohol (especially during Prohibition), American Legion halls were safe spaces where veterans could swap stories of youthful adventure and comic mishap without fear of seeming garrulous to the uninitiated. Indeed, a 1929 article in the *Writer's Monthly*, a how-to journal for aspiring authors, recommended that writers hoping to access the "market for war experience" should first contact "the local posts of the American Legion and Disabled World War Veterans."[18] At these community centers for war memory, the article asserted, writers would find promising anecdotes galore, both sobering and humorous, and stories of how medals were won, an especially marketable journalistic commodity (as the legion's own magazine demonstrates).

Thus, to understand the legion's version of war memory, this chapter will examine the kinds of narratives that legionnaires wrote and read during the 1920s and 1930s, especially the war-related fiction that appears so frequently in the organization's official magazine. Then, after establishing the general contours of the legion's vision of the First World War, the chapter will focus on the issues of race and gender as they fed into the organization's collective memory. Here particular attention will be paid to the controversial results of a war novel competition cosponsored by the legion in 1928. First, however, a formative influence on the organization's internal culture must be addressed. As Pencak observes, the legion drew its inspiration from numerous fixtures in early twentieth-century American life, including the model of neo-masculinity provided by Theodore Roosevelt, the rugged ethos of the American Boy Scout movement, the war nostalgia and commemorative ritual associated with the GAR and the UCV, and the public-service mission embodied in the YMCA.[19] However, an additional influence, perhaps more powerful than any of these, helped lay the foundation for the legion's preoccupation with the past—namely, the "memory culture" that formed an integral part of the AEF. As we will see, the American Legion, *the* driving force in American First World War commemoration, grew out of a military organization that was no less determined to keep the supposed glory of World War I alive for centuries to come.

Souvenirs and Snapshots: "Memory Culture" and the American Expeditionary Forces

Since the nineteenth century, Western cultures have associated the direct experience of war with heightened states of perception and intensified powers of recall. Veterans speak of their wartime memories standing out, with seemingly greater clarity, from all other recollections. And nations have privileged personal memories of war as well, making them the focus of massive oral history projects, for example, or highlighting them during commemorative rituals (as when an American Pearl Harbor veteran shares his personal experiences with visitors before they embark for the USS *Arizona* Memorial, an unforgettable moment still repeated daily in 2009). Among American soldiers in the First World War, the desire to preserve wartime experience, through mementos and personal records of various kinds, was overwhelming and, as we will see, fully sanctioned by the AEF's leadership. Urged at every turn to stockpile impressions of their part in the war, troops roamed bivouacs and battlefields equipped with their own portable cameras, commonly recorded daily events in pocket diaries (despite orders that forbade the possession of such potentially compromising documents), devoured print media (such as *Stars and Stripes*) that memorialized the war as it was happening, mailed home trophies taken from dead or captured Germans, and, in the manner of tourists, purchased a wide array of commercial souvenirs inscribed with memory-rich place-names like "Château-Thierry," "Verdun," and the "Argonne." Collectively, these activities comprise what we will call the "memory culture" of the AEF, a culture that reached out to every overseas American soldier with the message that involvement in the Great War was an experience to be cherished and contemplated (via relics, photographs, unit histories, and other paraphernalia) long after the armistice.

This impulse to retain and privilege wartime memories no doubt burned just as intensely within American Civil War soldiers. However, a pair of factors set the doughboys apart from their martial ancestors. First, the military and civilian progressives who ran the AEF exercised an unprecedented degree of control over virtually every area of a soldier's existence, including his sex life (reducing venereal disease was a near obsession among American war planners), perceptions of French culture, and, to the degree to which it was possible, the general shape of his wartime memories. Unlike past military commanders, the AEF's leaders wanted not simply to win the war but also to provide lessons in civic responsibility and moral uplift for the nation's citizen soldiers. From the beginning, then, their objective was to see the war become a truly usable past.

To keep this usable past fresh in the minds of veterans, the U.S. government offered an unprecedented array of commemorative regalia. Even before most troops had returned home from Europe, the War Department approved the design of an official Victory Medal ultimately issued to every American soldier. And unlike similar decorations produced by other Allied nations, the American Victory Medal identified the particular engagements in which its recipient participated. So-called battle clasps, attached to the medal's ribbon, publicly displayed the wearer's military record, thereby reinforcing personal pride and esprit de corps. Upon discharge each soldier also received a Victory Button, a lapel badge in the shape of a star that the War Department encouraged veterans to wear at job interviews and in other social situations where evidence of past military service would supposedly give them an edge. Wounded men received an official document, each copy personalized by a calligrapher, that depicted Columbia conferring "The Accolade of the New Chivalry of Humanity" upon a kneeling soldier. (The Purple Heart Medal, for which many World War I veterans later applied, did not become available until 1932.)

The War Department also made sure that trophies and other material reminders of service remained with veterans. Far more than any other soldiers in the First World War, the doughboys were voracious souvenir hunters, and each day the AEF's postal service willingly shipped literally tons of captured articles to homes spread across the United States. Indeed, *Stars and Stripes* reported that in January 1919 alone, "15,000 mailsacks full of German helmets" left the port of Bordeaux on American vessels.[20] Troops mailed home whatever they could grab—Luger pistols (which were especially coveted), Iron Crosses, pieces of crashed aircraft, shell casings, and so forth—and when the supply of desirable battlefield items began to run low, as it did for soldiers in the Army of Occupation in 1919, European manufacturers stepped in to ply the well-paid Americans with a seemingly endless variety of war-related bric-a-brac. According to the *Stars and Stripes,* which reported on the doughboys' penchant for keepsake collecting in almost every other issue (often lampooning it in cartoons), by March 1919 German plants that had once supplied equipment for the Kaiser's army now specialized in the production of "war mementoes." To satisfy "the insatiable American craze for souvenirs," such plants cranked out "rings with miniature Iron Crosses on them, buttons, ashtrays," and other knick-knacks.[21] War memory became big business.

However, the most evocative souvenirs of participation in the Great War came free of charge. In a move that once again confirmed its understanding of the importance of personal possessions as signifiers of memory—or, if one prefers, as memory fetishes—the U.S. Army allowed servicemen to keep all of their military clothing and equipment upon discharge, everything but their rifles or pistols, which many doughboys nevertheless smuggled home. The army was so accommodating in this regard that shortly before reentering civilian life soldiers could request replacements for lost or worn-out items. The military discharge document given to each departing member of the AEF actually included a check-off list, which verified that the soldier in question had retained his helmet, gas mask, overseas cap, and other military items. No one would leave without a full array of memory-summoning paraphernalia.

The second factor that defined the AEF's memory culture and set it apart from similar phenomena during earlier American wars involved technology. Recent inventions allowed the doughboys to mix together mass-produced imagery with more personal visual statements, in ways that were impossible fifty years earlier, and facilitated as never before the rapid transferal of memory into print media. Two innovations in the field of photography dominated the visual record of experience that veterans later hung on their walls or arranged in albums—the panoramic camera, typically employed by professional photographers, and the hand-held pocket camera or Kodak "Brownie," a more potentially subversive device carried to and from Europe by thousands of soldiers. The former, a massive contraption fitted with a concave lens, created so-called yard-longs, large rectangular photographs, sometimes more than three feet in length, that could capture an entire company of men (more than two hundred troops) in one portrait. Although the soldiers in the finished image appear to stand in straight lines, before taking the shot the photographer would arrange his subjects in a semicircle in front of the concave lens, a technique that explains why barracks or other buildings in the background of panoramic photographs appear to tilt or bend. Studios in the United States and Europe produced thousands of these images, and among members of the AEF they became a standard souvenir.

The appeal of such portraits is easy to understand. By bringing so many interchangeable figures together in one frame, panoramic photographs offered a reassuring sense of military solidarity and strength, especially when taken prior to a unit's arrival at the front. Thus, unlike the studio tintype of the Civil War era, which typically featured just one or two soldiers posing with especially ferocious-looking weapons or other eccentric props, yard-longs literally focused on the mass, not the individual. However, as if to defy this emphasis on uniformity, doughboys would often write the names of their buddies on these images, along with arrows that matched names with faces. In addition, the owner of a given photograph would usually mark his own visage, often nearly invisible, with an *X*.

Taken with the full support of military authorities, panoramic photographs furthered the interests of the AEF's progressive agenda—and of official memory—by depicting soldiers as homogenous blocks of military manpower. Such images are, if you will, snapshots of Americanization in action—that is, the notion, carried into the 1920s and 1930s through the American Legion's collective memory that the AEF served as a military melting pot, dissolving regional and ethnic differences among its members and strengthening their devotion to the nation. Personal cameras, on the other hand, allowed for individualized, vernacular expression. Seldom utilized, for obvious reasons, during combat, this portable form of memory technology provided recreation for soldiers during intervals of leisure. Military orders issued in the summer of 1918 restricted the use of personal cameras to officers; however, every other enlisted man seemed to have one—especially after the armistice. Doughboys mugged for one another's cameras with bottles of wine or beer in hand, documented the girth of their fifty-pound backpacks, posed with French (or German) girls, captured blurry images of Old World scenery as it moved past their railcars, and, whenever possible, recorded the devastation of the Western Front—the smashed tanks, mine craters, and other battlefield wreckage that American troops, in particular, found endlessly fascinating.

Handheld cameras gave American soldiers ample opportunity to mock the ideological pressures that the U.S. Army and its civilian partners brought to bear upon them—ample opportunity, that is, to *show* that which the AEF's leadership prohibited or denied. However, when examining personal photo albums or scrapbooks from the First World War, one detects surprisingly little tension between personal photographs and those provided by military or commercial sources. Individualized mementos sit comfortably next to the mass-produced variety. Vernacular expression coexists peaceably with official discourse.

One of the largest such albums, kept by Sgt. Thomas Fletcher of Base Hospital #4, resides in the Special Collections Department of the University of Colorado.[22] Fletcher, whose military serial number had just four digits, was among the very first American soldiers to reach Europe, arriving even earlier than Pershing and his celebrated team of handpicked men. Part of Cleveland, Ohio's Lakeside Unit of the U.S. Army Medical Corps, Fletcher's outfit landed at Blackpool, England, in May 1917, just weeks after the American declaration of war, and subsequently served in the British sector of the Western Front. Few objects passed through the sergeant's hands without winding up glued to a page inside his massive, folio-sized album, a personal archive so bulky, in fact, that one wonders how Fletcher moved its contents from place to place. Samples of French currency, British army insignia, cinema tickets, menus from restaurants in

Paris, typed military orders, identification documents, promotion papers, dog tags, Brownie snapshots of a leave spent in Monte Carlo—everything went in, along with literally hundreds of commercial postcards showing places that Fletcher had visited. Indeed, mass-produced images dominate more than 50 percent of this remarkable monument to the AEF's memory culture. And there is nothing perfunctory about their inclusion. Fletcher filled up every available page, and many of the postcards have handwritten captions beneath them detailing the sergeant's travels.

A sampling of photo albums compiled by other doughboys suggests that Fletcher's approach to personal remembrance, a blend of self-expression and commercial standardization, was the norm. For example, Pfc. Clyde James, a member of the 314th Signal Battalion (part of the 89th "Middle West" Division), filled the first half of his album with postcards purchased in France; in the second half, studio portraits of James and his comrades taken in Bitburg, Germany, along with Brownie snapshots of field exercises in the Rhineland, predominate.[23] In this case the soldier's assignment to a frontline unit that eventually became part of the Army of Occupation helps explain the even division between commercial imagery and more personalized mementos. Amid the notorious tedium of occupation duty, James probably had more time and (thanks to the post-armistice loosening of army regulations) more opportunity to take pictures. Cpl. Ray Wentworth of the 314th Mobile Ordnance Repair Shop (also part of the 89th Division) showed a taste for the macabre in his photo selections.[24] The personal snapshots in Wentworth's memory book indicate that he spent much of his time overseas in a machine shop located far from the front line; however, the dozens of commercial postcards contained in his album concentrate on battlefield horrors—piles of skeletons unearthed at Verdun, a headless German corpse, a horse dangling from a tree, and so forth. Perhaps Wentworth was struck, like so many American soldiers, by the weirdness of the Western Front, with its constant display of death. Or perhaps he intended these gruesome images as warnings for future children and grandchildren.

Beyond enabling doughboys to create their own photographic keepsakes—in a way that often reinforced, rather than undermined, official agenda—early twentieth-century technology also allowed AEF regiments and divisions to produce morale-boosting newspapers, which served at the same time as textual memorials of sorts, and even unit histories. The latter contained detailed narratives of a given outfit's stateside training and overseas service, usually supplemented with cartoons and rosters of the living and the dead. Combined with the ready availability of French and German printers eager to do business with well-paid American soldiers, the typewriter—"a potent symbol of modernity and high technology," according to British military historian Paddy Griffith—turned many doughboys into publishers.[25] During the spring of 1919, unit newspapers became the rage, working in tandem with *Stars and Stripes* to lift the spirits of soldiers who were increasingly frustrated with the slow rate of demobilization. Two samples demonstrate the polish and sophistication that these publications achieved. In the largely Kansan 137th Infantry Regiment, part of the 35th Division, a team of doughboy journalists produced no fewer than eight issues of the *Jayhawkerinfrance,* a four-page medley of news features, sports stories, and doggerel verse that helped the regiment endure a miserable winter spent cleaning up battlefield debris near Verdun. Even more elaborate, the *Skirmisher,* the official news organ of the Fourth "Ivy" Division (a seasoned outfit that became part of the Army of Occupation in Germany), ran up to twenty-six pages per issue before offering its "last spasm" in the form of its "Knights of Columbus" edition, published in May 1919.[26]

Both publications share a number of characteristics and in many respects anticipate the flavor of the American Legion's periodicals. Something of the spirit of these newspapers, along with that of the *Stars and Stripes,* would live on in the *American Legion Weekly* and *Monthly.* For example, the "in-group" feeling that Willard Waller later identified with the legion appears everywhere. Sometimes this feeling comes out as esprit de corps. Lead articles in the *Jayhawkerinfrance* proudly describe the 137th Infantry's triumphant inspection by General Pershing, the honorary decoration of the regimental flag with battle streamers, and words of praise offered to the Kansas doughboys by Gen. Robert L. Bullard, head of the Second Army.[27] By the same token, an editorial in the *Skirmisher* summarizes the Ivy Division's string of battles, from Château-Thierry to the Meuse-Argonne, and concludes, "Surely that is a record that every man in the Fourth Division should be proud of."[28] The variety of humor employed in these newspapers emphasizes solidarity as well. In both publications, gossipy news items poke fun at individuals (even sergeants and occasionally junior officers), but do so in a way that suggests no one in the unit, a family of sorts, is without foibles or absurdities. Less generous are pieces aimed at outsiders, especially slackers on the home front or claimants to undeserved military honors. A cartoon in the *Skirmisher,* for instance, angrily depicts a foppish character of deliberately mixed ethnicity, one "Percivle Socrates Alonzo," who "announced on November 12, 1918 that it had been his intention to enlist that very day."[29] Another cartoon, in the same newspaper, mocks "the guy that wears his service stripes before he earns them."[30] On leave the doughboy in question proudly displays his fraudulent insignia. But once back among his comrades, he nervously hides his sleeve.

Like the *Stars and Stripes* (and the legion's later periodicals), such newspapers also offered historical narratives intended to situate individual experience within the larger picture of army-level operations— or even prewar European history. Thus, in its first issue, the *Jayhawkerinfrance* described the capture of Louis XVI and Marie Antoinette in the French town of Varennes, the "same Varennes" (located in the Meuse-Argonne region) where the 137th Infantry fought 127 years later.[31] Remembrance of the dead played a central role in these publications as well. In its January 1919 issue, the *Jayhawkerinfrance* paid tribute, through a lead article, to the 137th Infantry's combat fatalities. "The Fallen," the newspaper announced, "Have Not Been Forgotten."[32] A similar piece in the *Skirmisher* urged the members of the Fourth Division to "remember our buddies who will stay in France."[33] And both newspapers stressed their own value not only as sources of news, but also as keepsakes—as textual memorials that would only become more precious over time. The staff of the *Skirmisher* urged members of the Fourth Division to purchase extra copies of the newspaper for relatives and sweethearts, who would treasure them. Going one better, the *Jayhawkerinfrance* ingeniously included a large blank box on one of its inside pages. Here doughboys could write a short letter before mailing the newspaper to "the folks at home." Blending the discourse of commercial advertising with remembrance rhetoric, the editors called upon the men of the 137th Infantry to "DO IT NOW!" or miss the opportunity to create a "souvenir that they will prize as long as they live."[34] Few newspapers in history have worked so hard to avoid being thrown away.

Often more concerned with commemoration than with breaking news, which was closely censored anyway, doughboy journalism reflected the memory culture of the AEF on many levels, especially as editors sought to transform newspapers into mementos. However, as demobilization approached, publishers in uniform often shifted their focus to an even more explicit expression of memory: the unit history. Some works in this genre proved to be too much for part-time amateurs. The AEF's divisional histories, massive volumes beyond the capabilities of anyone serving in France or Germany in 1919, would come later, most of them published between 1920 and 1930 (and advertised in the pages of the *American Legion Weekly* and *Monthly*). However, regimental and company histories were another matter. During the spring of 1919, literally hundreds of different titles poured out of French and German print shops. One can only imagine how German printers must have felt while producing texts that described their occupiers' victories and their own army's defeat. However, patriotism did not prevent German firms from taking credit, often on the front cover, for the quality typesetting and binding that such works display.

Again, a pair of samples reflect the time, care, and money that dough-boys lavished on textual memorials. The first of these, *The Ninth U.S. Infantry in the World War* (produced by a *Buchdruckerei*, or letterpress printer, in the Rhineland in 1919) presents the history of an exceptionally experienced and (concomitantly) casualty-ridden outfit. Part of the celebrated Second Division, the "old Ninth Infantry" fought at Belleau Wood and then in every subsequent AEF campaign, a gory record that produced a replacement rate of more than 100 percent.[35] As a result, nearly three-quarters of this somber volume, which features a funereal drawing of a no-man's-land on its cover, are taken up by lists—company-by-company rosters of those men who were with the regiment while it served in Germany preceded by "rolls of honor" that identify those killed in action, gassed, wounded, or "evacuated sick to hospital." The latter are, of course, far lengthier than the former. In the section devoted to Company C, for example, the "roll of honor" runs, double-columned, for seven pages. The list of men still standing, as it were, in 1919 takes up just four pages. Understandably, given such a grotesque ratio of casualties to survivors, *The Ninth U.S. Infantry in the World War* eschews the jokes and cartoons that so often appear in such texts. For this hard-hit regiment the war was no laughing matter. The volume also contains a minimum of commemorative iconography and inflated official rhetoric. The distinctive insignia of the Second Division, the profile of an American Indian set inside a star, appears just once—on the final page—and the one-sentence preface, while quietly expressing a deep sense of esprit de corps, avoids the grandiloquent Wilsonian discourse common to unit histories produced in 1919: "This history," writes the anonymous editor, "is published in answer to the many requests of members of the command, and in order to preserve the record of the gallant deeds, the valuable service, and the roster of all officers and men of the Ninth Infantry, we are offering the present edition to the public."[36] One senses in this carefully controlled language—so similar to the discourse later used by Eisenhower in the ABMC guidebooks—an implicit argument: the narrative set up by this preface will offer "pure" history, simple and straightforward, without boasting or embellishment. After all, the book exists only because members of the regiment asked for it.

Another unit history, likewise published in Germany in 1919, could not be more different in either style or content. While *The Ninth U.S. Infantry in the World War* is solemn in tone and appearance—as befitting the volume's hair-raising rolls of honor—*Company F Three Hundred and First Engineers* presents the Great War as an uncomfortable camping trip that was nevertheless not to be missed. No lists of KIAs or wounded appear in this volume, a beautiful leather octavo produced by one J. P. Bachem in Cologne, because no one in the unit, with the exception of six soldiers injured in an accident, met with harm. As the narrative makes clear, Company F's greatest trial by fire occurred following the Saint Mihiel offensive, when the 301st Engineers, attached to the Fourth Corps, received orders to build a new road in an area soon known, rather melodramatically, as "Death Valley." Here a German shell blew one of the company's mules to "mule heaven."[37] But there were no human casualties in "Death Valley"—just a good deal of hunger and frustration produced by "thirty consecutive meals of 'Corned Willy.'"[38] Company F's war, seldom genuinely dangerous and often anticlimactic, inspired an illustration-packed history that overcompensates in various ways for the unit's lack of combat honors. For example, the photographs of ruinous French farmhouses, churches, and bridges that appear sprinkled throughout the narrative create a misleading impression, suggesting weeks of perilous duty amid a violence-filled war zone. In fact, few of these structures were damaged while Company F served in the vicinity. Likewise, the collection of cartoons and sketches that takes up the final quarter of the volume, following the company roster, highlights the engineers' exposure to enemy shell fire—a memorable experience, to be sure, but one that occurred infrequently and with zero loss of life among the unit's two-legged members.

Titled "Objective Obtained," the final cartoon in *Company F Three Hundred and First Engineers* looks into the future, depicting a veteran of Company F comfortably smoking a pipe in his den and nostalgically revisiting his war experience (see fig. 2).[39] Over the fireplace mantel, in a traditional place of domestic honor, the former soldier's war souvenirs appear—his rifle, gas mask, and medals, along with a German spiked

2. "Objective Obtained." Cartoon in *Company F, Three Hundred and First Engineers* (1919).

helmet. As the veteran contemplates these mementos, the smoke from his tobacco forms the ghostly image of a doughboy marching in the rain. One might be tempted to interpret this spectral figure as evidence of lingering trauma. However, when placed within the context of Company F's far-from-harrowing war experience, the image points in a different direction, promising that time and distance will soften wartime hardship. Today's discomfort, the cartoon asserts, will become tomorrow's pleasurable recollections. Similar cartoons, likewise depicting middle-aged veterans parked next to fireplaces, appear in many other unit histories and newspapers. Indeed, such imagery was so familiar that a cartoon in *Sapper,* the newspaper of the 318th Engineers (part of the Sixth Division), reworked it as a piece of satire. Titled "1945 A.D.," this jab at the seemingly glacial pace of demobilization features an elderly veteran, again encamped next to the family hearth, talking with his grandchildren. When one of the children asks, "Say, grandpa, what did you do in the war?" (à la the famous British recruiting poster), the veteran replies that he spent "28 years" waiting for his discharge.[40] The cartoon is somewhat illogical—regardless of how long demobilization took, the war on the Western Front ended in 1918, not 1945—but its point is clear enough.

However, cartoons that projected into the future the frustration and bitterness felt by many members of the AEF in 1919, as they endured months of drill or physical labor while waiting to go home, were rare. Far more common was the anticipation of nostalgia presented in "Objective Obtained." In the end, the military and civilian progressives who set the ideological agenda of the AEF succeeded in creating a usable past, at least in the short run, for more than two million citizen soldiers. No one missed the message that service in the war was a transformative experience never to be forgotten. Indeed, as we have seen, troops returned home from the Great War laden with an unprecedented array of military memorabilia. Thanks to early twentieth-century technology and War Department decree, keepsakes of military service assumed a dazzling multiplicity of forms. Thus, the title "Objective Obtained" applies both to the veteran of Company F, who can at last relish his souvenirs in postwar comfort, and to the AEF policies that worked to nurture such imagery in the minds of American soldiers.

In a way, the presence of so many American troops in France and Germany during the spring of 1919 proved a short-term boon for collective memory. Although morale in the Army of Occupation, in particular, plummeted as months passed with no sign of demobilization in sight—a potentially explosive situation that led Pershing to develop a time-filling program of athletics and interunit competitions—post-armistice service, however resented, meant that doughboys digested their war experience en masse, with ample opportunity to stockpile souvenirs and to learn the usages of military remembrance. The more time spent in the AEF's memory culture, the more doughboys learned, in a sense, *how* to remember. The homogeneity of the personal artifacts, both photographic and textual, that these soldiers left behind is often surprising.

From 1919 onward the legion would borrow certain features of this memory culture, fusing them with commemorative practices established by earlier American veterans' organizations. For example, commemorative regalia became central to the organization's promotion of in-group feeling. In this way the legion capitalized on the love of distinctive insignia that so many American soldiers expressed when being photographed in France or Germany. In both studio portraits and Brownie snapshots, doughboys invariably pose with their left arm turned toward the camera, thereby showing off their divisional shoulder patches and overseas stripes (one per six months of European service). Soldiers with wound stripes (one per wound, worn on the lower right sleeve) usually fold their arms in such a way that all of their insignia are visible. The pride that AEF members felt in connection with these emblems, which set them apart visually from the millions of American troops who missed out on the fighting, is often evident on their faces. Not to be outdone, the American Legion created its own array of fetishistic regalia, likewise intended to inspire a sense of belonging and esprit de corps. Reproduced on everything from bass drums to flags, and used (to this very day) to mark the graves of veterans in American cemeteries, the organization's star symbol became one of the most familiar patriotic icons of the interwar period. And it was a symbol that legionnaires wore at post meetings, parades, and conventions. Few issues of the *American Legion Weekly* or *Monthly* failed to include advertisements for a seemingly endless variety of fashion memorabilia, including rings, tie pins, watch fobs, cuff links, hats (modeled after the overseas cap of World War I fame), and chrome parade helmets, all adorned with the legion's familiar celestial emblem. Partially inspired by the spread of distinctive insignia during the war years (divisional shoulder patches, for example, were something new in 1918), the American Legion's paramilitary trappings also owed much to the GAR, which used military regalia and rhetoric—the very term "post" is an example—to create a metaphorical *army* of veterans. This trope was not without political implications, as Edward Bellamy understood when he drew upon the GAR in his utopian vision of the "Industrial Army," a militaristic force for good, in *Looking Backward*.[41] The legion saw itself in similar terms.

The AEF's memory culture also influenced the kinds of articles and cartoons featured in the legion's periodicals. To a certain extent, doughboy journalism lived on in the *American Legion Weekly* and *Monthly*. Like their AEF predecessors, these magazines offered historical accounts of battles and campaigns, designed so that veterans could better understand how their individual experience fit into a larger strategic whole; tributes to the fallen that in terms of language and imagery might have appeared in either the *Jayhawkerinfrance* or the *Skirmisher;* reports on remembrance activities; and various examples of insider humor, including cartoons and comic strips that alternately revisited wartime absurdities (now from a safe distance) and gently mocked the social and domestic duties that defined middle age for these predominantly middle-class veterans. This is not to say, however, that the American Legion's magazines were tied entirely to the past. Although, again, less prominent than one might expect, political pieces that focused on familiar areas of the organization's concern (such as military preparedness, the need to purge American schools of leftist instructors, or the adjusted compensation question) carried these publications well beyond any journalistic formulas devised in 1918 and 1919. Likewise, the inclusion of war fiction, which became especially common from 1926 onward (thanks to the new monthly format), offered a venue for the expression of memory unseen in most AEF publications.

Nevertheless, the American Legion's ferocity as a remembrance organization, zealously pledged to keeping American soldiers of the Great War forever enshrined as heroes and patriots, cannot be understood without bringing the AEF's own memory agenda into view. The irony, in the end, is that the sense of homogeneity—of truly *collective* memory—imprinted on so many of the AEF's remembrance artifacts lasted only as long as soldiers remained overseas. Once free of the AEF's omnipresent progressive agenda, memory splintered like an artillery projectile, its shards and fragments tearing through postwar America to create the cultural "hole" or wound that David Kennedy has noted. Although it never stopped trying, the legion discovered during the 1920s and 1930s that it could not control memory of the First World War at a national level any more than it could convince the federal government to stockpile arms, reintroduce the draft, or forgo entry into international treaties. As we will see in chapter 2, even the Tomb of the Unknown Soldier, a national monument with close ties to the American Legion, took on a multiplicity of meanings during the interwar years, some patriotic, others antiheroic. Thus, the organization's version of the Great War, with its emphasis on Americanization and the masculine virtues of service, was just another piece of cultural shrapnel—albeit a large one with the power to maim those who stood in its way. When it came to collective memory, all the legion could ultimately do was to refine the vision of a glorious past kept alive in its more than ten thousand local posts and, where possible, spread that construct outward into the communities that surrounded these citadels of remembrance.

The contours of the American Legion's war, which quickly moved beyond the bankrupt idealism of Woodrow Wilson to a more subtle and arguably more dangerous form of idealism, serve as the focus for the next section of this chapter. Here we will examine the ideological alchemy that translated a failed national effort—for American intervention in World War I certainly did *not* make the world safe for democracy—into a worthwhile personal experience for each individual soldier.

"The things that made it hell, yet made us love it too": Memory and Idealism in America's Largest Veterans Organization, 1919–1941

Many veterans who attended the American Legion's 1939 convention, held in Chicago, purchased an especially revealing souvenir—a thirty-eight-page comic book titled *Memoirs of a Vet*. Written and illustrated by Nick Nichols, formerly a member of the 137th Infantry (the same unit that produced the *Jayhawkerinfrance*), the book recounts the experiences of an ordinary infantryman as he leaves his sweetheart to enlist, undergoes basic training, sails to France, fights on the Western Front, receives a nearly fatal wound (from a bayonet, of all things), and then returns home. Made up entirely of three-panel cartoon strips, many of which Nichols originally published in the *Chicago Daily Times*, *Memoirs of a Vet* seems, at first sight, to offer an irreverent, largely comic account of the Great War as experienced by an often bumbling enlisted man. Indeed, many of Nichols's panels depict the humorous vicissitudes of an especially pitiful sad sack: last to join the mess line, the protagonist goes hungry; lured into a craps game, he loses his army pay and even has to wire his parents for an additional ten dollars; he flirts with the colonel's daughter without knowing that she is the colonel's daughter; and so forth.

But many of the images are much darker. For example, as his troopship, a British vessel, heads to Liverpool, the hero encounters a hideously mutilated member of the crew, a once-handsome Englishman who became a wanderer after a shell blew up in his face during his first battle. And this "Gargoyle of the Galley" is just the beginning.[42] A few pages later, the protagonist reaches France just as a hospital train pulls into view. One of its occupants "left most of his body on the battlefield."[43] Then come the British "gas cases" with their bandaged eyes.[44] Nichols's increasingly panicked enlisted man subsequently prays that he may "go out like a light" and avoid becoming a "cripple or blind man."[45] In keeping with these revelations of the true face of Mars, the main character's single moment of combat, which comes near the end of *Memoirs of a Vet*, is both farcical and terrifying. Sent into no-man's-land as the member of a raiding party, he encounters a gigantic German and quickly demonstrates his ineptitude when it comes to hand-to-hand combat. Bayoneted and left for dead, the hero is subsequently rescued by a group of poilus (French soldiers) and eventually sent home on an American hospital ship. Looking out to sea, he reflects on his experiences: "what a terrible thing war is . . . the taking of the most precious of God's gifts . . . LIFE!"[46]

With its blend of humor and horror, *Memoirs of a Vet* could be interpreted as a reflection of the American Legion's endorsement of isolationism at the end of the 1930s. After all, the inside back cover of this twenty-five-cent souvenir depicts the sobering image of a war cemetery—endless crosses marked "Lest We Forget / 1918"—and bears the slogan, in bloodred ink, "Let's Keep America Out of War!" a message in keeping with the protagonist's somber ruminations during his return voyage to New York Harbor. However, as comic books go, Nichols's is a remarkably complex and thematically conflicted example. Indeed, the sense of ambiguity that permeates this seemingly modest narrative anticipates that of present-day graphic novels. How, then, does this visual war memoir undermine its own apparent attempt to de-glorify war? One feature that detracts from the antiheroic comedy and gore is the author's use of a frame narrative. *Memoirs of a Vet* opens not in 1917 but in 1939, and the imagery on the first page creates an atmosphere of comfort and nostalgia—precisely the atmosphere that military cartoonists in 1919 imagined for themselves in drawings like "Objective Obtained." In the opening three panels, Nichols depicts a portly middle-aged veteran rummaging through his army footlocker while surrounded by his curious children. The former soldier unearths the usual souvenirs and then discovers his wartime diary, which, of course, provides the narrative that follows. At the end of the story, we return to this cozy scene as the protagonist, now joined by his wife, closes his book of memories and takes stock of his good fortune, having exchanged "cooties" for "cuties."[47] Although the narrator's diary contains much that is disturbing or repellant, these images of middle-class domesticity (the veteran's vest and tie, worn on the weekend, establish his social status in the very first panel) effectively muffle the horror. Here war leaves no lingering trauma. The past is locked inside a book and buried deep within a footlocker, which the veteran can access as he pleases. Note, too, that family affection intensifies in the presence of war memory. As the hero closes his diary in the final panel, his son and daughter hang affectionately from his arms and shoulders, looking anything but frightened by the story they have heard (see fig. 3).

In addition, this frame narrative, with its images of an implicitly successful and well-dressed family man, performs an ideological linkage central to the American Legion's construction of its members' wartime past. Military service, the author implies, fosters the abilities needed for success, for achieving the American dream. Nichols's accident-prone enlisted man might seem a dubious vehicle for this message. After all, he twice narrowly avoids charges of desertion. In the first instance, he overstays his twelve-hour leave in New York City and nearly misses his troopship as it pulls out of the harbor. The second infraction is more serious. Fed up with marching in the Vosges Mountains, the protagonist decides to go AWOL with another soldier. The two men successfully slip away, but their guilty consciences, along with fears of the firing squad, soon force them back to their unit, where, fortunately, no one has noticed their absence. However, the hero's completion of his duty, when assigned to the raiding party, ultimately overshadows these instances of comic misconduct. Although clumsy and incompetent, he fights when he could have run away, and his red badge of courage (unlike the ironic wound that Private Fleming receives in Crane's novel) is just that—proof that even a sad sack has guts. The penultimate image in *Memoirs of a Vet*, a wedding picture of the protagonist (still in uniform) posing next to his sweetheart, steers the reader toward this interpretation. Beneath this panel Nichols writes, "And so we were married . . . your mother and I . . . How proud I was of her when we marched down the aisle of our little church . . . and I guess she was a little proud of me, too."[48] War, Nichols suggests, may indeed be "a terrible thing," but it has nevertheless made the protagonist a *man,* one worthy of his bride's respect and implicitly equipped for middle-class success.

The cover illustration for *Memoirs of a Vet*, a drawing titled *Zero Hour,* also seems out of keeping with the narrative's sometimes comic, sometimes gruesome content (see fig. 4). It is a scene of high drama that might have appeared on a film poster: while a platoon of doughboys prepares to go over the top, two officers in the foreground count down the last few seconds of safety. This suspenseful subject does not lack a certain glamour. As the soldiers wait for zero hour, exploding shells light up the distant horizon, sending flames into the night sky and illuminating the familiar barbed wire and ruins of an isolated war zone. The scene has an

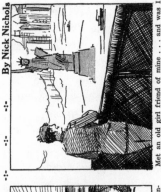

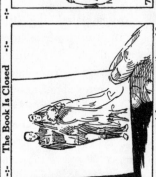

3. The final page of *Memoirs of a Vet* (1939) by Nick Nichols.

4. The front cover of *Memoirs of a Vet* (1939) by Nick Nichols.

eerie beauty that, again, gives little indication of the more hideous imagery contained within the comic book. Interestingly, an advertisement for this same drawing, available for twenty cents per copy, appears on the inside back cover—sandwiched between the previously mentioned drawing of a cemetery on the Western Front and the slogan "Let's Keep America Out of War!" Oblong like a panoramic photo, the drawing offers a dramatic, even perversely alluring vision of the past that works at cross purposes with both the cautionary image of soldiers' graves and the isolationist rhetoric.

Although a privately printed comic book might seem to be an eccentric sample, considerable evidence suggests that throughout the 1920s and 1930s the American Legion as a whole shared the vision of war experience that is recorded inside *Memoirs of a Vet* and displayed on its cover. Admitting to the horrors of war while simultaneously extolling the manly virtues of service (virtues that transcend the war's disappointing political results), linking wartime Americanization to middle-class mores and definitions of success (even as the legion pushed for pro-working-class entitlements such as adjusted compensation), and blending service comedy with images of wartime glamour—all of these memory-shaping maneuvers appear repeatedly in the legion's magazines. And as we will see, the organization's support for isolationism on the eve of World War II did not significantly alter any of the convictions that these maneuvers expressed. Even when arguing against a new American intervention into European affairs, the legion maintained its internal vision of the Great War as the original Good War—"Good" not in terms of progressive international outcomes but in terms of the masculine toughness, courage, and comradeship that the conflict had supposedly fostered in its American (or Americanized) participants.

Two issues of the *American Legion Monthly*—one published in April 1937, the other exactly ten years earlier—demonstrate the tenacity with which the legion clung to this specific construction of the past, regardless of changing times and politics. Marking the twentieth anniversary of America's entry into the war, the issue from 1937 acknowledges the organization's support for isolationism in no less explicit a manner than Nichols's comic book, published two years later. However, the largely positive version of World War I that the magazine encourages its readers to remember collectively, a version virtually unchanged since the previous decade, undermines this support at every turn. As in *Memoirs of a Vet,* ideological confusion and contradiction permeate this artifact as calls for the avoidance of foreign entanglements (supposedly inspired by the miseries of the last war) sit uneasily next to expressions of military nostalgia and pride. An example of the former, John H. Craige's editorial "Would We Get In Again?" endorses recent congressional efforts to limit trade with European nations during any future conflict. And in a rhetorical move common to such editorials, Craige roots his isolationist argument in the legion's firsthand experience of military violence: "No man who was a member of the American Army or Navy in the war with Germany will forget the anti-war sentiment that swept our uniformed establishments after the Armistice. Every soldier and sailor raised his hand and said, 'Never Again! No more war for me, now or ever.' "[49]

Ironically, Craige's articulation of a political position held by many— if not most—legionnaires in the late 1930s rests upon a recollection that very few former soldiers would have shared. As we have seen, artifacts produced by the AEF's memory culture hardly support the claim that a wave of antiwar feeling passed through the American army after its victories in 1918. On the contrary, doughboys rushed to collect souvenirs and to memorialize their exploits in newspapers and unit histories, hardly the behavior of individuals who had renounced war. Nor, for that matter, do the other writings in the April 1937 issue of the *Monthly*—a rich collection of editorials, feature articles, short stories, and cartoons—fit with the dark version of war experience that Craige establishes as the basis for isolationism. In fact, "Would We Get In Again?" is surrounded by texts that uphold the *experiential* value of American participation in World War I, whatever its illusory idealism or diplomatic failures.

In his opinion piece titled "Known But to God," war correspondent Frederick Palmer imagines the Unknown Soldier restored to life—a ubiquitous trope considered in more detail in the next chapter of this study. While writers outside the American Legion, such as Carl Sandburg and John Dos Passos, reanimated the Unknown Soldier in order to mock the government that had manipulated his remains into a false symbol, Palmer imagines a resurrected hero who cannot comprehend postwar disillusionment. In this instance, the man killed in 1918 knows the true meaning of the war while his supposedly wiser successors, victims of a cynical age, do not. Near the end of his essay, after detailing the many ways in which the Unknown Soldier would hear his sacrifice belittled by ignorant Americans in 1937, Palmer makes a remarkable (but, as we will see, far from unique) pronouncement on the significance of American involvement in the Great War:

> Ours was a high mission in which we believed. In return for victory we sought no reward in territory or money. If it is said that we fought for an illusion, then the answer is that men may fight as valiantly and endure as much hardship for an illusion as for a reality. No subsequent event can lessen the stupendous achievement of sending two millions of men to France and drilling more men to make it another million to win the war. For win we must and win we did.[50]

For Palmer, as for many legionnaires, the value of having served in the Great War resided in service itself—in the valor and endurance that the doughboys had displayed—and thus had nothing to do with the ideals, whether real or illusionary, to which this service was dedicated. That Wilsonian internationalism ultimately proved to be a chimera made no difference. To remember the war fondly, and in accord with the legion's version of collective memory, a veteran needed only to focus on his individual success as a soldier (again, the same message contained in *Memoirs of a Vet*), not on the larger causes or outcomes of American intervention.

Bernhard Ragner's article "D.S.C." (short for Distinguished Service Cross) focuses on wartime heroism and likewise eschews any discussion of the AEF's failed quest to make the world safe for democracy.[51] This article taps into a particularly rich vein of human-interest journalism. Indeed, were a full-fledged thematic inventory to be conducted of articles and short stories published in American Legion magazines between 1919 and 1941, courage under fire would almost certainly rank high on the list of preferred subjects.[52] Articles on heroic action, many written by recipients of the Congressional Medal of Honor, appear in the *Weekly* and the *Monthly* with a regularity surpassed only by that of advertisements for male girdles (guaranteed to take up to eight inches off the waistline), hair-loss cures, get-rich-quick schemes, and pre-Viagra solutions for waning male "vitality." Many of these articles go beyond personal reminiscences of combat. In November 1928, for instance, Congressional Medal of Honor winner Dan Edwards described the satisfactions and frustrations of being decorated (as opposed to the actions for which he was honored) in a lengthy article titled "The Hero Stuff."[53] And in October 1934, Edwards made a return appearance in the *Monthly*, tackling the question "Do War Stories Grow?"[54] Predictably, he concluded that most veterans actually downplayed their courage. However, the high drama of battle remained central to the American Legion's cult of heroism, as seen both in the illustrations that decorate these articles (the text of "Do War Stories Grow?" is dwarfed by the image of a fierce-looking doughboy leveling two pistols at a group of surrendering Germans) and in the advertising featured alongside them. Full-page advertisements for the *Chevrolet Chronicles,* a radio program devoted to "living national hero[es]," appear throughout American Legion magazines from this period.[55] Each week, legionnaires could tune in to the program to hear a number of medal recipients describe their adventures, including 1st Lt. Arthur McKeogh, of Lost Battalion fame, and Capt. Eddie Rickenbacker, the top American ace of the Great War.[56] Ragner's piece in the April 1937 issue of the *Monthly* represents, in many ways, the climax of this fixation on heroism, and, not surprisingly, the article completely demolishes the version of memory offered in John Craige's "Would We Get In Again?" (featured just four pages later).

Inspired by the release of an 846-page War Department document containing the citation for each and every Distinguished Service Cross awarded during World War I, "D.S.C." offers a statistical and anecdotal overview of just who won this coveted medal and, in the process, firmly ties the decoration to legion ideology. For example, when surveying the names of DSC recipients, Ragner notes with satisfaction that the list begins "with AAMODT (Morris H. G. of St. Paul), progresses through the alphabet via GONZALES (Benjamin, of Watrous, New Mexico) and SZCEZPANIK (Joseph of New York Mills, New York) and terminates with ZLOTNIKOFF, ZOBNOWSKI, ZUCKERMAN and ZYCH, for such is America."[57] *For such is America*—Ragner's closing comment on this alphabet soup of ethnic titles performs, in four words, the process of Americanization, removing the hyphen, as it were, from hyphenated Americans who have proven their loyalty on the battlefield. As we will see more fully in the next section of this chapter, not every American minority group found a place in the American Legion's conception of the Great War as the Great Assimilator. African American veterans, in particular, remained largely outside the rhetoric of inclusion. Nevertheless, Ragner's acknowledgement that diversity, however diluted in the melting pot of battle, *is* America typifies the organization's response to ethnicity. Rather surprisingly for a group aligned with the political right during a period of intense anti-immigration sentiment, the legion embraced foreign-born members—provided, of course, that these members had contributed honorably to the war effort. Ragner also makes a nod in the direction of American women who served in the war, reminding his readers that at least four nurses received the DSC for acts of extraordinary courage. Here again his article expresses values shared by the legion as a whole: although fully capable of behaving in a sexist manner, the organization nevertheless welcomed women veterans, nurses for the most part, into the ranks of its regular post members, a remarkable gesture of inclusion for the time.

However, perhaps the most interesting expression of American Legion ideology comes at the end of the article, where Ragner, like Palmer and Nichols, focuses on duty for duty's sake, thereby sidestepping the question of whether American valor was squandered in the service of a false cause: "In these latter days, when doubting Thomases and pessimistic Jonathans portray man as a selfish, helpless, burned-out atom doomed to incompetence, uselessness, and despair, the D.S.C.'s bring us a message of faith, of hope, of encouragement; that American manhood and womanhood have not degenerated; that self-abnegation, unselfishness and valor are still integral parts of the national soul."[58] Revealingly, Ragner never mentions the American war aims that necessitated this "self-abnegation, unselfishness and valor," an omission made all the more conspicuous by the closing sentences, which connect the wartime virtues displayed by DSC winners to the "colorful pageant of embattled America, fighting and winning an economic war against poverty and maladjustment on a nation-wide front."[59] Although the article eagerly builds the economic recovery of the late 1930s into a new crusade, complete with its own heroes, it remains silent on the political context for American bravery twenty years earlier. As the contents of this particular issue of the *Monthly* suggest, by 1937 that context had become a metaphorical no-man's-land for most legionnaires, who preferred to define the value of service in the Great War purely in terms of experiential benefits. Thus, collective memory in this case was also collective amnesia, as the progressive ideals that underwrote the war faded out of sight, leaving less historically specific (and therefore less vulnerable) values—such as "self-abnegation, unselfishness and valor"—to make sense on their own. This duality explains the ideological confusion evident in the April 1937 issue of the *Monthly*, which, on the one hand, denounces future interventionism, and on the other, works to depoliticize the American experience of World War I.

Not surprisingly, the short stories included in this issue also undermine the version of memory expressed in "Would We Get In Again?" One of these pieces comes from the *Monthly*'s most prolific fiction contributor—Leonard H. Nason, an author of hard-boiled war narratives (and a former AEF sergeant) best known for his 1926 novel, *Chevrons,* and its sequel, *Sergeant Eadie* (1928).[60] Between the mid-1920s and the Second World War, hardly an issue of the *Monthly* appeared without something by Nason, whose work fit the American Legion's ideology perfectly. Neither explicitly antiheroic nor offensively jingoistic, Nason's short stories and serialized novels (such as the wartime thriller *The Man in the White Slicker,* which appeared in several consecutive issues of the *Monthly* in 1929[61]) focus on a close-knit society of alpha males, who while drinking and brawling perpetually outsmart the military system and, when called on to do so, fight the Germans with courage and ingenuity. Nason doesn't skimp on violence or horror in his fiction, but, significantly, his doughboys are generally tough enough to withstand whatever the war throws at them. Perhaps the most striking feature of these works is the insularity of the military world that the author creates. Nason's hard-bitten enlisted men perpetually grumble, but because they apparently had no illusions to begin with, they never become disenchanted with the war effort. Indeed, for them there is no "war effort"; such an all-encompassing phrase becomes meaningless in narratives that boil military experience down to its local essentials—namely, dodging the wrath of (usually incompetent) junior officers, procuring alcohol, winning the affections of mademoiselles, and trying to stay alive in the midst of battle. With only scattered references to their prewar identities, Nason's conscripts and enlistees act the part of regular soldiers and thus have more in common with the crusty main characters in *What Price Glory?* (1924), Maxwell Anderson and Laurence Stalling's theatrical homage to the Marine Corps's Old Breed, than with the disoriented civilians in uniform who populate antiwar novels like Dos Passos's *Three Soldiers* (1921) or William March's *Company K* (1933).

The short story "Lafayette, That Was Us!" which immediately precedes Palmer's "Known But to God" in the April 1937 issue of *American Legion Monthly*, is classic Nason. Narrated by a tough-as-nails ex-sergeant, who periodically pauses in his narration to "aspirate a couple inches of brown liquid" in a tumbler, the story describes the protagonist's first few days in France—"a strange country"—and his very first run-in with military authority.[62] Stationed in a camp outside Bordeaux, Nason's hero quickly improvises a number of schemes in order to improve his situation. To bring in some extra francs, the sergeant pawns off his unnecessary gear—spare boots, bacon can, and so forth—on a detachment of Algerians, and by exaggerating his knowledge of French he receives a pass to Bordeaux, a sin city of forbidden delights. As it turns out, however, the sergeant is still a novice at playing the system. After the protagonist's return from Bordeaux, an officer spots one of the Algerians wearing an American bacon can tied to a string around his neck, traces the item back to the sergeant, and then arrests the sergeant for illegally trading in U.S. Army supplies. Simultaneously, another group of MPs shows up to incarcerate the sergeant for falsifying a roll call (the result of a deal arranged between the protagonist and another sergeant, who planned on overstaying his leave in town). Things look bad for Nason's inexperienced wheeler-dealer, but then suddenly his outfit receives orders to move out for the front, and the protagonist discovers that the records pertaining to his court-martial are stored in his wagon. He tears them up, and the matter is forgotten.

With only minimal suspense—the narrator's worldly voice, self-deprecating but hard-boiled, assures us from the beginning that he will beat the rap—"Lafayette, That Was Us!" operates primarily as a vehicle for military nostalgia. At the opening of the tale, the protagonist describes his wartime service, without apparent irony, as follows: "[I]t seems to me a long time since I was in France with the Army, and my blood ran hot, and the only care in life was a little question of getting a pass to town, or of being able to go there without one, without landing in the hoosgow. Gee, the world was my clam in those days, and I was going to open it with a bayonet, or a G.I. knife, or just with a strong kick of a hobnail."[63] It's hard to read this aggressive imagery without concluding that it is, in some degree, sexualized. On an explicit level, eroticism appears almost nowhere in American Legion magazines, which reflect the standards of middle-class propriety held by their subscribers (until, of course, they arrived at legion conventions). Unlike other periodicals with an all-male readership, the *Monthly* did not feature pinups or racy cartoons. Nevertheless, the sexual allure of wartime France is central to Nason's narrative—and an integral part of the nostalgia it expresses. Near the beginning of the story, the author treats the promise of French fleshpots with irony. On his first morning overseas, the narrator wakes to the sound of enticing female voices—only to discover that they belong to three middle-aged laundresses, each "fat" with "unkempt" hair.[64] However, in Bordeaux things are different. In a remarkable scene, Nason's protagonist pays a franc to enter a mysterious skating rink. Inside, a beautiful French girl, wearing a skimpy "pink gown . . . with a large bow in front," skates around the floor while pursued by one clumsy soldier at a time.[65] Whoever catches her, the protagonist learns, can untie the bow. Not surprisingly, the girl outskates all comers, including a dark-complexioned "Armenian, or Turk, or Bashie-Bazouke, or something like that" who lumbers after her, skating on all fours.[66] Nason's narrator spends "two hours" transfixed by this erotic spectacle, and when he returns to camp, his description of the skating rink inspires his comrades to "to find the looey [the lieutenant], for dental treatment, or eye treatment, or any excuse to get out of camp."[67] Here, as in much of Nason's work, voyeuristic pleasure intersects with the joys of military rule-breaking to create an attractive picture of American service life in 1918—a picture, again, that seems completely divorced from the legion's supposedly sobered and politically committed outlook on war in the late 1930s.

Moving back a decade, we find in the April 1927 issue of the *Monthly* the same ideological formulations—the same nostalgia and celebration of service for its own sake, and the same avoidance of larger contextual or historically based meaning. The outward appearance of this issue might lead one to conclude otherwise. Literally and figuratively over the top, Howard Chandler Christy's cover illustration, titled *The Spirit of 1917*, shows American servicemen of every description—soldiers, sailors, marines—swarming toward the enemy while the half-nude spirit of Victory (or is she Civilization?) hovers overhead, pointing forward (see fig. 5). Interestingly, this stirring image, provided by an American master of the World War I propaganda poster, appears directly above the title of the most noteworthy article in the issue: "Why We Went to War" by Newton D. Baker. Thus, by implication, the cover promises that Baker's explanatory essay will express the same grandiose idealism—the same Spirit of 1917—conveyed in the painting.

However, readers looking for winged deities in "Why We Went to War" would have been sorely disappointed. Characteristically dry and pedantic, the former secretary of war's article offers an anything but inspiring account—perhaps because the Spirit of 1917 was, in fact, dead where the American Legion was concerned. By 1927 the virtues of soldiering, independent of causes and crusades, had taken its place. In recognition of this reality, Baker never alludes to Woodrow Wilson's war aims in his article. There is no mention of the Fourteen Points or of making the world safe for democracy. Instead, the former secretary bases his case for the necessity of American intervention entirely upon the issue of freedom of the seas and conveniently never acknowledges America's pre-1917 sale of munitions and other war materiel to Great Britain and France. Near the end of the article, Baker's ordinarily tepid rhetoric heats up a bit, although without ever invoking Wilsonian idealism: "The situation [in April 1917], though tragic, at least had the merit of simplicity. A nation with which we were at peace had blockaded our ports and ordered us, at the peril of the lives of our people, to give up a right so elemental and so unquestioned that, with it surrendered, nothing in principle remained to save us from vassalage to a foreign power."[68] In the final sentences, battling Imperial Germany becomes a matter not of international progressivism, not of the New World rescuing the Old, but of much more traditional values— namely, the defiance of foreign tyranny and the assertion of American independence. "Spiritually," Baker writes, "it was the guns of Bunker Hill and Yorktown that answered and overcame the torpedo of the submarine."[69]

If Newton Baker, Wilson's right-hand man and a fellow progressive, was unwilling to evoke wartime idealism—in an article linked visually with Christy's propagandistic imagery, no less—then it comes as no surprise

5. The front cover of the *American Legion Monthly* (April 1927).
Painting by Howard Chandler Christy. Courtesy of the American
Legion National Headquarters.

that the other contributors to the April 1927 issue ignore the Spirit of
1917 as well. Perhaps the most illuminating example of the war's meaning redirected toward experiential particularities appears in "Why They
Want to Go to France," Frederick C. Painton's report on the results of an
essay competition (first prize: $350) open to all legionnaires who wished
to attend the Second AEF convention in Paris. One might expect the

prizewinners in this competition to express a sense of triumph; to gloat, perhaps, over the way that American intervention ten years earlier in the Great War had saved France from German autocracy; or to conceive of their return visit to Paris as an opportunity to savor the fruits of *their* victory. Yet these sentiments appear almost nowhere. Instead, a note of bittersweet nostalgia, by now familiar, hangs over these entries. For example, the top essay, by Robert McKinnis, a former member of the 28th Division (Pennsylvania National Guard), offers an impressionistic jumble of the wartime sights, sounds, and sensations that a pilgrimage to the former Western Front will evoke. Among "the things that made it hell, yet made us love it too," McKinnis lists the following: "lines of sweat streaking down dusty faces and necks, dangling hands swelling up to numbness as pack straps tighten across the shoulders, noisy mess wagons with clanking pans rolling along the rear, a passing outfit of Frogs trudging out of the lines for a rest, ambulances jammed with muddy, bloody, grinning Yanks going back to Blighty—and the distant boom of big guns banging away over the hills in front of us."[70] As is usually the case in American Legion discourse, horror and death are never far from the glamour. The gargoyle is always waiting in the galley. In the Marne region, McKinnis hopes to revisit the remains of a trench where two of his buddies were found, "leaning over their rifles on top of the parapet just as the Jerries had knocked them off."[71] But such dark scenes merely add a sense of solemnity to the nostalgia and are never allowed to raise questions about the causes or conduct of the American war effort. Ultimately, joining the Second AEF convention will allow McKinnis to "live again" as a soldier in a "land of romance" where, if his essay is to be believed, he just *happened* to fight.[72]

Leonard H. Nason is unusually absent in this issue. However, the pieces of short fiction that appear alongside "Why They Want to Go to France" mine the same vein of hard-edged service comedy as "Lafayette, That Was Us!" published a decade later. One of these pieces, "A Pass to Paris" by William Slavens McNutt, is especially Nasonesque in its presentation of enlisted characters who manipulate foolish superiors, outrun the military police, and enjoy the forbidden fruits (alcoholic and otherwise) of wartime France. At the opening of "A Pass to Paris," two loggers from Dahlia, Oregon—Web Hawley and Boze Grout—join the U.S. Army primarily so that they can visit the fabled city of Paris. Once overseas, both characters realize the impossibility of their dream. The AEF, they learn, has established its own leave areas far from the metropolis and devoid (thanks to the watchful presence of the YMCA) of Parisian temptations. But then Web gets a break. After rescuing his major from a jealous French husband, who nearly breaks in on a romantic tête-à-tête between the American officer and the village beauty, Web receives a pass to Paris in exchange for his silence. However, while celebrating his good fortune with Boze, he fails to notice that his friend has slipped cognac into his champagne. After Web passes out, Boze steals his pass, proceeds to Paris, and leads the military police on a monthlong chase. When finally caught, Boze is unrepentant: "I've had mine," he tells the MPs. "Try an' take it away from me, you guys."[73] As for Web, his hatred for his former friend fuels one act of battlefield heroism after another until, by the end of the war, he is "the most decorated man in his regiment."[74]

The story closes with the two characters' comic reunion back in Oregon. When the townspeople of Dahlia hold a homecoming rally for Web in front of the courthouse, they ask him to give a speech about his acts of valor. The veteran doesn't know what to say. But then he hears a familiar voice from the back of the crowd: "Tell them about Paris."[75] The speaker is, of course, Boze, who has just returned from several months in a penal labor battalion. At this point Web finds his voice, delivering a torrent of profanity to which "strong men listened enviously" while "weak women blushed and covered their ears." The town hero then leaps over the rail of the bandstand, chases Boze across the courthouse grounds, and tackles him. Ironically, the appalled citizens of Dahlia attribute the doughboy's bizarre behavior to war trauma. "Poor fellow," remarks one of the town matrons. "Shell shock. It takes them that way."[76] Web is about to beat his former buddy senseless—but then, suddenly, he forgives him. Despite Boze's act of betrayal, wartime comradeship conquers all, and on the story's final page Web listens in wonder to Boze's account of his month in Paris, a mesmerizing string of "lies, half lies, facts and fancies."[77]

Humorous in the rowdy, any-excuse-for-a-brawl fashion of Leonard Nason and, in its concluding scene, unabashedly sentimental, "A Pass to Paris" strikes a number of familiar chords. Once again the army is a world of its own, and when civilians attempt to understand its mysteries, as they do when misinterpreting Web's "shell shock," the results are appropriately ridiculous. In addition, the AEF's idealistic mission is, as usual, irrelevant to the action: Web and Boze's mission is to see Paris, not to rescue Civilization from the Hun. And, finally, the narrative's ironic treatment of heroism (ironic, as we will see, in a way that promotes "in-group feeling" as opposed to antiwar sentiment) is consistent with other legion artifacts, including *Memoirs of a Vet* and the short story "Eggs," which also appeared in the April 1927 issue.

Written by Drew Hill, a regular contributor to the *Monthly*, "Eggs" focuses on yet another sad-sack figure: Pvt. Orville Bostle, a soldier whose awkward, unmilitary appearance has, by the beginning of the story, earned him the dubious honor of a truly unique nickname: "The Busted Sofa." Whether hard-boiled or prepared as an omelet, eggs, we quickly learn, are Bostle's culinary passion—his idée fixe, in fact—and no one in his unit proves more adept at finding them, even on the most barren of battlefields. However, unlike Kat in *All Quiet on the Western Front,* or other famous scroungers in war literature, The Busted Sofa does not share his plunder. He hoards his eggs or sells them to his comrades at three francs apiece. Ultimately, this unlikeliest of heroes makes good through an act of courage ironically inspired by his food obsession. After being captured by the enemy, Bostle spots a basket of eggs in the front seat of a German wagon. The temptation is too great. He waits until his guards are distracted and then makes a run for the vehicle, which he subsequently drives away with. Once safe behind the American lines, the protagonist discovers a German colonel in the wagon's covered compartment—an intelligence bonanza—and receives praise for his exploit not only from his fellow enlisted men but also from an officer who had earlier written him off as "a disgrace to the outfit."[78] As for the eggs? Bostle jokingly offers them to his buddies at a dollar apiece, because they are "imported from Germany."[79] Once a source of alienation, Bostle's mania now ties him to his comrades.

In both "A Pass to Paris" and "Eggs," unlikely enlisted men accomplish the extraordinary. Web, who joins the military with only Paris nightlife in mind, wins more medals than anyone else in his unit. Bostle, once a "disgrace," makes a daring escape. But these courageous actions proceed from farcical motivations. Web superimposes Boze's face on each of his German adversaries. The Busted Sofa—or, as he comes to be known after an especially egregious display of hoarding, The Busted Egg—risks his life for "a lotta hen-fruit."[80] Neither story has much to do with the Spirit of 1917 celebrated so flamboyantly—and, by 1927, so archaically— in Christy's cover illustration. However, these narratives are not exactly antiheroic either. No one would mistake them for the work of John Dos Passos or William March.

What kind of collective memory, then, do these stories enact? In its public discourse, aimed at policy makers and audiences of nonveterans, the American Legion happily emphasized abstractions such as "sacrifice" and "heroism." Such official language, nearly indistinguishable from that employed earlier by the GAR, can be found in abundance on the thousands of community war memorials that the organization helped to establish in the 1920s and 1930s. And as we will see in the next chapter, this language would dominate the ceremonial interment of the Unknown Soldier, a commemorative spectacle created largely through the legion's influence. However, within the pages of its periodicals, insider space where ex-soldiers could write for one another without the need to persuade non-veterans of anything, abstractions give way to nostalgia-summoning details tied directly to experience—"the things that made us hate it and love it too." Indeed, it is not impossible to imagine writers like McNutt or Hill—or even Nason—actually agreeing with Hemingway's famous pronouncement, in *A Farewell to Arms* (1929), that words like "sacred" and "glorious" have no meaning next to place-names, the numbers of roads, and so on.[81] The difference is that for these American Legion writers, the tangibles of war, the very things that Hemingway elevates above the discourse of nationalistic crusades, add up to an experience of such intensity and wonder that no disillusionment over causes or outcomes can dim its appeal.[82] In other words, at least where the version of memory expressed in the legion's magazines is concerned, nostalgia operates independently of abstraction.

And in this regard, "A Pass to Paris" and "Eggs" are, for all their seeming eccentricity, typical works of American Legion fiction—especially when one considers the evocative illustrations that accompany these narratives. For example, although Boze and Web are to some extent comic grotesques, Kenneth Camp's illustrations for "A Pass to Paris" offer detailed scenes of lifelike soldiers, the standard mode for artwork included inside the *American Legion Weekly* and *Monthly*. On the first page of the story, Camp presents the moment of Boze's arrest: while the AWOL soldier sits in a Paris eatery, wearing a radiant expression, a pair of MPs stand close by, ready to take him in (see fig. 6). The scene is exquisitely detailed: empty white plates and a drained bottle of *vin rouge* sit on Boze's table; a collection of small paintings and prints, distinctively French with their wide mats, covers the wall behind him. The illustration offers an expressive snapshot of Parisian elegance certain to stir the memory—and appetite—of any former doughboy. Likewise, Camp's rendering of the scene in which Web warns his major of the French husband's approach features a luxurious domestic interior—and a beautiful adulter-

A PASS to PARIS

By
WILLIAM
SLAVENS
McNUTT

*Illustrations
by
Kenneth Camp*

A month later the M. P.'s got Boze Grout. "I've had mine," he said. "Try an' take it away from me, you guys"

WEB HAWLEY and Boze Grout stood on the corner watching the parade pass.

It was the year of our excitement, 1917. Flags were flying. Bands were playing. Four-minute speakers were telling the world that they would go over personally and slit the Kaiser's throat with their own pen knives only for the unfortunate fact that they all had flat feet and were needed at home. Prize-fighters were wreaking their fury on red-hot rivets in mushroom shipyards. Expert accountants were driving trucks. Truck drivers were being taught to count so they could keep books for the Q. M. C. All cowboys were drilling in infantry outfits and every professional pedestrian in the country had joined the cavalry and was out for to see the world from the hurricane deck of a war horse. The war was on and every man was in his place. That is to say all square pegs were in round holes and all round pegs were in square holes and all was efficiency.

The corner that Web Hawley and Boze Grout stood on was located in the town of Dahlia, Oregon. The town was filled with excitement. Web and Boze were filled with beer. They were just down from a long job in the woods and they had money in their pockets and civilian clothes on their backs. That was only the half of it. They were loggers, and loggers were needed at home. The airplanes had to have spruce, didn't they? Well, then! Don't be silly.

Web Hawley was short and lank. Boze Grout was long and wide. Also thick. He was thicker than Web from the neck down. He was known, however, to have a longer head than Web. The tape measure wouldn't agree to this, but it was true.

A column of infantry passed. Boze Grout shook his head and sighed sympathetically.

"Thirty dollars a month," he murmured. "Thirty a month to join a travellin' jail with no roof to it! Thirty a month to go play tag with a lot o' loose bullets an' cannon balls just 'cause a lot o'

foreigners nobody ever heard of before in a lot o' places nobody's ever been to are all fightin' for a lot o' countries nobody wants to live in if they win 'em. The thing looks like a lot o' gooseflesh to me, I'm here to say."

Web grinned contentedly. "We got nothin' to scream about," he reminded Boze. "Wages is better'n they ever been yet."

"I ain't screamin'," Boze declared. "I'm just wonderin' out loud, that's all. What do you suppose all them guys got in their heads, tryin' to beat this army game? What do they go into it for? If they live they don't get enough to live on an' if they die they're dead. What's the big idea?"

"Maybe they think they're goin' to be heroes," Web suggested.

"Heroes!" Boze exclaimed scornfully. "What a fine graft that hero thing is for a young guy tryin' to get along in the world! I know about them heroes. They bury 'em young an' forget 'em fast an' then put up statues of 'em for the birds to sit around on. Say, you never seen a statue of one o' them heroes any place with a grin on his face, did you?"

Web considered. "No," he admitted. "Don't know 's I ever did."

"That ain't no accident," Boze assured him. "There's a reason. What have they got to grin about?"

Spud Lenihan came around the corner. Spud had worked with Web and Boze in the woods. He was in khaki, brand new khaki that hung on him like an elephant's hide.

"Well, would you look at what went an' jumped off the dock!" Boze greeted him.

"'Lo, boys," said Spud, grinning. "What do you think o' me?"

"You'll never know," Boze said sadly. "The fix you're in you got trouble enough without findin' out what I think o' you."

"You think I'm a sucker, don't you?" Spud asked.

"You guessed part of it," Boze admitted.

Spud laughed. "You ain't ever been to Paris, have you?" he

APRIL, 1927

9

ess. Wallace Morgan's charcoal drawings for "Eggs" offer a grittier but no less compelling version of wartime glamour. With the "shoulders of a gorilla, the neck of a swan, and the arms of a kangaroo," The Busted Sofa cries out for caricature, but Morgan depicts the protagonist and his fellow soldiers in a realistic manner.[83] His drawings look convincingly like wartime combat art (not surprisingly, perhaps, since Morgan was one of the AEF's eight official artists), their bold, intentionally sloppy lines reminiscent of sketches made at the front in 1918. Unlike Camp's, Morgan's illustrations are dark—most of them set at night—and their considerable appeal derives chiefly from the artist's skillful use of light and shadow. The scene on the opening page, for instance, depicts Bostle's commandeered wagon racing past a German position. Like a flashbulb, an exploding shell in the distance eerily silhouettes the doughboy's vehicle. Another drawing offers a similarly impressive chiaroscuro effect: amid the shadowy interior of a French barn, Bostle reads a letter by the light of a single candle, his pile of eggs illuminated at his side (see fig. 7).

The interplay between text and illustration in this pair of stories creates what must have been for the average legionnaire an especially seductive construction of memory. As we have seen, the text in each narrative removes the notion of heroism from its official pedestal. Web and Bostle are not conventional heroes; they are monomaniacs of the sort playfully ridiculed in 1919-era unit newspapers, which often ran short news stories or cartoons focused on the foibles and eccentricities of individual soldiers. The Paris-obsessed Web and the egg-gobbling Bostle probably have dozens—if not hundreds—of counterparts in AEF publications. Thus, in "A Pass to Paris" and "Eggs," the thematic emphasis falls less heavily on heroism (if anything, the protagonists' adventures are mock-heroic) than on the sentimental restoration of comradeship and solidarity. Web forgives Boze. The Busted Sofa wins the respect of his outfit. However, while these texts explore the ridiculous side of soldiering (something all too familiar to any legionnaire) in an almost cartoonish fashion, the illustrations romanticize the past. Camp's detailed drawings present wartime France as a place of epicurean splendor and enticing vice. Cruder but no less effective, Morgan's illustrations cast the front line as a place of shadows and mystery, eerily compelling. In a way, then, these stories have it both ways. The veteran reading them can laugh, with a sense of recognition, at the way fools become heroes; however, he is just as likely to find a lump in his throat when military comradeship is charitably extended even to thieves and slovenly losers. Moreover, while the texts de-

"Will you look at them eggs!" shouted Norcross

A number of men swore they'd beat The Busted Sofa at his own game. But at the end of a hot day's trudge, very few of them were able or willing to compete with Bostle's tireless, ceaseless search for eggs. His keen appetite for this edible rose far above any physical weariness he felt—and also proved greater than the early-morning threats of his customers. Twenty kilometres or so with full packs left them primarily interested in the restful solace of their billets. Besides, as one man somewhat grudgingly admitted:

"Aw, Busted will get most of 'em anyway. So what's the use of breakin' yer neck over a lotta hen-fruit?"

And when the long hike ended, and F Company pitched shelter tents near the shell-ruined city of Voorde, on the Belgian border, Private Bostle's *nom de guerre* had been changed to The Busted Egg. He accepted it as he had the other—without comment.

It wasn't necessary to inform the men that they were within a few miles of the front lines. The constant roar of nearby British batteries, and the shattering frequency with which enemy shells dropped into deserted Voorde, told them all they needed to know. As to what lay ahead of them, veteran British Tommies supplied more specific details.

"It's a bit of a nawsty show, you fellows," the Tommies would say.

"Yeh?" was the usual American reply. "Well, whata we care, Buddy? We're kinda tough, too." They wanted to get into it —wanted to see for themselves.

And during the week they remained there, tuning up for their first trip "in," the one man in F Company who wasn't especially excited about this forthcoming event was Private Orville Bostle. Not that he feared going into battle—no. As a matter of fact he didn't think much about it. His mind was struggling with a far more serious problem. And that was eggs—or rather the lack of them. Every spare hour of his time he had spent combing the surrounding countryside for eggs—or even one egg if he could have found it. But there were none; simply because the usual producers of eggs were totally wanting in that desolated area. Neither hens nor the owners of hens could he find.

Private Bostle still had that problem to deal with, the afternoon the regiment started up to the lines for its baptism of fire.

TWELVE days went by, during which time the different battalions of the regiment alternated tours of duty in the front, support, and reserve line systems. They had taken over a thousand-yard front in part of the Ypres Salient which, among comfortably-housed staff officers back at Division H. Q.. was spoken of as "quiet." But any number of (Continued on page 64)

7. One of Wallace Morgan's illustrations for "Eggs" by Drew Hill. Courtesy of the American Legion National Headquarters.

glamorize for the sake of humor, the illustrations *re-glamorize*, transforming comedy into scenes of nostalgic beauty.

Remembering, American Legion magazines remind us, is also forgetting. And the version of World War I cultivated between the world wars by the largest veterans organization in American history involved forgetting on a massive scale. As we have seen, in order to retain an affirmative interpretation of the Great War, the legion jettisoned Wilsonian idealism and conveniently ignored the causes and outcomes of American intervention. One might think that such a glaring historical omission would have a crippling effect on memory. But the opposite was the case. Leaving the Spirit of 1917 behind allowed the legion to create a new combination of shared memories (some derived from the AEF's memory culture, others shaped by ideological forces predating Progressivism) with far more power and resilience than anything concocted during the war years. Indeed, this body of collective memory proved so vital that even the organization's endorsement of isolationism did not substantially alter its composition or lessen its appeal.

For virtually the entire interwar period, then, the American Legion's construction of the First World War remained remarkably consistent, weathering federal corruption (the Veterans Bureau debacle), changing tastes within popular culture (the influx of antiwar novels and films in the late 1920s and early 1930s), repressive violence (the attack on the Bonus Marchers' camp), and the national drift toward isolationism (which implicitly challenged the virtues of war experience). Thus, it is time to summarize the essential features of this body of collective memory. Laid out in story form, as if all the fiction published in the *American Legion Weekly* and *Monthly* between 1919 and 1941 were distilled into a single master plot, legion war memory translates into the following narrative: In 1917, American males of varying ethnicity entered a military organization that toughened them into *real* men and forged their loyalty to the nation. Once overseas, these soldiers proved themselves on the modern battlefield and won the war for the Allied side, although their heroism was not always of the conventional kind portrayed by wartime propagandists. In France the doughboys encountered much horror and death, but, on balance, they enjoyed more good times than bad. Tight-knit groups of comrades made the most of the Old World. War brought a magical sense of intensity—of glamour—to existence, and military life proved enjoyable enough provided one knew how to navigate the system in the tried-and-true fashion of professional soldiers. After the armistice, discharged servicemen returned home to a society that had allowed war-time factory workers and other opportunists to earn far more than they should have. In addition, ex-doughboys discovered that America, a forgetful place, would require constant reminding of their sacrifices. However, the experience of war—truly a Great Adventure—was nevertheless worthwhile, providing personal memories (more pleasant than unpleasant) that would last a lifetime and fostering personal virtues, such as confidence and maturity, that would aid former soldiers in their pursuit of the American dream. The end.

Such was the story that legionnaires told one another over and over again in the nostalgia-drenched pages of their national magazine and in their more than ten thousand community posts. Such was their shared memory, their truth. And such was the vision of the past that shaped the American Legion's political activity in the present, as well as its goals for the future. In some respects, legion politics fed off the positive dimensions of this collective memory. For example, from fond recollections of wartime Americanization and the rugged virtues of service life came the organization's support for a peacetime draft and other pro-military measures viewed with alarm by pacifists (and with indifference by Washington politicians). However, a bitter grudge, a dark spot in the legion's otherwise affirmative memory, played an important role as well, ultimately shaping the organization's entitlement agenda: the American Legion never forgot and never forgave when it came to the wage disparity between servicemen and civilians employed in crucial wartime industries. As every veteran knew, the former had performed their patriotic duty for a dollar a day while the latter had earned "the highest wages in American history."[84] In other words, the federal government had expected the doughboys to bleed—some literally, all metaphorically through lost wages and lost career opportunities—while slackers at home grew rich. It was an outrage about which World War I veterans never tired of complaining.

From the standpoint of organizational solidarity, this convenient issue served the legion well, helping to ease the class tensions that sometimes surfaced between its middle-class members, who tended to dominate state and national conventions (as well as the worldview offered by the *American Legion Weekly* and *Monthly*), and its working-class rank and file. Thus, the remainder of this section will briefly consider how the legion's campaign for adjusted compensation, a matter of compassion (and political necessity), intersected with the Bonus Army, an example of World War I remembrance at its bitterest and most volatile.

During its first several years of existence, the American Legion adhered to the lofty principles of its (mostly wealthy) founders by refusing to wave the bloody shirt in an appeal for federal benefits. Service, the organization's leadership intoned, was its own reward, a view welcomed with relief by Congress and by President Wilson, since the GAR's success in establishing pensions for Union veterans had once threatened to bankrupt the U.S. Treasury. However, hard times quickly led the legion to discard this ethos. In the early 1920s, as the economy remained sluggish due to canceled war contracts and as an alarming number of veterans faced chronic unemployment, the American Legion came out in support of adjusted compensation (in the form of a so-called bonus payment for each former soldier that would retroactively make up the difference between wartime military wages and those earned by prosperous civilian workers). The organization took this position because it had to. Too many of its working-class members had landed on skid row, a reality registered visually as well as editorially, in the *American Legion Weekly*. Titled "No Man's Land," Cyrus LeRoy Baldridge's cover illustration for the March 17, 1922, issue, for instance, depicts a former soldier trapped in a field strewn with barbed wire. In the distance, the wire forms the word "unemployment."[85] Other covers from the same period likewise conveyed the working-class veteran's precarious footing in the postwar economy. On one, a threadbare former soldier gazes at a broken-down war monument, the Help Wanted section of a newspaper tucked under his arm.[86] Another, drawn by the ubiquitous Baldridge, contrasts the doughboy of 1917, marching off to glory amid a shower of roses, with the unemployed veteran of 1922. Beneath this pair of images, the caption reads, "Make It a Job Shower This April."[87]

Such arresting visual statements prepared readers for articles like "Practical Benefits of Compensation" by pro-Bonus senator Arthur Capper of Kansas and cartoons like "The Great 'Bonus Raid' on the United States Treasury," a satirical depiction of veterans as fiscal conservatives imagined them—masked bandits plundering the federal budget.[88] Both the covers and the political content of these magazines suggest the speed and intensity with which the American Legion responded to the needs of its members, adjusting its ethics and economic philosophy in the process. Indeed, by 1924 the organization that had pledged not to follow the example of the GAR had become thoroughly immersed in special-interest politics. Results, however, were mixed. Legion lobbying in Washington, DC, that year led to the Adjusted Compensation Act, a quasi-victory at best that set aside bonuses for the nation's World War I veterans but with the stipulation that no money could be collected, either by a veteran or by his surviving family members, until 1945. Seeking immediate relief for unemployed veterans, the legion instead received what was, in effect, a form of guaranteed life insurance. In this respect, the act was an insult on par with the wartime wage situation that had inspired the bonus demand in the first place. However, as the economy improved and the 1920s began to roar in earnest, interest in the bonus issue subsided and the rhetoric of financial disinterestedness returned. For most veterans it now made little difference if the government waited twenty years to correct a financial injustice. After all, prosperity had become the new norm.

Or so it seemed. Not surprisingly, once the Great Depression hit, producing waves of fiscal mayhem that made the recession of 1919 look trivial in comparison, the bonus issue returned—and with more urgency than ever. With the economy in free fall, veterans demanded their money *now*. Otherwise, many argued, they would not live to see the promised payment in 1945. At first the American Legion dealt with the matter in a way that threatened to drive away much of its constituency. In 1930 President Herbert Hoover spoke at the legion's national convention and convinced the delegates to table a proposal for bonus payment. One year later, somewhat mollified by a new policy that allowed desperate veterans to *borrow* against the value of their bonuses, the delegates backed down again. However, by 1932, with the Depression in its fourth year and no end in sight, the legion could no longer ignore the plight of its working-class members. The convention that year produced an official demand for immediate adjusted compensation, and politicians in Washington, now under direct political pressure from the nation's largest veterans organization, responded with a flurry of proposals. As Jennifer Keene writes, "In its first session, the Seventy-Second Congress debated no fewer than thirty-four versions of payment legislation."[89]

While members of Congress wrangled over the ins and outs of an exceedingly thorny issue—few in Washington knew whether the bonus could be paid at once, given the state of the federal budget, or what kinds of economic consequences might result if it were—an event transpired that no one, including the leaders of the American Legion, expected: down-and-out veterans began to pour into the nation's capital, promising to remain there until new bonus legislation became a reality. In all, nearly forty thousand former soldiers would participate in what came to be known as the Bonus March.[90] Triggered by the legion's renewed push for adjusted compensation, but never officially sanctioned by any major veterans organization, this unprecedented event became an edgy spectacle of remembrance in the service of public protest and civil disobedience. To make their point that former soldiers had received a raw deal, the Bonus Marchers evoked their shared military past at every turn—and always with a sardonic twist.

The entire event became an ironic parody of the Great War. No longer members of the AEF, marchers now served in the BEF, short for Bonus Expeditionary Force. A subversive camp newspaper, the *BEF Times,* took the place of the *Stars and Stripes,* and even popular songs of World War I became part of the Bonus Army's topsy-turvy appropriation of the past. To the chorus of "Over There," BEF members sang, "The Yanks are starving / The Yanks are starving / The Yanks are starving everywhere."[91] Bizarre images abounded. As they massed outside the U.S. Capitol building, middle-aged veterans, many wearing their 1918-vintage overseas caps, drilled as if back at boot camp, thereby evoking the now-distant days when they had enjoyed the nation's admiration as uniformed crusaders. A placard carried by many of these men made this incongruous appeal to war memory explicit: "Wilson's Heroes, Hoover's Bums."[92] In the end, the parody turned grotesque as regular U.S. Army forces led by Douglas MacArthur routed the former citizen soldiers, driving them out of Washington, DC, at bayonet point and setting fire to their shanties.

Rumors of a Communist conspiracy swirled around the Bonus Army; however, most marchers were not political radicals. Indeed, contrary to appearances, the BEF stood closer to the American Legion, an organization long associated with law and order (and with the Republican Party), than to any left-wing revolutionaries or "Reds." As we have seen, the kinds of narratives written and read by legionnaires, textual barometers of the group's collective memory, tended to reinforce middle-class values. A man's education as a soldier, such narratives insisted, gave him the discipline, confidence, and "pep" to succeed in an open economy. This vision of American war experience fit well with the legion's brand of hyperpatriotism, which stressed each citizen's sacred obligations to the nation (rather than vice versa), and, for a time, helped to squelch any discussion of GAR-style benefit procurement. However, the wartime salary gap between soldiers and civilians, an open wound in the legion's vision of the past, created a powerful rationale for the pursuit of entitlements— after all, the logic followed, any bonus paid to veterans by the federal government would represent an equity adjustment, not a "reward"—and the growing hardships faced by working-class veterans quickly made that pursuit an inevitability. Power, in this case, flowed upward. To hang on to its working-class members, the legion had no choice but to take up the cause of adjusted compensation. Thus, while the organization may have deplored the Bonus Marchers' tactics of public protest and intimidation, the mobilization of the BEF simply represented a grassroots version of the legion's own attempt to renegotiate the relationship between the state and its citizen soldiers. After many setbacks, that attempt would succeed. In 1936, years of American Legion lobbying in Washington finally paid off: World War I veterans at last received their bonuses. And in 1944, with the social contract between soldiers and the federal government now recast, the legion engineered the GI Bill, the most generous piece of veterans legislation in American history.

Thus, although the social biases of its collective memory remained generally intact between the wars, the American Legion nevertheless overcame internal class divisions by focusing on an economic injustice remembered with bitterness by every veteran, rich or poor. More than any of the legion's other political initiatives, the adjusted compensation crusade changed the complexion of the organization, shifting it from a remembrance society that eschewed the pursuit of entitlements to a special-interest group fully capable of wielding memory as a political weapon. At the same time, however, the bonus issue probably prevented the legion from breaking apart along class lines. Though not without moments of political vacillation, the legion's campaign to expand the federal government's sense of obligation toward its citizen soldiers proved to many working-class veterans that the organization understood their difficulties and would fight for their interests. Ultimately, class differences never impeded the legion's progress, on any of its various fronts, to the degree that they could have. But other divisions in American life would bring out the organization's less enlightened side. And so it is to the issues of race and gender that we now turn. How did the American Legion negotiate these potentially explosive issues as it carried its resilient body of memory from the end of one world war to the start of another? And who qualified to occupy a place in the version of the past that the legion remembered?

Wildcat and the Case of Mary Lee: Race and Gender in the American Legion's Memory of World War I, 1919–1941

Two of the American Legion's most prominent founding fathers envisioned a nonsegregated and therefore boldly progressive brotherhood of former soldiers. Theodore Roosevelt Jr., the chief organizer of the legion's 1919 Paris convention, shared the racial views of his father, who famously invited Booker T. Washington to dine in the White House—a gesture regarded as unthinkable by many white Americans at the time. For Hamilton Fish Jr., Roosevelt's right-hand man at the 1919 gathering and the author of the legion's preamble, fair treatment of black veterans was a passion, one that would surface throughout the future congressman's career in Washington, DC. As an officer in the Harlem Hellfighters, Fish saw up close the courage and resourcefulness of African American soldiers as well as the stupidity of the AEF's racial policies, and he never forgot the troops with whom he served (or the way that Pershing had treated them).

However, as Roosevelt and Fish quickly learned, 1919, a year of explosive racial violence across America, was an inopportune time to challenge the color line—despite the U.S. government's implicit promise to grant equality to African American soldiers and war workers in exchange for their wartime loyalty. By the end of its first convention, the legion not only rejected a policy of nonsegregation but it also ensured that Southern black veterans would remain largely excluded from the organization's ranks. Nothing in the legion's preamble or its set of national policies directly mandated this outcome. Instead, Southern legionnaires, fearful of well-organized groups of black veterans (men trained to kill) living in their midst, blocked the proliferation of African American posts by successfully advocating a seemingly innocuous policy: *state* legion headquarters, not the organization's national leadership, would have the power to grant or to deny charters to individual posts. In Southern states this policy meant, in effect, that former white officers could keep the number of black legionnaires under control. Thus, while some African American posts eventually became established below the Mason-Dixon Line, provided they were run by the "right" sort of deferential Negroes, thousands of Southern black veterans in 1919 discovered that whites had already blocked their way into an organization that supposedly represented the interests—and memory—of *all* former soldiers and sailors. As the NAACP bitterly noted in a 1919 issue of the *Crisis,* state legion headquarters in Georgia and South Carolina even went so far as to make racial discrimination explicit in their bylaws, which stated in incontrovertible black and white that only Caucasians could apply for post charters. Mississippi and Alabama followed the same policy, only "without any written declaration."[93]

Meanwhile, in the North (no racial paradise, either), where the wartime migration of black workers to industrial cities had triggered riots and lynchings, rigid segregation became the norm for virtually all American Legion activities. There were, of course, exceptions. In eastern Pennsylvania, the artist Horace Pippin, a veteran of the Harlem Hellfighters, enjoyed friendly relations with several white legionnaires, even painting their portraits. However, Pippin's legion post in West Chester was entirely black (and named after an African American casualty) while those of his white acquaintances admitted only Caucasian members.

Relegated to the status of separate and *unequal* through a chartering process that perpetuated Jim Crow, African American veterans also found themselves mocked and humiliated inside nearly every issue of the *American Legion Weekly* and *Monthly*. As far as the treatment of blacks in the legion's periodicals was concerned, Roosevelt and Fish might never have existed. First published in 1919, the *Weekly* established two unofficial policies regarding race that would remain in place throughout the interwar decades: first, as *legionnaires,* African Americans would be invisible, the activities of their community posts denied almost any news coverage (in sharp contrast with those of Native Americans and other racial minorities); second, as *soldiers,* they would be cast as clowns, minstrels in olive drab. Examples of the latter painfully abound, liberally sprinkled throughout "Bursts and Duds," the magazine's joke section. "Bursts and Duds" for September 12, 1919, offers this typical example:

There was with the A.E.F. one regiment of especially good-natured and willing negroes, whose sergeants always wore their chevrons pinned on their sleeves. One of these non-coms was asked why he did not sew them on.

"Ah, boss, what's the use?" he replied. "We jes passes dem around in our unit."

And this one:

The following conversation ensued between two colored troopers in an outpost while Jerry was putting over a barrage.

"Sam, Ah don't like the hum them shells has; they talks to me."

"You neveh see me turning white, niggah. What they say?"

"They say, Y—o—u ain't going back to A—la—BAM!"[94]

Each of these pieces illustrates a familiar formula of early twentieth-century racial "humor." In the first, a white observer notices something unusual, asks a question of a "good-natured" Negro (who invariably responds with a deferential "sir" or "boss"), and then receives a ridiculous answer that underscores the old caricature of African American childishness and simplicity. In this instance the white "boss" learns that African American soldiers regard rank insignia as playthings—a comforting revelation given the large number of African American officers demoted and denied leadership roles in 1917 and 1918. The second example employs a situational device likewise common to many racial gags: the overheard conversation. Here, African American infantilism is established through what black soldiers—invariably a comic duo, like Charles E. Mack's popular blackface act, Two Black Crows—say to each other. For the white reader who "eavesdrops" on this particular exchange, the frightened soldier's confession that he hears the shells talking to him is clearly meant to be taken literally, as evidence, again, of the inherent foolishness and unreliability of African American combat troops.

Unfortunately, racist jokes and cartoons contained in other issues of the *Weekly* make the samples provided above seem tame in comparison. For instance, a three-panel cartoon in the March 3, 1922, issue of the *Weekly* depicts a black soldier, his racial features grotesquely exaggerated, fleeing from the front line. A white officer stops him. White officer: "Halt, is there a battle going on there?" Black soldier: "Yas suh!" White officer: "Well, what are *you* doing?" Black soldier: "Ah's spreadin' the news, suh, ah's spreadin' the news."[95] The notorious collapse of the 368th Infantry, the African American unit that inadvertently allowed the Germans to encircle the Lost Battalion in the Argonne Forest, lurks in the background of this cartoon. Indeed, as we will see more fully in chapter 3, that particular regiment became a symbol, via AEF scuttlebutt, of African American cowardice, one that effectively blotted out the achievements of highly decorated units like the Harlem Hellfighters.

However, the *Weekly* occasionally spun the notion of black heroism for laughs as well, depicting soldiers of color who *could* fight and even perform acts of valor, but only as minstrel stereotypes. "Bursts and Duds" for December 17, 1920, features a full-page cartoon with the following caption: "Private Snowhite carves his way through single-handed to the battalion objective."[96] Offered as one in a series of "Unpublished Pictures of the War," the cartoon depicts a black soldier, a doll-like figure with white clown eyes and lips, literally slicing his way through a German tank, then a howitzer, and finally a general headquarters, thereby throwing the entire German army into a panic. Private Snowhite's weapon? A straight razor. Although perhaps well-intentioned, this comic tribute to the supposed ferocity of African American soldiers denigrates while it praises. The private's choice of weapon reflects his primitive, "savage" inclinations (according to legend, Senegalese troops in the French army, notoriously bloodthirsty, also preferred the use of a blade) and is consistent, once again, with minstrel shows, which presented razor fighting as a popular pastime among African American gangsters.

Indeed, the negative implications inherent in equating blackness with an innate capacity for physical violence (albeit a capacity that could be praised within the context of military combat) stand out in "The Rhine 'Horror,'" a news story published in the April 1, 1921, issue of the *Weekly*. Essentially, this piece mocks the German government by contrasting two sets of statistics: the number of "French negro troops" reported in the occupation sector by one Dr. von Mach, a former officer in the Prussian army and therefore a disreputable source, versus the number confirmed by, among others, the commander of the American Legion Department of France, Francis E. Drake.[97] According to von Mach, forty thousand such troops served at one time or another in the French Army of Occupation zone, where numerous "crimes of violence against white women occurred."[98] Not so, according to Drake and other American watchdogs, who contend that "the number was never more than 5,200" and that sex crimes committed by these soldiers were "surprisingly few."[99] Note how for both sides the animalistic nature of black soldiers is a given—hence the German government's eagerness to exaggerate their numbers, in the way that a foreign government today might exaggerate the civilian death toll of a counterterrorism operation, and the desire on the part of French and American authorities to set the record straight. Set next to the blade-wielding Private Snowhite, "The Rhine 'Horror'" reveals a grotesque double vision on the part of many white veterans: as seen in the cartoon, the only way for a black soldier to modify his image as a coward and incompetent is to perform an act of *savage* violence (in contrast with Sergeant York's skilled marksmanship or Eddie Rickenbacker's sophisticated application of geometry); at the same time, however, this capacity for primitive aggression, once revealed, makes him a threat to white women—a monstrous "Horror." Snowhite's charge leads him into dangerous territory indeed. Thus, for the most part, the legion's cartoonists, feature writers, and fiction authors would keep their African American subjects as far removed from battle as possible. Better to have shuffling fools than primitive warriors (no matter how useful in battle) with savage appetites.

One particularly interesting expression of this need to, in a sense, disarm the African American soldier, right down to his lethal straight razor, appears in an article that, ironically enough, takes the side of black veterans, albeit in the most patronizing and self-serving manner imaginable. Written by Wiley M. Pickens, commander of the legion's North Carolina Department, and published in the June 1937 issue of the *Monthly,* "Be It Ever So Humble" argues for the establishment of a new colored veterans hospital in North Carolina, citing the unwillingness of local veterans to travel all the way to the all-black facility in Tuskegee (the only hospital for African American veterans in the entire country). Pickens opens his argument by highlighting the tragic story of one particular North Carolina veteran, Sgt. Nori White, an African American infantryman introduced to the reader as a "good soldier" who saw "front-line action" in France.[100] At first it appears that the article will describe the unthinkable—a capable black foot soldier who is neither a comic minstrel nor a bloodthirsty savage. The accompanying illustration, a charcoal drawing by the popular AEF illustrator Cyrus Leroy Baldridge, promises as much by depicting a handsome soldier of color without any demeaning touches (see fig. 8). Rifle in hand, Sergeant White stands in full combat gear, gazing purposefully into the distance. And the concertina wire and shell-blasted tree trunks behind him leave little question that he is at the front line, exposed to the same death and horror as white soldiers. Baldridge's respectful and dignified illustration might have been called "The Spirit of the African American Doughboy."

However, just a few sentences after his introduction, this capable infantryman begins his inevitable descent into stereotype. When Pickens encounters Nori in Charlotte, nineteen years after the war, the conversation that ensues might have come straight from "Bursts and Duds." After Pickens notes the veteran's cadaverous appearance, Nori explains that he has been in poor health ever since his service in France and that he is still waiting for his money from "Mistah Roosevelt" to come in.[101] "What money?" asks Pickens. Predictably enough, as Sergeant Nori answers, the stalwart doughboy depicted by Baldridge dissolves into a minstrel figure, complete with exaggerated African American vernacular:

tion of their trust in their white folks. When the form was filled out and Nori had made his mark, the official said that Nori would be sent to Roanoke for treatment. Nori looked at me and I explained that Roanoke was a general hospital for treating ailing veterans, and that he would get good attention there.

"Roanoke, suh?" cried Nori, aghast. "Leave all mah folkses 'n go way up theah? Please, Capt'n Pickens, suh, kain' Ah stay right yeah 'n you give me mah money?"

I went into detail. That if it wasn't Roanoke it would be a hospital at Oteen, Asheville or Johnson City. When I finished he backed slowly toward the door, a stubborn, reproachful light in his eyes.

"I ain't goin' theah," he said. "Ah kain't go off like that. Ah'd get wusser jest thinkin' 'bout Beulah 'n the chillun. Nawsuh, if y'all kain't get me mah money, Ah 'spects Ah'll jest have to stay heah 'n die. Ah'd die quicker way up theah anyways."

Nori continued to refuse hospital treatment and a short while later I learned that he had died of a tumor. I found out because the Veterans Administration office sent a flag which was to be draped over Nori's casket.

The single purpose in telling this story is to show the Negro's reluctance to leave his environment, the scenes with which he has been familiar all his life. It is a fact well known to physicians and others who have had experience with Negroes that they respond to treatment more satisfactorily in familiar surroundings. It is equally the fact that, unable to get treatment in their own territory, they stay at home and die.

In 1936 a total of 318 North Carolina veterans, mostly Negroes, died outside of a Veterans Administration Facility. That is the official total as tabulated from the number of flags sent to drape coffins. That there are others unreported because they did not know of this veteran privilege I have not the slightest doubt.

Yet there is only one veterans' hospital devoted solely to Negroes, in the United States. That is at Tuskegee, hundreds of miles away. There is no facility for them at all in the eastern or plains country of North and South Carolina and Georgia where they could be hospitalized without suffering from the climatic changes to which a Negro is peculiarly susceptible. Physicians having knowledge of the Negroes have often said that they should be hospitalized whenever possible where the climate is not essentially different from that to which they are accustomed. Which makes the situation in North Carolina singularly difficult.

We sent a total of 21,609 colored men to the Army in 1917, and of this total, eighteen thousand live in the eastern part of the State, which section's climate differs radically from that of the west or mountainous section. From this fact two hardships are worked. First, it is an (Continued on page 55)

8. Cyrus Leroy Baldridge's illustration for "Be It Ever So Humble" by Wiley M. Pickens. Courtesy of the American Legion National Headquarters.

Well, suh, it's thisaway. When Ah was in France, the cunnel he say to me, "Nori," he say, "you go out there 'n capture some of dem Germans 'n Ah pays you a lot of cash." Yessuh, hope for to die, dat what he say. 'N Ah goes out there in some of dat Oregon woods wheah it's blackah dan de inside of de whale, 'n Ah cotches me a mess of them Germans—ten Ah cotched, foah Gawd, Capt'n Pickens. 'N dat cunnel done gets hisself killed 'n dey ain't paid me mah money. Nossuh, 'n Ah need it. Reverend Hyacinth, he say wif interest it most a million dollahs now.[102]

His childishness now established through a question-and-answer routine that follows the familiar outline of racial jokes and cartoons, Nori "contentedly and trustfully" accompanies Pickens to the local Veterans Administration office, where the legion commander completes the appropriate paperwork. The former sergeant will at last, it seems, receive medical attention. However, Nori's story ends unhappily, as it must in order to support Pickens's argument for a new colored veterans hospital in North Carolina. When he discovers that he will have to travel out of state for treatment, the veteran backs toward the door with "a stubborn, reproachful look in his eye" and explains that he would "get wusser jest thinkin' 'bout Beulah 'n the chillun."[103] Months later, after repeatedly refusing to leave his family, Nori dies of a tumor, a victim of the Veterans Administration's failure to understand that "Negroes . . . respond to treatment more satisfactorily in familiar surroundings."[104] Although supposedly presented with the interests of North Carolina's African American veterans in mind, Pickens's argument is, of course, anything but politically disinterested. Continued white dominance in Southern communities required that blacks remain in their place, both socially and geographically. Self-interest was behind the wartime efforts in some Southern states to prevent cheap African American labor from moving to industries in the North. And self-interest explains the call, in Pickens's article, for a new medical facility from whose windows the ailing Negro can "see the familiar scenes that keep him contented and singing when he is well."[105]

Various short stories in American Legion magazines also offer "sympathetic" portrayals of African American troops, and in each case they focus on soldiers who, like Sergeant White, are comfortable with Jim Crow—so much so that they resist attempts, on the part of outsiders, to improve their circumstances. One such soldier is the AEF laborer Wildcat Marsden, celebrated in a 1922 issue of the *Weekly* as "the greatest black-face character in American literature since Uncle Tom."[106] Wildcat's creator, Hugh Wiley, made a career out of racial caricatures, supposedly basing his popular African American figures on various real-life members of the 18th Engineer Regiment, the writer's unit in France. In March 1919 Wiley published his first short story, "Four Leaved Wildcat," in the *Saturday Evening Post*. Dozens of Wildcat tales followed, most of them appearing in legion magazines, along with successful books, such as *The Wildcat* (1920) and *The Prowler* (1924), constructed out of minstrel comedy.[107] Beginning in 1934 Wiley brought his dubious talents to bear on another minority group—Chinese Americans. In a series of detective stories, featuring the super sleuth James Lee Wong, the writer exposed the criminal underbelly of San Francisco's Chinatown, and Boris Karloff would eventually play Wong in several B movies designed to compete with the Charlie Chan and Mr. Moto franchises.

Before Asian mystery became Wiley's forte, he probably did more to shape white America's collective memory of black doughboys than any other writer—except, perhaps, Charles E. Mack, a vaudeville artist (and blackface performer) whose 1928 novel *Two Black Crows in the A.E.F.* represents, as Richard Slotkin observes, the absolute "nadir" of postwar racial mockery.[108] At first sight Wildcat seems an unusual vehicle for fiction that ultimately reinforces the racial status quo. As his name suggests, he is an energetic figure, an inveterate trickster, whose skill when it comes to dodging military regulations (and watchful MPs) rivals that of Leonard Nason's white soldiers. Although he speaks in minstrel colloquialisms, Wildcat is no fool. Nor, for that matter, are his cronies, who help Wiley's clever protagonist execute one rule-breaking scheme after another. However, Wildcat's rascality has limits. Securing a steady supply of cognac, supplementing army rations with desirable French dishes, raising funds for craps games (the black soldiers' favorite recreation), and ducking out of work details represent his chief objectives. Liaisons with French women are never mentioned—Wildcat and his buddies are, in fact, sexless—and, importantly, whenever the subject of racial advancement enters one of Wiley's narratives, Wildcat uses his considerable talent for mischief to block or undermine do-gooders.

One of the most striking instances of Wildcat's talents turned against his own interests appears in the short story "Private War," Wiley's contribution to the May 1936 issue of the *American Legion Monthly*. Set in the AEF base camp outside of Bordeaux, the same camp where Nason's "Lafayette, That Was Us!" takes place, "Private War" brings together Wiley's two main literary preoccupations—the comic world of African American soldiers and Asian exoticism, represented, in this instance, by a detachment of idolatrous Annamites (incorrectly identified by the author as "Chinese"). At the beginning of the story, Wildcat and his companions eagerly prepare for payday and for a subsequent foraging expedition in Bordeaux. But to their chagrin, an "uplifter" by the name of Marmaduke C. Raleigh, presumably a representative of NAACP, arrives at the colored section of the camp, and with the cooperation of the men's white officers begins a course of instruction in reading and writing. All passes are canceled, and each evening the unit's mess hall is converted into a schoolroom. Desperate for some real food and fed up with their forced education, Wildcat and his comrades momentarily slip away from the "sour-faced" Marmaduke and raid an Annamite tent, where they discover—and promptly devour—a roast chicken and other delicacies laid out on a shelf beneath a statue. Unfortunately, what Wildcat mistakes for dinner is, in fact, an offering to the Goddess of Mercy, Kwan Yin, and the doughboys manage to escape an angry mob only by combining their cash and making a donation to Dong Gut, the Annamites' spiritual leader, who doubles as a gambling-den operator.

But this nearly disastrous expedition gives Wildcat's squad leader, Sergeant Kinzie, an idea. Over the next few days, a succession of roast chickens and ducks disappear from Kwan Yin's altar, leading the superstitious Dong Gut to conclude that the goddess is accepting his offerings. Then the Annamites receive a mysterious tip, which leads them to Marmaduke's tent, where they discover the uplifter feasting on duck—the standard ration (or so he was told) for guests of Wildcat's unit. At this point, Dong Gut's "heavy teakwood walking stick beat[s] the cadence of sweet revenge on Marmaduke's skull," and Wildcat and his crew are at last freed of their unwanted schoolmaster.[109]

In his Wildcat stories, Wiley grants a measure of intelligence and sophistication to African American soldiers that is unmatched elsewhere in American Legion magazines from the interwar period. However, as seen in "Private War," Wiley carefully sets this intelligence on a course that perpetuates black servitude. Wildcat may be clever, but his appetite for pleasure drives his reasoning—to the point of pitting the black soldier against "uplift" when it interferes with his recreation.

Interestingly, the American Legion's depictions of other racial minorities often celebrate the social advancement that Wiley makes his African American characters reject for the sake of gambling and cognac.

For example, photographs of various "exotic" legion posts, located in such unexpected locales as Eskimo communities or urban Chinatowns, appear regularly in legion magazines, usually with captions that praise these chapters as evidence of Americanization at work. In these instances the legion defines *itself* as a form of uplift, boosting racial outsiders to the status of true Americans through shared symbols (such photographs often show nonwhite children grouped around the legion's star emblem) and shared memory (since only black troops were segregated, other racial minorities could claim to remember the same war as white veterans). Again, one must recall that images of African American posts, citadels of memory that numbered in the hundreds even after careful gleaning by Southern state-level headquarters, never appear in either the *American Legion Weekly* or the *Monthly*—at least not in the approximately 150 magazine issues examined, from cover to cover, by this author. In contrast, veterans activities within Great Plains Indian reservations attracted dozens of colorful articles, including "The 4th Comes to the Rosebud," a lengthy piece written by Joseph Mills Hanson for the July 1928 issue of the *Monthly*. Focused on the Dakota Indians, Hanson's article places the wartime sacrifices of Native Americans, and their energetic involvement in postwar commemoration, within an overarching narrative of racial improvement that ends with the assimilation of a once-scorned minority group into mainstream America—precisely the narrative denied African Americans. For Hanson, the cultural gap between Sitting Bull's forces, which stripped and mutilated the bodies of Custer and his Seventh Cavalrymen, and the brave Dakotas who fought on the Western Front "denotes . . . a progress from almost complete barbarism, and is good evidence that eventually the evolution [from savage to everyday American] will become complete."[110] Hanson's ethnocentrism is appalling, but the collective racial mind-set reflected in American Legion magazines leaves African American soldiers in an even worse position than their Native American counterparts—namely, that of second-class citizens *who prefer it that way.*

As one might expect, women appear in American Legion magazines between 1919 and 1941 linked primarily to either wartime glamour or the comic realities of middle age. War-related short stories in the *Weekly* and *Monthly* abound with French love interests—and with sexy femmes fatales (German agents, for example). In cartoons set in the present, wives of legionnaires most frequently appear as rolling-pin-wielding shrews who bully former doughboys into watering the lawn or taking out the trash.

However, the legion could not remain entirely aloof from the dramatic impact of the First World War on American gender roles, and in many respects the organization showed flexibility in the face of changing times. For example, the legion welcomed into its regular posts all women who had served as naval yeomanettes or as army nurses, switchboard operators, or truck drivers. Such veterans enjoyed the full rights and privileges of any other legionnaire. In addition, while legion magazines tended to either deify or caricature the fairer sex, they sometimes included cartoons and articles that celebrated female power and independence. A cartoon from 1920, the year of the Nineteenth Amendment, shows a formidable-looking woman, equipped with soap and water and the ubiquitous rolling pin, stomping up to the doorway of a house labeled "politics" while terrified male faces appear at the windows.[111] Although playing to domestic stereotypes, the cartoon asserts that women voters will bring about a much-needed housecleaning in Washington, DC. Even more striking is Joanna W. Harting's article "The Girl Who Took a Soldier's Job," which appeared in a 1919 issue of the *Weekly*. In her lengthy analysis of the wartime sexual revolution and the unwillingness of many young women, such as those employed in munitions factories, to return to their pre-1917 lives, Harting asserted the following: "The girl who was left behind, who kept the hearth fires burning and the pot a-boiling and all the rest of it, while the American man was over there, is not trying to usurp his place in the industrial world but she is certainly determined to find one of her own. If search proves it to be nonexistent she is ready to create one."[112] Needless to say, these are not the sentiments that one expects to find in the main news organ of a notoriously conservative and overwhelmingly male organization.

However, in the late 1920s, at the height of the international boom in First World War literature and film, a now-forgotten literary controversy revealed a dangerous gap between the legion's masculine construction of memory, within which direct exposure to violence remained central, and a new, broader definition of war experience endorsed by feminists and upheld by modernist writers of both sexes. A product of the ongoing gender reorientation introduced by the war itself, the latter decentered combat (that ultimate male proving ground) and conferred the privileged status of *participant* upon both soldier and civilian, combatant and noncombatant—an expansion of meaning regarded by most legionnaires as an anathema. Ironically, in 1929 the *American Legion Monthly* found itself essentially forced to publish a serialized novel shaped by this new definition of war experience and written by a woman to boot. As a result, the organization would indulge in a less-than-flattering form of payback, an ethical low point in its defense of collective memory.

The story of how this strange situation came to pass begins one year earlier with the announcement of a literary prize competition cosponsored by the American Legion and the Houghton Mifflin publishing company. Open to anyone writing in English, the competition promised twenty-five thousand dollars—more than a quarter of a million dollars in today's currency!—to the author of the best new novel "dealing with the period of the World War."[113] And the prize didn't end there. To sweeten the pot even more, Houghton Mifflin promised to publish the winning novel, at a lucrative royalty rate of 25 percent, while the *American Legion Monthly* pledged copious advertising in the form of full or partial serialization. Five distinguished judges were recruited to make the selection: Alice Duer Miller, a member of the head council of the Authors' League of America; Ferris Greenslet, Houghton Mifflin's literary director (and Willa Cather's editor until 1922); Richard Henry Little, a prominent journalist with the *Chicago Tribune;* Maj. Gen. James G. Harbord, former commander of the AEF's Service of Supply; and John T. Winterich, editor of the *American Legion Monthly.* Fifteen hundred writers from around the world declared their intention to participate in the competition; of these, approximately five hundred sent in manuscripts before the deadline of May 1, 1929. Staff members at the *American Legion Monthly* and Houghton Mifflin forwarded the best of these submissions to the judges, whose final decision, reached only after "protracted debate," appeared in the August 1929 issue of the *Monthly.* In a surprise move, the judges split the prize between two completely antithetical novels: William Scanlon's *God Have Mercy on Us!* a gritty combat narrative focused on U.S. Marines, and Mary Lee's *It's a Great War!* a massive—more than 250,000 words—portrait of wartime as seen through the eyes of Anne Wentworth (an idealistic, upper-crust New Englander modeled after Lee herself), who serves with the AEF first as a secretary, then as a YMCA canteen worker. The only thing these texts have in common are the exclamation marks in their titles.

As it turned out, the decision to announce two winners was a compromise that satisfied none of the judges. Not surprisingly, given their ties to the American Legion, Harbord and Winterich were adamant that Scanlon's manuscript, a straightforward depiction of military violence, deserved the prize. Representing the interests of art, Miller and Greenslet felt the same way about Lee's text, which offered a more self-consciously "literary" approach to the subject of the Great War. And Little, who concluded that neither work was worthy, argued unsuccessfully to have the competition extended for another year.[114] In retrospect, Little was the most prescient of the five judges, for neither novel is particularly good. Offering nothing new, *God Have Mercy on Us!* describes the same battles and explores the same psychological terrain as Thomas Boyd's *Through the Wheat* (1923), a far superior combat narrative. And Scanlon's staccato prose style reads like a bad parody of Hemingway. A notice by Martha Gellhorn (coincidentally, Hemingway's future third wife) in the *New Republic* typified the reviews. For Gellhorn, *God Have Mercy on Us!* captured life at the front line with "faithfulness and monotony." However, "it is impossible to feel sympathy for the people in Mr. Scanlon's book, and since it is only in this oblique, personal way that a civilian can understand what the War was—the book simply does not jell."[115]

In contrast, *It's a Great War!* shares some affinities with the canon of modernist classics inspired by World War I—works such as E. E. Cumming's *The Enormous Room* (1922), Virginia Woolf's *Mrs. Dalloway* (1925), Willa Cather's *The Professor's House* (1925), and John Dos Passos's *1919* (1932). Like these texts, Lee's novel depicts the Great War's terrifying reach through time, space, and consciousness—how the conflict, the first total war in history, wounded combatants and noncombatants alike. In addition, *It's a Great War!* is boldly modernist in its narrative structure and prose style. Written in the present tense, the narrative consists of hundreds of brief vignettes, which impressionistically (via one intentional sentence fragment after another) describe the wartime sensations that wash over Lee's protagonist. For a World War I scholar, her text offers a treasure trove of details that few other writers bothered to record. However, as a novel, it is rough going. Reviewers objected to both the book's length and its technique. The unsigned notice in the *New York Times Book Review*, for example, noted that "Miss Lee makes the mistake of believing that the more photographically life is reproduced, the closer it comes to being great art. But nothing could be less true."[116] Commenting on Lee's nearly incessant use of sentence fragments, Byron Darnton of the *New York Evening Post* remarked, "One longs for a verb as a doughboy longed for a beefsteak."[117] And in the most blistering review of all, the *Times Literary Supplement* mimicked the novel's clipped, impression-istic style: "Wherever Anne goes, there is a shortage of verbs. Life is al-ways enormously exciting. Anne arrives in England, then in France. It is very unsanitary."[118]

As far as most male veterans were concerned, Lee's novel upset far more than conventional aesthetics. For example, content, not form, pro-voked Harbord's displeasure with the book, which quickly leaked to the press. As the *American Legion Monthly* reported, the former Service of Sup-ply commander believed that "Mrs. Lee's book places undue and mislead-ing emphasis on certain phases of the war."[119] From the legion's perspec-tive, *It's a Great War!* was "misleading" indeed, and one can only imagine how the staff of the *Monthly* felt when, bound by rules of the contest, they published a "generous two-part sample" of the novel in 1930.[120]

In what ways, then, did the novel offend—beyond, of course, its focus on a woman in the midst of war rather than a man? First of all, Lee's story asserts through its sheer variety of incidents and flood of impres-sions that the Great War had been a much larger and more chaotic expe-rience than the narrative of comradeship and frontline danger that stood at the core of the American Legion's collective memory. Indeed, the nov-el's avalanche of details and modernist fragmentation suggest disconcert-ingly that the war had no center of meaning—the last thing that an orga-nization built around collective memory wished to hear. Second, the title of Lee's book is sarcastic. The phrase "It's a Great War!" becomes a re-frain, somewhat overused, as Anne Wentworth and her fellow female vol-unteers encounter one disillusioning situation after another. As we have seen, arguments that the war had been for naught, in terms of political outcomes, or even less than brilliantly conducted posed little threat to the legion's sense of identity. Such arguments ricocheted off the orga-nization's nostalgia-encased model of the past, which celebrated the vir-tues of wartime experience independent of larger historical issues. How-ever, Lee's novel goes after that very experience, implying through its seemingly endless succession of often lurid details that the actual sensa-tions of wartime were far less pleasant than remembered. *It's a Great War!* might have been called "It's a Seedy War." While serving as an officer's secretary at a base hospital, Anne scours a French latrine, achieving the American standard of cleanliness after literally paragraphs of excruciat-ing effort—so much for the glory of French culture. Likewise, wartime sexual romance, a staple in legion magazines, becomes in Lee's narrative mere promiscuity. And chickenshit, not comradeship, dominates the interaction among Lee's doughboys. Lee's "cynical pen spares neither officer nor private," remarked the *Boston Herald*.[121]

Only slightly more palatable than giving an award to, say, John Dos Passos's *Three Soldiers* (1921), a book that many legionnaires would have loved to burn, the American Legion's grudging endorsement of Lee's novel was guaranteed to provoke a backlash, and when it came the writer was more than ready. While patronized by many male reviewers as an ultrafeminine "lady idealist," the author of *It's a Great War!* was in fact a seasoned journalist and a formidable woman of the world.[122] After her return to the United States in 1919, Lee completed a master's degree in "government, history, and economics" at Radcliffe and then became a reporter for the *New York Evening Post*.[123] In 1923 and 1924 she served as an overseas correspondent, covering stories in Greece and Italy. Photographs of Lee taken around the time of her receipt of the war novel prize show an athletic-looking woman with bobbed hair, something of a flapper, and a face that conveys both shrewdness and determination. Lee would display both attributes during the controversy that ensued.

Within a week of Houghton Mifflin's publication of *It's a Great War!* in October 1929, the American Legion moved to distance itself from Lee— despite the fact that the organization remained bound by the terms of the contest to serialize at least a portion of her prizewinning novel in its monthly magazine. Since 1919 Lee had served as a member in good standing of the Newton post of the American Legion, located in her home neighborhood of Chestnut Hill, Boston. Now, suddenly and suspiciously, her qualifications for membership came under question. Without any official prompting from legion headquarters in Indianapolis, one Emily Williams, a former nurse with the AEF, wrote to the national adjutant, James F. Barton, to point out that Lee had never served officially in any branch of the U.S. military, a technical requirement for all legionnaires, male or female.[124] Thus, without warning, Lee received word on October 25 that the legion had struck her name from the roster—a transparent form of revenge for her scandalous war novel.

Ironically, Lee had joined the Newton post ten years earlier at the personal invitation of its commander, and in 1928 she rode at the head of the post's Armistice Day parade. Not once before October 1929 did anyone challenge her eligibility. However, if the novelist was at all stung by the American Legion's vindictive behavior, her papers, preserved in Harvard University's Schlesinger Library, give little indication of it. On the contrary, Lee quickly retaliated in a way that made the organization look even pettier—and that boosted the sales of her book in the process. She started by requesting reimbursement of the annual dues that she had paid, apparently in error, since 1919. As if determined to come across poorly, the legion ignored her request—a fact that Lee subsequently made available to the Associated Press, along with all the other shadowy details of her expulsion.[125] Typical of the news stories that resulted was a lengthy piece in the *Boston Herald* titled "Newton Legion Ousts Mary Lee." Above the novelist's picture appeared a single word—"Dropped."[126] Lee then asked the *American Legion Monthly* to formally announce her removal from the roster, a request obviously designed to create maximum embarrassment for *Monthly* editor John Winterich, who had to work closely with Lee on the forthcoming serialization of *It's a Great War!* despite his own misgivings about her novel and despite the punitive action of his own organization.[127]

Through all of this, Lee enjoyed a friendly correspondence with Ferris Greenslet of Houghton Mifflin, and her letters to the experienced editor show just how thoroughly she understood the promotional value of negative publicity. On February 18, 1930, she remarked, "Since the American Legion racket I have been getting about twice as many letters per day about 'It's a Great War!' as I was getting before." And she added that she had been "asked to speak about three times as often. . . . There seems to be a general curiosity to see what I look like."[128] As for her view of the legion, Lee pulled no punches, and in a letter to Greenslet dated April 16, 1930, she let fly: "I think it's the world's worst organization and only stayed in because I rather fancy taps as a funeral, and nothing else. However, I can get along nicely without that."[129] By early 1930, buoyed by the extensive press coverage of Lee's controversial ouster, sales of *It's a Great War!* doubled those of *God Have Mercy on Us!* and Lee, as they say, laughed all the way to the bank. The American Legion had tangled with the wrong "lady idealist."

~

In many respects, the twenty-five-thousand-dollar war novel contest, an event intended to produce *the* literary masterpiece of the First World War, became a perfect cultural storm that revealed the unsettled position of the conflict in postwar imagination—and the limits of the American Legion's control over the past. In terms of memory, the judges' split decision mirrored a nation likewise torn between traditional conceptions of war—and war novels—and a more modern sensibility. Indeed, in retrospect it seems remarkable, given the incongruous partnership of the legion with a mid- to highbrow publishing house, that anyone ever believed the contest could produce a single winner. Since there was no national consensus over the meaning of the war—no monolithic body of collective memory shared by all—the effort to select the finest literary vehicle for memory was doomed from the start. Moreover, once the legion went on the attack to discredit Lee, its efforts backfired, again revealing that the organization's version of the Great War held only limited purchase beyond the pages of its national magazine and the nostalgia-echoing walls of its posts.

Unfortunately, African American veterans, cast as buffoons through two decades of American Legion journalism, never had the chance (as Lee did) to defend themselves against the organization in a prominent public forum. However, as we will see in the next chapter, the voices of black Americans joined with those of whites in a contest over memory that was far larger than the controversy surrounding the 1928 war novel competition: the battle to determine the meaning of America's Unknown Soldier.

2
Soldiers Well-Known and Unknown
Monuments to the American Doughboy, 1920–1941

Everyone knows about the Unknown Soldier, but no one knows about the Well-Known Soldier. Makes you think, doesn't it? Maybe not.
—George Carlin, *Brain Droppings* (1998)

If judged by the number and scale of public memorials that it inspired, the First World War produced an outpouring of pride and patriotism unparalleled in American history. Indeed, in some regions of the country today, more World War I memorials exist than any other kind of public commemorative artifact, and the total number of such memorials in the United States would almost certainly run in the tens of thousands. Within this commemorative outpouring, the federal government, the most powerful official agent of remembrance, played a surprisingly modest role. Whereas Washington spent generously, though far from lavishly, on permanent cemeteries and memorials in France, Belgium, and England (the original appropriation request made by the ABMC to Congress in 1925 estimated the start-up cost of overseas memorials at just three million dollars[1]), the domestic surge in remembrance came mostly at the local level as official and vernacular forces negotiated the nature and cost of memorial gestures that quickly assumed a dizzying variety. Some towns, neighborhoods, and campuses erected stone or bronze statuary, particularly mass-produced works depicting triumphant doughboys. Others invested in stelae (boulders with plaques attached to them), commemorative obelisks, or victory arches. A reflection of the early twentieth-century outdoor recreation movement and the 1920s vogue for gardening and park planning, tree planting became a popular commemorative effort as well, along with memorial flower gardens and shrubbery. And then there was the vast array of functional memorials (known as "living memorials" by their proponents) from which communities could choose. Building companies completed thousands of contracts in the 1920s and 1930s for memorial halls, auditoriums, student unions, high schools, bridges, and roadways. As historian Kurt Piehler has observed, intense competition between fine-arts studios, which regarded functional commemoration as vulgarity, and the construction industry, which defined monuments as a waste of public funds, made World War I memorialization a lively and controversial topic not only in trade journals (such as the cleverly titled *Monumental News*) but in popular magazines and newspapers as well.[2] Hardly an issue of the *American Legion Weekly* or the *American Legion Monthly* appeared without at least a short article on memorials and the public debates that they inspired. Likewise, the interwar-period files of memorial-related articles and editorials in the *New York Times* are immense.

Within the well-known "living memorial" debate was a larger theme that permeates the entire subject of American First World War commemoration—namely, the relationship between tradition and modernity. Although the concept of functional memorials predated the armistice (by several decades, in fact), its advocates stressed the appropriateness of this concept to the Jazz Age. An event as vast and inspiring as the Great War, they argued, required a *new* approach to commemoration, and Civil War remembrance, identified with courthouse statues of questionable aesthetic merit and monument-cluttered battlefields, became one of their favorite examples of how *not* to memorialize war. Not surprisingly, sculptors and monument companies countered by invoking the sanctity of commemorative traditions. Both sides utilized official, rather than vernacular, language in their appeals (grandiloquent pronouncements on sacrifice and glory served, of course, to camouflage the commercial interests at stake), but at its core the debate presented two very different visions of the war itself—one that placed the conflict in line with America's wars of the past, and thus stressed that sense of continuity through familiar forms of remembrance, and one that, in a sense, broke the war off from the history that predated it and therefore called for a "new" approach to commemoration.

However, within most American First World War memorials, whether nonfunctional or "living," tradition and modernity actually prove much more difficult to disentangle than the dichotomizing "living memorial" debate might suggest. More often than not, the old found expression through the new, and the new borrowed from the old. The ambiguities of America's First World War made for strange commemorative bedfellows, inspiring often awkward mishmashes of the traditional and the modern. As a result, the messages expressed in memorials erected during the interwar decades are frequently muddled, contradictory, or (anticipating the National Vietnam War Veterans Memorial) seemingly left entirely up to the viewer. Indeed, a sense of liminality—of being caught betwixt and between—characterizes American World War I memorialization in general. The visual elements of memorials often waver between the old-fashioned and the avant-garde, the familiar and the strange, and the messages expressed are frequently liminal as well, hesitantly veering back and forth between affirmation and sorrow, celebration and condemnation. This chapter will explore the themes of tradition and modernity in post–World War I commemorative culture, and the many contradictions and ironies that arise from the tension or interplay between the two, through a pair of monuments to the American soldier of 1917–1918: sculptor E. M. Viquesney's *Spirit of the American Doughboy*, one of the most replicated military statues of all time, and the Tomb of the Unknown Soldier at Arlington National Cemetery.

As we will see, Viquesney's almost quaint representation of the "American Doughboy," an obvious throwback to Civil War statuary, became an almost unavoidable presence within 1920s visual culture by offering a revealingly awkward blend of the official and the vernacular. The Tomb of the Unknown Soldier, on the other hand, seems at first sight to break all ties with commemorative tradition. The very fact that the tomb honors an "Unknown," a body so brutalized by high explosives that it could not be identified, points to the terrifying newness of the Great War itself, a conflict that saw the killing power of military technology carried to a grotesque extreme. However, in the way that the federal government attempted, through pomp and circumstance, symbolically to fill in the Unknown Soldier's identity as a fighting man and a patriotic American, traditional cultural formulations proved central—though, for a time, ineffectual. For a period during the 1920s and 1930s the official rhetoric and imagery that was intended to shape the meaning of the Unknown Soldier for the American public broke down, and what began as a top-down effort to impose a lasting interpretation of the First World War became a spectacle of contested meaning driven from the bottom up.

"The things the statue speaks": E. M. Viquesney's *Spirit of the American Doughboy* and American War Memory

Although George Carlin might have disagreed, everyone *does* know about the Well-Known Soldier described at the opening of this chapter. They just don't know that they know. The Well-Known Soldier is, of course, E. M. Viquesney's *Spirit of the American Doughboy,* a seven-foot-tall statue depicting a World War I infantryman, identical copies of which currently stand on display in nearly 140 communities in 35 states spread from coast to coast (see fig. 9). Literally millions of Americans have seen this work, perhaps the most popular American military statue of the twentieth century, but few know its title, the name of its artist, or its history.

In recent decades a small group of hobbyists, known as the Doughboy Searchers, has latched on to Viquesney's best-known work, tracking down forgotten copies of the statue and posting ultra-detailed information about this World War I icon on an impressive Web site. The group has also made some provocative pronouncements about the cultural importance of the statue. For example, Viquesney expert Earl D. Goldsmith remarks that some enthusiasts "believe that except for the Statue of Liberty, Viquesney's Doughboy replicas have collectively been seen by more people than any sculpture in the U.S., even though many don't realize that they have seen them."[3] This claim may or may not be accurate, but one thing is certain: this still prominent World War I monument was nearly ubiquitous during the interwar period—and not only outdoors. In addition to the seven-foot-tall version, designed to adorn traffic intersections, parks, and courthouse lawns, Viquesney's American Doughboy Studios also produced a popular twelve-inch-tall model, perfect for a veteran's mantelpiece or desktop, as well as a version that supported a lightbulb and lamp shade. Like the full-scale statue, these miniatures are hardly trivial cultural artifacts. They are more than ephemera. Between 1921 and 1926, reportedly twenty-five thousand statuettes and lamps found their way into American homes, and various versions of both remained available, in furniture stores and via direct mail order, until the outbreak of the Second World War.[4] And advertising for miniature copies of *Spirit of the American Doughboy,* filled with dubious but revealing claims made by the statue's aggressively entrepreneurial creator, offers a treasure trove of information about memory during the interwar period. Not surprisingly, most of this advertising appeared in the American Legion's periodicals. As we will see, the spread of Viquesney's popular doughboy into both public and domestic space resulted not only from the sculptor's formidable marketing acumen, but also from the thematic ambivalence that characterizes his simultaneously realistic and idealized American soldier.

The creator of *Spirit of the American Doughboy* is a fascinating individual, more P. T. Barnum than Michelangelo, and his career intersects with

9. E. M. Viquesney's *Spirit of the American Doughboy.* This particular copy of the statue stands in Axtell, Kansas. Photograph by the author.

the memory of three American wars. The son and grandson of French sculptors, Ernest Moore "Dick" Viquesney (1876–1946) grew up in Spencer, Indiana, where he lived for most of his life, and he learned his craft from his father—though the latter reportedly warned him that he would "die a poor man" if he devoted his life to art.[5] Viquesney seems to have heeded this warning insofar as his creative endeavors seldom lacked an explicit commercial agenda. After his service in the Spanish-American War, Viquesney plunged into a career in the monument business. In 1904 he married his first wife, Cora Barnes (he would be twice widowed), and one year later he accepted the first of several positions with various monument companies and marble works in Americus, Georgia. At the same time, he helped fashion the stone memorials at the nearby federal cemetery located on the Andersonville Prison site, thereby playing a role in the controversial remembrance of a particularly ugly facet of the American Civil War, one that some Southerners today regard as misremembered. Ever pragmatic, however, Viquesney may not have limited his Civil War–related work to pro-Northern commemoration. Rumors persist that he may have known the celebrated sculptor of Mount Rushmore, Gutzon Borglum, and assisted him with the early stages of the gargantuan Stone Mountain Confederate Memorial (eventually completed in the 1970s).[6]

Viquesney was still living in Americus at the end of the First World War when, sensing that the market for war memorials would soon explode, he focused his energy on the creation of a statue that would honor the American soldiers who had proved victorious on the Western Front. From the beginning the sculptor aimed for a high degree of verisimilitude. Returning veterans, including Walter Rylander, one of Viquesney's business associates, posed for the sculptor in full combat gear, and according to legend, the soldier's face in the finished statue faithfully mirrors Rylander's handsome features.[7] Other pieces of Viquesney folklore, most of them spread by the artist himself, assert that he studied "hundreds of photographs" of AEF members and that his doughboy's face is that of an American everyman, a composite of features displayed by the nation's ethnically and racially diverse fighting men.[8] Regardless, the artist aspired to more than a mere three-dimensional likeness. He sought to infuse his statue with emotion. As Goldsmith explains, although Viquesney "wanted to depict an American soldier in battle, he didn't want to depict excessive might or power by portraying a soldier charging or running forward. Instead, he wanted to depict the 'spirit' of the American Doughboys' determination to preserve freedom for their country and mankind. So he portrayed a Doughboy striding firmly forward in an erect posture through 'no man's land.'"[9]

Viquesney patented *Spirit of the American Doughboy* in December 1920 and around the same time founded the American Doughboy Studios in Americus. Sales of the statue gained momentum in 1921 when the national headquarters of the American Legion supposedly selected Viquesney's creation over all other competitors in a nationwide search for a monument to stand outside the legion post in Centralia, Washington, the site of a then-recent and bloody clash between legionnaires and Wobblies, members of the radical International Workers of the World (IWW). In subsequent advertising Viquesney milked this purported honor for all it was worth, claiming, among other things, that his was the only war monument endorsed by the legion as "100% perfect." But whether his statue actually won the legion's competition remains unclear. Inexplicably, the monument erected outside the Centralia post is by another sculptor. Still, Viquesney's story must have contained some truth, since the legion never contested his claims—claims that Viquesney repeatedly broadcast from advertisements run in the legion's own magazine, no less.[10]

In 1922, with his already famous statue in full production (along with the statuette and lamp versions), the sculptor encountered a serious reversal of fortune: the American Art Bronze Foundry in Chicago, which manufactured a series of doughboy monuments by Viquesney's chief competitor, John Paulding, sued him for copyright infringement. According to the American Art Bronze Foundry, Viquesney's "100% perfect" creation was in fact a blatant rip-off of *Over the Top,* a soldier statue that Paulding had registered at the U.S. Patent Office several months ahead of *Spirit of the American Doughboy.*[11] Both works depicted a helmeted soldier in an attitude of triumph, his right arm held aloft. Though similarities between the two statues may have been coincidental, Viquesney apparently lost the case—or agreed to pay a settlement—because unspecified financial difficulties subsequently prompted him to sell all rights to his statue to Walter Rylander, who assumed control of the business in Americus.[12] Ironically, during most of the period when *Spirit of the American Doughboy* enjoyed its greatest popularity, from 1921 through 1929, Viquesney did not own his own design. However, he continued to cook up marketing strategies for the statue and remained a source for its often ingenious advertising.

Undaunted by this setback, Viquesney returned to Spencer, Indiana, where he quickly founded a new studio and, within a few years, regained his financial footing through an unlikely new product line—a series of paperweights, plaques, and ashtrays depicting the "Imp o' Luck," a leprechaun surrounded by four-leaf clovers, lucky horseshoes, and the like. Profits from the aptly fortuitous "Imp o' Luck" enabled Viquesney to buy back the rights to his doughboy statue in 1926, and for the rest of the interwar period he produced both the full-scale and miniature versions of his best-known statue in Spencer. However, the heyday for *Spirit of the American Doughboy* soon came to an end. In the 1930s, as the Depression wore on, sales of the statuettes and lamps declined steadily, and fewer and fewer communities ordered copies of the seven-foot-tall statue. During two years, 1932 and 1937, the American Doughboy Studios did not sell a single full-size replica.[13] When the United States entered World War II, Viquesney responded with a new line of patriotic statues, once again offering miniatures as well as monuments. And although it was never as famous as Viquesney's doughboy, one of these works, the statue of a World War II infantryman titled *Spirit of the Fighting Yank*, achieved a measure of popularity. Several full-scale replicas still stand in public spaces today. But the age of the war statue had come and gone, as evidenced by the absence of statuary in most American war monuments constructed from the end of the Second World War through to the present day. Indeed, the three most familiar American military statues of the past sixty years—the National Marine Corps Memorial, with its stirring three-dimensional rendering of the flag raising on Mt. Surabachi; the bronze trio of infantrymen at the National Vietnam War Veterans Memorial, who stand near the lesser-known monument to women veterans of that conflict; and the National Korean War Veterans Memorial—are exceptions to the rule. Walls, plaques, and simple stone blocks carved with names have come to typify contemporary American war monuments. Thus, by 1945, at age seventy, Viquesney was a holdover from an earlier era. And in the end, his optimism and energy failed him. On October 4, 1946, distraught over the death of his second wife, Betty Sadler, this little-known but enormously influential participant in twentieth-century American war remembrance shut himself inside the garage at his Spencer, Indiana, home and left his car running.

However, while Viquesney embodied a tradition of patriotic statuary that had largely run its course by mid-century, his work, like that of so many artists involved in World War I commemoration, also blended the old and the new. For example, to outprice his competitors, Viquesney utilized newly developed materials and methods of production. Unlike the statues manufactured at the American Art Bronze Foundry and elsewhere, the seven-foot-tall version of *Spirit of the American Doughboy* weighed less than two hundred pounds and was constructed through a process that, at the time, was highly unorthodox—and economical. As Goldsmith explains, "The most replicated version of the Doughboy is of pressed sheet copper (or copper/bronze alloy) formed by machine die-stamping more than 75 separate pieces which were then welded together over an internal metal frame."[14] Construction in this manner meant that Viquesney's statue was much lighter than the bronze castings offered by other studios and far less expensive—one reason, perhaps, for the work's popularity. A community in 1921 could purchase its very own Viquesney doughboy (excluding the pedestal) for as little as $1,100 to $1,500, plus shipping—roughly $14,300 to $19,500 in today's currency—a far from outrageous price tag for a public monument.[15] And the miniature versions were af-

fordable as well. The twelve-inch-tall statuette and the "American Doughboy Art Lamp" retailed for just $6.00 and $9.85, respectively.[16] However,
then as now, consumers got what they paid for. Viquesney's studio made
all of its miniatures out of cheap pot metal, which broke easily, and then
covered them with a "bronze spray" finish—in other words, a blackish-
brown spray paint.[17] So crude was the casting that the soldier's left hand,
clutching his rifle, came separately and had to be glued to his arm. In
terms of taste, these domestic versions of *Spirit of the American Doughboy* are
a bit questionable—not quite in the same category as velvet paintings, garden cherubs, or lawn flamingos, but close. However, part of Viquesney's
entrepreneurial genius was his rejection of the high-end market and his
refusal to kowtow to sophisticated urban art circles. Whether located in
Americus or Spencer, and whether officially overseen by Rylander or by
Viquesney, the American Doughboy Studios consistently produced memorial art priced within the grasp of ordinary Americans. Thus, the company cornered a market that monument studios more attuned to highbrow aesthetics and wealthier patrons ignored entirely.

Viquesney's inventive advertising and unique marketing gimmicks also
put a new spin on war remembrance. His advertisements in the American Legion's magazines are inspired. Consider, for example, the pitch
that appears in a 1922 issue of the *American Legion Weekly*:

> IT WAS HELL and we're all glad it's over. But you and I, Buddy,
> both feel mighty good to know that we did our part when we were
> needed. And it's going to be a lot of pleasure to us when our kids get
> to the history class in school and can say, "My dad helped lick 'em."
>
> You can show them how their dad looked by having a "spirit of
> the American doughboy" statuette or lamp, the only representation
> of the American soldier there is showing him as he really was in
> action. An exact representation of the famous life size [*sic*] bronze
> statue of the same name made only by us.
>
> Your name on a postcard will bring FREE and without obliga-
> tion a beautiful gold embossed book telling the wonderful story of
> this attractive statue and lamp that every true ex-soldier wants.[18]

In this instance Viquesney eschews official rhetoric entirely and instead
parrots the vernacular voice of the down-to-earth veteran ("Buddy," "mighty
good," "licked 'em," and so forth). And he appeals directly to central
tenets of American Legion ideology. Consistent with the organization's

construction of memory, the speaker in the advertisement casts warfare as a "Hell" to be avoided. But this recognition of war's horrors does not diminish the veteran's pride in having served or his sense of pleasure in contemplating the past. In addition, Viquesney zeros in on the legion's preoccupation with education and youth; a quick reference to the history classroom, where patriotic youngsters will boast of what their fathers did in the Great War, leads to a description of the statuette and lamp, which the advertisement would have its reader take seriously as true domestic *memorials* as opposed to mere pieces of décor. Indeed, the advertisement cunningly presents its products as nothing less than foundational agents of collective memory; these doughboy miniatures will show the sons and daughters of veterans the American soldier "as he really was," thus shaping the narrative that the children will share at school.

Another advertisement from 1922, this one nearly a full page in size, focuses specifically on the "American Doughboy Art Lamp" and displays Viquesney's salesmanship working at full throttle.[19] In this case, several different styles of discourse flow in and out of one another, creating an almost polyphonic effect. Official rhetoric makes its appearance in several places. For example, the lamp "immortalizes America's Peace-Makers" or "Democracy's greatest son—the American Doughboy" or "the American doughboy, author of America's hard-won peace and security." But the plain-spoken voice of the veteran periodically cuts through this grandiloquent language, almost like a commercial anticipation of Dos Passos's Unknown Soldier in "The Body of an American." After several passages of heady Wilsonian prose, the advertisement lurches into the vernacular: the lamp will be "Your pal for life—a buddy in your home that you'll appreciate more and more as the days go by." Also of interest in this particular advertisement is the tension between passages that describe Viquesney's product as a bona fide work of art and those that underscore the object's utility. In places the two descriptions merge. Thus, the lamp is a "useful art fitment" (whatever that is) and "a work of real art" that "is likewise wholly practical." In effect, the advertisement plays off both sides of the "living memorial" debate, assuring the connoisseur of fine art that he is buying more than just a lamp while simultaneously promising the more practical-minded consumer that aesthetics have not compromised functionality.

By 1927 Viquesney had moved to a somewhat different approach. In the advertisement for the *Spirit of the American Doughboy* statuette that appears in several issues of *American Legion Monthly* that year, the text is dwarfed by a photograph that seems to depict the product (see fig. 10). Closer inspection, however, reveals that the photograph is of the seven-foot-tall statue, not the pot-metal, spray-painted miniature. Misrepresentation aside, Viquesney may have felt that his most successful creation, now a familiar public icon, could sell itself. This perhaps explains the secondary role played by the text, which in microscopic type describes the statuette as, among other things, "a striking memory-reviving likeness of the American fighting man and his part in the World War."[20] Three additional items in this particular sample became more or less standard in Viquesney's advertisements during the late 1920s (the period after he reacquired the rights to his statue). The sculptor's own photograph appears alongside his creation, thereby adding a personal stamp of approval, and two blurbs, separated from the main body of the text, emphasize the statue's verisimilitude through emphatic redundancy: "'Amazing Realism' Says American Legion Commander" and "Authentic Accurate 100 Per Cent Perfect." However, Viquesney was never one to pass up a good sales pitch, and though his later advertisements typically contain the elements described above, he would sometimes mix in other appeals, including the bandwagon approach—"Already [the statuette version of *Spirit of the American Doughboy*] holds a place of honor in thousands and thousands of American homes"[21]—and celebrity endorsements, among them a somewhat ungrammatical plug from Alvin York: "I consider your Doughboy a wonderful life like [*sic*] work of art and from personal knowledge of the equipment used by the Doughboy, this statue is correct to the smallest detail."[22]

Beyond his facility with advertising, Viquesney also masterminded sales plans that made his full-size statues available to communities that otherwise could not have afforded them. For example, a city council or American Legion post could purchase statuettes, raffle them off at fund-raisers, and then deduct their cost from the total owed for the seven-foot-tall version. As part of a fund-raising packet guaranteed to bring his creation within the reach of any town, no matter how small, Viquesney included a three-by-five-foot poster printed with an image of his statue and covered with a grid, somewhat like a bingo board. As the members of a given community bought tickets, the squares on the poster would fill up (not unlike the props used on later charity telethons)—until the statue was paid for.

Viquesney's cost-cutting manufacturing methods, aggressive advertising campaign, and innovative fund-raising materials (complete with dra-

10. Advertisement for a *Spirit of the American Doughboy* statuette. *American Legion Monthly* (April 1927). Courtesy of the American Legion National Headquarters.

matic visuals) all helped to turn *Spirit of the American Doughboy* into one of the most prominent collective-memory phenomena of the 1920s and 1930s. However, the content and design of his statue also played a role in its success. Interpretations of what Viquesney's doughboy means, independent of those offered in his abundant marketing, vary. For example, historian Jennifer Wingate plausibly suggests that the statue offers an image of vigor and muscularity that Americans found reassuring in the aftermath of the Spanish flu epidemic. And she makes much of the connection between Viquesney and Centralia, the site of an especially bloody clash between legionnaires and IWW members during the Red Scare. Interpreted against this backdrop of paranoia and violence, the sculptor's depiction of a robust fighting man—potentially a street-fighting man—

serves as a visual "antidote to radicalism."[23] Jennifer Keene, on the other hand, emphasizes the doughboy's realistic equipment and his "purposeful" gaze, thereby reading the statue as a three-dimensional expression, frozen in time, of legion-defined war memory.[24]

As an embodiment of memory, however, Viquesney's creation is surprisingly awkward (both aesthetically and ideologically), which leads one to wonder whether the work's popularity had more to do with its contradictions—contradictions that mirror the ambiguities of the Great War—than any perceived aesthetic merits. A closer look at the most popular American statue of the First World War reveals a conflicted icon, one whose uneasy blend of down-to-earth realism (signaled by the vernacular "Doughboy" in the title) and romantic idealization ("Spirit") sends profoundly mixed messages. As Keene observes, the statue is scrupulously lifelike in many of its details—"100 percent perfect," in fact, when it comes to World War I clothing and equipment. The soldier's hobnailed boots, gas-mask carrier (hung around his neck), ammunition belt, backpack, bayonet scabbard, and Model 1903 Springfield rifle would all pass an AEF veteran's inspection. On the statue's base, which is meant to depict no-man's-land, shell-blasted tree stumps and actual barbed wire (frequently removed for safety reasons) add to the realistic effect. However, the soldier's heroic posture undermines these lifelike details—almost absurdly so. "Spirit" looks ominously like suicide. The figure stands far too erect to represent credibly a soldier advancing into enemy fire. And his raised right arm, frozen in mid-swing as he hurls a hand grenade, is the phoniest touch of all. Since the doughboy is carrying his rifle in his left hand, we can only assume that he has just removed the grenade's cotter pin with his teeth, a common enough practice in Hollywood war films, but a near impossibility in reality.

Moreover, the doughboy's unhurried stride and air of calm resolve are completely out of keeping with the aggressive military action that the sculpture supposedly depicts. Viquesney may, as Goldsmith asserts, have wished to avoid any suggestion of brutality or violence in his stature, preferring to depict his subject as a Wilsonian interventionist who is part of the war but simultaneously above the ignoble emotions and motivations that characterized America's enemies and allies alike. But "war fought without rage," the idealistic vision of America's First World War embraced by Willa Cather's naïve protagonist in *One of Ours,* is difficult to swallow.[25] Thus, one finds it hard to believe that Viquesney's soldier is pitching anything more lethal than a baseball—could the sculptor have intended a visual echo of America's greatest pastime?—and in any event, the height of the doughboy's swing, which looks as if it will launch the grenade at a downward angle, does not bode well for the soldier's safety. In fairness it should be noted that these major lapses in realism, which nearly push the statue into the realm of parody, also appear in the work of the competitor who sued Viquesney for copyright infringement. Although the doughboy figures in John Paulding's *Over the Top* series are not armed with hand grenades, they display the same basic posture as Viquesney's figure—back straight, right arm held heroically high—and are just as implausible. One of these statues depicts a soldier advancing while apparently shaking his fist at the enemy.

Thus, Viquesney's *Spirit of the American Doughboy* presents a visual tug-of-war between photographic accuracy and creative heightening—between vernacular realism and official idealization. Neither of these elements is quite strong enough to overpower the other, and so the meaning of the statue remains uncomfortably suspended. At the same time, tradition and modernity clash in Viquesney's iconic doughboy. As we have seen, with his celebrated eye for detail, the sculptor equipped his infantryman with all the familiar accoutrements of modern industrialized warfare, including shrapnel helmet and gas mask, thereby acknowledging the impersonality of combat on the Western Front and the narrowed scope for heroic action. But the figure's confident stride, combined with his unbending posture and upraised arm, direct the viewer's attention skyward, away from the mud and debris of the battlefield and create an impression of triumph and transcendence. In other words, Viquesney's sculpture is modern in its details but essentially Victorian in its aesthetic, like an updated Civil War statue of the triumphant variety that stand atop Grand Army of the Republic monuments. Reminders of the industrial nature of the First World War, a war of artillery and machine guns that reduced the individual soldier to the status of a serial number (recall that more than fifty thousand American troops were blown up or mowed down in less than six months of major combat operations), appear in the soldier's equipment and the chewed-up, barbed-wire-strewn earth over which he advances. However, his "Spirit" lifts him out of this reality—or at least tries to. While the traditional and the heroic work to liberate the soldier from his specific place and time, the modern features of the sculpture stubbornly tie the doughboy to that reality of mud and destruction seen on the monument's base.

By focusing his statue on an ordinary American infantryman (as opposed to abstract or purely symbolic figures such as Columbia, Uncle Sam, or Joan of Arc), Viquesney contributed to the postwar enshrinement of the citizen soldier, a commemorative phenomenon that played out in both Europe and the United States. As many historians have observed, since the end of the First World War, governments that practice wartime conscription have felt compelled to honor ordinary citizens and to do so in as equitable a fashion as possible. The political realities of total war necessitated the silent cities of the dead that line the former Western Front, each fallen soldier in his own burial plot with his own headstone (regardless of rank), and the appearance of enlisted men at the center of war monuments and remembrance rituals. Such egalitarianism was unheard of during the Napoleonic Wars, fought a century before World War I, and was by no means the norm during the American Civil War, which saw its share of mass gravesites (one of them, in fact, located in Arlington National Cemetery) and the separate and unequal commemoration of officers and enlisted men. In the case of *Spirit of the American Doughboy,* we see egalitarian commemoration driven from the bottom up. Nearly 140 American communities took Viquesney up on his offer of surefire fundraising strategies and ultimately erected a monument not to the military elite but to the ordinary American foot soldier. And on that monument, in most cases, appear *all* the names of the citizens who represented a particular town or county in the war. That Viquesney's statue is visually and ideologically awkward, offering no easy answers on the meaning of the war, says less about the artistic taste of these communities, or the talents of the sculptor, than it does about the formidable challenges that Americans faced when attempting to distill an ambiguous war into coherent collective memory.

Viquesney's best-known creation might seem the antithesis of the Tomb of the Unknown Soldier, the former a revival of nineteenth-century commemorative aesthetics, the latter a grotesquely innovative solution to the modern problem of how to honor the war dead when their sheer numbers, by necessity, made state-driven commemoration impersonal and non-cathartic. However, *Spirit of the American Doughboy* perhaps has more in common with the shrine at Arlington than we might at first imagine. One final dimension of meaning remains to be teased out of the Well-Known Soldier. In 1923 the local newspaper for Wayne County, Kentucky, the *Wayne County Outlook,* published an unattributed poem, titled "He Lives," that probably appeared in other news venues as well. Since the poem describes a miniature soldier statue, contains the phrase "Spirit of the Doughboy," and was quite likely written by none other than E. M. Viquesney, it warrants full-length quotation:

I have a few art treasures
In this little house of mine,
But something's lately come to it
That seems almost divine.

It's the statue of a Doughboy,
And as at it I look
I'm far, or very far away
From mine own inglenook.

I'm visioning the trenches and
Flanders Field afar—
I see through hot and burning tears
A wee, gold star—

And it doesn't seem to matter
About the lesser things
When I think of what they did for us—
Those heroes who were kings.

Oh Spirit of the Doughboy,
You hope and solace bring!
Taking away the anguish
That was made by Death's deep sting.

And though in Flanders Field there sleeps
The only son I had,
In spite of bitterness and pain
I cannot be but glad.

Glad for his life—his patriot soul
That saw where duty lay;
That held the torch of courage high,
Though steep and rough the way.

These are the things the statue speaks;
Shall I not lift my head
And greet his Spirit shining through?—
He lives—HE IS NOT DEAD![26]

Whether Viquesney wrote this poem may never be known for certain. However, there are tantalizing hints of the sculptor's salesmanship at work within the doggerel verse. The image of the "torch of courage held high," for example, perhaps points not only to the obvious similarities between Viquesney's soldier, with his raised right arm, and the Statue of Liberty, but also to the literal illumination offered by the "American Doughboy Art Lamp." And who else but the founder of the American Doughboy Studios would describe his statuette as "almost divine"? Yet authorship in this instance is less important than the sentiments expressed. Probably only E. M. Viquesney would have written so effusively about a twelve-inch-tall, pot-metal figurine, but the *Wayne County Outlook* apparently found nothing outlandish about his tribute in verse—or the notion of a mass-produced statuette as a reassuring symbol of the war dead. Whatever its probable commercial motivations, the poem offers a culturally resonant interpretation of the best-known American statue of the Great War.

Indeed, "He Lives" sends us back to *Spirit of the American Doughboy* with a new set of questions. Could the word "Spirit" in the sculpture's title carry a double meaning? Does the statue capture the Wilsonian "spirit" that motivated an army of crusaders to wage "war without rage," or does it present an actual spirit—a phantom doughboy eternally advancing? Could it be that instead of depicting soldierly vigor, ready to be unleashed on any potential Red Menace, the statue presents manhood already spent and buried on the Western Front? If *Spirit of the American Doughboy* does in fact carry these funereal associations, then the statue participates in what historian George L. Mosse has called the Cult of the Fallen Soldier, a set of cultural expressions, pervasive in both Europe and the United States, that enlisted the war dead in the service of perpetuating nationalism after 1918. Fittingly, Mosse emphasizes the visual and tactile intimacy of this cult: through public monuments, domestic art objects (such as the American Doughboy Studio's statuettes and lamps), and aesthetically pleasing cemeteries, "the fallen were transformed into symbols which people could see and touch and which made their cult come alive."[27] Whether Viquesney's statues performed this transformation or not, "He

Lives" describes the process perfectly. The poem is a textbook example of the Cult of the Fallen Soldier at work. For the grieving narrator of the poem, the miniature doughboy, an "art treasure," becomes a stand-in for the lost son. Contemplation of this memorial simulacrum then leads to an idealized vision of the dead, a vision that reinforces nationalistic concepts of service and sacrifice ("where duty lay").

Near the end of the poem, the imagery shifts from visual to aural. The patriotic consolation offered by the statue becomes something metaphorically spoken. Duty and courage, in the service of the country, are "things the statue speaks." Thus, the poem ingeniously combines the best-known American visual memorial of the First World War with the popular aural trope of the war dead speaking to the living. Communities that erected *Spirit of the American Doughboy* in public spaces—or individuals who purchased miniature versions for their homes—may or may not have interpreted the statue in this fashion. However, it seems likely, given the prominence of the war dead in American culture during the early 1920s, that the poem "He Lives" describes yet another layer of meaning contained within Viquesney's awkward but expressive creation. Contemplating the sculptor's incongruous arrangement of the traditional and the modern, the official and the vernacular, Americans of the 1920s and 1930s could both *see* an image of the men who had returned home from battlefields of Europe, vigorous and ready to combat radicalism, and *hear* the voices of the dead. Thus, within interwar culture, both the Well-Known and the Unknown Soldier spoke to Americans. In the case of the latter, however, the soldier's voice would increasingly turn against the official forces that attempted to script its utterances.

Voices from the Tomb: The Unknown Soldier and American Culture, 1921–1941

As many commentators noted at the time, the site selected for the reburial of America's Unknown Soldier on Armistice Day 1921 conveyed, with almost unbearable poignancy, the scenic beauty and spaciousness of the United States. Interred one year earlier, the anonymous fallen soldiers selected by the governments of France and Great Britain received anything but pastoral resting places. France's Unknown Soldier resides beneath the Arc de Triomphe in Paris, at the center of one of the busiest traffic circles in the world; Great Britain's, in Westminster Abbey, amid the gothic gloom shared by the nation's poets and notables. America's

Unknown Soldier, on the other hand, "sleeps beneath the stars" (as the cliché would have it), atop a hill that overlooks the Potomac River and central Washington, DC. At sunset, in particular, it is a place of stunning beauty. Yet the sense of timelessness and pastoral calm associated with Arlington National Cemetery was—and is—illusory, and the instability of the Unknown Soldier as a national symbol perhaps begins with his resting place, the scene of multiple memory wars and contested cultural narratives.

As is well known, before its seizure by federal forces during the Civil War, the ground that is today known as Arlington National Cemetery belonged, through marriage, to Robert E. Lee. Thus, the history of Arlington's transformation into sacred space begins with a punitive action that underscores not unity but division. And as historian William A. Blair has shown, often heated conflict, involving multiple constituencies, was the norm at Arlington during its first half century as a federal center for commemoration.[28] At the heart of that conflict stood the dead, whose teeming presence on the grounds of Lee's former estate had less to do with the federal government's desire to punish the Confederate commander (that desire was satisfied through legal maneuvers that blocked the Lee family from ever repurchasing their property) than with overcrowding in Washington, DC's existing graveyards. During America's bloodiest war, demand for cemetery space often threatened to exceed supply.

Among the first bodies interred in what would eventually become hallowed ground were those of runaway slaves, members of an African American community that sprang up at the estate, shortly after its seizure, and that cultivated grain for the U.S. Army Quartermaster's Department. Next came the remains of several hundred Confederate soldiers who had died in nearby Union hospitals, along with ever larger waves of Union dead, both black and white. In 1864 the site officially received its designation as a federal soldiers cemetery—just in time to accommodate the thousands of Union corpses produced by Ulysses S. Grant's notoriously casualty-ridden campaign in Virginia that year.[29] With the cemetery's official status came segregation of the dead, something that had not been practiced there previously. Thus, while cemetery officials henceforth separated the Blue from the Gray and the black from the white, establishing separate burial zones for each, hundreds of bodies remained intermingled, including Confederates buried with African Americans, an intolerable situation to many white Southerners (and just as intolerable to many blacks). Although the staggering body count of the Civil

War, rather than any commemorative impulse, led to the establishment of Arlington National Cemetery, the place soon took on an air of prestige enhanced by its proximity to the nation's capital and spectacular setting. Thus, by the end of the 1860s Arlington was already fixed in the national consciousness as *the* cemetery of cemeteries, the burial ground of choice for the nation's distinguished soldiers and heroes.

But controversy haunted the site. Indeed, throughout the decades leading up to the First World War, the seemingly placid, monument-covered lawn at Arlington was, in Blair's words, "a place of sectional discord."[30] The Reconstruction years, for example, saw Confederate graves placed off limits during Decoration Day functions. In the view of the GAR, which had not yet entered its all-forgiving reconciliation phase, Decoration Day (later retitled Memorial Day) was a holiday to honor Union losses, not those of a traitorous former enemy. Nor did cemetery officials allow the erection of any Confederate memorials at this time. Meanwhile, African American leaders noted with anger that soldiers of color were buried as far as possible from their white compatriots. And they discovered that no one at Arlington bothered to see that the graves of African American soldiers received flags or flowers. According to the Jim Crow formula, followed to the letter by the Arlington staff, the bodies of white soldiers went to the heights, to the area nearest the Lee family's elegant mansion and the site of Decoration Day ceremonies, while negro remains stayed below in the cemetery's shallow north end, among (as black leaders in Washington, DC, put it) "paupers and rebels."[31]

While African American concerns went largely unaddressed, discord between Northerners and Southerners at Arlington diminished over time, thanks in part to the conciliatory stance of President William McKinley at the close of the nineteenth century.[32] In a deft political move designed to secure Southern support for the Spanish-American War, McKinley vowed to make the federal government responsible for all Civil War graves, both Union and Confederate, thereby honoring the fallen of both sides equally. By the outbreak of the First World War, the spirit of reconciliation had grown so strong that the United States government approved the construction of the Confederate memorial at Arlington that still stands there today, complete with its bronze image of a loyal slave following his master off to battle. Ironically, as Blair points out, this monument, paid for with funds raised by the United Daughters of the Confederacy, is among the tallest and most conspicuous in the entire cemetery.[33] But even as late as 1914, wounds left behind by the Civil War could suddenly open at Arlington—and nearly swallow an unwary politician. That year, Southern Democrat Woodrow Wilson snubbed the GAR by declining an invitation to speak at Arlington on Memorial Day. And, to make matters worse, word soon got out that the president had agreed to attend the unveiling of the new Confederate memorial. After some political back-peddling, Wilson reconsidered the Union veterans' invitation, and the incident eventually blew over.[34] Nevertheless, such clumsiness on the part of an ordinarily shrewd politician demonstrated that "sectional discord" could still rise without warning, like an angry phantom, from the nation's most celebrated burial ground.

Perhaps because of its history of friction between Northern and Southern commemorative interests, Arlington was not the first choice for the Unknown Soldier's resting place. Hamilton Fish Jr., who introduced the legislation calling for the selection of an American Unknown, preferred the rotunda of the U.S. Capitol Building. Fish also lobbied vigorously to have the Unknown Soldier reburied on Memorial Day, not Armistice Day, so that the unity of North and South, reaffirmed on the battlefields of Europe, would be emphasized before the entire nation.[35] In the end, the Harding administration rejected both proposals. However, the lavish ceremonies conducted at the nation's capitol and at Arlington National Cemetery in November 1921 could not help but underscore Civil War reconciliation. After all, the Unknown Soldier might just as easily have come from either side of the Mason-Dixon Line. Although the GAR played a far more prominent and official role in the proceedings than Confederate remembrance organizations—indeed, GAR representatives received more time than any another group when they visited the flag-draped coffin as it rested in state on November 10[36]—veterans of the Blue and the Gray alike marched in the Unknown Soldier's funeral procession as it wound its way from the Capitol Building to the Arlington heights. For most Americans on that solemn occasion, the ghosts of discord that had long haunted the former property of Robert E. Lee finally seemed to be at rest.

But one especially volatile division remained. While North and South metaphorically embraced over the body of the Unknown Soldier, African Americans stood apart, sidelined during the reburial proceedings just as they had been during the war. There were token gestures of inclusion. For example, the Harding administration allowed a delegation from the NAACP to lay a wreath on the Unknown Soldier's casket and admitted representatives from the Colored Veterans of the War into the funeral procession, where they marched alongside the members of forty-three other patriotic organizations, including the Knights of Columbus and the Jewish Veterans of the World War. However, as Kurt Piehler observes, no one among the multitude of speakers featured on November 11 ever raised the possibility "that the [Unknown Soldier] might come from a black sharecropper's cabin or from Harlem."[37] Obviously, there were limits to how far the trope of the Unknown as an American everyman would be carried—limits that were consistent with the segregated cemetery within which the Memorial Amphitheater stood. Just as the bodies of white soldiers had traditionally ascended to the highest, loveliest area of Arlington while blacks stayed below, the African American dead of the Great War were barred, metaphorically, from climbing into the flag-draped casket that received so many honors in November 1921.

Nor were African Americans alone in being told—without being told directly—that the Unknown Soldier was not one of their own. Authorities apparently found the notion of a Jewish or Catholic Unknown Soldier just as unthinkable, despite the participation of non-Protestants in the procession and reburial ceremony. As Piehler writes, "Many of the rituals and symbols associated with the Unknown Soldier defined the ideal American as a white, most likely Protestant, Christian. The Cavalry Band played 'Onward Christian Soldier' as the Unknown Soldier was escorted from the Washington Navy Yard on 9 November. Protestant hymns dominated the amphitheater service, and when the former Chaplain of the [AEF], Episcopal bishop Charles Brent, read the committal service, he prayed that this fallen hero would be resurrected in the name of 'Jesus Christ our Lord.'"[38] Further evidence of official bias came several years later when the Commission of Fine Arts considered a design for the Unknown Soldier's finished tomb (until 1932 the anonymous remains rested beneath a simple concrete marker, without any distinctive monument) that featured a Christian cross. Ironically, the Jewish Welfare Board, speaking for a portion of the national population that had in fact been statistically overrepresented in the AEF,[39] had to remind the commission that the Unknown Soldier might have been a Jew.

The eleven-year delay in selecting a monument to stand above the Unknown Soldier's tomb points to a lack of clarity in the official meaning of the site—a lack of clarity that, ironically enough, fits well with the turbulent history of Arlington National Cemetery, with its "sectional" remembrance and racial hypocrisy. On an emotional level, this ambiguity makes little difference. Even now, nearly a century after that memorable

Armistice Day in 1921, a visit to the Tomb of the Unknowns remains a moving experience. Although mostly curious tourists, not mourners, form the daily crowds that spill over the steps and balcony of the Memorial Amphitheater to look out on the changing of the tomb guards, few visitors leave the site without having felt, however fleetingly, connected to a deep and painful body of collective memory—not the "period rush," in this case, but its solemn opposite. Audiences at the tomb turn off their cell phones and speak in whispers. And tears come unexpectedly—even for those who have given little thought to America's past (or current) wars. But stepping back from the site, and momentarily resisting its almost hypnotic emotional pull, one cannot help but be struck by the oddity—indeed, bizarreness—of the Unknown Soldier as a form of remembrance. Why would a government select an unidentifiable cadaver and enshrine it with so much pageantry, with nothing less, indeed, than the full honors ordinarily reserved for a head of state?

Historians have provided various answers. For example, Mark Meigs notes that the Unknown Soldier's selection and ceremonial reburial "raised a whole population's pain to the level of tragedy."[40] In other words, the civic spectacle that surrounded the Unknown's return functioned as a kind of theater—tragic theater that, like the sorrowful dramas of the ancient Greeks, provided catharsis for its audience. Kurt Piehler, on the other hand, reads the spectacle politically, as an expression of the federal government's need, noted earlier in this chapter, to honor the citizen soldiers without whom modern total warfare would be impossible. "Symbolically," Piehler writes, "the Unknown Soldier raised the status of the common soldier to that of a general or head of state," a powerful democratic message and one perhaps necessary in an age of total warfare.[41]

Arguing along a quite different track, Aviel Roshwald, a historian of nationalism, observes that the Tomb of the Unknown Soldier "has become a widespread nationalist tradition whose power lies not only in the anonymity of the individual remains lying within it, but also the nonspecificity of the time it refers to." For Roshwald, the tomb functions for the nation as the means by which "[c]onflicts fought in vastly different periods and for fundamentally different reasons are all conflated into a single, institutionalized commemoration."[42] Such an interpretation might seem like a stretch, except that the inscription on the Tomb of the Unknown Soldier identifies him only as "An American Soldier, Known But to God," not as a casualty of the Great War (in contrast, it should be noted, to the far more specific inscriptions on the graves of the British and French Unknowns). Indeed, Roshwald's assertion of a nationalist agenda behind the Tomb of the Unknown Soldier proves no less persuasive than the conclusions presented by Meigs and Piehler. As we will see more fully later in this chapter, progressive hopes for lasting peace and international goodwill, inspired by a major disarmament conference that opened in Washington, DC, on the day after the ceremony at Arlington, tended to reinforce the connection between the Unknown Soldier and the specific conflict in which he fell, a conflict that many Americans in 1921 were still optimistic enough to call the "War to End All Wars." But the icon's murky symbolism also accommodated a different interpretation. For those less hopeful or less desirous of improved international relations and disarmament, the conflation that Roshwald notes served as a way of directing the Unknown Soldier's significance away from a dubious cause and toward values—duty, honor, country—thought to be ahistorical and distinctly American. Much of the cliché-ridden verbiage in Harding's amphitheater address strived for precisely this kind of historical transcendence, and the presence in the procession of veterans (or the children of veterans) representing so many different conflicts in American history also served to expand the ritual's significance well beyond the First World War. So was the Unknown Soldier a symbol of American sacrifice in a war that would bring lasting peace? Or did he represent a noble martial tradition, one that was likely far from over? Official versions of the Unknown Soldier's significance allowed the public to embrace either one of these interpretations; vernacular versions would ultimately deny them both.

Thus, the array of explanations (all of them plausible) offered by historians for this strangest of public monuments underscores the multi-dimensionality—and elusiveness—of the Unknown Soldier as a national symbol. And in this regard it is worth noting that the ceremonial honors conferred upon the American Unknown had surprisingly little to do with the issue of "missing" soldiers—that is, those troops whose remains were unrecognizable or irretrievable. Approximately forty-five hundred members of the AEF remained unaccounted for by 1921, in contrast with the *hundreds of thousands* of European soldiers whose bodies simply vanished.[43] Thus, whatever—and whoever—the Unknown Soldier was, the icon drew its power from the war trauma (and resulting hunger for meaning) that had been inflicted on the nation as a whole rather than the specific needs of those Americans who had no grave to visit. That the symbol spoke to this national trauma in a way that varied from American to American only increased its appeal.

However, the Unknown Soldier's capacity for expansion and redirection as a signifier was not limitless, at least not from the official perspective. As illustrated in Harding's funeral oration, along with the speeches delivered by other prominent political and military dignitaries, three specific assumptions came from the top down: (1) that the tomb housed a white Christian (most likely a Protestant), an assumption at variance, as we have seen, with the note of ethnic and racial inclusion not infrequently struck during the reburial service; (2) that the Unknown Soldier fully deserved and would have wanted the honors that he posthumously received, honors that defined him exclusively as a soldier, as an obedient agent of the state; and (3) that the Unknown died for a reason—if not for lasting peace, then at least in the name of timeless martial virtues that made service in any American war, no matter how misguided or bungled, a matter of pride and distinction. Thus, although the enshrinement of an unknown soldier was unprecedented in American war remembrance, and born of the thoroughly modern conditions of the Great War, his official meaning evoked long-standing conceptions of military service, manhood, and purposeful warfare.

For millions of Americans during the interwar decades, the assumptions listed above remained as fixed and impervious as the reinforced concrete that hid the Unknown Soldier from view. But for others, the soldier's symbolism, a strange brew of the traditional and the modern, was more vaporous and spectral; it seeped easily from the ideological casket built to contain it. Thus, within just a few short years of the Unknown Soldier's return, dozens of poets, fiction writers, editorialists, and clerics appropriated this national symbol and turned it against its official makers. The works produced by these commentators comprise a significant subgenre of American war literature during the 1920s and 1930s and an important reflection of collective memory, one largely unexplored by scholars. Thus, the remainder of this chapter will focus on selected literary responses to the Unknown Soldier, including poems, short stories, sermons, and novels. As we will see, most of these writings expose the gruesome military realities masked by the patriotic ritual, question the ethics of foisting a patriotic military identity upon a fallen citizen who could not speak for himself, or (anticipating Mosse) deconstruct the pomp and circumstance of the Unknown Soldier's return as an expression of the Cult of the Fallen Soldier, revealing the militaristic dimensions of a ceremony that purported to honor a dead warrior in the name of peace.

However, before turning to works that typify this body of protest literature, we must first consider a piece whose vernacular reworking of the Unknown Soldier's symbolism moved in a quite different direction. In "Saint Peter Relates an Incident of the Resurrection Day" (1930), Harlem Renaissance poet James Weldon Johnson did the unthinkable—or, rather, what was implicitly prohibited at the Armistice Day ceremony in 1921: he claimed the Unknown Soldier as one of Black America's own, thereby redirecting the icon's meaning toward the very divisions and injustices recorded in the history of Arlington National Cemetery.

By his own account, Johnson wrote "Saint Peter Relates an Incident of the Resurrection Day" in a fury after learning that African American mothers who participated in the Gold Star Mother Pilgrimage of 1930 traveled to and from France aboard second-class vessels while their white counterparts sailed in luxury. The original edition contained the following dedication: "Written while meditating upon heaven and hell and democracy and war and America and the Negro Gold Star Mothers."[44] Set in heaven ages after the Resurrection, the poem opens with a scene reminiscent of Thomas Hardy: An eternity-weary band of angels entreat St. Peter, known for his knowledge of history, to tell them yet another story of human folly. St. Peter agrees and recounts the following tale of the Unknown Soldier and his return to life. Wakened by Gabriel's trumpet on the morning of the Resurrection, the dead of "every land and clime" rise and are restored to health, "their faces radiant and their bodies new." Within the United States, however, "the grand roll call" reveals that one reanimated citizen has not yet been liberated from his grave— the Unknown Soldier. Thus, a "special order" goes out, and various patriotic organizations, headed by the Ku Klux Klan, swing into action, forming a grotesque reenactment of the processional march to Arlington on November 11, 1921:

> The word went forth, spoke by some grand panjandrum,
> Perhaps, by some high potentate of Klandom,
> That all the trusty patriotic mentors,
> And duly qualified Hundred-Percenters,
>
> Should forthwith gather together upon the banks
> Of the Potomac, there to form their ranks,

March to the tomb, by orders to be given,
And escort the unknown soldier up to heaven.

Compliantly they gathered from each region,
The G.A.R., the D.A.R., the Legion,
Veterans of wars—Mexican, Spanish, Haitian—
Trustees of the patriotism of the nation;

Key Men, Watchmen, shunning circumlocution,
The Sons of the This and That and of the Revolution;
Not to forget, there gathered every man
Of the Confederate Veterans and the Ku Klux Klan.

The Grand Imperial Marshal gave the sign;
Column on column, the marchers fell in line;
Majestic as an army in review,
They swept up Washington's wide avenue.[45]

Once at the tomb, the Unknown Soldier's rescuers hear a "faint commotion" inside, "like the stirring of a child," and they set to work with picks, crowbars, and drills. At last, after heroic effort, they force an opening in the concrete, and a figure rises, growing "bigger and bigger." But then comes the terrible discovery:

"Great God Almighty! Look!" they cried,
"he is a nigger!"[46]

In the riot that ensues, the Klan offers to hide this monstrous revelation by re-imprisoning the body inside the tomb, but it is too late: the Unknown Soldier ascends to heaven, a "tall, black soldier-angel marching alone," singing of crossing over to Jordan. And so St. Peter's story ends, leaving his celestial audience "'twixt tears and laughter."[47]

Johnson's poem achieves its remarkable power by turning the story of the Unknown Soldier upside down. In this topsy-turvy rendition, Arlington National Cemetery becomes a place of life, not death, and a parade of patriotic rescuers representing every war in American history, the Grandest Army of the Republic ever assembled, takes the place of the mournful column that marched to the heights of Arlington in 1921. But as the poem goes on to demonstrate, even the transmogrifications wrought by the Resurrection have little impact on racial prejudice, a force too deeply buried in God's Country for any divine intervention to take effect. And so for the stunned whites who witness the revelation at the tomb—a sardonic rewriting of Christ's resurrection—the day of deliverance instantly becomes a day of mourning, and celebration gives way to hellish bedlam. Johnson also offers a biting critique of American memory. From the Ku Klux Klan to the "Sons of the This and That," the "Hundred-Percenters" cannot imagine a black man inside the tomb, because they refuse to remember African American contributions during the Great War or any other conflict in American history. For them, all black soldiers are Unknowns—a collective delusion that makes the irony of the scene at the tomb that much more delicious. Thus, in "St. Peter Relates an Incident," whites exercise hegemonic control over the past, and they manipulate the master narrative of American military glory to serve their own interests—that is, until history ends and the truth comes out.

While Johnson wrenches the Unknown Soldier as far as possible out of his official framework of meanings, in order to expose the racism at the heart of American war memory, Laurence Stallings's 1924 novel, *Plumes,* shows that "Hundred-Percenters," no less than blacks, are ill served by a government that offers an artillery-shredded corpse as a patriotic symbol. Like Carl Sandburg's "And So To-Day" (1922), Stallings's narrative offers an early indication of the Unknown Soldier's possibilities as an anti-symbol—possibilities that would be explored more fully by writers in the late 1920s and early 1930s as dissatisfaction with the outcomes of the Great War grew and calls for disarmament or isolationism became more strident.

Before his wounding at Belleau Wood, Stallings's autobiographical protagonist, Richard Plume, shares much in common with the WASPish neopatriots who gather on the banks of the Potomac in Johnson's poem. Raised in a middle-class household in Georgia and educated at an insular denominational college (modeled after Wake Forest, where Stallings majored in English), Plume has been drawn since birth to all things military, and shortly after the American declaration of war in 1917 he pursues a commission in the Marine Corps as a matter of course, giving little thought to the wife and son he will leave behind. Plume's racial attitudes are also in line with those of Johnson's resurrected white warriors. The novel's only scene in wartime France highlights Plume's physical vitality (before German machine-gun bullets shatter his right leg) and his ingrained sense of racial superiority. When the second lieutenant's platoon refuses to share its boxcar with a group of Sengalese "casuals," a fistfight erupts, during which Plume grabs one of the African soldiers, refers to him as "Sambo," and "send[s] him sprawling" with a kick to his backside.[48] That the black troops, members of another army, have a legitimate claim never occurs to him. Like other moments in the novel when Plume's bigotry rises to the surface, this episode would be unreadable except that Stallings treats his protagonist ironically. Thus, in this instance, Plume's racist bravado nearly leads to his demise: one of the Sengalese soldiers, it turns out, is armed with a bayonet—and he is not afraid to use it on a white American officer. The racial deference that Plume expects (at his peril) simply doesn't exist in a country without Jim Crow.

By the same token, Stallings underscores the blindness inherent in Plume's gung-ho attitude toward war, a blindness shared by his ancestors. A genealogical history of the Plume family, presented near the beginning of the novel, reveals that its male members (war lovers one and all) all pay dearly for their martial enthusiasm. After plunging into war, few escape death or mutilation. And, economically, the family is worse off after each conflict. However, those Plumes who manage to return home from the battlefield, typically missing an arm or a leg, never talk of their physical suffering and financial sacrifice; instead, they dutifully take their place in commemorative rituals that stress the virtues of war for the next generation. Thus, Stallings makes it clear from the beginning that his protagonist is a dupe—in a line of dupes. However, after multiple operations on his leg, which leave him in constant pain, Plume resolves that he will defy family tradition and reject the role of the stoic war veteran. Thus, he refuses to return to Georgia, where a comfortable college appointment awaits him, and takes up residence in Washington, DC, where he flirts with political radicalism, seeking some way to protest against cultural forces that have led to his physical ruin.

However, in *Plumes,* as in Stallings's other First World War writings, attraction to war—particularly as an expression of manhood—is too deeply rooted in the male American psyche for any protest to succeed. And so, in the end, Plume gives up his quixotic effort and accepts the inevitable: like his ancestors, he will hobble home and play the role of noble Southern warrior, never again to speak of the pain he has endured or the horrors he has witnessed. Appropriately enough, Plume reaches this bitter conclusion at Arlington National Cemetery, on the day before the Unknown Soldier's funeral. After his young son, Dickie, another war lover in the making, scrambles to collect brass casings (as they fall at the feet of an honor guard that has just fired a salute), Plume looks out on the acres of grave markers and senses the futility of his protest. "I can't do anything," he tells his wife, Esme. "What chance has that poor little boy yonder against all these dead men? I'll go home with you any time you say. I'm through."[49]

But after granting the power of Arlington as a repository of war memory and as a site where militaristic passions are cyclically renewed, Stallings closes the novel with a final note of protest—and faint hope. Plume's friend Gary, another maimed veteran of the Great War, takes the protagonist's son to the open crypt where the Unknown Soldier will be placed and offers a haunting lesson on the cruelty of war:

> Dickie was puzzled by the marble hole in the ground.
>
> "What's that for?" he asked Gary.
>
> "A grave."
>
> "What's a grave for?"
>
> "For a soldier to sleep in."
>
> "Why doesn't he sleep in his bed?" Dickie was puzzled.
>
> "General won't let him," Gary said solemnly.
>
> Dickie scrutinized the dark face above him to make sure there was no insincerity in the answer. He studied the marble receptacle.
>
> "What's a general?" he said finally.
>
> "A man," said Gary, "who makes little boys sleep in graves."
>
> Dickie was frightened. His lip trembled. He looked about to where Richard and Esme sat above him. "I'll ask Esme," he said, "not to let a general get me."[50]

This powerful scene, the finest in the novel, draws its force from several elements—the child's first apprehension of evil, the veteran's cruel but well-intentioned bluntness, and the sinister ugliness of the tomb, which is, of course, both literally and figuratively hollow. Indeed, in an ingenious move, Stallings presents the Unknown Soldier's "resting place" (Gary's stark comments play off this familiar euphemism) before any commemorative apparatus has kicked into motion—before any speeches have been delivered or wreathes laid. Thus, in the place of a national monument, surrounded by ritual and patriotic iconography, the reader confronts a "marble hole" or "receptacle," the cold accommodations of the dead.

By 1928, four years after the publication of *Plumes,* writers had begun to reconstruct the identity—and voice—of the soldier inhabiting the tomb, thus filling in the space that Stallings intentionally left empty. One measure of the Unknown Soldier's power and popularity, both as an official symbol and as an emerging anti-symbol (in the hands of vernacular forces), appears in an illuminating cultural artifact from that year—an anthology of poetry and prose intended to capture the spirit of Armistice Day. Edited by A. P. Sanford and Robert Haven Schauffler and part of a book series devoted to "Our American Holidays," *Armistice Day* mirrors the First World War's turbulent and divided memory a decade after its conclusion. And even apart from its value as a source for written responses to the Unknown Soldier, the volume offers considerable insight into American war remembrance in the 1920s. One notes, for example, that throughout its various sections, the book sprinkles antiheroic pieces among predictably patriotic and affirmative selections. Thus, antithetical versions of war memory sometimes sit side by side on the same page—and without any commentary by the editors. Few documents of the time more vividly reflect the lack of a national consensus regarding the conduct and outcomes of the Great War. Equally fascinating is the preponderance of British and Canadian works, which suggests that the literature and culture of Great Britain and its dominions played a far larger role in American First World War remembrance than one might assume. Surprisingly, alongside selections by Woodrow Wilson, Alan Seeger, Dorothy Canfield, and Vachel Lindsay appear writings by John Galsworthy, Philip Gibbs, Rupert Brooke, and Siegfried Sassoon (these last two names represent a particularly striking collision between the idealistic and the antiheroic). Moreover, several of the sample Armistice Day programs provided at the back of the book (revealing documents in themselves) highlight non-American literary texts. Canadian John McRae's "In Flanders Fields," then (as now) the most famous poem of the Great War, appears as a recommended selection for recitation in three of the programs, including one provided by the American Legion; Kipling's "Lest We Forget" is endorsed in two others.

The spectral figure of the Unknown Soldier looms large in the volume. No fewer than thirty poems and stories, collected mostly from newspapers and magazines, appear in the section titled "The Unknown Soldier and His Brothers," and they reflect a broadening range of interpretations inspired by this nebulous icon. Some pieces, such as Harry Kemp's "The Unknown," tow the official line. After noting that the Unknown Soldier's name will remain "Unspelled" until "Time . . . Goes Back to God" (an anticipation of Johnson's "St. Peter Relates an Incident"), Kemp marvels in his final stanza at the elevation of an anonymous common man into the pantheon of the great:

Here, under sacred ground,
   The Unknown lies:
Dim armies gather 'round
   His sacrifice;
Kings, Princes, Presidents
   Attest his worth:
The Generals bow before
   His starry earth,
In the World's heart inscribed
   His love, his fame—
He leads the Captains with
   His Unknown Name![51]

Like "He Lives," that equally atrocious hymn to *Spirit of the American Doughboy,* Kemp's poem is a veritable catalog of patriotic clichés ("sacred ground," "dim armies," "sacrifice," and so forth) that shift the reader's attention as far as possible from the tragic object supposedly at the center of the poem. Indeed, the poem illustrates perfectly culture critic Elaine Scarry's observation that official discourses of war refuse to acknowledge the chief "product" of armed aggression—namely, broken or lifeless bodies.[52] Within such discourses, Scarry argues, war's victims remain *bodiless,* caught in an endless loop of solipsistic signifying that never connects with the reality of physical harm. The grisliest passages in John Dos Passos's aptly titled "The Body of an American"—where, for example, Grave Registration workers handle the Unknown Soldier's bones and "dried viscera" and rats lap up his blood—restore the body denied in texts such as "The Unknown."[53] However, before Dos Passos could offer his horrifying reminder of the soldier's physicality (or, for that matter, before Johnson could appropriate an icon defined by "Hundred-Percenters" and turn it against them), readers first had to see the Unknown Soldier through a lens other than that offered by official rhetoric—and hear his *voice.*

Two pieces in *Armistice Day* look ahead to more radical responses. Though sentimental, E. O. Laughlin's "The Unknown" eschews the note of democratic celebration struck in Kemp's poem of the same name. Here a mood of quiet grief predominates as the Unknown Soldier, only half aware of what has happened to him since his death, describes his peculiar situation:

I do not understand . . .
 They bring so many, many flowers to me—
Rainbows of roses, wreaths from every land;
 And hosts of solemn strangers come to see
My tomb here on these quiet, wooded heights.
 My tomb here seems to be
One of the sights.[54]

Although the last line of this opening stanza suggests possibilities for irony—is the tomb simply a *sight*, a tourist attraction, rather than a *site* of memory?—the poem does not explore them. Instead, the Unknown Soldier goes on to describe his absolute separation from the living. Mothers visit the tomb and whisper the names of their dead sons. The speaker wishes "they knew" his true identity, but he cannot reach them. And when his "sweetheart" stops at the tomb, he is likewise powerless.[55] She alone speaks his real name, but then goes on her way. He has no means of recalling her. While Laughlin's poem may be clumsy—even trite—in its emotional appeals, it does not (as Kemp's poem does) sidestep tragedy and grief. To Laughlin's Unknown Soldier, posthumous honors and praise make little difference. Only his loss of connection matters.

A prose selection titled "Unknown," by congressman and advertising mogul Bruce Barton, also introduces elements that would soon become commonplace in the vernacular redefinition of the Unknown Soldier's significance. While Laughlin employs the soon-to-become-standard trope of the Unknown speaking from the grave, Barton shows his reader apparitions at night. The tomb at Arlington becomes a portal into the beyond, not unlike the British Menin Gate Memorial at Ypres, Belgium, which Australian artist Will Longstaff famously depicted as a gathering place for phantoms in his spiritualist painting *The Menin Gate at Midnight* (1927).[56] In Barton's story, three "dim figures"—Unknowns from earlier wars— gather at Arlington to read the inscription on the newly constructed tomb.[57] Each ghost tells his story. The first, one of the three hundred Spartans slain, after legendary resistance, at Thermopylae, reports that his grieving mother received consolation from her neighbors, who celebrated Leonidas's band as the saviors of Greece. And yet, the phantom remarks, the Greece that resisted the Persians eventually fell to Rome. What did his death ultimately achieve? The second, a medieval knight killed at Tours, likewise describes his commemoration: "'It is splendid,' they said to my mother, 'splendid to sacrifice a son on the altar of peace and good-will.'" However, centuries after helping to save the "Christian continent" from Islam, the spirit finds no evidence of a better world.[58] And the final ghost, a British foot soldier "who stood with Wellington at Waterloo," offers the most discouraging account of them all. He died to free the world of "tyranny and wrong" only to see the worst war in history—one "beside which ours seemed a little thing"—erupt a century later. This phantom raises the central question: Do the honors heaped on America's Unknown "mean that the hearts of men have changed"?[59] The story holds out hope that these hearts *have* changed and that the "real" inscription on the tomb may someday read,

WAR
AN ARMED CONTEST BETWEEN NATIONS—
NOW OBSOLETE
UNKNOWN[60]

However, Barton's reference, near the end of his story, to men gathering in Washington, DC, "to speak of peace" on the morning after the ghosts' visitation—that is, the 1921–1922 Naval Disarmament Conference—would have been only mildly encouraging to readers in 1928.[61] Politicians and journalists made much of this conference in 1921. Speaking before the House of Representatives two days before the Unknown Soldier's funeral, Rep. Phil D. Swing of California, for example, expressed his hope that "out of the conference will come the beginning of a new era in which truth and justice and right will prevail in place of greed and avarice and might, and that the war to end war shall not have failed."[62] (Ironically, several days before Swing offered his vision of lasting peace, Rep. Royal Johnson of South Dakota presented Congress with the "slacker lists," state-by-state inventories of men who had dodged the draft in 1917–1918 and who were still at large.[63] Thus, while one member of Congress urged the nation to put war behind it forever, another called for the public disgrace of individuals who had refused to risk their lives in the last conflict.) President Harding referred directly to the disarmament talks in his address at the Memorial Amphitheater, assuring the "gentlemen of the conference" that the republic's "hundred millions . . . want less of armament and none of war."[64] Indeed, this imminent gathering of eminent diplomats, which held out the possibility of lasting international harmony to a nation still reeling from the League of Nations vote, only added to the emotional intensity of the Unknown Soldier's return. And high hopes persisted for weeks afterward. Reporting in the November 23 issue of the *Outlook*, Ernest Hamlin Abbott wrote, "The beginning of this Conference has given good reason to believe that simplicity, honesty, and honor are to be more highly valued and more characteristic of the proceedings here than in any former council of nations."[65] History would make a mockery of these words. Largely forgotten by the time Sanford and Schauffler's *Armistice Day* was published, the disarmament talks of 1921–1922 hardly ushered in a brave new world. The meeting arguably prevented a major war during the 1920s, but growth in Japanese naval power, one result of the various treaties that the conference produced, contributed directly to Japan's military clash with the United States twenty years later.[66] Thus, like the infamous Kellogg-Briand Pact of 1928, a renunciation of armed conflict signed (ironically enough) by all the major combatant nations of the Second World War, the conference ultimately demonstrated the irrelevance of diplomacy in the face of resurgent militarism and nationalistic fervor.

Through the rather clunky device of three spirits (one cannot help but think of Dickens's *A Christmas Carol*), Barton places the Unknown Soldier next to—but, importantly, not *within*—a tradition of idealistic warriors who have been "lied to and cheated and fooled."[67] Thus, his story uses the supernatural to make the same central point offered in *Plumes*—namely, that war, a patently insane social activity, continues to exist by offering each new generation of combatants its own set of false promises. In believing that this cyclical process, active throughout history, could at last be confronted rationally and circumvented, the conviction presented at the conclusion of "Unknown," Barton, along with other postwar peace activists, paradoxically resembled the president who had led the United States into war in 1917. Postwar calls for disarmament evoked the same vision of American-led international progressivism that had underwritten the country's intervention in a European conflict. And both sets of activity, the Great Crusade of wartime and the Great Peace Crusade that followed, drew their energy from deeply rooted conceptions of American exceptionalism and Manifest Destiny. In each case, America would lead other civilized nations to lasting peace because it was America. Thus, in Barton's story, the only Unknown who doesn't speak, who doesn't relate a doleful story of betrayal and disenchantment, is the American inside the tomb. The story leaves the reader with the hope that this soldier, and all of those whom he represents, will, by virtue of his uniquely enlightened countrymen, be spared the disappointments so commonplace in the history of the Old World.

Readers familiar with Dos Passos's "The Body of an American," the best-known example of a vernacular attack upon the Unknown Soldier's official meaning, may be surprised to learn of the progressive, Wilsonian roots of the postwar pacifist movement and of the many Unknown Soldier poems, stories, and sermons that this movement inspired. After all, Dos Passos's prose poem refers to America's wartime leader just once—in its final sentence, a terse jab at the culpable former president who squandered the Unknown Soldier's life (along with more than a hundred thousand others) in the pursuit of an impossible dream: "Woodrow Wilson brought a bouquet of poppies."[68] However, peace advocates in the 1920s and 1930s more typically presented the Unknown Soldier and Woodrow Wilson not in opposition to each other, but in alignment, as mutually reinforcing symbols of international progressivism betrayed. Thus, in *The Red Harvest: A Cry for Peace,* an anthology of antiwar pieces edited by Vincent Godfrey Burns and published in 1930, one encounters a chapter titled "The Unknown Soldier and Poems to Woodrow Wilson" and, within that section, an elegy titled "The Known Soldier." Written by M. A. De Wolfe Howe "For the Day of President Wilson's Burial" (February 7, 1924), the latter employs an obvious play on words to equate the sacrificed soldier entombed at Arlington with the fallen former president. Indeed, the poem's opening lines refer to a resurgent sense of America's international mission that might have been inspired by the commemoration of either figure:

> Now through the stifling air, thick with the murk
> Of self and pettiness—shame's perfect work—
> A sense of greatness spreads from sea to sea;
> For greatness was, when, bound in unity
> Of generous aim, men of our blended race
> Stood looking each into his neighbor's face
> And said, "This towering thought, this cleaving word
> Speaks for America"—and the world heard.[69]

Other poems in *The Red Harvest* explicitly transform the Unknown Soldier into a symbol of the pointlessness of *any* war—the last thing the War Department had intended when enshrining an anonymous "hero."

References to lasting peace had, of course, appeared throughout the Unknown's reburial ceremony in 1921, but these references consistently served the soldier's portrayal as a martyr (as opposed to a victim) whose sacrifice would usher in a new age of international understanding and peaceful coexistence. Although the Harding administration's isolationist stance had already crystallized by November 11, 1921 (the new president had, in fact, renounced Wilsonian internationalism in his inaugural address), the timing of the Unknown Soldier's return with a major disarmament conference fueled hopes that his death would prove meaningful within the context of international progressivism. However, by 1930 that hope had faded, and pacifists who might earlier have accepted the Unknown Soldier as an officially sanctioned peace symbol—or rather as a symbol of peace achieved through war—now expressed a new conviction, namely, that the establishment of this national icon had nothing to do with preventing war and everything to do (as Stallings had suggested in *Plumes*) with perpetuating militarism.

Thus, many of the Unknown Soldier poems included in *The Red Harvest* attack official discourse and commemorative pageantry with a ferocity surpassing anything seen in *Armistice Day*. Some of these works turn patriotic rhetoric against itself, lamenting the way that courage and loyalty, noble virtues in themselves, are squandered in the service of military violence. For example, Margaret Stineback's "The Unknown Soldier" focuses on heroic qualities misspent:

> This is the Unknown Soldier. His dear grave
> Is hallowed. So we, very grateful, say:
> "He signifies the bravest of the brave:
> He is above the common run of clay."
> Yet what is bravery—if it must show
> Its potency in carnage? . . .[70]

The selection by Arthur B. Rhinow, an unorthodox dialogue poem featuring a conversation between "I" and "Myself," raises a different issue: if the Tomb of the Unknown Soldier celebrates the common man, then will the common man be consulted before America enters another war? As "I" insistently pursues this question during the service at the Memorial Amphitheater, "Myself" revels in the "beautiful flowers," "oratory," and "music."[71] In the end, the sensual spectacle, cunningly manipulative and deceptive, smothers the divided speaker's ability to probe the true political significance of the event. Hopelessly duped, "Myself" gets the last word. For Stineback, tribute paid to the Unknown Soldier enshrines the false god of war; for Rhinow, such tribute is part of an elaborate fraud that fools ordinary citizens into ignoring their own interests.

At the same time, the trope of the Unknown Soldier speaking from beyond the grave takes on a new intensity in *The Red Harvest*. Now the Unknown Soldier denounces—and renounces—his posthumous service to the country. Of the several poems that adopt this first-person perspective, the most compelling is Charles A. Wagner's "The Unknown Soldier," which opens with an arresting reminder of battlefield realities:

> One man's shoulder, another man's thigh—
> The unknown soldier, here I lie.[72]

At first Wagner uses the Unknown Soldier's thrown-together corpse to mock the patriotic tribute that this false icon receives—tribute unknowingly delivered not to an anonymous American "hero," but to a collection of body parts that once belonged to several different men. In other words, the poem presents an Unknown who is more unknown—gruesomely so—than the architects of his official meaning can imagine. By the second stanza, however, this notion of the fallen soldier as a composite shifts from the literal to the metaphorical, and Wagner eventually equates the Unknown Soldier with all Americans lost in the Great War. The "mingled thought" of this multitude turns scornfully to its supposed memorial, dismissing the notion of the tomb at Arlington as "a symbol of the end of war" and ridiculing the "wreaths and speeches" offered by Harding and others.[73] Near its close, the poem's scope expands still further as the speaker imagines a Grand Army comprised of the fallen of every war (à la Johnson's "Saint Peter Relates an Incident"). But this is no army of jingoistic "Hundred-Percenters." Wagner's phantom legions consist of men who "falsely fell and bled," and the poem concludes with the Unknown Soldier's pledge to work through the "ranks of the unborn" to achieve a permanent end to war.[74]

The Red Harvest is dedicated to none other than the prominent Protestant theologian Harry Emerson Fosdick—a reminder of the crucial role played by clergymen both in the peace movement of the 1920s and 1930s and in the pacifist redefinition of the Unknown Soldier. A Baptist minister, well known (and widely criticized) for his break with Fundamentalism and advocacy of liberal Protestantism, Fosdick had not always opposed war. He preached in support of American military intervention in 1917, and his brother, Raymond Fosdick, another clergyman, managed the AEF's War Camp Community Activities, a program of moral improvement and healthy recreation (carried out by civilian organizations such as the YMCA) intended to keep American troops away from European fleshpots. Both men shared the same vision of the American war effort as a glorious and *clean* crusade. However, in the 1920s, soured by the Great War's disillusioning aftermath and probable resumption, Fosdick took up the cause of peace with the same passion and indifference to criticism that characterized his call for religious tolerance and a more flexible conception of Protestant doctrine. And guilt over his earlier complicity in the spread of militarism gave his pacifist writings a special edge.

In his sermon for Armistice Day 1933 (subsequently published in *Christian Century* and eventually included in *Riverside Sermons* [1958] under the title "The Unknown Soldier"), Fosdick eschews the tone of confident moral superiority that is characteristic of most pacifist texts and instead emphasizes his personal role in the Unknown Soldier's betrayal: "I have an account to settle between my soul and the Unknown Soldier. I deceived myself first, unwittingly, and then I deceived him, assuring him that good consequence could come out of that."[75] The sermon becomes a penitential act as Fosdick dismantles his past assumptions with self-mortifying thoroughness, revealing the practical and spiritual costs of modern warfare. At one point, in an allusion to the then-fashionable pseudoscience of eugenics, he decries the loss of good (presumably white) stock: "Mad civilization, you cannot sacrifice on bloody altars the best of your breed and expect anything to compensate the loss."[76] Yet it is finally the godlessness of war, rather than its genetic toll, that stirs Fosdick's most impassioned renunciation: "We can have this monstrous thing [war] or we can have Christ, but we cannot have both. . . . I renounce war and never again, directly or indirectly, will I sanction or support another! O Unknown Soldier, in penitent reparation I make you that pledge."[77]

The Unknown Soldier also inspired an impassioned oration from the celebrated Unitarian minister John Haynes Holmes. Like Fosdick, Holmes was no stranger to controversy. His unwavering commitment to racial equality, admiration for Mahatma Gandhi, and espousal of Zionism made him a clerical lightning rod. So, too, did his pacifist convictions, which were as well known and widely discussed in the 1920s and 1930s as Fosdick's. Delivered on Armistice Day 1928 and later published in *The Sensible Man's View of Religion* (1932), Holmes's sermon "The Unknown Soldier Speaks" inspired a film documentary of the same title and became common currency, integral to the growing canon of peace literature, among multiple denominations and faiths. Indeed, the influential Jewish cleric Rabbi Harold I. Saperstein almost certainly drew from Holmes's best-known work in his own Armistice Day sermon "Must There Be War?" (1936), which argued that even the horrors of Nazism should not turn American Jews away from the cause of peace (a position that Saperstein reluctantly abandoned soon after).[78] Like Fosdick and Holmes, Saperstein constructed his oration as a tribute to the *real* Unknown Soldier, someone who knew the horrors of war firsthand and would not want them repeated.

Holmes's influential sermon belongs to what we might call the gothic branch of Unknown Soldier writings, works (such as Barton's short story) featuring phantoms and clairvoyance. However, in "The Unknown Soldier Speaks," the supernatural trappings are largely metaphorical and of secondary importance to the eloquent message that the Unknown Soldier delivers once he miraculously materializes. At the opening of the sermon, Holmes imagines himself in a hotel room in Washington, DC, on the evening following his visit to the tomb. Curious to know what the hilltop at Arlington looks like at night, he suddenly finds himself there (he proves to be dreaming) and confronts a "shadow" that "like a ship emerging ghostlike from a fog" takes the shape of a man.[79] This apparition is, of course, the Unknown Soldier, and Holmes uses the ensuing conversation between clergyman and phantom to knock down all three of the assumptions that determined the Unknown's official meaning. The notion of the anonymous soldier as a white Protestant is the first sacred cow to be dispatched. The apparition that we meet in the sermon has shifting physical features and indeterminate social and regional origins. He is "a white man, yet the shadow of his helmet, under the stars, made his face look like that of a colored man." "[B]orn on a farm in the Middle West," he speaks with the "cultivated accent of Boston," and his name, which the minister fails to catch, sounds Jewish.[80] In this way, Holmes sets his Unknown Soldier, a true everyman, apart from the federal government's ethnocentric version. The sermon then goes on to reveal the arrogance inherent in turning an anonymous corpse into a patriotic symbol. Holmes's Unknown Soldier, a conscript who would have avoided military service if he could have, emphatically does *not* approve of his posthumous glorification. Indeed, he wishes that his country had allowed him to remain in the "little corner" of a French graveyard where he had found peace, and he denounces his manipulation as an agent of nationalist propaganda: "they bring little children to my grave, to teach them how beautiful it is to be a soldier. . . . And they hold festivals on holidays, with prayers and songs and magic rites, to show that here is the altar of the nation's life. Every day they kill me again. Every hour they lay me fresh upon the altar, and spill my blood."[81] And, finally, "The Unknown Soldier Speaks" gives the lie to the entire notion of beneficial warfare or progressivism through arms. Looking at the world ten years after the armistice, the Unknown Soldier sees the "same armies and navies, the same insecurity and fear, the same hatreds and suspicions and preparations for war—and the same superstition in the hearts of men that it's noble to fight and heroic to kill for one's country."[82]

Eloquent and mercilessly thorough in their dismantling of official discourse, Fosdick and Holmes took the vernacular redefinition of the Unknown Soldier to a new level. However, it would fall to two novelists, John Dos Passos and William March, to offer the fullest—and most terrifying—exploration of the Unknown Soldier's capacities as an anti-symbol. Frequently approached in terms of cinema, Dos Passos's "The Body of an American," the modernist prose poem that concludes *1919* (the second volume of his *U.S.A.* trilogy), can also be interpreted as the literary equivalent of a Mahler symphony. Sound, even more than sight, is central to the piece's effect. Discordant voices (some official, some vernacular) and disparate prose styles flow in and out of one another, creating a polyphonic texture not unlike Mahler's musical pastiche with its sudden shifts in tone and strung-together parodies of popular tunes. Indeed, "The Body of an American" is Dos Passos's symphonic requiem to American losses in the Great War, and his melodies, intentionally jumbled and dissonant, come from the decade-old tradition of Unknown Soldier poetry, fiction, and ecclesiastical writing that predates his novel.

In exposing the banality of official commemorative discourse, for example, Dos Passos echoes one of the earliest poetic responses to the Unknown Soldier—Carl Sandburg's well-known poem "And So To-Day" (1922). The very title of Sandburg's work, with its hyphenated "To-Day," evokes the mechanical, overly precise intonation of a public speaker who is simply going through the motions. And in the poem itself, Sandburg makes his contempt for such hollow gestures explicit:

> The honorable orators,
> Always the honorable orators,
> Buttoning the buttons on their prinz alberts,
> Pronouncing the syllables "sac-ri-fice,"
> Juggling those bitter salt-soaked syllables—
> Do they ever gag with hot ashes in their mouths?
> Do their tongues ever shrivel with a pain of fire
> Across those simple syllables "sac-ri-fice"?[83]

Dos Passos goes one better, refusing even to dignify the empty language of "honorable orators" with proper punctuation and spacing. "The Body of an American" opens with official rhetoric reduced to a nearly inaudible and unintelligible drone, white noise:

> Whereasthe Congressoftheunitedstates byaconcurrentresolu-
> tionadoptedon the4thdayofmarch lastauthorizedthe Secretaryofwar
> to cause to be brought to theunitedstatesthe body of an American
> whowasamemberoftheamericanexpeditionaryforceineuropewholost-
> his lifeduringtheworldwarandwhoseidentityhasnot beenestablished
> for burial inthememorialamphitheatreofthe nationalcemeteryat-
> arlingtonvirginia[84]

Jarringly, after this halfhearted recording of purely perfunctory speech, Dos Passos points us directly at what is missing in the official proceedings: recognition of the "Body of an American" *as a body*. We suddenly swing from oratorical nothingness to gruesome tangibility. Building on Wagner's sardonic refrain, "One man's shoulder, another man's thigh," the prose poem unflinchingly presents the charnel-house realities of the Western Front. For the Graves Registration workers who less than reverently handle his remains in the "tarpaper morgue at Châlons-sur Marne," the Unknown Soldier is nothing more than another cadaver that stinks with "gagging chloride" and the "puky dirtstench of the yearold dead." And with a nod to James Weldon Johnson, Dos Passos ties the soldier's physical body, denied throughout his commemoration, to the issues of race and ethnicity. We overhear a Graves Registration officer or NCO express his prejudices to workers who, ironically enough, are probably African American:

> Make sure he ain't a dinge, boys,
> make sure he ain't a guinea or a kike
> how can you tell a guy's a hundredpercent when all you've got's a
> gunnysack full of bones, bronze buttons stamped with the screaming
> eagle and a pair of roll puttees?[85]

The intertextual richness of "The Body of an American" also becomes apparent in Dos Passos's treatment of the Unknown Soldier's voice. In Holmes's sermon the Unknown Soldier begins his conversation with the minister by welcoming him as a "buddy."[86] However, by the end of the piece, the soldier has dropped all colloquialisms. Indeed, his voice becomes indistinguishable from Holmes's own as he, in effect, delivers a sermon within a sermon. In contrast, Dos Passos's Unknown Soldier plays the part scripted for him by the nation—that of an eternal doughboy, forever in uniform, who continues to speak the AEF's unique slang even in the hereafter. But the phantom who speaks in "The Body of an American" is not to be confused with the triumphant "Spirit" depicted by Viquesney. Dos Passos's soldier is lost and scared, and his increasingly plaintive request—"*Say soldier for chrissake can't you tell me how I can get back to my unit?*"—makes a mockery of the patriotic blather spoken in his honor.[87] Moreover, only the reader can hear him. Ironically, to the officials who pay tribute to this "hero," the real soldier is voiceless and invisible, undetected and unwelcome at his own funeral. Here again Dos Passos draws on Sandburg, who likewise juxtaposes the vitality of colloquial expression with the inert speech of ceremonial functionaries. When Sandburg imagines the Unknown Soldier suddenly coming back to life in the midst of his entombment, he offers a string of possible verbal reactions:

> . . . the first shivering language to drip off his mouth
> might have come as, "Thank God," or "Am I
> dreaming?"
> or "What the hell" or "When do we eat?"
> or "Kill 'em, kill 'em, the . . ."
> or "Was that . . . a rat . . . ran over my face?"
> or "For Christ's sake, gimme water, gimme water,"

or "Blub blub, bloo bloo. . . . . . ."
or any bubbles of shell shock gibberish
from the gashes of No Man's Land.[88]

These snippets of soldier's speech, ranging from the sacred ("Thank God") to the profane ("For Christ's sake") to the lunatic ("Blub blub, bloo bloo"), suddenly evoke the physical experience of warfare in the midst of a ceremony that has buried that experience in euphemism and platitude. Eating, drinking, killing, going insane—here, Sandburg suggests, is the visceral reality behind the syllables "sac-ri-fice." By the same token, Dos Passos employs his own form of colloquial subversion, condensing all the terror and sadness of war into a lonely request, a crude but forceful musical signature sung by a ghost, that no one among the "honorable orators" can hear. The gothic tradition of Unknown Soldier writing—earlier given shape by Barton, Holmes, and others—here reaches its chilling climax.

A symphonic summary of themes and motifs introduced by various literary artists over the course of a decade, "The Body of an American" is arguably the one true masterpiece to emerge from the subgenre of American war literature (and peace literature) that utilized the Unknown Soldier as a multidimensional symbol. However, Dos Passos hardly offered the last word on this American icon. One year after the publication of *1919*, the Unknown Soldier appeared in another major novel of the First World War—William March's *Company K*. A Marine Corps veteran who received the Distinguished Service Cross, along with other medals, for his courageous actions during the battle of Blanc Mont in 1918, William March (the pen name for Alabama-born William Edward March Campbell) had more combat experience and more decorations than perhaps any other American First World War writer. However, readers expecting a gung-ho tribute to the Old Breed, along the lines of John W. Thomason's popular memoir *Fix Bayonets!* (1926), were shocked by March's highly modernist and blisteringly antiheroic text.[89] Consisting of 113 vignettes, each narrated by a different member of a fictional Marine Corps company, *Company K* presents war as the ultimate irredeemable social evil. Here, more than in any other American First World War novel, violence and depravity reign supreme. As critic Philip Beidler points out, "[I]n narrative after narrative [in *Company K*], there is mainly just one fundamental fact of modern warfare: the fact of violent, ugly, obscene death. Men die of gas, gunshot, grenade. They die by bayonet. They are literally disintegrated by high explosives. They commit suicide. They murder prisoners. They murder each other."[90]

Along with repellent and pointless violence, the theme of memorialization permeates this grim work, determining even the physical appearance of the text. For example, the first edition features a military insignia on the front cover—crossed rifles over the letter *K*. A veteran glancing at the volume in 1933 might easily have mistaken it for a company history. As we saw in chapter 1, hundreds of these histories—textual memorials, in effect, that record a specific unit's movements and battles—went to press even before the soldiers who wrote them returned from Europe. Many were produced in France, still more in Germany, during the Army of Occupation's long and tedious watch on the Rhine. March further reinforces this connection with supposedly nonfictional company histories by calling his table of contents a "Roster"—rosters were, of course, standard in unit histories—and by actually parodying the style of such texts. In one of the novel's 113 vignettes, Company K's would-be historian, Cpl. Stephen Waller, offers a laconic account of the company's overseas service that might have come from almost any unit-produced history published between 1919 and 1933: "Company K went into action at 10:15 P.M. December 12th, 1917, at Verdun, France, and ceased fighting on the morning of November 11th, 1918, near Bourmont, having crossed the Meuse River the night before under shell fire; participating, during the period set out above, in the following major operations: Aisne, Aisne-Marne, St. Mihiel and Meuse-Argonne."[91] Ironically, nothing could be further from this dispassionate chronicle than the catalog of horrors that March presents in the other vignettes. The rest of *Company K*, filled with killing and suffering, shows what phrases like "went into action" and "major operations" actually mean at an experiential level. And we catch Corporal Waller in a lie. After mechanically listing the number of medals and citations given to members of the company, along with tallies of casualties, Walker praises the unit's commander, Capt. Terence A. Matlock, as an "able and efficient" officer who "retained throughout the respect and admiration of the men who served under him."[92] Not so. As the novel makes clear elsewhere, Company K's enlisted men and officers alike loathed Matlock as a sadistic bully. Indeed, it is none other than Matlock who orders the massacre of a group of German prisoners—the most obscene atrocity in the novel.

In this way March asserts that memorials, textual or otherwise, are not to be trusted. The novel *Company K*, a collage of personal disappointments and shocking displays of inhumanity, tells the real story of the war, the story that a unit history of the same group of men would presumably leave out entirely. Thus, for March, as for Dos Passos, the memory of the Great War preserved through official acts of remembrance is nothing more than a collection of dangerous omissions and outright falsehoods. And, not surprisingly, the Unknown Soldier emerges as the biggest lie of them all. At the novel's climax, March presents this soon-to-be-venerated symbol of duty and honor during his final agonizing moments of life. Caught on the barbed wire of the battle zone, his entrails exposed "like a badly arranged bouquet of blue roses," the Unknown Soldier speaks for the final time in a major work of interwar literature, and his words are terrible.[93] Realizing that "military music" and "high sounding words" have led him to his doom, the marine vows that he will never become part of war's seductive commemoration. By hiding his identity, he thinks he sees "a way out": "I took off my identification tags and threw them into the wire, as far as I could. I tore to pieces the letters and the photographs I carried and scattered the fragments. I threw my helmet away, so that no one could guess my identity from the serial number stamped on the sweatband. Then I lay back exultant!"[94] Thus, in a cruel twist, the soldier bound for the Memorial Amphitheater, for the largest patriotic spectacle of them all, dies believing that he has "beaten the orators and the wreath layers at their own game"—that he has "defeated the inherent stupidity of life."[95]

When the New York firm Harrison Smith and Robert Haas published *Company K* in 1933, March was working as an executive in the Hamburg, Germany, office of the Waterman Steamship Corporation (headquartered in Mobile, Alabama), his employer for two decades. Watching the rallies and celebrations that followed Hitler's election to the Reich chancellorship, the part-time fiction writer realized that his freshly published novel was precisely the kind of war book that the Nazis would burn. Everything in it was an anathema to Third Reich ideology. With the ascent of the National Socialists, who glorified the Great War and attributed Germany's defeat to a stab in the back by traitorous Jews and Communists, the German version of the Cult of the Fallen Soldier swung into high gear. Nazism demonstrated that "orators and wreath layers" could indeed be dangerous. Invoked through remembrance rites, collective memory of the storm of steel on the Western Front, where Hitler and many other veterans had felt a sense of belonging and purpose, helped to fuel Germany's rearmament and territorial ambitions. However, to see evidence of militarism's resilience, in the wake of an unimaginably costly conflict, one did not have to be in Germany. Within just a few years of the publication of *Company K*, official forces in Washington, DC, would recapture the Unknown Soldier from the pacifists and myth-debunking novelists who had momentarily made off with him. And this time the federal government would hold on to this symbol for good.

↤

In the early 1920s, appalled by reports that visitors to the Tomb of the Unknown Soldier had used its stone marker "as a bench or picnic table," the American Legion repeatedly requested that the U.S. Army place the monument under armed guard.[96] Ironically (given the popularity of the military spectacle that this request would ultimately produce), the army resisted the idea, citing budgetary restrictions. However, in 1926 the legion finally prevailed. Elite troops from Fort Myer, Virginia, members of the famed "Old Guard," were assigned to stand guard at the tomb, and eleven years later they began to do so twenty-four hours a day. Since then the Unknown Soldier has never been without uniformed company. As legion spokesman Frederick Palmer approvingly wrote in 1937, the Unknown Soldier "is under a simple block of stone before which a soldier of the Regular Army paces. One will continue to pace in his honor . . . as long as the nation survives."[97] *As long as the nation survives.* Regardless of weather, the cycle never varies: one immaculately dressed and groomed sentinel remains near the tomb, performing a precise series of movements, until relieved by a comrade in a ceremonial transfer of responsibility that occurs at exact half-hour intervals during the summer months and hourly in the wintertime. Even the high winds and torrential rains of Hurricane Isabel in 2003 could not drive the Unknown Soldier's military companions from his side.

Visitors to the tomb today would find it difficult to believe that there was ever a time when they could have touched this monument, let alone irreverently climbed or rested upon it. Over the years, the sentinels' shoes have worn impressive paths in the flagstones, and everything about the site now gives the appearance of a commemorative practice as old as the republic itself. Indeed, the very density of the ritual that has become part of guard duty at the tomb suggests timelessness—identical mechanical motions passed from soldier to soldier at precise intervals, a ceremony seemingly without beginning or end. Nothing in this unbroken chain of tribute and fidelity is accidental. Movement and duration, for example, are bound by the number twenty-one, a reference to the traditional twenty-one-gun salute. In this respect the ritual seems almost obsessive-compulsive. According to the Society of the Honor Guard, Tomb of the Unknown Soldier, each sentinel "stops on the 21st step, then turns and faces the Tomb for 21 seconds. Then he turns to face back down the mat, changes his weapon to the outside shoulder, counts 21 seconds, then steps off for another 21 step walk down the mat. He faces the Tomb at each end of the 21 step walk for 21 seconds. The Sentinel then repeats this over and over until he is relieved at the Guard Change."[98] Given the precision and mental focus that this almost masochistic duty demands, the tomb's sentinels, once grudgingly assigned to the site by a financially strapped War Department, have now become an elite within an elite. Drawn only from the ranks of the already exclusive Old Guard, the Tomb Guards, as they are officially known, follow their own creed (literally), must meet demanding physical requirements, and are expected to memorize word for word a seven-page history of Arlington National Cemetery. Over the years, fewer than five hundred of these sentinels, the very best of the best, have qualified to wear the Tomb Guard badge, one of the rarest and most coveted insignias in the entire American armed forces.

Clearly, more is at work here than protecting a monument from the ravages of insensitive picnickers. The military pageantry that is now part and parcel of the tomb as a site of memory—that holds center stage for the millions of Americans who tour Arlington each year—represents a restoration of official meaning, a successful counterattack aimed at the vernacular forces that once threatened to define this national icon not simply as a symbol of peace but as a symbol of the pointlessness of *all* wars, past, present, or future. Truly, the Unknown Soldier is kept under close guard. In the 1920s and 1930s, poets, clerics, and novelists could imagine him as a restless, anarchistic figure breaking free of his commemorative enclosure to warn his countrymen of war's true face, seek out his old outfit, or reveal his unforgivable blackness before ascending to heaven. Such subversive possibilities are almost impossible to imagine today. One simply cannot contemplate the Unknown Soldier without bringing his dedicated military guardians into the picture. After all, they are hard to miss. One could even say that in the early twenty-first century the relationship between the Tomb of the Unknowns and its elite protectors *is* the memorial. This relationship fuels a symbology, a refinement of the monument's original array of meanings, that movingly depicts the ties between American soldiers of different eras and different conflicts and, at the same time, promotes martial virtues that appear to transcend time and individual identity. Once amorphous, the tomb's official significance is now more tightly focused and less vulnerable to redefinition. And the Unknown Soldier no longer speaks. The living soldiers who guard this once eloquent icon keep him silent, one could say, by defining him exclusively through the terms of ritualistic military brotherhood.

Thus, while collective memory of the First World War is no longer central to America's best-known war monument—too many other conflicts have obscured the tomb's origins, too many additional unknowns added to its sacred space—the stirring ritual that has dominated the site since 1937 stems directly from the post-armistice contest between official and vernacular agents of remembrance. Without knowing it, visitors to Arlington's chief attraction gaze upon a monument to a now-distant *memory* war, a war that ended with the illusion of tradition and timelessness imposed upon what had in fact been an ambiguous response to a thoroughly modern conflict.

In contrast, there is no mistaking E. M. Viquesney's *Spirit of the American Doughboy* as a monument to the citizen soldiers of America's first overseas crusade. The doughboy's "100% perfect" World War I attire, along with his stylistic blend of the Victorian and the modern, tie him firmly to a specific conflict and a specific commemorative aesthetic. And yet for all its artistic and ideological awkwardness, Viquesney's statue has withstood the passage of time surprisingly well. Casualties have, of course, occurred. The copy of *Spirit of the American Doughboy* that once stood in Omaha, Nebraska, became a victim of vandalism in 1943 and ultimately wound up as a contribution to a wartime scrap drive. In Liberty, Kentucky, a utility truck smashed into the town's doughboy in 1982, completely demolishing it. However, as documented on Earl Goldsmith's definitive Web site, communities have, by and large, replaced or restored damaged statues. (For example, a new casting of *Spirit* today stands in Liberty.)[99] And, as with the Tomb of the Unknown Soldier, memories of later conflicts have, ironically enough, become part of this symbol of the War to End All Wars. Although the doughboy himself may look quaint, most Viquesney replicas now honor the servicemen and -women not only of World War I but also of World War II, Korea, Vietnam, and even the Gulf War. On the pedestals of these statues, the rosters of warriors born in some cases decades after the armistice sit side by side with those of "Democracy's Defenders" in 1917 and 1918, thus merging all twentieth-century American conflicts into one seamless narrative of service and sacrifice—the same nationalistic conflation detected by Roshwald in the Tomb of the Unknowns.

In the end, then, both the Well-Known and the Unknown Soldier carried official versions of memory—one established, paradoxically, from the bottom up, the other literally secured by federal troops—through the turbulent memory conflicts of the 1920s and 1930s. Each monument in its own way reflected the ambiguities of World War I while simultaneously contributing to the postwar Cult of the Fallen Soldier. And despite the efforts of peace activists both during the interwar decades and later, as the nation confronted a spectacularly disastrous intervention in Vietnam and the specter of nuclear Armageddon, both monuments remain vital expressions of military remembrance to this very day. However antiquated aesthetically, Viquesney's statue stands ready to honor new rosters of American soldiers. There is still space on the monument's base for plaques commemorating future wars. And although DNA testing probably means we have seen the last anonymous fatality added to the Tomb of the Unknowns, the emotions stirred by the changing of the Tomb Guards remain as powerful—and as critically unexamined—as ever. Given the sentinels' unceasing vigilance, it is unlikely that picnickers will ever return to the site—and just as unlikely that the Unknown Soldier will ever again slip beyond the confines of his official meaning.

3
Painters of Memory
Harvey Dunn, Horace Pippin, and John Steuart Curry

> When a war poses for its picture . . . it will sit with hands folded for
> those who wish it to, or it will strut with clanking sword, or pose as
> a mother of mercy, or the invading barbarian, or the valiant hero, or
> the cringing coward, or, better yet, a composite of all of these envel-
> oped in a fury of sound and sight and horror.
>
> —J. André Smith, *In France with the American*
> *Expeditionary Forces* (1919)

Two large-scale projects, each unprecedented in the history of the American military, reflected the AEF's preoccupation with memory. The first
was an effort to document, through photographs, nearly every conceiv-
able facet of the U.S. Army's activities in France. From 1917 to 1919 the
Photographic Division of the U.S. Army Signal Corps assembled a collection of no fewer than forty thousand images and, incredibly, recorded
the identity of each and every American face captured on film. Doughboys who wound up having their pictures taken could later look themselves up in the massive *Catalogue of Official A.E.F. Photographs* published
by the U.S. government in 1919.[1] Unlike the portraits of static subjects
taken fifty years earlier on the battlefields of the Civil War, by photographers such as Matthew Brady, the Signal Corps' visual record included
snapshots of American soldiers in the heat of battle. Portable cameras
and photographers willing to risk life and limb brought a new level of
realism and intimacy to war photography. The second project involved
painting and drawing. Eight American artists received commissions to
accompany the AEF during its combat operations and to translate what
they saw onto canvases and sketch pads. Not surprisingly, the works created by these artists in uniform (totaling more than five hundred pieces)
have, along with the Signal Corps' photographs, dominated visual repre-
sentations of the AEF ever since. Indeed, they are a ubiquitous presence

in books, museum displays, documentaries, Web sites, and course materials devoted to the United States and the First World War.

However, American First World War visual art did not end with the armistice. War-related paintings, drawings, and etchings (to say nothing of the commemorative statues addressed earlier in this study) appeared throughout the 1920s and 1930s, and many of these pieces present direct challenges—counter memories, if you will—to the seemingly "documentary" works created by the AEF's official artists. Thus, this chapter will explore the sharply contrasting visions of World War I expressed in the post-1918 work of three American painters—Harvey Dunn, Horace Pippin, and John Steuart Curry.

The best known and perhaps most talented of the eight artists assigned to the AEF, Harvey Dunn belongs to this discussion because his wartime paintings, surprisingly few in number, marked only the beginning of his artistic engagement with the First World War. From 1928 until 1938 Dunn regularly painted cover illustrations for the *American Legion Monthly,* thus revisiting his war experience from the distance of a decade or more. Heroic and mournful by turns, his ambivalent compositions tie in well with the legion's ideology, exaggerating the strength and resilience of the American soldier while at the same time acknowledging the horrors of war (albeit in a way that does nothing to diminish patriotic pride). In work that contrasts sharply with Dunn's, Horace Pippin, a veteran of the Harlem Hellfighters, offered a modernist vision of the war. Mistakenly characterized as "primitive" or "naïve" by the artist's white patrons, Pippins's war paintings—again, produced after a decade of reflection and recovery—feature flattened perspectives and crude, almost abstract figures. At first sight, his work appears, disconcertingly, to offer little in the way of judgments or conclusions about the war. Closer inspection, however, reveals Pippin's engagement with collective memory on both sides of the color line. The final artist, Midwestern regionalist John Steuart Curry, entered the Student Army Training Corps too late in 1918 to see action with the U.S. Army. However, tragedy kept the war fresh in Curry's memory for the rest of his life and inspired one of his most fascinating works—the somber depiction of a friend's stateside burial titled *The Return of Private Davis from the Argonne* (1928–1940). The final section of this chapter will focus entirely on this single painting, an especially revealing case study in the dynamics of personal and collective memory.

"He didn't have to . . . but he went over the top":
Harvey Dunn, the *American Legion Monthly,* and Masculine Memory

In its September 1936 issue, the *American Legion Monthly* paid tribute, in the form of a brief article, to the most distinguished artist ever affiliated with the magazine—Harvey Dunn. Titled "He didn't have to . . . but he went over the top," the article praised the painter, who by this point had provided cover illustrations for the *Monthly* for nearly a decade, by tying him to critical components of legion ideology. Born in the Dakota Territory, Dunn came from good stock, the son of "pioneer parents" who left him with a true "pioneer spirit."[2] A self-made man (and thus quintessentially American), he paid his own way through a course of study at the Chicago Art Institute, where he "suffered the struggles and privations of an art student without means."[3] And in line with the American Legion's unceasing emphasis on education (of the right sort, of course), Dunn excelled in teaching, passing his gift on to other illustrators, including many "whose work has won recognition."[4] However, the article reserved its highest praise for Dunn's physical courage, by implication his most legionnaire-like trait. As an official artist with the AEF, Dunn performed his duties "with characteristic verve" and even "went over the top without orders to see with his own eyes what actual combat looked like."[5] Here, the *American Legion Monthly* assured its readers, was no beret-wearing pansy. Dunn was a *man's* artist, no less rugged than his muscular subjects, and he possessed an inherent affinity for the legion's conservative ideals and its patriotic brand of collective war memory. How Dunn's depiction of the war changed as he became so strongly embraced by the American Legion, and thus came to share the organization's collective memory of the past, is the focus of this section, a study in the intersection between art and ideology.

Dunn's prominent connection with the legion was, in many respects, inevitable. After all, the artist's physical appearance, personality, and reputation for daring had earlier captivated the doughboys of the AEF. While most soldiers in 1918 would have been hard-pressed to name even one of the seven other official artists, everyone seemed to know Dunn. A gigantic figure, more than six feet tall, with an unforgettable visage, described by one observer as "a cross between an Indian chief and a Viking," the artist couldn't help but stand out.[6] Even his art supplies were larger than life. Famously, Dunn carried an unusual sketch pad into battle—

a large rectangular box, outfitted with scrolls so that a continuous ream of paper could be advanced. Soldiers who saw Dunn with this cumbersome device noted that the contraption would have been impossibly unwieldy for a man of ordinary size. And everywhere the big man went, he talked, lecturing foot soldiers and fellow artists alike on his philosophy of art, the conduct of the war, and the benefits of Christian Science (Harry Townsend, one of the AEF's eight commissioned artists, found the loquacious painter's discourses on the latter topic particularly irritating[7]). At the front, Dunn's willingness to share the hardships and hazards endured by the ordinary grunt became legendary, so much so that a cartoonist famously depicted him painting in the middle of no-man's-land, indifferent both to German artillery and to orders from General Pershing that he move his "easel back a foot or two" in order to avoid an American barrage.[8] Press coverage such as this did not always sit well with the other official artists, who felt (not entirely without reason) that Dunn's frontline antics had as much to do with self-promotion as they did with gathering material for combat art.

However, Dunn's physical presence, charisma, and undeniable (if sometimes opportunistic) bravery did not entirely explain his appeal. Soldiers simply liked his pictures. Writing of Dunn in the late 1960s, military historian Edgar M. Howell attributed the artist's popularity to his "ideal of the 'universal man at war' and his forceful representation of this point of view."[9] In Dunn's work, doughboys invariably saw something of themselves; however, this response perhaps had more to do with the artist's dramatic, emotive style than with his rendering of a universal warrior. The faces on his soldiers, for example, are never expressionless; depending on the situation, they convey shock, grim resolve, jubilation, exhaustion, terror, or alarm. Dunn's rendering of posture is always emotive as well. For example, in his famous wartime watercolor *The Machine Gunner* (later used on the cover of Laurence Stallings's popular history of the AEF, *The Doughboys* [1963]), Dunn captures the body language of a soldier—neck straight, arms akimbo—who is comfortable in his uniform and apparently perfectly at home in the strange world of war (see fig. 11). Another piece of official art, *The Engineer*, portrays a hapless doughboy buried in gear (see fig. 12). Here again Dunn's attention to body language makes the piece come alive. Trudging forward in a heavy overcoat, the man wears a grotesquely swollen backpack, complete with an extra pair of boots dangling from one of its straps, and carries his rifle (whose weight the viewer can almost *feel*) in his left hand. But this human

11. *The Machine Gunner* (1918) by Harvey Dunn.

packhorse isn't giving up. The forward tilt in his posture (subtly different from the look of a man who is about to collapse under the weight of
his equipment), combined with the perfectly level angle of his head and
helmet, suggests a weary determination. The engineer will make it to the
end of the march.

As works such as these vividly attest, Dunn placed feeling above all
other artistic considerations—this was, in fact, the central tenet of his
teaching—and he had little patience with realism as an end unto itself.
In a report to the War Department the painter explained that although
they were not always factual (that is, based on direct observation), his
paintings still offered a truthful depiction of "the struggle and the men
involved."[10] Art, in other words, captured a higher truth than any mere

12. *The Engineer* (1918) by
Harvey Dunn.

record of actualities, precisely *because* the former is creative and expressive. Indeed, Dunn's determination to get as close to the actual fighting as possible, presumably so that he would get each and every detail right, conveniently obscured the fact that many of his wartime paintings are highly imaginative and employ perspectives never made available to the artist even in the heat of battle. For instance, Dunn's *In the Front Line at Early Morning* (a painting to which we will return in a moment) portrays an American sentry exactly as he would have appeared to a German raiding party in no-man's-land (see fig. 13). Although there is nothing in the picture to suggest that an attack is imminent, this unnerving perspective adds to the atmosphere of tension, amplifying the sentry's obvious exhaustion and vulnerability.

Yet the most striking example of Dunn's creative license—or, rather, his emphasis on feeling independent of direct observation—appears in *The Hand Grenade,* his rendering of a French cellar being violently cleared of its German occupants. Astonishingly, Dunn presents this terrible scene from the enemy's point of view. The viewer is *inside* the underground

13. *In the Front Line at Early Morning* (1918) by Harvey Dunn.

chamber as an American grenade lands near the entrance and the Germans scatter in terror. The details tell the full story. One notes, for example, that two of the soldiers are wearing their *feldmutzes,* or "pillbox" caps, instead of their helmets, an indication that this attack is completely unexpected. In addition, the men's rifles are stacked against the wall. No one, in other words, has given the helpless Germans a chance to surrender. Firsthand accounts of World War I combat attest to the authenticity of this painting, however impossible its point of view. Dunn had seen enough during his frontline excursions to know that American troops sometimes shot prisoners, bombed dugouts and cellars without warning (often out of fear, just as often out of indifference), and plundered the dead. In short, he knew—at least at this point in his career—that "Pershing's Crusaders" were no more humane or inhumane than their European counterparts. His works from 1918 never gloss over violence or brutality.

In this respect, Dunn's small (just thirty completed pictures) but accomplished output as an official artist hardly served the interests of the

War Department, which hoped not only for accurate depictions of the AEF in action but also for paintings that would inspire Liberty Loan contributions at home. A handful of works, it is true, make concessions to motivational stereotypes. In *The Boche Looter,* for example, Dunn depicts a simian-looking German who, like an evil Santa Claus, drags a huge sack stuffed not with presents but with plunder, an image straight from "Rape of Belgium" iconography. Here again the artist has painted what he could not have seen firsthand, and the result, in this instance, is pure propaganda. For the most part, however, Dunn depicts sympathetic human beings, regardless of nationality. Since wartime censorship prevented him from portraying American fatalities (except in pictures that cast the fallen as heroic), the abundant corpses in his paintings typically wear field gray. However, there is nothing triumphal in his portrayal of the enemy dead. Obviously gunned down at close range (probably while running for their lives), the crumpled pile of German machine gunners depicted in *Study, September 26,* for instance, underscores the brutality of combat. Tellingly, not one of the American soldiers who have just killed these men looks in their direction; the doughboys in the picture are intent on the next stronghold and anxious not to become casualties themselves. Likewise, in the sardonically titled *Harvest Moon,* Dunn takes a potentially propagandistic image—a field strewn with enemy cadavers—and, once again, avoids any note of triumph. Eerily lit by the full moon, the dead are not slain monsters, but pitiable figures. One corpse, frozen in rigor mortis, holds his left arm raised. Another almost looks as if he is kneeling in prayer. There is little to distinguish these dead soldiers from American fatalities—just the shape of their backpacks and helmets.

However, while Dunn was drawn to scenes of horror, some of his official works capture the adrenaline-charged sensations of battle. His series conveys both the terrible waste of war *and* its seductive moments of excitement. Perhaps the most famous of Dunn's wartime paintings, *Street Fighting,* depicts a pair of American soldiers set against a shell-blasted house. While one doughboy lies facedown in the rubble, either dead or mortally wounded, his comrade blazes away with his rifle at an enemy located somewhere outside the frame. The face of the infantryman left standing is hidden (a rare departure for Dunn), but his posture—legs spread, helmet tucked in close to the rifle sight—tells us all we need to know. The soldier has momentarily become a killing machine, utterly indifferent to danger, his body seemingly fused with his weapon. Doughboys who admired this picture perhaps saw that Dunn had captured one of the most powerful (and irrational) of all soldierly emotions—the desire for vengeance against an enemy that has killed one's buddy. The War Department, on the other hand, found in *Street Fighting* an image of American toughness and courage under fire. For once, Dunn had come up with the kind of picture that the AEF's official artists were supposed to provide. In 1920 this already iconic painting received further publicity when Dunn's pair of doughboys—one fallen, one defiant—appeared in relief on the front cover of *U.S. Official Pictures of the World War,* a nearly eight-hundred-page collection of photographs (drawn from the tens of thousands taken by the U.S. Signal Corps) published by the federal government.[11] Advertising for this popular volume, which remained in print throughout the 1920s, frequently appeared in the *American Legion Weekly* and *Monthly,* and this advertising seldom failed to feature the book's embossed cover, one indication, among many, of Dunn's high profile and marketability among veterans.

Painted during the summer of 1918 and based on the artist's personal experience of house-to-house combat at Château-Thierry and elsewhere, *Street Fighting,* which accommodates (at least for some viewers) a heroic interpretation, differs strongly from the works that Dunn completed in the fall of that year. His paintings inspired by the Meuse-Argonne offensive are darker, at times almost nihilistic. By this point Dunn's view of the Great War had changed, and his theatrical exterior concealed a growing sense of revulsion and weariness. When first commissioned, Dunn, "a super patriot," made a near boast of the ugliness he expected to encounter.[12] He would, he told a friend, paint war in the raw—"the shock and loss and bitterness and blood of it."[13] However, months of exposure to "shock and loss" carried a greater psychic and emotional strain than the rugged painter anticipated, and it is perhaps important to remember in this regard that although technically a noncombatant, Dunn saw more frontline action than many of the doughboys he depicted in his paintings—more, in fact, than the vast majority of men in the AEF. In his history of the AEF's eight official artists, Peter Krass asserts that Dunn's greatest theme was the "vulnerability" of soldiers, a theme born of the artist's intuitive understanding that in war "each man had his own limits."[14] Whether Dunn, a man of granitelike strength to outside observers, had come to feel his own vulnerability after so many days at the front is unknown; however, the emotional intensity of his final—and best—wartime paintings suggests that he had. And so does the curious absence of emotion in his wartime letters. After his passage through the killing fields of the Meuse-Argonne battle, the artist seemed, as Krass observes, to force himself "not to reflect on the horrors that he had witnessed."[15] While "on the surface, Dunn would still have his flashes of exuberance, . . . inwardly, he was evolving into a subdued and restless man."[16]

Among the works that this increasingly introspective artist created in response to the Meuse-Argonne fighting is his masterpiece, *Prisoners and Wounded*, a picture that explodes from its frame with brutal honesty and power (see fig. 14). Produced in October 1918 as the American offensive degenerated into a contest of attrition, the painting depicts a group of less-than-formidable-looking German prisoners (one spectacled, one obviously middle-aged) as they wearily carry an American casualty on a stretcher. Staggering alongside these pathetic figures in field gray are American "walking cases" slowly making their way to the rear, their faces twisted in agony. The battle that the soldiers of both armies have just left is somewhere behind them, invisible and now irrelevant. One of the doughboys in the foreground, his shoulder and chest wrapped in bloody linen, looks straight at the viewer with a disconcerting thousand-yard stare. The pain and exhaustion recorded on the canvas are palpable. Nothing, one suspects, could have been further from the kind of art that the War Department hoped to receive from Dunn—except perhaps *No Man's Land*, a depiction of apocalyptic ruin completed around the same time as *Prisoners and Wounded*. Here Dunn presents a smoke-shrouded moonscape that is utterly devoid of life. At first glance there is nothing to hold the eye. Then, slowly, details emerge—a dead mule, an American helmet and rifle (marking a soldier's grave), a crashed aircraft (dimly seen in the distance), and a single human skull, which grins at the viewer.

By the time of the armistice, Dunn had completed a body of work that communicates, perhaps more fully than any other series in twentieth-century combat art, the complex emotional palette of war. The artist's highly varied canvases record the thrill of battle, as well as the ugly brutality of killing; soldierly strength, as well as vulnerability; and dramatic military spectacle, as well as mournful ruin. Dunn had indeed managed to convey "the shock and loss and bitterness and blood" in war. But he had also captured something else—the perverse allure and satisfaction that men find in destruction. More than anything, Dunn wished at war's end to continue with his work, to create additional paintings based on the hundreds of rough drawings contained in his sketchbook scrolls. Thus, in December 1918 he requested that the U.S. Army continue to subsidize his art until he could finish his complete oeuvre of war pictures. As his-

14. *Prisoners and Wounded* (1918) by Harvey Dunn.

torian Alfred Emile Cornebise writes, Dunn "envisioned many months, even years, of painting, maybe at the War College, and of having the leisure to turn his sketches, his visions and impressions of the war, into finished works of art."[17] Unfortunately, with Germany's defeat the War Department almost immediately lost all interest in the official artists program, and Dunn's request went nowhere. It was the greatest disappointment of his career. Depressed and somewhat embittered, he received his discharge from the U.S. Army on April 26, 1919. As a sole concession to the artist's scheme, the AEF sent him home with a crate full of military props—helmets, gas masks, a machine gun—everything, in short, that Dunn would need to complete war paintings that no one in Washington, DC, apparently wanted.

With demand for military illustrations suddenly all but nonexistent, Dunn had little choice, once back in the United States, but to set aside his rough sketches of the AEF in action. These would have to wait until another day. But what he had seen during his months on the Western Front was never far from his thoughts. Indeed, the more important of the nonmilitary paintings that he produced in the early 1920s indirectly reflected the immense and still-unfolding impact that his frontline experiences had upon him. Although the famous illustrator continued, in his teaching, to preach the value of magazine work, dismissing any distinction between "serious" and "commercial" art, he focused more and more of his energy on paintings intended to stand alone. And, increasingly, his more personal and ambitious canvases depicted the Dakota Territory of his childhood, a sun-drenched world of wildflowers, windswept grasses, distant horizons, and vast skies. A world far from the shattered forests and cratered fields of the Meuse-Argonne. Stunningly beautiful, these paintings betray a yearning for a simpler time located decades before the First World War and its industrialized slaughter. Dunn's High Plains landscapes burn with the same romantic intensity and share the same creative urgencies as the early chapters of Willa Cather's *My Ántonia* (1918), prairie paintings in words composed during the war that Cather would subsequently call the "the great catastrophe."[18]

Photographs taken of Dunn as he worked on these Dakota paintings—and other nonmilitary pictures—in his Tenafly, New Jersey, studio contain a suggestive detail: On the fireplace mantel, located to the right of the artist's easel, sits a row of imperial German helmets. Beneath them, a World War I shovel, gas mask, and other trench paraphernalia hang from nails. Part of the trophy collection given to Dunn by the AEF in 1919, these mementoes signify the painter's continued fascination with the war (and, perhaps, his lingering ambition to dominate its artistic representation), even as he sought refuge from battlefield horrors through a nostalgic return to childhood scenes. As with all the artists considered in this chapter, ambivalence and contradiction would define Dunn's relationship with war—and with memory.

In 1928, nearly a decade after his frustrating exit from the AEF's official artists program, Dunn finally found an outlet for his long-interrupted series of war studies. Or, rather, the outlet found him. Instructed by the American Legion's national commander to create "more virile covers" for the *American Legion Monthly*, assistant art editor William MacLean sought Dunn out and after a couple of visits to the artist's studio convinced him to relinquish a battle scene, titled *Doughboys Going Over the Top*, that he had painted earlier for a calendar company.[19] This dramatic work appeared on the *Monthly*'s January 1928 cover. Dunn was, of course, already familiar to most legionnaires. Some had seen the legendarily courageous painter in action on the Western Front; others had encountered Dunn's wartime artwork in earlier issues of the legion's magazine. In 1919 the periodical's editors placed Dunn ahead of his seven colleagues in "Painted at the Front," a series of articles profiling the work of the AEF's official artists.[20] For "virile" paintings that would enliven the *Monthly*'s appearance and attract new readers, Dunn was the logical first choice. However, since the artist's work regularly commanded prices far beyond what the magazine's meager budget could support, the kind of long-term relationship that MacLean had in mind was by no means certain. Dunn was busy with other projects, and although friendly, he seemed less than inclined to sell his paintings at a discount.

Fortunately for the *Monthly*, Dunn and MacLean went on to become good friends, and the painter, an active member of his local American Legion post in Tenafly, eventually warmed to the idea of revisiting his war experience on a regular basis before a receptive audience of fellow veterans. Once won over, Dunn showed characteristic industriousness, supplying MacLean with one war scene after another until he became to the *American Legion Monthly* what Norman Rockwell was to the *Saturday Evening Post*. Indeed, Dunn's dramatic cover art boosted the legion's magazine, previously little known to non-legionnaires, to a new level of public prominence by giving it an instantly recognizable visual style. For the artist, the arrangement was somewhat less than ideal. Because of the *Monthly's* financial constraints, Dunn worked practically for free, and magazine covers, with their obvious limitations in terms of composition, were a far cry from the kind of grandiose pictorial record that earlier he had hoped to complete while drawing a federal salary. Nevertheless, his output was impressive. Between 1928 and 1938, while juggling his work for the *Monthly* with other, more lucrative commissions, the artist sent MacLean nearly twenty war pictures, almost two-thirds as many as he had completed during his service with the AEF.

The differences between these cover paintings and Dunn's earlier war scenes are pronounced—and revealing. Not surprisingly, the sense of immediacy that makes his wartime work so compelling is now almost entirely absent. For many of his finest official pieces, such as *The Machine Gunner* and *Prisoners and Wounded*, Dunn quickly sketched his subjects with charcoal, in bold, scraggly lines, which he then overlaid with watercolors. The resulting images look rough and unstudied—especially in comparison with the more polished productions of the AEF's other official artists—and for precisely this reason give the impression of absolute verisimilitude. In contrast, Dunn's post-1928 paintings seem mannered, more like commercial illustrations (which, of course, they were) composed with a particular effect in mind as opposed to the spontaneous expression of feeling. However, the most striking differences appear in the soldiers whom Dunn presents. While some of the doughboys depicted on the *Monthly* covers convey vulnerability, the majority do not. The troops in Dunn's second round of war pictures are more muscular than those he painted in 1918, and their rugged, somewhat stylized faces only rarely betray fear.

This shift in representation becomes especially noticeable if we set two paintings of the same subject—one from 1918, the other from 1937—side by side. Discussed above, Dunn's wartime painting *In the Front Line at Early Morning* depicts an American sentry, noticeably thin and narrow shouldered (as most men in the AEF actually were), peering into no-man's-land with eyes that simultaneously convey watchfulness and sleep deprivation. And as we have already seen, the artist portrays this lonely figure from a disconcerting angle of vision—that of the enemy. For his April 1937 cover of the *Monthly*, Dunn reworked this image, creating a completely different effect (see fig. 15). Like its precursor, this new painting, titled *Standing To,* focuses on a solitary sentry, and it reproduces many of the details included in the original picture. Both doughboys have their 1903-pattern Springfield rifles at the ready, as well as an assortment of grenades, including captured German "potato mashers." But the 1937 painting offers a close-up view, thus eschewing the eerie perspective of the 1918 version, and the soldier it depicts is a massive man (built rather like Dunn himself) with almost impossibly broad shoulders and a rugged visage that expresses not weariness, but unwavering resolve.

The majority of Dunn's covers feature similarly formidable Americans. And, more often than not, we see these muscular figures in the thick of battle. Several scenes, for example, focus on urban warfare and echo the élan of *Street Fighting.* The cover illustrations for the March 1928 and September 1928 issues show hardened troops, with visages worthy of later Hollywood noir films, fighting from house to house, intent on "mopping up." Other covers present doughboys resolutely holding their foxholes against an attack (July 1928 and November 1930), using their strength to dislodge an artillery piece stuck in the mud (September 1936), and laying down a rapid-fire barrage (September 1929). Not without reason, one twenty-first-century viewer of these illustrations has described them as "painted with testosterone."[21] Stylized almost to the point of anticipating DC Comics' Sergeant Rock—or, for that matter, the impossibly lethal protagonists of modern military video games—Dunn's soldiers exude masculine toughness, and thus are a far cry from the haunting, all-too-human subjects depicted in *Prisoners and Wounded.* Indeed, even when the painter returned to the subject matter of his 1918 masterpiece, the

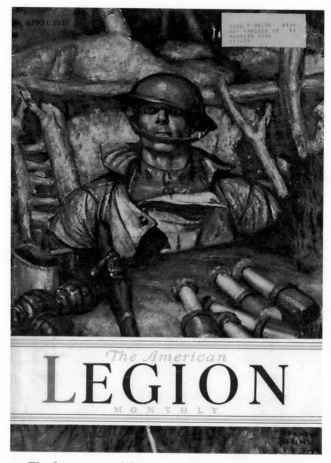

15. The front cover of the *American Legion Monthly* (April 1937). Painting by Harvey Dunn. Courtesy of the American Legion National Headquarters.

results are curiously flat. His March 1929 cover, for instance, shows a trio of wounded doughboys—two of them obviously too exhausted to move, the third leaning on a walking stick. With his usual attention to facial expressions, Dunn registers the soldiers' psychic withdrawal from the battle that rages in the background, but perhaps because of its carefully executed details this illustration seems distanced from its subjects, in sharp contrast with the artist's less formal—indeed, seemingly frenzied—treatment of the same theme a decade earlier.

What had happened to Dunn's war art? For one thing, the artist's milieu had dramatically changed. Paradoxically, in 1918, as an initiate surrounded by the unfamiliar sensations of war, Dunn had been largely free from the pressure to explain, interpret, or justify. He could paint the war as it came to him—as a jumble of discordant elements. Although the directors of the AEF's official artists program served, at times, an explicitly propagandistic agenda and were not above criticizing their artists when they failed to deliver the quantity or perceived "quality" of work that the project demanded, the War Department mostly left Dunn and his companions alone. As Peter Krass observes, each artist, in his own way, sorted out the "serious moral issues" presented by his situation as a "recorder of history" who was also loyal to the flag; each determined for himself whether his first duty was to "humanity or to the Allied cause," to "country or to truth."[22] As we have seen, despite some anomalous forays into propaganda imagery, Dunn painted the truth of war as he saw it— or, rather, a set of conflicting truths. Taken as a whole, his thirty wartime paintings and completed sketches do not offer a thematically unified body of work—far from it. More than anything, Dunn conveyed the contradictions of military experience, registering both the boredom of service life (vividly captured in the almost comatose doughboy who stares at the viewer in *Off Duty*) and its moments of sudden terror or bloodlust. On Dunn's eclectic wartime canvases, grotesquery and death sit cheek and jowl with comradeship, joy, *and* tedium. Ugliness communes with beauty, drama with banality.

Perhaps inevitably, Dunn's sense of war's multidimensionality and amorphousness—what Australian writer Frederic Manning called its "myriad faces"—settled over time into a more coherent (albeit simplified and less artistically satisfying) pattern of meaning.[23] And it is interesting to note that the start of the painter's second series of military pictures coincided with a proliferation of cultural activities related to memory. Just weeks before MacLean met Dunn for the first time, sixteen thousand legionnaires returned home from the Second AEF convention in Paris, one of the most dramatic remembrance events of the 1920s. Eisenhower, we should recall, was immersed in his commemorative work for the ABMC as Dunn's illustrations began to appear regularly on the *Monthly*'s covers. And Dunn's return to war art occurred alongside the international surge of war books, including Remarque's *All Quiet on the Western Front* (1929), and films that marked the end of the first post-armistice decade. Gold Star Mothers, many of whom maintained close ties with the legion (and received its magazine), might have seen Dunn's new war paintings before embarking for the former Western Front on their pilgrimages. In short, that Dunn's second engagement with war subjects, which began ten years after his AEF service, produced a more thematically uniform body of work should not surprise us. In the late 1920s the artist became part of an effort to understand the Great War—through various forms of remembrance—that was more culturally pervasive than ever before.

Changes in Dunn's role and responsibilities as an artist perhaps also influenced his post-1928 war paintings. But this factor is less important than one might assume. No longer a supposedly objective "recorder of history," the painter commissioned by MacLean in 1928 was unapologetically commercial in his outlook. In fact, Dunn's no-nonsense attitude toward money formed part of his iconoclastic persona. When asked what a painting was for, Dunn would always reply, "For sale!"[24] However, it seems doubtful that the painter consciously crafted his cover illustrations to meet specifications—ideological or otherwise—explicitly set forth by the American Legion. Dunn did not work that way. Indeed, as his biographer Robert F. Karolevitz observes, Dunn lost much of his enthusiasm for magazine illustration in the 1930s because he disliked dealing with the new breed of art editors, known as "art directors," who micromanaged the content and design of each and every image.[25] During his heyday in the 1910s and 1920s, Dunn navigated the marketplace better than most twentieth-century artists, but he did not prostitute himself by accepting "direction" from editors—in fact, he later ended his long-standing relationship with the *Saturday Evening Post* when he refused to correct a supposed error in one of his illustrations—or by becoming the visual spokesman for organizations or causes in which he did not believe.

Instead of simply giving the American Legion what it wanted, as any commercial illustrator could have done, Dunn painted the war as he now remembered it. Thus, the tight fit between the themes in his cover illustrations and legion ideology says less about his commercial savvy—after all, his work for MacLean was practically charity—than it does about his investment, by 1928, in the version of collective memory for which the legion stood. In other words, after ten years of reflection and interpretation Dunn had moved away from his sense of "the myriad faces of war" and had come to embrace a less multidimensional version of war experience, a version shared and reinforced by more than a million of his fellow veterans. In some respects, little changed in his military paintings. To the casual observer, Dunn's post-1928 war pictures are just as gritty—just as filled with destruction and drama—as his works completed in 1918. There are the same ruinous French villages, the same barbed wire and mud. But, as we have seen, Dunn no longer stressed the vulnerability of the American troops who fought their way across this modern battlefield. Instead, he now highlighted the opposite—the determination and power of the AEF's members. In his covers for the *Monthly*, works that in effect form a multi-canvas memorial, we see Dunn's own version of *Spirit of the American Doughboy*.

Through images of brawny combatants who no longer appeared to have a breaking point, Dunn reinforced a key tenet of American Legion ideology—namely, the notion that although America's entry into the First World War had failed to make the world safe for democracy, it had nevertheless given American males the opportunity to become *real men*. As we saw in chapter 1 of this study, the *American Legion Monthly* stressed this theme wherever possible. Profiles of veterans turned prize fighters, combat accounts by Congressional Medal of Honor winners, and hard-edged war fiction by Leonard Nason and others all underscored the virtues of the World War I battlefield as a manly proving ground and as a place where, regardless of international causes and outcomes, true *Americanization* (the merger of individual ethnic groups into a fighting whole) had gloriously occurred. Importantly, bloodshed and suffering remained part of this neo-masculine version of memory—the legion never sanitized war experience, as the GAR had—but in ways that reinforced, rather than undermined, pride in service and calls for military preparedness. If anything, acknowledging the horrors of war (as generously depicted in Dunn's often violent covers) only strengthened the legion's image of former soldiers as patriotic martyrs and, at the same time, served the organization's ongoing campaign for a national policy of peace through military deterrence.

Thus, Dunn's paintings of tough, weathered, and anything-but-idealistic doughboys facing—and withstanding—all that the Western Front could throw at them captured the American Legion's war as well as any illustrations could have. Although less familiar today than his 1918-vintage works, which continue to dominate pictorial histories of America and the First World War, Dunn's second series of war pictures represents one of the most ambitious remembrance projects of the 1920s and 1930s—and (at least from the standpoint of the legion) one of the most successful artistic efforts to recover the "real war."

However, Dunn's talent sometimes wandered in alternative directions, momentarily disrupting his otherwise unified and consistent version of memory. Two works in particular showed that the artist's earlier, more unsettling vision of war could resurface without warning. For his November 1929 cover, titled *Armistice,* Dunn depicted a ruinous no-man's-land lit up by sun rays breaking through a gray sky. In the foreground, a dead body, unmistakably American, lies next to an improvised marker, a rifle stuck in the ground and topped with the soldier's "tin derby." A German helmet, its owner unseen but presumably likewise dead, rests nearby. At first glance the image looks hopeful, as gloom gives way to sunlight. But the vista disclosed by this burst of illumination is anything but encouraging: in the background, the denuded battlefield seems to stretch on forever. Dunn's cover for the August 1938 issue, among the last that he completed for the *Monthly,* takes a rare turn into nonliteral representation (see fig. 16). In this haunting, untitled work, set in a veteran's hospital, we see a haggard former soldier—presumably a "psychiatric case"—sitting up in bed while terrifying images of World War I combat swirl above his head. On the contents page, the *Monthly's* editors put a predictably pro-legion spin on this disturbing image: "Legionnaire Harvey Dunn's cover design should recall to all of us the fact that the war after the war is always the harder war for some of us. The Legion won't fail them."[26] Dunn may well have shared this sentiment, but his moving depiction of post-traumatic stress, perhaps the most memorable of his post-1928 war pictures, nevertheless has more in common with his wartime paintings than with his other *Monthly* covers. Here, in one of his last war pictures (produced on the eve of the Second World War), Dunn eschewed masculine bravado and once again reminded his viewers that no soldier is without a breaking point—the central theme in his finest paintings created nearly twenty years earlier.

Defamiliarizing War: Horace Pippin, the Harlem Hellfighters, and African American Memory

In the early 1930s, while Harvey Dunn worked on the magazine covers that brought him renewed national attention, Horace Pippin, one of the most important modernist American painters of the First World War, labored in obscurity, slowly and painfully translating his wartime memories into a collection of paintings that few Americans would see—let alone

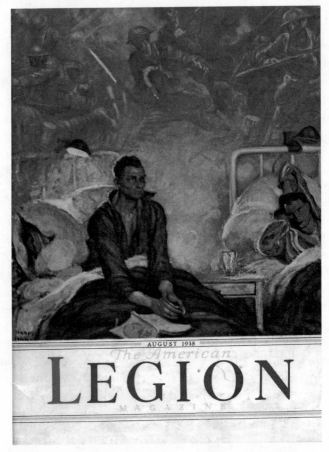

16. The front cover of the *American Legion Monthly* (August 1938). Painting by Harvey Dunn. Courtesy of the American Legion National Headquarters.

appreciate—until decades later. Indeed, even after Pippin was "discovered" by white art critics and patrons, his war pictures remained the least familiar component of his oeuvre, despite the fact that his first serious painting, begun in 1928, is a battle scene. In the 1940s the artist achieved national attention primarily though his paintings of domestic African American life (as in *The Domino Players,* arguably his masterpiece), American history (focused on the likes of Lincoln and John Brown), and biblical subjects, not his scenes of the Western Front. And Pippin's war art remains nearly as obscure today. While Dunn's work continues to appear regularly in World War I histories—including, most recently, Edward Lengel's *To Conquer Hell: The Meuse-Argonne, 1918*—Pippin's name remains unfamiliar to most scholars of the period.[27]

Originality, not lack of talent, explains this neglect. With their flattened perspective, "primitive" absence of shadows, and borderline abstraction, Pippin's war paintings defamiliarize their subject in often surprising ways, as if making us see military violence (or its consequences) for the first time, and represent a modernist challenge to artistic convention. They look nothing like the pictures produced by the AEF's official artists. At the same time, these are subtly political artworks. Although small in scale, Pippin's paintings fill in a vast gap in postwar collective memory, providing a visual record of African Americans in combat—a subject either misremembered or forgotten by most white veterans.

Unlike Dunn, Pippin enjoyed renown as an artist for less than a decade. His fame came late—during the last nine years of his life—and after decades of setbacks and physical suffering. Born in West Chester, Pennsylvania, in 1888, Pippin grew up with four siblings in a fatherless household, where he displayed his artistic ability at an early age. After moving to Goshen, New York, in 1891, he completed an eighth-grade education and then embarked on a series of low-paying jobs, including a seven-year stint as a porter at the St. Elmo Hotel. In 1914 Pippin became an iron molder for the American Brakeshoe Company in Mahwah, New Jersey, his highest-paying and most secure position to date (although as an African American he was denied union membership). Told that his job would be waiting for him when he returned from the war, the twenty-nine-year-old enlisted in 1917 in the 15th Regiment of the New York National Guard, a legendary outfit headquartered in Harlem. Retitled the 369th Infantry and nicknamed the "Harlem Hellfighters," Pippin's regiment saw more action and earned more honors than almost any other American unit in World War I but was shunned by the U.S. Army. Sent overseas in advance of most American troops because of racial tensions in its stateside training camp (the army, in its infinite wisdom, assembled the black New Yorkers in Spartanburg, South Carolina!), the Hellfighters served within a French division and under French command. For a time, the men even wore French helmets and carried French rifles.

Promoted to corporal and highly regarded within his company, Pippin survived a series of costly battles unscathed. Then, in October 1918, as the Hellfighters participated in a French assault staged alongside the massive American offensive in the Meuse-Argonne region, his luck ran out. A burst from a German machine gun lacerated his neck, fractured his right shoulder, and tore apart his right arm. Dazed, Pippin fell into a shell hole. Minutes later a mortally wounded French soldier tumbled into the same crater, pinning the American to the ground. Fortunately, Pippin could reach the dead man's canteen, along with his bread and coffee. Helpless and freezing, the Hellfighter lay there all night, drifting in and out of consciousness, until he was finally located by stretcher bearers and taken to the rear, where probably no one expected him to survive.[28]

Pippin's nearly fatal wounding left him permanently disabled and made painting a torturous exercise. Nerve damage caused his right arm to hang limp at his side, and for the rest of his life he could not raise a paint brush any higher than his shoulder. Photographs later taken of the artist at work show him seated in obvious discomfort, his left hand used to prop up his right wrist. By January 1919 he had recovered enough of his strength to participate in the Hellfighters' famous homecoming march through New York City. But his days of steady employment as an iron molder were over. Unable to return to the American Brakeshoe Company, he moved back to West Chester, where he lived on a meager pension grudgingly doled out by the federal Veterans Bureau. After marriage in 1920 to Jenny Giles, a widowed laundress, the former soldier supplemented his income by delivering laundry and decorating cigar boxes. In 1928 his long dormant artistic passion resurfaced as he began his first oil painting, *The End of War: Starting Home* (1930), a chaotic scene of German and African American troops locked in battle moments before the armistice. Other war scenes followed, including *Outpost Raid: Champagne Sector, Gas Alarm Outpost: Argonne, Shell Holes and Observation Balloon: Champagne Sector,* and *Dog Fight over Trenches.* These are small paintings—most on canvases less than two feet by three feet in size—and Pippin spent months working on each of them. With the war momentarily out of his system, he moved on to the historical scenes, portraits of contemporary African American life, and religious subjects for which he would become famous.

In 1937 Pippin entered two paintings in a West Chester art show, where they caught the attention of famed illustrator N. C. Wyeth and art critic Christian Brinton. From this point on, Pippin's fortunes rose steadily. Within three years he joined the list of artists represented by Philadelphia art dealer Robert Carlen; staged a one-man show in the prestigious Bignou Gallery in New York; and saw four of his works featured in Alain Locke's groundbreaking study, *The Negro in Art: A Pictorial Record of the Ne-*

gro Artist and of the Negro Theme in Art (1940).[29] Patronage from a wealthy collector allowed Pippin to study painting formally for the first time in his life, and by the beginning of the 1940s his yearly output of works more than doubled. Major museums purchased his paintings, and in 1944 *Vogue* magazine commissioned him to create a pair of works depicting—of all things—Southern cotton fields. By the time of his death in 1946, he was one of the best-known African American painters in the country.

Pippin's success owed much to timing. However, the art world within which he was praised and supported closed some doors even as it opened others. In the leftist political climate of the 1930s, many American art collectors and patrons sought "authentic" visions from supposedly unsophisticated members of the proletariat. This sensibility explained the 1930s phenomenon—essentially a marketing phenomenon—of Midwestern regionalism, as Grant Wood, Thomas Hart Benton, and John Steuart Curry became, in the hands of their respective dealers and promoters, simple painters of the American heartland, unsullied by East Coast fashion or European influence. The same attitude drew white sophisticates to "Negro" art, with its—to use the critical discourse of the day—refreshingly "naïve," "primitive," and "instinctive" qualities. As art historian Judith Stein observes, such potentially reductive descriptors did not necessarily carry the negative connotations attached to them today.[30] Nevertheless, race determined the perspective through which Pippin's art was both celebrated, perhaps for all the wrong reasons, and in terms of its significance and complexity *contained*. Indeed, Pippin's blackness, as constructed by his white audience, formed the basis for nearly everything said about him. N. C. Wyeth remarked that Pippin's work had "the jungle . . . in it," thereby manifesting "a basic African quality."[31] (One thinks here of Duke Ellington's early compositions, described as "jungle music" by white visitors to Harlem.) And a well-meaning Philadelphia art critic made the following pronouncement, intended as praise: "The Modern world admires Pippin because it is subconsciously jealous of the natural expression of a crude, simple soul. Pippin had something most of us have lost: something that was trained out of us."[32]

In Pippin's war paintings, in particular, there is nothing crude or simple. On the contrary, his depictions of the Harlem Hellfighters reflect a complex, politically charged background. And contested memory is central to their meaning. Indeed, two events in the regiment's wartime history, each a central feature in the Hellfighters' collective memory of their experience, informed Pippin's artistic vision: first, the desperate struggle between Henry Johnson, the most famous African American hero of the war, and a score of German attackers; and second, the emergence of the Harlem Hellfighters Band, led by the gifted composer James Reese Europe, as the premier musical performers of the Great War. Combined, these events create a complicated political and cultural platform for Pippin's anything but naïve paintings of black soldiers in World War I.

Johnson's feat helped make the regiment famous and for a time captured the imagination of Americans on both sides of the color line. Sadly, however, the poor performance of another black regiment later in the war would push the episode from the memory of most whites. On the night of May 13, 1918, while Pippin's unit held a section of frontline trenches near the Argonne Forest, a German raiding party closed in on an isolated position protected by just two sentries—Needham Roberts and Henry Johnson, a volunteer from Albany. Badly wounded by "potato masher" grenades and shot several times, the two men refused to be taken prisoner. A furious hand-to-hand struggle ensued. Johnson fired his rifle until it jammed and then used the long arm as a club, crushing the skull of at least one attacker. When he saw a pair of enemy soldiers attempting to drag his comrade away, he took on the Germans with his bolo knife, disemboweling one soldier, who cursed him in "good New York talk."[33] The relief party that reached Johnson's position the next morning beheld a gory spectacle—Roberts and Johnson, both barely alive, surrounded by the bodies of five dead Germans. Red stains in no-man's-land showed where other members of the raiding party, dead or wounded, had been dragged away. In all, Pippin's fellow Hellfighters had dispatched perhaps as many as a dozen adversaries.

One week later the "Battle of Henry Johnson," as the episode came to be known, reached the American press, and the 369th Infantry, more accustomed to being treated as a pariah, enjoyed widespread, if fleeting, acclaim for its ferocity and courage. As Richard Slotkin observes, Johnson's feat provided ideal copy during a news lull. In mid-May 1918 the AEF's major battles were still in the future, and war correspondents were hungry for stories of American valor.[34] Such, indeed, was the appetite for frontline heroics that *even* a black hero would do. However, as Pippin would later discover when celebrated as a "primitive" or "instinctual" artist by his supposedly liberal patrons, approval from the mainstream media carried a reductive undercurrent. The physical violence of which Johnson had proven capable evoked for white reporters images of African "savagery" or the razor fights, supposedly a popular African American pastime, enacted in minstrel shows. A patriotic cartoon featured in the *New York Herald* summed up this combination of celebration and belittlement. Titled "Two First Class Americans!" the cartoon depicts Johnson supporting his wounded comrade while fending off the Germans. The African American's posture suggests strength and defiance. But stereotyping undercuts the tribute: Johnson's massive knife, dripping with blood, and his exaggerated racial features create a figure who is, in Slotkin's words, "at one and the same time a 'first-class American' hero and a blackface minstrel."[35]

Already complicated by race, Johnson's fame had a short life, at least where most whites were concerned. Three months after the Battle of Henry Johnson, another African American regiment, the 368th Infantry (part of the all-black 92nd "Buffalo" Division), earned the contempt of white troops when two of its battalions fled from the enemy. The episode could not have happened at a worse time or place. Assigned to the left flank of the American divisions that went over the top in the opening phase of the Meuse-Argonne offensive, the 368th Infantry was supposed to keep pace with the 77th "New York" Division as it advanced through the Argonne Forest. Thus, the black regiment's collapse created a gap in the American line, which the Germans then exploited in order to encircle the famous Lost Battalion. Just as circumstances had conspired earlier to make Johnson a national hero and to boost the image of African Americans as capable soldiers, they now conspired to make black troops laughingstocks. *Everyone* knew the story of the Lost Battalion, so everyone knew (or thought they knew) just who had let down Maj. Charles White Whittlesey and his brave men—and why. One Southern white officer later reported that he had discovered the cause of the debacle firsthand: Several disgraced enlisted men in the 368th told him, "Ef we'd a had some white officers, we wouldn't run, no suh."[36] This same source alleged that the soldiers had panicked at the sound of their own artillery. Even worse, however, than the rapid distribution and embellishment of the regiment's failure through AEF scuttlebutt was the episode's impact on Pershing and his fellow generals, who now became more convinced than ever of African American inferiority. Indeed, so thoroughly did the dishonor of the 368th efface the successes of the Hellfighters and other black regiments serving under French command that racial segregation, something that was *not* a given when the United States entered World War I, would remain a fixture of American military life until the Korean War. Collective memory at its most selective made this so. The reality that many white units had performed just as poorly in the Argonne battle (enough to produce an estimated two hundred thousand stragglers) was conveniently forgotten. Nor were morale problems within the 92nd Division (produced, not surprisingly, by the demeaning treatment of its men, particularly its black junior officers) ever taken into consideration.

As we will see, through his war paintings, Pippin grappled with this collective memory in subtle and sophisticated ways. At the same time, his visual art has a cross-media connection with the Hellfighters' best-known artists—the members of its legendary regimental band. While the combat performance of black troops remained dubious in the eyes of most white American soldiers, no one contested the astonishing talents of the musicians led by Lt. James Reese Europe, who not only outplayed rival bands in the AEF but were also largely responsible for establishing the French love affair with American popular music. Allegedly subsidized with a "check for 10,000 dollars," which Europe used to enlist only the finest Harlem musicians, the band dazzled American troops at leave centers and hospitals and gave dozens of goodwill performances in French towns and cities, where audiences whistled as loudly as they could after each number, a form of praise that the band members initially mistook for catcalls.[37] Although later credited with introducing the French to jazz, the Hellfighters played music that was, in fact, transitional—syncopated marching numbers and songs, many written by Europe and tenor Noble Sissle, that form a bridge between the ragtime of the 1910s and the later, more improvisational music of Louis Armstrong and Duke Ellington.[38] Neither the French nor the Hellfighters' fellow Americans could get enough of this distinctive sound, and Europe's musicians soon became accustomed to a strange existence that involved frontline duty one week and a concert tour the next.

On one level the band's success trivialized the regiment's reputation, drawing attention to African American musicianship rather than fighting skill—hence the remark in the regimental history, wishful thinking on the author's part, that with the Battle of Henry Johnson, the 369th Infantry "passed out of the category of a merely unique organization of the American Army, a regiment with its chief bid for fame based upon the music of Jim Europe's Band."[39] Unfortunately, few observers outside the regiment attached so much importance to Johnson's quickly forgotten exploit. Less than a month after the Battle of Henry Johnson, the *St. Louis Post Dispatch* reported, "The first and foremost Afro-American contribution to the French fighting line is its band."[40] However, while white American audiences tended to separate the black entertainer from the black combatant, praising the former and disparaging (or ignoring) the latter, Europe and his band sought to unite the two. Their best, most innovative music represents a challenge—not unlike Pippin's paintings—to stereotyped notions of African Americans in uniform.

The first black musician to lead his own ensemble—the "Europe Orchestra"—on a major recording label; a formidable entrepreneur, whose musical comedies played in African American theaters across the country; and an accomplished musical director, whose collaboration with British-born dancers Irene and Vernon Castle carried his name into the white mainstream, the multitalented Europe initially resisted the notion of heading up a regimental band. The thirty-eight-year-old Harlem celebrity wanted to lead men in battle, not entertain. However, once Europe submitted to the inevitable, he approached his new musical duties with a sense of mission. As Slotkin points out, the band leader's artistic trajectory was clear before 1917: during the early, prewar stirrings of the Harlem Renaissance, Europe shared with other black artists and intellectuals his vision of a "distinctly African American music," which would form "part of the larger struggle to achieve a coherent racial identity." White musicians, he argued, had debased ragtime, reducing this black art form "to something not much better than minstrel show 'coon song.'" In response, Europe imbued his compositions and arrangements with "powerful and distinctive rhythms," and he beefed up the percussion section in his orchestra, establishing a more muscular style of ragtime that paved the way for modern jazz.[41] The Harlem Hellfighters Band gave him the opportunity to lift this expression of "racial identity" onto an international stage. At the same time, Europe would use the band to respond, in a nonthreatening but eloquent manner, to the racial politics of his homeland and, more specifically, the AEF.

Some of the Hellfighters' music fell short of this ambitious mark. For example, the medley "Plantation Echoes," recorded (along with the rest of the compositions mentioned below) for Pathé Discs in the spring of 1919, paints an aural picture of the antebellum South and ends with a nostalgic rendition of "Dixie." Like the pictures of apparently contented slaves in cotton fields that Pippin painted for *Vogue*, this syrupy tone poem is hardly music to shatter minstrel-show stereotypes. However, other numbers carry a political edge. In the song "All of No Man's Land Is Ours," a soon-to-be-discharged soldier—a *black* soldier—phones his sweetheart with plans for their future happiness. Significantly, the chorus, with its plural possessive pronoun ("Ours"), places the African American singer within an American collective and implicitly puts him on an even footing with white soldiers. Moreover, Europe and Sissle's lyrics accommodate an even more radical reading: Is "No Man's Land" an oblique reference to the color line? Do the lyrics describe the fruits of the social contract, promoted by Du Bois and other African American leaders in 1917, that promised advancement and opportunity in exchange for wartime loyalty? Probably composed soon after the Hellfighters' homecoming in 1919, the song's exuberant imagery, filled with the promise of birth and fair weather, carries political as well as romantic connotations:

> Wedding bells in June-y June
> All will tell by their tuney tune
> That Vict'ry's won
> The war is over
> The whole wide world is a-wreathed
> in clover!
> Then hand in hand we'll stroll
> through life, dear
> Just think how happy we will be—
> I mean we three!
> We'll pick a bungalow among the
> fragrant boughs
> When I come back to you with the
> blooming flow'rs
> All of No Man's Land is ours![42]

Sadly, for returning African American veterans, the world would not remain "a-wreathed in clover" for long. As 1919 brought more lynchings than ever (several victims were veterans, hanged while wearing their uniforms), the bright social forecast offered in Europe and Sissle's lyrics would prove brutally ironic. Indeed, with its theme of homecoming, "All of No Man's Land Is Ours" should be contrasted with the ballad "Sam Smiley," composed a few years later by Howard University professor Sterling A. Brown. In Brown's grim ditty, the title character, a black AEF veteran, returns home to discover *his* sweetheart on death row, condemned for murdering her infant, the offspring of a white man. Inevitably, the sardonically named "Smiley" finds himself pursued by a lynch mob "in fine fettle," and in the last stanza the black doughboy performs his final "buckdance" at the end of a rope.[43] So much for a peaceful "bungalow among the fragrant boughs."

The most remarkable song in the Hellfighters' repertoire, "On Patrol in No Man's Land," focuses on the capabilities of African American line officers. Written by Europe as he recuperated from a dose of poison gas in the summer of 1918, the lyrics take the form of a series of orders, a monologue in effect, delivered by an officer before and during a raid on the German trenches. Sound effects, created by the Hellfighters' percussion section, make this tune especially memorable. A snare drummer realistically imitates the rhythm of a Maxim machine gun. A Klaxon rings as a gas attack is announced. And a bass drum mimics the hollow boom of shells exploding in the distance. Set against this eerie cacophony, the officer's voice, provided by Noble Sissle, reassures the members of the raiding party and displays an intimate knowledge of trench warfare:

There's a *Minenwerfer*
coming—look out (bang!)
Hear that roar (bang!)
There's one more (bang!)
Stand fast—there's a Very light
Don't gasp, or they'll find you all right
Don't start to bombin' with those hand
grenades (rat-a-tat-tat-tat)
There's a machine gun, holy spades!
Alert! Gas! Put on your mask!
Adjust it correctly and hurry up fast[44]

A wartime hit in the United States, "On Patrol in No Man's Land" offered an aurally realistic but still patriotic representation of Americans in battle, acknowledging the horrors of trench warfare—*Minenwerfers,* machine guns, and poison gas—while countering them with the speaker's frontline expertise. The lyrics themselves contain nothing threatening or overtly political. However, the notion of a black composer in uniform writing of military leadership *and doing so on the basis of personal experience* was, in itself, radical. And so was the mere fact that a black performer sang the lines that Europe had authored. Indeed, the U.S. Army expended considerable energy during the First World War to discredit and humiliate African Americans who qualified for leadership positions. Evidence of this unspoken policy appeared everywhere. For example, bigotry within the War Department undermined a well-intentioned training program for African American officers set up in Des Moines, Iowa. Meanwhile, within the Harlem Hellfighters and other black National Guard units, black officers above a certain rank had to step aside for white replacements, regardless of experience or documented successes. And as we have already seen, in the much maligned 368th Infantry, African American officers (those not yet replaced) received an inordinate share of the blame for the regiment's failings. Thus, in perhaps his boldest response to the AEF's racial policies, Europe used an infectious piece of ragtime, complete with crowd-pleasing sound effects, to plant a deeply subversive image in the minds of his white American listeners—namely, the image of a capable black officer taking *his* men over the top.

Both Johnson's heroics, the focus of brief but groundbreaking media attention, and Europe's popular music—among the most popular American music of the First World War—may seem far removed from Pippin's miniature paintings of the Western Front, deeply personal works created in relative obscurity. However, throughout the 1920s and 1930s, Pippin actively participated in public war remembrance, and he would have understood the extent to which his individual vision of the Great War, as recorded on his modernist canvases, reinforced or undermined the collective memory of white soldiers. In fact, the disabled former Hellfighter was very much a part of the postwar culture of commemoration. A member of the American Legion until his death, Pippin served for a time as the commander of the all-black Nathan Holmes post in West Chester and, segregation notwithstanding, became friends with several influential white legionnaires. In 1937 he painted portraits of two of these men: Paul Dague, a local law enforcement officer and future congressman, and retired Marine Corps general Smedley M. Butler. Both paintings emphasize military and commemorative regalia. Dague's portrait features its subject seated at a table in his dress uniform with a gavel and block, the latter embossed with the American Legion symbol, placed before him. Although inspired, as art historian Linda Roscoe Hartigan observes, by Pippin's sincere desire "to honor his civic-minded friend" the painting nevertheless offers a striking image of the white veteran's power over collective memory—as implied by the ceremonial gavel and prominent legion insignia (interestingly enough, Dague was not a post commander at the time) that the artist has included.[45] In his portrait of Butler, Pippin sets the imposing general, a hawk-nosed figure with a chest full of medals, against a background of blue sky and churning clouds. Aloof from

17. *Outpost Raid: Champagne Sector* (1931) by Horace Pippin.

the world of peace-loving men, the retired marine looks like a statue—
the top of a memorial perhaps.

When examined in light of the Harlem Hellfighters' history, both military and musical, and the artist's personal engagement with collective
memory, the series of war paintings that Pippin produced in the early
1930s take on new shades of meaning. Consider, for example, *Outpost
Raid: Champagne Sector* (1931) (see fig. 17). One of Pippin's most atmo-
spheric war scenes, this canvas depicts two soldiers—one African American (the lead member of a raiding party), the other German—as they
confront each other amid a landscape of gray, ambiguous tones. Everything looks washed out. The snow on the ground, for example, reflects
the smoky color of the early morning sky, as does the German soldier's
field-gray uniform. Fittingly, the situation that Pippin has recorded is ambiguous as well. Will the American soldier use his bayonet? And what kind
of weapon is the German holding in his concealed right hand? Both men

stand at the ready but seem hesitant as well, as if wishing to avoid violence at such close quarters. Pippin has perhaps captured that split second of hesitation before two adversaries on the battlefield realize that they must either kill or be killed. At the same time, like news accounts of the Battle of Henry Johnson or the lyrics of "On Patrol in No Man's Land," the painting affirms the skill and determination of African American combat troops. There is no white American officer in the scene. Caught, as if in a snapshot, on the brink of hand-to-hand combat with a resolute opponent, the black infantryman in the foreground is propelled forward, however warily, by his own initiative and sense of duty.

The first painting in Pippin's Hellfighters series, *The End of War: Starting Home* (1930), offers a similar blend of ambiguity and tribute (see fig. 18). The strangeness of this work begins with its title, for no one in the picture is starting home. Instead, Pippin offers a scene of senseless violence as soldiers continue to fight and die in the moments leading up to the armistice. By virtue of their lighter-colored uniforms, the enemy soldiers stand out on this thickly layered canvas, and their varied responses to the African American troops who have overrun their position accurately reflect the confusion at the close of the Meuse-Argonne offensive, when some German infantrymen surrendered or quickly retreated while others fought to the bitter end. Thus, one field-gray figure stands with his arms raised, hoping for mercy. Another, still defiant, clutches his rifle. And a third topples backward, shot by one of the advancing doughboys. In contrast, the victorious Hellfighters whom Pippin depicts are resolute and professional as they close with the enemy, each man holding his rifle and bayonet in the same position, thus creating a sense of collective strength and willpower. Once again, Pippin offers an image of disciplined African American combat troops, a counter memory aimed squarely at the overemphasis on the 368th Infantry's supposed incompetence and cowardice. In this case, however, discordant visual elements lead the viewer's attention away from the Hellfighters—the American troops are, in fact, difficult to see against the green and gray landscape—and create a disorienting effect. Indeed, this work seems barely able to contain the apocalyptic violence that it depicts—violence that moves outward and *toward* the viewer on three different visual planes. In the background Pippin has created a scene of fiery death as German planes crash toward the earth and reddish shrapnel bursts fill the sky. In the foreground the ground troops fight on, even though the armistice is at hand. The hor-

18. *The End of War: Starting Home* (1930) by Horace Pippin.

rors of war then spill onto the picture's frame, which Pippin has decorated with carvings of grotesque military implements—gas masks, stick
grenades, helmets, and tanks. Paradoxically, this painting suggests that
war is too much for the artist's eye, that memory in this instance has produced a rush of images too powerful for the frame to enclose.

Other paintings in Pippin's war series from the early 1930s likewise
negotiate personal and collective memory while sometimes manifesting
an almost hallucinatory quality. *Gas Alarm Outpost: Argonne* (1931), which
shows three African American troops standing guard next to a barri-
caded train track, evokes the sense of mystery and menace felt by soldiers
in close proximity to an unseen enemy. The painting also conveys, once
again, the fighting skills and instincts acquired by the Hellfighters as successful *combat* troops. Rifles in hand, gas masks at the ready, all three of
the infantrymen seem prepared for whatever lurks on the other side of
the barricade. *Shell Holes and Observation Balloon: Champagne Sector* (1931)

has a disturbing, dreamlike atmosphere, not unlike the work of Salvador Dali. Painted entirely in grayish tones, this eerie canvas depicts a ruinous farmhouse, next to two flowerlike shell craters. A German observation balloon, a mere blotch in the overcast sky, hangs in the distance. And that is it. There are no people in the picture, just a ghostly set of footprints running past a cracked and crumbling edifice. With its focus on devastation and emptiness, this work explores the same territory as Dunn's *No Man's Land* (1918), but with completely different results. Pippin's painting depicts a psychological, as well as literal, landscape, employing gothic touches that edge the work toward surrealism and abstraction.

These quietly revolutionary pictures clash with White America's collective memory of black combatants in numerous ways. White officers, so essential to discipline in African American units (according to the War Department), never once appear, a telling omission. Determined and aggressive (although not "ferocious" in the manner of stereotyped French colonial soldiers or the African American berserkers portrayed in American Legion cartoons), Pippin's infantrymen close with the enemy. They do not run away; nor are they simpletons. The black doughboys in these paintings appear as competent students of modern warfare and its horrifying technologies (as in *Gas Alarm Outpost: Argonne*). And the surreal destruction to the landscape caused by long-range artillery, so memorably captured by *Shell Holes and Observation Balloon: Champagne*, emerges as a psychological force that affected African American soldiers no less than their Caucasian counterparts.

However, if Pippin's war paintings pose a subversive challenge to the prejudicial recollections of white AEF members—in much the same manner as James Reese Europe's more daring song lyrics—then they likewise take issue with a particular body of African American memory: Pippin's war is not the racial and political crusade envisioned by the NAACP. Indeed, a comparison of paintings like *The End of War: Starting Home* and *Outpost Raid: Champagne Sector* with articles contained in post-armistice issues of the NAACP's national magazine, *Crisis*, demonstrates that the artist steered a course between *two* dominant constructions of African American war experience—one established by whites, the other by blacks. Thus, through its lack of alignment with either camp, Pippin's work suggests that collective memory of World War I in African American communities was hardly uniform.

What kind of war memory, then, did the NAACP promote? To answer that question we should start with the vision offered by the organization's most eloquent rhetorician, *Crisis* editor W. E. B. Du Bois. In an editorial published in September 1920, Du Bois expressed a sense of disappointment and weariness shared by many African Americans who had joined the war effort with high hopes only to see their dream of civil rights in exchange for wartime loyalty disintegrate amid race riots (many of them in Northern cities), lynchings (more, in fact, than recorded before the war), and renewed Southern efforts to squelch black voting. "The reaction of war is upon us," Du Bois wrote. "We sit back, exhausted, depressed. What is the use? we groan. What has this world madness meant to us? We are still in bonds; wages lag behind mounting costs of life; lynching flourishes—what's the use of it all!"[46] However, after giving way to despair, Du Bois characteristically turned his comments in a morale-building direction, and in a manner that hints at the NAACP's construction of the recent past: "Steady, comrades, you have seized from the Hell of War, Self-Knowledge and Self-Control. These are priceless. They are worth all."[47] What did Du Bois mean by "Self-Knowledge" and "Self-Control"? The latter perhaps partially referred to wartime instances when black soldiers or civilian workers had refused to respond to white provocation, thereby boosting the reputation of their race. Kelly Miller, a dean at Howard University and a popular author whose works were regularly advertised in *Crisis,* emphasized this kind of rational restraint in his *History of the World War for Human Rights* (1919). For example, the trainees at Camp Des Moines in 1918 "held on" when news of the East St. Louis riot, "the most savage pogrom Anglo-Saxon culture has ever revealed," reached their barracks.[48] By not responding violently, these soldiers passed their "acid test."[49]

But the "Self-Knowledge" and "Self-Control" emphasized by Du Bois also have more heroic connotations and thus reflect the many celebrations of African American courage under fire presented in *Crisis* during the years immediately following the war. In a military context, "Self-Knowledge" referred to the realization on the part of black troops that they could master the art of soldiering as well as—if not better than—whites; "Self-Control" signified their capacity for valor, their mastery of fear. The magazine stressed both of these characteristics through a veritable cult of military heroism no less striking than the obsession with military decorations and citations displayed in the *American Legion Weekly* and *Monthly.* Initially, politics, as well as pride, drove this constant display of African American combat honors. In order for black participation in the war to translate into political benefits for African Americans in general (a hope to which *Crisis* clung even as racism intensified after the armistice), soldiers of color had to be *more* effective, when it came to killing Germans, than their white counterparts—and more stoic.

Thus, since the majority of black AEF members had served in labor battalions, less-than-ideal sources for politically inspiring examples of heroism, *Crisis* focused its attention on the two African American combat divisions (the 92nd and the 93rd)—and exaggerated where necessary. Readers of the November 1918 issue, for example, discovered that during one attack infantry regiments in these divisions refused "rations and rest" and "almost annihilated four fresh divisions of German reserve troops," a dubious claim for any segment of the AEF.[50] *Crisis* provided even more memorable instances of individual valor, including the story of a "negro soldier from Alabama" who "put a rifle ball through the skulls of twenty-one Germans."[51] Another news report focused on the Distinguished Service Cross recipient Cpl. Isaac Valley, who saved his comrades by pushing an enemy grenade into the mud with his boot. Valley's only comment, after losing part of his foot, showed his nobility: "I saved the others even if it did get me."[52] At times this emphasis on superhuman military performance came close to reinforcing the white stereotype of the "savage" or innately bloodthirsty Negro soldier. Indeed, *Crisis* often ran testimonials by white officers who were eager to praise the physical ferocity of black troops. For instance, according to Lt. James E. Black of Lewiston, Pennsylvania, soldiers of color were more "thorough" than any other warriors: "They slit Boches' throats with their bayonets when they get within reach, and take no prisoners."[53] Lt. O. W. Weatherford of New York City described a "giant Negro" in an attack across no-man's-land: "The Negro stuck his bayonet into the Huns, and then took his foot and pushed their bodies off. When his bayonet could not be used, he used his gun as a club."[54]

Du Bois added to this celebration of African American valor and lethality wherever he could. For example, in "An Essay toward a History of the Black Man in the Great War," published in June 1919, he concluded his description of the 92nd Division, the division that contained the notorious 368th Infantry, with a stirring set of anecdotes obviously intended to counterbalance that unit's negative association with the Lost Battalion legend. According to Du Bois, on the final morning of the Meuse-Argonne offensive, the 56th Infantry, a white regiment, became trapped in a thicket of barbed wire, completely surrounded by enemy machine-gun nests. Black troops in the Buffalo Division came to their rescue. An officer in the 367th Infantry (presumably one of the few black commanders who managed to keep their commissions) "maneuvered several pla-toons to a position where they could hit the Germans from the flank" and thus "probably saved the 56th from annihilation." Another unit in the 92nd Division, the 365th Infantry, occupied "800 yards of the battle-front" by the time of the cease-fire on November 11 and "held against odds five to one under intense shell and machine gun fire."[55]

Such testimonials, regularly offered by Du Bois and others, attempted to salvage a positive political message from African American war experi-ence. At first, stories of black soldiers as military supermen served the so-cial contract (service in exchange for an end to second-class status) that the NAACP's leadership attempted to draw up with the federal govern-ment. Tales of African American valor and battlefield sacrifice offered dramatic evidence that Black America had held up its end of the bar-gain. Then, as this contract collapsed, the successes of African American combat troops became, if anything, even more important. As Du Bois suggested in his affirmation of a new "Self-Knowledge" and a new "Self-Control" among blacks in the postwar world, battlefield heroism did not have to bring direct legislative benefits in order to be worthwhile. On the contrary, the revelation of African American valor in the Great War had become, he implied, a foundational component of racial identity, one that stood ready—along with the vision of France as "the only real white Democracy"—to inspire even loftier social goals.[56]

Significantly, however, Pippin's canvases contain no such heroics—just soldiers, black soldiers in this case, coping with the bewildering con-ditions of modern warfare. Ironically, his paintings would have seemed equally out of place in either the NAACP's national magazine or the *American Legion Monthly.* Ideologically, they fit neither venue. Or to put it another way, the memory that they convey has little to do with mar-tial glory, a preoccupation in both periodicals, albeit for very different reasons. The only World War I painting by Pippin that even remotely re-sembles a *Crisis*-style depiction of military triumph and racial achievement is *The End of War: Starting Home,* the first work in his Hellfighters series. Indeed, this painting depicts the same moment in time—Armistice Day morning—as Du Bois's dramatic account of heroic action by the 92nd Division. As we have seen, the black doughboys in this picture project a sense of soldierly professionalism light-years removed from the comic rascality of Wildcat and his cronies. And there is no question that the advancing Hellfighters are victorious. In these respects the painting over-turns demeaning stereotypes perpetuated throughout the interwar period by the American Legion. At the same time, however, the mood of the painting is somber, closer to the poetry of Wilfred Owen, with its compassionate ruminations on the "pity of war," than anything featured in *Crisis*. The Germans in the painting—some fighting, some dying, others surrendering—are painfully human, and they bear little resemblance to the dehumanized "Boches" that black troops supposedly dispatched with such enthusiasm. Nor do the Germans' adversaries, who seem to press forward out of grim necessity rather than joy, exult in their victory. Confusion and waste stand out as the central themes in this disturbing painting, as opposed to the selfless courage and gleeful military violence celebrated by the NAACP.

Likewise, in *Outpost Raid: Champagne Sector,* Pippin captures the hesitation and anxiety felt by combatants on both sides. Again, there is nothing heroic about the scene. Neither soldier—German nor African American—seems eager to engage in hand-to-hand combat. And in *Gas Alarm Outpost: Argonne,* the artist manages to convey more than the sinister mystery of no-man's-land: the troops in his painting look prepared, but also *bored*—a reality of military life seldom, if ever, acknowledged in *Crisis*. Thus, Pippin's Hellfighters series adds up to much more than a response to racial prejudice and its distorting effects upon war memory. By refusing to idealize his subjects, the artist simultaneously defied an ideological agenda that was operative on his own side of the color line. In other words, his vernacular art rejects *two* sources of official meaning— the American Legion *and* the NAACP. Freed of the overemphasis on heroism that might have resulted if Pippin had been more dependent on convention (or more driven by political concerns), these paintings form a multi-image war memorial that is similar, in terms of its varied situations and emotions, to Harvey Dunn's war series from 1918. And as with Dunn's work, the strength and fascination of Pippin's canvases derive from the artist's ability to defamiliarize his subject, an effect that is possible only when official meaning—or in Pippin's case, official memory of two varieties—is resisted.

Although Pippin produced his last World War I painting in 1935, his war experience, and the painful memory issues that surrounded it, continued to surface in his work well into the 1940s. However, his depiction of war changed, becoming more explicitly political and symbolic. For example, in *Mr. Prejudice* (1943), Pippin uses an African American doughboy as part of an allegorical appeal for racial harmony during the Second World War (see fig. 19). On the top half of the painting the artist por-

19. *Mr. Prejudice* (1943) by Horace Pippin.

trays a brutish white figure, the Mr. Prejudice of the title, as he drives
a wedge into the center of the "V for Victory" symbol. A Klansman and
the member of a lynch mob, noose in hand, look on approvingly. On
the bottom half Pippin presents a crowd of World War II servicemen
and home-front workers, both white and black—all the people, in other
words, whose efforts will be for naught if prejudice prevails. The painting's message could not be blunter. But Pippin includes a mysterious detail: one of the soldiers, a black man, wears the uniform of the preced-
ing war—right down to his wrap leggings (also known as puttees) and
World War I box respirator (or gas mask). Art historian Judith Wilson
interprets this figure as an accidental anachronism.[57] However, the artist's attention to detail when reproducing the World War II–vintage attire
of the other servicemen—note, for instance, the pilots' authentic flight

jackets and helmets—suggests otherwise. Perhaps Pippin included this solitary Hellfighter as a reproach, as a reminder of Mr. Prejudice's work in 1917 and 1918.

World War I would also find its way, hauntingly, into a series of works that at first sight seem far removed from Pippin's experience of the Western Front. Between 1944 and 1946, at the height of his popularity and near the end of his life, the artist produced what came to be known as his Holy Mountain paintings, each a variation on the vision of Edenic harmony described in the Book of Isaiah and popularized a century earlier by Quaker artist Edward Hicks. Like Dunn's luminous scenes of the Dakota frontier, Pippin's Holy Mountain works express a yearning for peace and simplicity made all the more poignant by the artist's war experience. All three paintings depict the same essential scene: amid a lush grove, covered in wildflowers, a black shepherd (presumably Pippin himself) watches over a group of exotic animals that rest together, no longer predator and prey, while small children of both races play in the grass. It is a moving portrait of a world without violence—or, rather, *almost* without violence. A closer look at the forest in the background reveals the tiny figures of soldiers running through the trees, white crosses amid red flowers (suggestive of the poppies in Flanders Fields), and even a rifle stuck into the ground and topped with a helmet—a battlefield grave marker. Pippin described these incongruous details as "little ghostlike memor[ies]" of World War I, a comment interpreted by art historian Richard J. Powell as follows: "In the context of Isaiah's vision, one can translate Pippin's statement to mean that the specters of discord and destruction are never very far removed from the concepts of peace and harmony."[58] However, the presence of Hellfighters on the Holy Mountain perhaps also carried a deeper personal significance for the artist. These "specters of discord and destruction" show that for Pippin there was no entering the Peaceable Kingdom; traumatic memories of war's horrors, made even more painful by racial injustice, remained with him to the end. Imagining a refuge from the past, where no doughboy would ever fight or die again, ultimately proved impossible.

Pippin grappled with that inescapable past in a collection of highly idiosyncratic, deeply personal war paintings. As we have seen, however, political and cultural issues informed these works from the start—as one might expect given the artist's involvement in commemorative ritual and public war remembrance. Indeed, Pippin's war art was, to a large degree, both *shaped by* and *directed at* various versions of collective memory, both white and black. The Harlem Hellfighters' effort to occupy a position of honor, as combat troops, in the historical narrative of the war—an effort spectacularly strengthened by Henry Johnson's heroism and then tragically undermined by the conduct of another unit—marches on in Pippin's portrayal of competent and determined African Americans serving at the front. Likewise, the crowd-pleasing but simultaneously subversive song lyrics of James Reese Europe and Noble Sissle can be "heard," in a sense, in the painter's scenes of battle. However, Pippin never carried this memory agenda to the point of idealization. His iconoclastic art refuses to glorify African American war experience, and thus it challenges *two* versions of the past, one created by whites, the other by blacks.

The complex, multilayered "remembering" at work in Pippin's war paintings—and in his paintings of peace—hardly lines up with descriptors like "naïve" or "primitive." Such adjectives might more accurately be applied to the supposedly sophisticated art critics and dealers who promoted Pippin's work while, albeit with good intentions, patronizing the artist who produced it. The next section of this chapter focuses on a single painting, John Steuart Curry's *The Return of Private Davis from the Argonne* (1928–1940), which likewise displays a complexity, depth, and ambivalence completely out of keeping with the reductive image manufactured for—and to some extent by—its creator. Indeed, Curry's painting, a masterpiece of ambiguity and conflicting visual elements, is, in terms of collective memory, perhaps the most revealing American war painting of the interwar period.

The Western Front Comes to Kansas: John Steuart Curry's *The Return of Private Davis from the Argonne*

On June 5, 1921, the citizens of Winchester, Kansas, and many neighboring communities turned out for an event that would later be immortalized by the so-called regionalist painter John Steuart Curry: the reburial of William L. Davis, the artist's high-school friend, in a small cemetery two miles southeast of town. Davis had been dead for nearly three years. In August 1918, while serving in the ordinarily quiet belt of trenches that wound through the Vosges Mountains of Alsace, he had become one the first soldiers in the Kansas National Guard to die of wounds in the Great War. Now, thanks to the federal program that allowed families to repatriate the remains of their fallen loved ones (at governmental expense), Private Davis was at last back in the heartland. And he received a hero's welcome. According to the *Winchester Star,* services for the repatriated soldier began at 11:00 AM (armistice hour) in the Winchester Christian Church, where a packed house listened to a series of uplifting sermons and patriotic speeches. The program then culminated in a graveside ceremony led by a "firing squad, under the command of a sergeant from Leavenworth" and "the local chapter of the American Legion." Involving the entire community, along with scores of visitors, Davis's funeral was, the newspaper remarked, "one of the largest gatherings ever held in Winchester."[59]

Whether Curry actually attended this event is unknown. Ironically, ties between "Curry of Kansas," as the painter later came to be known, and his home territory had loosened early in the artist's life. At sixteen Curry had left the Sunflower State to study at the Kansas City Art Institute in Missouri. Then came a sojourn at the Chicago Art Institute, followed by additional instruction at Geneva College in Iowa and, eventually, informal tutelage under none other than Harvey Dunn at Tenafly, New Jersey. To be close to Dunn, Curry took up residence in the nearby town of Leonia, and it was there he was living in 1921. Years later, Curry implied that he had journeyed all the way from the East Coast to Kansas to see his former schoolmate put to rest, but a gap in his correspondence from the early 1920s makes this claim difficult to substantiate. By the same token, only sketchy information about Curry's friendship with Davis has survived.[60] In the years after the funeral the painter spoke affectionately of Davis as an "old school chum"; however, he did not offer any details.[61] Nor does oral tradition in the Davis family go beyond a general recollection that the two young men were quite close.[62] Like many of the claims used by Curry to establish himself as a painter of "authentic" Kansas subjects, his personal connection to Davis may have been exaggerated. This is the same artist, after all, who became famous for painting tornadoes (without ever having seen one); who perpetuated the stereotype of Kansas flatness by smoothing out the hilly countryside around Winchester (as in, for example, *Baptism in Kansas,* the painting that established Curry's reputation as a Midwestern regionalist), and who donned overalls for photographers in order to enhance his image as an unsophisticated rustic (when in fact Curry had spent nearly a year in the Paris of Ernest Hemingway and Gertrude Stein).

However, while it is probably impossible to know whether Curry was in Winchester, Kansas, on June 5, 1921, there is little question that the *notion* of Private Davis's posthumous return from "Over There"—a homecom-

ing at once poignant and macabre, patriotic and subversive—ultimately
stirred the painter's deepest reflections on modern warfare and its consequences. Into his depiction of a heartbreaking scene that he may or
may not have witnessed firsthand, he would pour his sense of frustration
as another world war erupted in Europe, thereby (in Curry's view) setting back the cause of art for a century or more, and as American isolationism, which the painter strongly supported, became untenable. At
the same time, he would express an uncertainty shared by many of his
countrymen in the 1920s and 1930s over the meaning of the conflict in
which Private Davis had died.

Curry began to paint Davis's return in 1928 and almost immediately
ran into difficulties. If one believes in the painter's affection for his childhood "chum," lack of emotional distance may have been a problem. If
not, technical dilemmas provide an alternative explanation. Retouched
again and again, Curry's depiction of the graveside service, ultimately
titled *The Return of Private Davis from the Argonne,* would not be completed
until 1940, one year, ironically enough, before the entry of the United
States into the Second World War. Born of his growing fears (already
confirmed by the time he finished the piece) of another global conflict
and his ongoing engagement with the cultural memory of the First World
War, this tragic canvas, which most studies of twentieth-century war art
have curiously ignored, offers an extraordinary window into the work-
ings of American military remembrance during the 1920s and 1930s (see
fig. 20). Indeed, *The Return of Private Davis from the Argonne* captures, in a
Midwestern microcosm, all the interpretive tensions and ideological divisions that prevented both Jazz Age and Depression-era Americans from
achieving a true consensus over the meaning of the Great War. And, thematically, the painting goes even further than that. Among its creator's
most ambiguous works, this cryptic scene both harnesses the energy of
commemorative ritual, one of the primary means by which communities
construct and perpetuate their sense of the past, and ultimately underscores the terrifying hollowness of that very ritual. To view this canvas
is to feel simultaneously the force and the failure of war remembrance
when confronted with a conflict fought far away—somewhere far over the
Kansas rainbow—for a questionable cause and with dubious outcomes.

However, before interpreting *The Return of Private Davis from the Argonne* as a rumination on war memory, we must first turn to its multiple
contexts: to the young soldier whom Curry immortalized (and *may* have
mourned); to the initially controversial program, run by the War Depart-

20. *The Return of Private Davis from the Argonne* (1928–1940) by John Steuart Curry. Oil on canvas, 38 x 52 in. Courtesy of the Westervelt-Warner Museum.

ment, that between 1920 and 1923 transferred the remains of more than forty thousand fallen soldiers from AEF cemeteries in France and Belgium to American communities spread from coast to coast; to the artist's exposure to World War I remembrance through memorials and literature; and, finally, to Curry's isolationist political convictions. The painting's social-historical milieu and biographical origins help to explain its thematic complexity and, ultimately, its many contradictions.

One especially poignant thread in the work's tangle of meanings is the sad, almost grotesquely ironic story of Pvt. William L. Davis, who died at age twenty-three as a result of wounds received on his very first night in the trenches. Indeed, British war poets such as Siegfried Sassoon or Wilfred Owen could not have devised a more sardonic illustration of war's senseless cruelty. Eager to play his part in the war, Private Davis had traveled thousands of miles and endured months of training in preparation for his single night of frontline service. According to Davis's father, who filed a short biography of his son with the Kansas State Historical Society, William "was among the first" to respond to "his country's call."[63]

He enlisted in Company B of the Third Kansas Infantry Regiment (head-quartered in Oskaloosa, Kansas) in June 1917, just two months after the American declaration of war, and trained at Camp Doniphan, Oklahoma, where the National Guard units of Kansas and Missouri were merged to create the 35th Division.[64] After six months, the Third Kansas, now known as part of the 139th Infantry, moved by rail from Camp Doniphan to Hoboken, New Jersey, where it set sail for Liverpool, England.[65] Fourteen days later, Davis and his comrades reached the western British shore, then traveled overland to Southampton, where they boarded the ships that would take them across the English Channel—the most dangerous leg of their journey. Following a tense but uneventful crossing, the regiment began a new round of training under British instructors in Normandy. Three months later the 139th finally entered the trenches, assuming control of a sector in the Vosges Mountains, about fifty miles from the Swiss-Alsatian border, the southern tip of the Western Front.[66]

Although the Vosges Mountains had seen their share of fighting, especially at Hartmannsweilerkopf (where tens of thousands of French and German combatants died), by 1918 the region was relatively quiet, the perfect place for green American troops to become acclimated to modern warfare—and to demonstrate their belligerency. While French forces in the area happily practiced a policy of "live and let live" by staying to themselves and not provoking their adversaries unless absolutely necessary, the men of the AEF, new to the war and eager to prove themselves to their skeptical allies, pursued a more aggressive policy—one that would cost Private Davis his life. In the 139th Infantry, as in other units, officers regarded American control of no-man's-land as imperative, and in addition to eagerly organizing raids against the enemy, they established outposts far forward of the American frontline trenches.

On the night of July 31, 1918, their first night at the front, Davis and another soldier received orders to stand guard at one of these hazardous positions. What happened next will probably never be known for certain. According to the account published in the *Winchester Star* on September 27, 1918, as soon as the two sentries entered the outpost, Davis "was wounded and captured by a squad of Germans, but he put up such a hard fight that his captors beat him over the head with their rifle butts and left him for dead, near the German wire entanglements, where he was found by his comrades next morning."[67] The interests of wartime propaganda, one suspects, partially shaped this narrative. Davis, the article is careful to point out, had not willingly allowed himself to be captured. Instead, he had struggled valiantly until bludgeoned by the Huns, who then "left him for dead." In this version of the story, Davis's pluck combined with the Germans' brutality overshadows the terrible irony of his early demise.

By 1921, the year of Davis's return and reburial, the story had become more ambiguous. Indeed, an article on the funeral published in several Jefferson County newspapers included testimony from an anonymous "comrade" in Company B, who related a somewhat different version of Davis's death. His account, apparently taken from a wartime letter composed while Davis was hospitalized, ran as follows:

> Immediately after entering the outpost trenches Davis and other Sentry were challenged by four big Boche. Davis opened fire on them. They threw a bomb into the trench, wounding both Davis and the other man. Well, the Boche jumped into the trench and dragged Davis out, kicking and beating him, until Ralph Nichols [another member of Company B] saw them and opened fire on them. But he couldn't see Davis. Next morning Davis was missing, so they sent out a patrol to look for him and found him caught in the barb wire entanglement. They got him back into the trenches and sent him to the hospital. He has a scalp wound that is pretty bad.[68]

In this version the specific cause of Davis's death, which occurred one week later as a result of "blood loss and exposure," remains concealed in the fog of war.[69] The private may have received his presumably fatal "scalp wound" when the German grenade detonated or when he was violently taken prisoner. However, the story also accommodates an even more terrible possibility never mentioned in 1918—namely, that Davis died as result of so-called friendly fire. Could Ralph Nichols have shot him without knowing it? Was Davis mortally wounded by one of his own comrades? As if to ward off such unsettling questions, the article ends with a predictably patriotic gloss on the narrative: "Those who can read between the lines of this brief sketch can find a story of true heroism beginning with enlistment and ending with a brave and hard fight hand to hand with an attacking force that was two to one. He died for the honor of his Country and for the Liberty of Humanity and the World."[70]

Private Davis's father and stepmother (John W. Davis's first wife died in 1906) were well acquainted with such grandiloquent rhetoric. The couple's first news of William's injury and subsequent demise came in the usual fashion—in a series of less than expansive telegrams from the War Department that indicated first that William Davis had been seriously wounded, then that no details on his condition could be provided, and finally that he had died of his wounds. However, such matter-of-fact discourse was largely limited to these telegrams, and after a time it was replaced by more compassionate correspondence from a number of sources, beginning with the Red Cross, which sent the family a photograph of the wooden cross marking Davis's grave. As documented in the collection of family materials recently donated to the National World War I Museum by William's nephew, Donald Davis, nearly everything else that John and his wife received related to William's death valorized his enlistment as service to civilization—or to Christ, the two being nearly synonymous. Among the expressions of sympathy that the Davis family received, for example, was a "Gold Star" greeting card sent by the Military Sisterhood of Oskaloosa, Kansas. Bearing the celestial symbol of military sacrifice, the card also featured a poem, the first lines of which read: "His life in the balance, Jesus / Counted not dear / But poured it out for truth."[71] Similarly, the commercially produced remembrance card that the Davises mailed to friends and family offered reassurance that William had "heard Humanity's / Clear call / And knew the voice Divine."[72] Not surprisingly, John W. Davis internalized this idealistic language of consolation and used it when describing his son for the Kansas State Historical Society. His biography of William L. Davis ends with the following: "He was a lover of home and friends and never shrank from his life's duties. He died for humanity which will make his memory sacred to peace loving Americans."[73]

These words, composed by a grief-shaken parent, contain a revealing tension. John W. Davis finds solace, first, in the notion that his son died not for a nation, but for "humanity." All nations, in other words, will benefit from his sacrifice. Thus, the father's word choice evokes the lofty vision of international progressivism—making the world safe for democracy—that underwrote the American war effort. However, the rest of the sentence locates Private Davis's *memory* in his fellow countrymen and through the phrase "peace loving" points implicitly in the direction of American exceptionalism. Davis may have died for humanity, the passage implies, but his sacrifice will be understood best by his progressive homeland with its inherent abhorrence of armed conflict.

The ideological tug-of-war in this sentence—between defining the meaning of William Davis's death in international terms versus a more narrowly patriotic construction—reflects a national debate that would soon have a direct impact on John W. Davis and his family. Even before the armistice, the question of where America's war dead would ultimately rest drew fiery editorials in newspapers across the country. Forces on both sides of the issue quickly mobilized. In line with the AEF's international mission, as summarized by President Wilson's Fourteen Points, the War Department preferred that the dead remain in Europe, where they would serve as enduring reminders of the United States' selfless *intervention* in a conflict that might otherwise have destroyed European civilization. American war cemeteries in France and Belgium would let no one forget that the New World had saved the Old. In the summer of 1918 this position received a boost from Theodore Roosevelt, who insisted that the remains of his son Quentin, perhaps the most famous American casualty of the war, be left at the exact spot in the Aisne-Marne region where the flier's bullet-riddled aircraft had crashed. Discussed in more detail in the next chapter, Roosevelt's instantly famous metaphor for burial abroad— "where the tree falls there let it lie"—became a rallying cry for proponents of overseas cemeteries.[74]

Predictably enough, the American funeral industry, which obviously stood to lose a good deal of revenue if the dead remained in Europe, squared off against the War Department and the former president. Lobbyists representing the interests of morticians descended on Washington, DC. However, it would be a mistake to identify the repatriation campaign entirely—or even mostly—as arising from economic self-interest. Grieving families, not funeral home directors, formed the core of organizations such as the Bring Home the Soldier Dead League, one of the more prominent (and bizarrely titled) pressure groups to emerge during the controversy.[75] In the end the federal government elected to satisfy both camps. Legislation signed into law by President Wilson in 1919 gave families the option of either allowing their fallen loved ones to be memorialized in permanent overseas cemeteries or having their dead returned to them at governmental expense. Moreover, each family would have until 1923 to decide, a generous time frame subsequently narrowed by diplomatic problems. Lack of cooperation from the French government, which was understandably concerned about the possible health risks posed by the transportation of tens of thousands of cadavers on French trains, delayed the start of the repatriation program until March 1920.[76]

The details of Private Davis's homeward journey were more or less standard, as reflected by the formulaic governmental correspondence that John W. Davis received during the weeks leading up to the body's return. For example, a form letter from the head of the Cemeterial Division of the Quartermaster General's Office reminded the Davis family that the War Department could not share information with the American Legion or any other patriotic organization.[77] Thus, if the Davises wished to include an honor guard in the funeral proceedings, then they would have to contact their local legion post directly, which they did. Another piece of official correspondence, signed by an officer in the Graves Registration Service, explained that Private Davis's war risk insurance provided up to one hundred dollars for funeral expenses.[78] To collect, the family would have to fill out a notarized form and attach the undertaker's bill. Perhaps the largest mass migration of the dead in American history—nearly half of the nation's one hundred thousand fallen soldiers were brought home—the repatriation program of 1920 to 1923 involved, by necessity, bureaucracy and paperwork, as well as patriotic spectacle.

On June 1, 1921, John W. Davis at last received word that his son was back in the United States; a telegram from the Graves Registration Service announced that Private Davis's remains would leave Hoboken, New Jersey, the terminus for ships carrying bodies from France, at 10:30 AM and arrive in Winchester "Via [the] Union Pacific Railroad" in a matter of days.[79] As it turned out, the trip from the eastern seaboard to the heart of the American Midwest took more than seventy-two hours. Davis's flag-draped casket finally reached Winchester on Saturday, June 4, one day before the memorial service that Curry would spend twelve years fashioning into art.

In many respects *The Return of Private Davis from the Argonne* re-creates that event with considerable accuracy. According to Donald Davis, Curry's depiction of John Davis, seen kneeling by the side of the coffin, is a nearly perfect likeness.[80] And the news coverage published in the *Winchester Star* and elsewhere attests to the accuracy of other features, especially the phalanx of soldiers (from nearby Fort Leavenworth) and uniformed American Legion members who stand in the left side of the crowd. A close examination of the painting reveals that the words "Winchester, Kansas," and "Legion" appear, along with the legion's star emblem, on one of the three flags carried by the honor guard—a meticulously rendered historical detail.

At the same time, however, Curry exercised his artistic license and made creative adjustments where necessary for the sake of his themes. Note, for example, that the very title of the painting is a factual inaccuracy that nonetheless amplifies the work's cultural resonance. As we have seen, Private Davis did not return from the Argonne. He was actually buried in Alsace, where he died more than a month before the Argonne battle began. Curry probably knew this.[81] Davis's heroic struggle when accosted by the "four big Boche" no doubt figured prominently in the sermons and tributes delivered on June 5, 1921. And even if Curry did not attend the funeral, it seems likely that this story concerning a celebrated classmate, one of the earliest Kansas casualties, would have reached him in some form. By tying Private Davis to the Argonne, the biggest battle in American history, Curry erased the distractingly anomalous circumstances of the young man's death and in so doing made him a more representative symbol of the nation's war dead. Thus, nowhere does the painting hint at Davis's peculiar destiny as a possible victim of hand-to-hand combat (the ultimate rarity on the World War I battlefield) or, worse, friendly fire. Nowhere does the canvas acknowledge the absurdity of Davis's real-life demise, his cosmically ironic misfortune on his very first night in the trenches. Instead, Curry shifts his irony away from the details of Davis's death to the broad outline of his ideologically dubious return. The title of the painting not only transplants Davis to a battle where more than twenty-six thousand Americans were killed (including seventeen members of Company B), but it also underscores the central tragedy of any war.[82] *The Return of Private Davis from the Argonne* reads like a happy picture of a warrior's triumphant homecoming from a hard-fought battle. What the painting actually depicts, however, is the return of some bones in a flag-covered box. Chillingly, the title of the painting reminds us that only the lottery of combat—particularly cruel and capricious in Davis's case—determines which kind of return a soldier will have.

Curry's other significant departure from fact involves the painting's unsettling perspective. In an early sketch of Davis's graveside service, the artist set the point of view much closer to the ground, nearly on an even level with the figures.[83] In this version we see the ceremony as if we, too, are in the cluster of mourners. The finished painting creates a very different effect. Here we are above the crowd, looking down—almost as if we are the disembodied spirit of Private Davis himself. And the countryside is tilted in such a way that the vast immensity of the prairie, against which Winchester's water tower shows up as a mere speck, appears to mock the spiritual ceremony in the foreground, making it small even as it occupies nearly half of the canvas. To achieve this point of view, Curry modified the landscape of his youth—just as he had done for different artistic (and arguably commercial) purposes in his other famous Kansas paintings. In this case, considerable topographical manipulation came into play. The Winchester City Cemetery (known in 1921 as the Wise Cemetery), where William L. Davis is actually buried, sits on a hillside that slopes eastward at a relatively steep pitch two miles southeast of the town. From Davis's gravesite it is impossible to see Winchester in the distance—the slope is just too steep, the grave too far from the summit. Indeed, even if a twenty-foot tower were erected at the spot, it would not offer the view that Curry has painted.

Clearly, then, Curry did not aspire to create a completely realistic depiction of Davis's reburial. Commercial considerations perhaps explain why. As historians Marjorie Swann and William M. Tsutsui have persuasively demonstrated, Curry of Kansas (who spent much of his career living in Connecticut) was adept at giving his East Coast audience what it wanted: scenes, the more violent or grotesque the better, of exotic flatlanders inhabiting a strange, monotonous landscape.[84] Unfortunately for Curry, this approach to Kansas subjects proved less successful when practiced within his home state. The controversial imagery in his Kansas statehouse murals, especially the towering figure of a crazed John Brown, led to a falling out between Curry and the Kansas legislature and, ultimately, to the termination of his commission in 1941, a blow from which the artist never completely recovered. In the case of *The Return of Private Davis from the Argonne*, however, Curry has done more than capitalize on Kansas oddity, topographical or otherwise. Here the landscape of the Great Plains, as much imagined as real, provides the perfect setting for a complex work that addresses both the unsettled memory of World War I and the likelihood of the United States becoming entangled in an even bloodier European conflict.

Beyond the sad and ironic story of William L. Davis, Curry's artistic milieu and personal experiences, both during the First World War and afterward, also helped shape the content of his painting. As Charles C. Eldredge has recently shown in his book-length analysis of *Hoover and the Flood*, Curry's historical paintings operate on multiple levels and draw upon far more cultural and biographical sources than one might at first imagine.[85] In *The Return of Private Davis from the Argonne*, a painting with an especially lengthy gestation period, this density of meaning is particularly striking. For example, at least two works by other painters probably influenced Curry's composition. While studying drawing in Paris in 1927, he may have seen Gustave Courbet's *A Burial at Ornans* (1849), a twenty-foot-long canvas that inspired heated controversy within Paris art circles by depicting a commonplace ceremony, attended by ordinary middle-class citizens, on a scale ordinarily reserved for scenes of epic historical events. Like Curry's painting, Courbet's emphasizes landscape. The rocky bluffs depicted in the background of his burial scene mirror the craggy emotional texture of the ceremony in the foreground, where some of the participants weep decorously while others look away or talk among themselves. Satire inhabits the literal and figurative margins of Courbet's painting—just as it does in Curry's treatments of Kansas subjects. A more somber and straightforward canvas by Harvey Dunn, Curry's mentor in the early 1920s, probably also had a direct influence on *The Return of Private Davis from the Argonne*. Completed shortly before Curry began work on his own depiction of a burial on the Great Plains, Dunn's *I Am the Resurrection and the Life* (1926) portrays a small group of mourners perched atop a bleak, windswept hill in the Dakota Territory. Once again, landscape is central to the painting's effect. Over the shoulders of the pioneers, open grassland stretches for miles in a series of wavelike crests. The only houses one can discern appear as mere dots on the horizon, looking more like ships on the Atlantic than domiciles anchored in the earth. As Henry Adams observes of this painting, "Dunn focuses on the seriousness of the scene" and avoids any hint of irony or satire.[86] Nevertheless, his emphasis on the threatening vastness of the frontier, set against the determined efforts of its inhabitants to find meaning in death and comfort in ritual, anticipates Curry's approach.[87]

Combined, Courbet and Dunn provided Curry with a compositional template full of thematic possibilities. However, the themes that Curry ultimately chose to explore had as much to do with his recent past (and fears for the future) as they did with the paintings that he appears to have partially imitated. Like many men of his generation—including, for example, F. Scott Fitzgerald and William Faulkner—Curry was haunted by the war that he had narrowly missed. Guilt and disappointment, born of the artist's inability to join in the Great War, perhaps initially dominated his feelings toward the conflict. In 1917, while studying at the Chicago Art Institute, he had hoped to join one of the U.S. Army's camouflage units, common destinations for artists. However, he unknowingly passed the deadline for voluntary enlistment, which came much earlier than expected, and the war ended before his draft registration number was called. A photograph from 1918, taken shortly after Curry transferred to Geneva College, shows the artist in uniform, his head shaved above his ears, looking very much the part of a doughboy. However, Curry's service never went beyond a few weeks in the Student Army Training Corps. As if to compensate for his civilian status, his letters to his parents from this period expressed a youthful bellicosity. He repeatedly conveyed his desire to join the fighting in France, and in the martial spirit of the time he noted slackers among the service workers at the Chicago Art Institute: "Everybody talks war and nobody goes. There is an unpatriotic bunch at the cafeteria. They are all Germans or sympathizers."[88]

In the 1920s Curry's attitude toward the war changed considerably, thereby setting the stage for his well-documented support of isolationism in the late 1930s. Among the events that shaped this reassessment, Private Davis's funeral in 1921 probably played a lesser role. Curry's disenchantment with the war seems to have come later as the painter became more intimate with loss, via a sudden family tragedy, and as antiheroic literature and film redefined popular memory of the conflict. In other words, for Curry, Davis's reburial acquired over time a set of meanings that it did not necessarily possess in 1921. Later events combined to magnify its significance. Much of this process apparently occurred toward the end of the first postwar decade. During his period of European study in 1927, Curry visited and, in fact, sketched one of the American battle cemeteries on the former Western Front, an already emotional experience made more poignant still by a subsequent bereavement, which may have colored and intensified the artist's reflections on the loss of so many young men.[89] Within several months of Curry's return to the United States, his younger brother, Paul, who had fallen ill while enrolled at Harvard Law School in 1916, suddenly died at the Mayo Clinic in Rochester, Minnesota. In her account of this sudden tragedy, Curry scholar M. Sue Kendall notes that Paul's untimely death "may help to explain the origins of *Baptism in Kansas*."[90] Seeing his sibling struck down so unexpectedly "spurred Curry to recall a powerful religious experience from his youth and to explore that memory in paint."[91] A similar connection can be drawn between Paul's demise and *The Return of Private Davis from the Argonne,* which Curry started less than a year after his return from Europe and just months after losing his brother. Perhaps the terrible spectacle of a promising life cut short led Curry's imagination back to the American memorials and grave markers that he had just seen in France—and then further back, to a schoolmate's posthumous and bitterly ironic return from a war that had killed him on his very first night as a combatant. In short, by 1928 Curry had no shortage of personal reasons to reflect artistically on death and commemoration, albeit in a way that would once again play to his East Coast clientele.

The painter's exposure to works of First World War literature and other cultural engagements with war memory perhaps also played a role in his depiction of Private Davis's homecoming. According to Curry's biographer, Laurence E. Schmeckebier, the painter's sensitivity to the "tragedy, suffering, and death" produced in such superabundance on the Western Front came partially through his reading, which included Alfred Noyes's famous poem "The Victory Ball" (1918), a work that in some respects anticipates *The Return of Private Davis from the Argonne*.[92] Like Curry's painting, "The Victory Ball" focuses on a patriotic ceremony, in this case a dance to mark Germany's defeat, and on a homecoming of sorts. While the dancers celebrate, the phantoms of dead soldiers, who have at last returned from France, move about the ballroom unseen, undercutting the gaiety with their spectral presence. Curry's painting creates a similar effect through its ghostly point of view: as discussed previously, we look down on Davis's patriotic burial from an odd, unearthly perspective— as if witnessing the event through the dead man's eyes. Noyes's mockery of the idealism that led these soldiers to their deaths perhaps also struck a responsive chord in Curry. While the participants in the Victory Ball abandon themselves to sensuality—"Gripped by satyrs"—the dead look on, surprised at how little the world has changed as a result of their passing:[93]

"What did you think
    We should find," said a shade,
"When the last shot echoed
    And peace was made?"
"Christ," laughed the fleshless
    Jaws of his friend,
"I thought they'd be praying
    For worlds to mend."[94]

As we will see, Curry's use of space in his treatment of Davis's burial, combined with various satirical touches, offers a similarly unsettling critique of the ultimate value of military sacrifice.

It is also important to note that Curry began work on *The Return of Private Davis from the Argonne* at a time when efforts to grapple with the meaning of the First World War took on a new level of intensity in the United States and found a greater variety of cultural expression than ever before. Like Dunn's covers for the *American Legion Monthly*, Curry's painting should be set against the backdrop of the Second AEF, the Gold Star Mother Pilgrimages, and the international boom in First World War literature and cinema. This wave of war-related cultural activity at the end of the 1920s perhaps provided the market-savvy painter with yet another form of inspiration: from a commercial standpoint, the time was right for Curry to paint a Kansas scene that would intersect with the larger subject of America and the Great War. Personal tragedy, various artistic and cultural influences, and (last but not least) the marketplace all form part of the backdrop for the work.

During the late 1930s politics joined this tangle of influences and creative stimuli. Ordinarily reticent on matters of state, Curry openly expressed his isolationist views. In an interview conducted shortly before he delivered a public lecture in Cincinnati, the painter remarked, "I studied in France—but [I] don't think we ought to feel it our duty to go to war every time France and other European nations resume their 1,000 year-old quarrels."[95] Moreover, he warned that another large-scale conflict would extinguish the artistic renaissance of which regionalism was a part: "After the World War there began a splendid resurgence in Art in America, and we are in the midst of this movement now—but war will kill it before it can reach its flowering. . . . War and beauty," the painter added, "do not go together."[96] Established, by this point, as the official artist in residence at the University of Wisconsin (the first such position in American history), Curry found a like-minded friend in the outspoken governor of Wisconsin, Philip F. La Follette, a leader in the America First movement.[97] Indeed, in 1938 Curry painted the inauguration of La Follette's National Progressive Party, which included the avoidance of foreign entanglements as a central feature of its platform, at the University Stock Pavilion in Madison. Further evidence of Curry's support for isolationism came in 1940, when he wrote to Kansas senator Arthur Capper to congratulate him on his opposition to the Lend Lease Act: "You're 100% right," Curry declared, "in your stand on our Foreign policy in the Senate."[98]

The myriad sources and influences outlined above help to explain the ambiguities that permeate Curry's canvas. Is *The Return of Private Davis from the Argonne* a tribute to a lost friend and an American hero (albeit one whose death could not have been more ironic)? A depiction of mourning colored by Curry's own family tragedy? A vision of pointless military sacrifice, of waste, inspired by antiheroic war literature and film? A grim warning of war's costs delivered by an openly isolationist painter? Or yet another somewhat exploitive rendering of Kansas exotics produced with non-Midwestern buyers in mind? Remarkably, the painting lends itself to all of these interpretations. Tension and contradiction appear everywhere. Note, for example, that Davis's casket, decorated with the Stars and Stripes, actually leads our eye away from the American scene for which it serves as the epicenter. Forming a vertical line, in a painting dominated by horizontals, the coffin points toward the distant horizon, reminding the viewer, as art historian Henry Adams has observed, "that Davis died in a far-away place, for remote and mysterious reasons."[99] This feature of the painting raises a question that goes to the heart of American memory of the First World War, memory that failed during the 1920s and 1930s to settle into a coherent body of cultural myth shared by most Americans. Does the true meaning of Davis's death reside in the nation to which he has returned or in the "far-away place" from which he has come? Indeed, one can read Curry's painting, on this level, as an ambivalent response to the specific policy debate that surrounded the postwar commemoration of America's fallen soldiers. Whose agenda offered the most meaningful form of remembrance—advocates of repatriation, who wished to reconnect the fallen with the commemorative traditions of their homeland, or supporters of overseas cemeteries, who hoped, in a sense, to keep America's war dead permanently enlisted in the cause of international progressivism? By splitting the viewer's attention between the patriotic ceremony and the distant skyline, which no one attending Davis's reburial could actually have seen, Curry suggests that this question has no answer. Thus, his painting simultaneously evokes the passions of isolationism and internationalism (passions that the painter had felt at different points in his life), but sides with neither as a response to the Great War.

The painting's perspective, almost cinematic in the way that it zooms over the crowd (as if drawn irresistibly by that distant horizon), also creates a sense of emotional distance between the viewer and the scene. And what appears initially as an almost sentimental celebration of Midwestern patriotism and heartland religiosity soon takes on darker, more ironic significance. On the surface the painting offers a touching display of small-town unity and military fidelity. Indeed, unlike Courbet, Curry has painted his provincial mourners in attitudes of genuine grief. There is nothing perfunctory about their participation in the service. Heads bowed, the townspeople lean toward the coffin with an air of protectiveness, as if reassuring the dead man that he is still part of their community. The military participants in the ceremony, regular soldiers and uniformed legionnaires, likewise claim Davis as one of their own; these olive-drab figures stand stiffly at attention, absorbed in paying the proper ritualistic tribute.

Such, it is worth noting, were the thematic elements that presumably appealed to the painting's buyers in 1940. Through donations from thirty local individuals (collected over the course of a yearlong subscription campaign), the Alonzo Cudworth American Legion Post No. 23 in Milwaukee acquired *The Return of Private Davis from the Argonne* for fifteen hundred dollars, less than half the price listed by the artist's New York gallery.[100] On May 31, 1940, Curry presented the painting to the legionnaires at a formal dinner held in the post's Cudworth Memorial Building. The subject of stories in both the *Milwaukee Tribune* and the *Milwaukee Journal,* this ceremonial gathering added yet another chapter to the story of William Davis's posthumous commemoration as the piece of art that bore his name became part of a sacred space (itself named after a dead man) devoted to the memory of the Great War. On the surface at least, *The Return of Private Davis from the Argonne* became fused through this event with an institutionally sanctioned version of war memory—namely, that of the American Legion, which continued (even as it embraced isolationism) to glorify military service and sacrifice. Not surprisingly, patriotic officialdom dominated the proceedings. Just as dignitaries of various kinds had spoken over the private's remains nearly twenty years earlier, official representatives ranging from the mayor of Milwaukee to two U.S. Army colonels now paid homage to Curry's painting.[101]

Perhaps the most interesting—and revealing—comments made during the dinner came from Alfred G. Pelikan, the director of the Milwaukee Art Institute. Tellingly, Pelikan acknowledged that a "few post members" had earlier questioned the appropriateness of the painting for a legion "clubhouse."[102] (Did these members, one wonders, already perceive the many tensions that lurked beneath the work's veneer of sentimentality?) As the occasion's sole spokesman for high culture and aesthetics, the director took it upon himself to defend the painting. After praising the picture as a "great work of art," he promised "those who had doubts that months from now they would find a depth of feeling wrought in the canvas by the artist that they do not find today."[103]

In his assertion that Curry's painting requires more than one viewing before its full "depth" becomes apparent, Pelikan was accurate. However, the meaning revealed by such repeated examination is quite different from what the director had in mind. A closer look at this supposedly patriotic and sentimental canvas reveals discordant details. As we have seen, Curry does not call the sincerity of his mourners into question. Thus, in this regard his painting bears a stronger resemblance to Dunn's *I Am the Resurrection and the Life* than to Courbet's *A Burial at Ornans*. However, there is something *off* about the Protestant preacher at the center of the painting. Captured at a moment of dramatic gesticulation, in the midst of a sermon whose clichéd, neo-patriotic content is easy enough to imagine, the preacher seems curiously animated for such a solemn occasion; thus, he is perhaps a satirical figure consistent with Curry's tongue-in-cheek depiction of Bible belt evangelicalism in such works as *Baptism in Kansas* and *The Gospel Train*. Here again the artist defines Kansas exoticism in terms of quirky religious practice. Notice, too, that the preacher's grandiloquent gesture does not lead the eye upward. Lost in the crowd of mourners and swallowed by the vastness of the prairie, it is an empty gesture delivered in empty space—despite the sun rays that *almost* appear to deliver a benediction. This may seem like excessive interpretation except that gestures that call attention to themselves are one of the hallmarks of Curry's style. For example, in *Hoover and the Flood,* the centrally positioned figure of an African American Moses, arms lifted in praise to the heavens, conveys the painting's central themes of deliverance and salvation. More ambiguously, John Brown's outstretched arms in *The Tragic Prelude,* one of Curry's statehouse murals, simultaneously suggest his Christlike martyrdom and his destructive fanaticism (reinforced by the Kansas cyclone that spins and the fires that burn behind him). In *Hoover and the Flood* the central figure's hands stand out against a neutral background; in *The Tragic Prelude* John Brown's hands are bloody red compared to the coloring of his tanned, weathered face and the blue of the Kansas sky; in *The Return of Private Davis from the Argonne,* however, the preacher's hands blend entirely into the background of the mourners. It is his face—his speech, perhaps—that is highlighted. The preacher's raised hand can, of course, be read as a conventional invocation of the heavenly spirit. At the same time, however, the gesture accommodates a quite different interpretation, signifying a speaker who is lost in his own platitudes, pompously holding forth on a subject of which he knows nothing—namely, the war from which Private Davis has "returned."

The line of identical black Model T Fords that is visible behind the crowd likewise complicates the painting's meaning. In terms of composition, this string of automobiles creates a solid line of demarcation between the foreground and the background—between the cemetery and the distant expanse of fields—and thus contributes considerably to the illusion of depth. However, the townspeople's appropriately funereal vehicles also carry thematic significance by hinting at the deadening conformity of small-town America. This may seem to be a stretch. However, by the time Curry began work on *The Return of Private Davis from the Argonne*, the cult of the automobile had became a well-established target in the "revolt against the village" school of American fiction, a Midwestern literary movement with close thematic ties to Curry's more satirical Kansas paintings. For example, in Sinclair Lewis's *Main Street* (1920), the preoccupation with motoring displayed by small-town physician Will Kennicott, along with virtually all of his male cronies, becomes a prominent measure of the cultural vacuity of Gopher Prairie, Minnesota.[104] Willa Cather's Pulitzer Prize–winning novel, *One of Ours* (1922), likewise constructs the automobile as a symbol of rural Midwestern malaise. Significantly, the best driver in Cather's narrative of early twentieth-century Nebraska is the unsympathetic Enid Royce, a temperance advocate, vegetarian, and would-be missionary. Used primarily to carry its operator from one meeting of self-righteous reformers to another, Enid's Ford is described unpleasantly as a "black cubical object."[105] In both of these works, automobiles connote not freedom—not the open road—but the values of an oppressively insular small-town world where technology is valued over art, total compliance to social convention is demanded, and intellectualism is scorned. Would Private Davis, we wonder, have wanted to return to such a world? Curry, we know, left it as quickly as he could.

And then there is the honor guard, whose members stand ready with their rifles and bugle, beneath flags that one can almost hear flapping in the prairie wind. Disconcertingly, the faces of these men—those that we can see—are interchangeable and expressionless, as if stamped out with a military mold. And two of the uniformed standard bearers look almost sinister, their features blotted out by the shadows of their steel helmets, giving them the eerie appearance of doughboys in gas masks. Indeed, these spectral figures—Curry's version, perhaps, of the phantoms

21. *Parade to War, Allegory* (1938) by John Steuart Curry (American, 1897–1946), oil on canvas, 47 13/16 x 63 13/16 in. Gift of Barnett Banks, Inc., AG.1991.4.1. Courtesy of the Cummer Museum of Art and Gardens, Jacksonville, Florida.

who show up for the Victory Ball—remind one of the enlistees featured in the artist's 1938 painting *Parade to War,* living men, marching to glory amid ticker tape and applause, who simultaneously assume the appearance of corpses (see fig. 21). Thus, into what appears initially as a stirring portrait of martial tribute, Curry inserts a subtle critique of military regimentation as well as a grim reminder of the horrors of modern industrialized warfare.

In the end, then, *The Return of Private Davis from the Argonne* presents the First World War as an event that—in America, at least—defied translation into a stable body of collective memory. Whether representing the community, the church, the American Legion, or the army, the mourners depicted on Curry's canvas all labor to fit Private Davis into various social narratives—metaphorical equivalents of the flag-draped casket that houses his remains. The preacher, his face dramatically lit from above, Bible clutched to his chest, eulogizes a fallen Protestant crusader. The legionnaires, on the other hand, enfold Private Davis into a stern tradition of service and manliness that joins together American soldiers of all wars—regardless of their causes or outcomes. Flags, flowers, sermons, and salutes—the painting brings together multiple forms of commemorative apparatus, all of which are intended to make sense of a young American's death in the Great War, a death that in Davis's case constituted an ironic "satire of circumstance" worthy of Thomas Hardy. But the Kansas plains that seemingly extend forever in the background of the painting, an essential feature that Curry accommodated only by refashioning the topography of Jefferson County, are unmoved by the pomp and circumstance. Limitless and indifferent, they form an existential void within which the preacher's rhetoric and the honor guard's salute seem hollow and puny. Moreover, none of the consolatory narratives offered by either church or state seem to reach John Davis, who kneels alone, bent with grief, and lost in his private pain. Although completely surrounded by his fellow townspeople and dressed in his Sunday best, he is as removed from the ceremony as the lonely water tower on the horizon—perhaps the most devastating of the many ironies that Curry packs into this haunting study of war and remembrance.

By the time of its completion in 1940, Curry's exploration of the ambiguities of the First World War had also become a warning. Here again, Midwestern space lent itself particularly well to the national themes that the painting addresses. By depicting a burial in the landlocked heartland, *The Return of Private Davis from the Argonne* vividly demonstrates how far the tragic consequences of foreign intervention had reached in 1918—and might reach again. In this sense the painting carries a clear isolationist message, which is reinforced by the strange line of clouds, thunderheads in the making, that billow upward beyond the water tower, looking almost like the smoke produced by exploding artillery projectiles. Are these the clouds of another war waiting both literally and figuratively on the horizon? One year after finishing *The Return of Private Davis from the Argonne*, Curry depicted America's entry into the Second World War through a similar meteorological metaphor. Commissioned by *Esquire* magazine, Curry's painting *The Light of the World* (or *America Facing the Storm*) eschewed conventional patriotism in favor of apocalyptic imagery. Allegorical rather than realistic, the painting shows a group of Americans on the eastern seaboard, set against a medley of buildings that include a small-town church and Manhattan-style skyscrapers, as they gaze at a terrifying storm approaching from the Atlantic. With the arrival of war, the ominous belt of clouds depicted in Curry's Kansas painting has become a hurricane.

In his study *Renegade Regionalists*, James M. Dennis writes that "Wood, Benton, and Curry were entirely capable of hitting upon visual ideas of immediate social-political relevance."[106] The term "regionalism," he asserts, is a reductive misnomer for a body of work that is, in fact, highly modernist and engaged with issues of national, even international importance. Dennis's argument applies with special force to *The Return of Private Davis from the Argonne,* a so-called regionalist painting that captured the doubts and divisions of an entire nation as it struggled to "remember" the First World War—and as it contemplated the approaching storm clouds of an even worse conflict.

What conclusions, then, can we draw from the First World War paintings of Dunn, Pippin, and Curry? How does the study of these works add to our understanding of war remembrance in the 1920s and 1930s—or, more specifically, the failure of postwar culture to produce a cohesive master narrative for the war (or a stable body of collective memory) that lined up with the personal memories of most Americans? In the case of Dunn and Pippin, the conflict between the official and the vernacular came into play, just as it did in the discourse battle over the Unknown Soldier. For the African American artist, this conflict was twofold: Pippin's modernist paintings challenge far more than aesthetic orthodoxy; they square off against an official assessment of African American soldiers (an assessment backed by the American Legion, among others) that dismissed their abilities with egregious unfairness. At the same time, Pippin parted company, memory-wise, from the NAACP, which promoted its own official version of the war. Dunn's negotiation of the official and the vernacular carried the artist to a very different destination, demonstrating once again that memory is a "messy business." Paradoxically, as an official war artist in 1918, Dunn created an essentially vernacular mode of war painting, one rooted in direct frontline experience and largely indifferent to the War Department's expectations. It was not until the late 1920s that Dunn began, in a sense, to tow the official line that he had brashly ignored ten years earlier while serving as an artist in uniform. Dunn's covers for the *American Legion Monthly,* expressions of a neo-masculine version of war memory that celebrated toughness and "guts" (despite the questionable outcomes produced by American intervention and despite the legion's own eventual support for isolationism) should give scholars pause. Not everyone in American interwar culture dropped the supposedly discredited view of World War I as a worthwhile and affirmative national experience. Indeed, many veterans—like Dunn and his fellow legionnaires—found that they could continue to celebrate their service in the war, and do so in a way that reached out to American youth, without having any further connection with Wilsonian internationalism.

In John Steuart Curry's *The Return of Private Davis from the Argonne*, the official and the vernacular appear simultaneously, layered on top of each other in a way that creates a truly disturbing effect. While the viewer cannot help but feel the emotional power of the remembrance ritual that Curry depicts, an event achingly expressive of state-sanctioned meaning (not unlike the changing of the guard at the Tomb of the Unknown Soldier), a satirical undercurrent, manifest in certain incongruous details and in the painting's use of landscape, provides a sardonic gloss on the proceedings. Gazing at this troubling canvas, the viewer cannot decide which interpretation to embrace—which is why, perhaps, the painting can be said to express the conflicted state of American war memory in the 1920s and 1930s with far more intensity than any other artwork from the period.

However, Curry's conflicted masterpiece does have one rival—not a painting, in this case, but an etching by the accomplished artist and peace activist, Kerr Eby.[107] An anti-Dunn in almost every way, Eby was born in Tokyo in 1889, to missionary parents, and trained in New York City, where his uncle, the founder of the prestigious Frederic Keppel and Company art gallery, helped boost his career. By 1917 Eby already enjoyed a reputation as one of the top etchers in the United States. However, the War Department rejected his application to the official artists program. Undeterred, Eby joined the AEF as a lieutenant in a camouflage unit (the kind of assignment that Curry tried to obtain), and during the American army's main operations he bore witness to the tortured zone just to the rear of the front line—a place of seemingly endless troop columns, massive accumulations of war materiel, ruinous villages, and dead bodies (both German and American) left in the wake of the fighting. Simultaneously fascinated and repelled, Eby sketched each and every terrible sight. Some of these sketches he subsequently turned into prints without any modification. Others provided the basis for more polished etchings, the artist's forte.

In the early 1930s, after a decade of additional success as a landscape artist (especially known for his New England scenes) and master printmaker, Eby became connected with various pacifist movements, and in 1935 the Keppel Gallery staged a one-man show that highlighted his

22. *September 13, 1918, Saint Mihiel* (1934) by Kerr Eby.

war scenes. One year later Yale University Press published a collection of these drawings and etchings, along with an eloquent preface by the artist, under the title *War*.[108] Brutally frank, at times even shocking, the pieces reproduced in this volume, a landmark collection in the history of American war art, turn Dunn's *American Legion Monthly* covers inside out. Indeed, it is hard to believe that Eby did not have the other artist in mind as a target. For example, while the doughboys featured in Dunn's second war series are, as we have seen, muscular and stalwart, but at the same time individualized, Eby's soldiers appear as faceless automatons, drooping with fatigue and lost amid the military mass. And his depictions of frontline carnage, devoid of any redemptive heroism, surpass even the grotesquery of Goya. Eby's sardonic titles only heighten the horror. A sketch of a severed head, for example, appears above the title *A Bit of the Argonne*. *One of Ours*, a blistering reference to Cather's novel, shows a dead body hanging from a tree. *Mama's Boy* depicts a soldier writhing on the ground with both feet shot off. And so forth.

However, the most powerful piece in *War* (and arguably Eby's masterpiece) is the etching *September 13, 1918, Saint Mihiel* (1934) (see fig. 22). Here, as in Curry's cryptic portrayal of Private Davis's homecoming, Eby pulls the viewer in several directions at once, thereby mirroring the confused state of postwar collective memory. It is an ingeniously ambivalent image. Beneath a gigantic thunderhead, which takes up nearly four-fifths of the paper, Eby has placed a column of antlike soldiers, stretching from one side of the picture to the other. Despite the ominous atmosphere created by such a dark sky, the scene seems at first sight heroic. Leaning forward, as if in a stiff wind, the American troops in the formation create a strong sense of motion, carrying the viewer's eye from right to left. The black cloud above somewhat resembles a giant wing, a symbol of victory. Pershing's unstoppable crusaders apparently have the Hun on the run. Closer examination, however, reveals that the soldiers are bent over with fatigue. One group struggles to dislodge a howitzer from the mud. And the vast cloud suddenly looks like a smear of blood effacing the heavens. Stepping back from this etching, one sees glory. Stepping toward it, exhaustion and futility. To return to the words of AEF artist J. André Smith, which serve as the epigraph for this chapter, war indeed changes as it poses for its portrait. And sometimes the portrait changes, too, as conflicting versions of memory collide and do battle in the same work.

4
Memory's End?

Quentin Roosevelt, World War II,
and America's Last Doughboy

All monuments are efforts, in their own way, to stop time.
　　　　　　　　—Sanford Levinson, *Written in Stone* (1998)

On July 14, 1918 (Bastille Day), Lt. Quentin Roosevelt, the youngest son of former president Theodore Roosevelt, was shot down and killed when his patrol of American airmen encountered a German force over Chamery, France. Accounts of the aerial battle vary greatly. German witnesses, members of the famed Flying Circus (led, at this point, by Hermann Goering, who had assumed command after Manfred Von Richtofen's death three months earlier) testified that the American fliers, part of the 95th Aero Squadron, had held the advantage through superior numbers. American reports maintained the opposite. The details of Roosevelt's final moments also remain unclear. According to one popular newspaper account, as Roosevelt's comrades fled toward their airfield, the Flying Circus closing in from above, Roosevelt banked his plane toward the pursuers and engaged them single-handedly, bringing down no fewer than two enemy aircraft during the last few seconds of his life.[1] A disgusted Eddie Rickenbacker later described this story as "absolute piffle."[2] Another version of the flier's demise, probably more accurate, describes a chaotic melee as the Germans descended on the American patrol without warning.[3] In this version of the dogfight Roosevelt displayed no more or less courage than his squadron mates. The novice fighter pilot simply found himself caught in the gunsite of a more experienced adversary, the identity of whom has become a matter of long-standing debate.[4] And then there is the erroneous legend, which grew up after the war, that Roosevelt, "a short-sighted man," died as result of mistaking German planes for American aircraft and joining them in formation.[5] Just days before his death,

Roosevelt had made this very blunder but managed to escape after scoring his first and only victory.

Whatever the facts (and they were quickly irrelevant), during the days and weeks that followed his demise, Quentin Roosevelt became *the* American casualty of the Great War. Killed on Bastille Day, youngest son of a bellicose former president who had delighted France and Great Britain with his white-hot condemnations of American neutrality, and likeable to boot, the twenty-year-old flier quickly inspired a veritable cult of remembrance. Poems written in the young aviator's honor appeared in scores of American newspapers, along with cartoons and editorials that contrasted Sagamore Hill's wartime record—all four of Theodore Roosevelt's male children saw action (one killed, two severely wounded)—with the kaiser's decision to assign his own sons to posts located far from harm's way. At the same time, the flier's name became a badge of honor. In the summer of 1918 one American airfield after another changed its name to Roosevelt Field. Some of these fields, now airports, bear the title still. The town of Bismarck, Pennsylvania, became Quentin, Pennsylvania. The French navy christened one of its vessels the *Quentin Roosevelt*. And the French community of Mauperthuis, where the pilot was billeted during the final weeks of his life, renamed its centuries-old public square Place Roosevelt.

Anything associated with the fallen flier took on the aura of the sacred. At the American aviation camp in Issoudun, where Roosevelt had trained air cadets while impatiently awaiting his assignment to the front, his first French aircraft (a training vehicle not outfitted for combat) was wheeled into a hangar by itself and treated as a holy relic. An officer from a nearby unit reported that mechanics and trainees who had known Roosevelt would invite visitors to sit in the cockpit so that they would have "something to remember him by."[6] Smaller mementoes that produced almost religious reverence included the "twisted, mutilated" axle from Roosevelt's crashed Nieuport, which assumed a place of honor alongside other pieces of family memorabilia in the North Room of Sagamore Hill, and a radiator and broken propeller (both allegedly taken from the same wreck) placed on display by a hotel owner in Château-Thierry. Here, as with so much of the story of Quentin Roosevelt's death and remembrance, irony abounds. Archie Roosevelt, Quentin's brother, noticed decades later that National Park Service officials at Sagamore had removed the axle from view for fear that it would disturb younger visitors. "People," he commented in response, "do not understand the Roosevelts and do not understand what we did in the war, who we were before the war, and who we were after."[7] And the aircraft parts displayed at Château-Thierry? They were a fraud, according to World War I guidebook authors Tonie and Valmai Holt. The radiator, they observe, comes from a different type of French aircraft than the one flown by the president's son.[8]

However, it was Roosevelt's solitary grave in a field near Chamery, located just a few yards from the place where his Nieuport fighter had slammed into the earth, that formed the epicenter of his commemoration (see fig. 23). Since he was shot down over occupied France, German troops conducted the burial service, and an American POW, captured during the Aisne-Marne fighting, later reported that he had witnessed Roosevelt receiving full military honors on July 15: "In a hollow square about the open grave were assembled approximately one thousand German soldiers, standing stiffly in regular lines. . . . Officers stood at attention before the ranks. Near the grave was the smashed plane, and beside it was a small group of officers, one of whom was speaking to the men."[9] On July 18, American troops retook Chamery, located the wreckage of Roosevelt's plane (soon ravaged by souvenir hunters), and found the flier's grave marked by a wooden cross inscribed "Lieutenant Roosevelt / Buried by the Germans." Members of the American 302nd Engineer Regiment subsequently erected their own cross-shaped marker, which identified Roosevelt as a member of the "Air Service U.S.A." resting "on the field of honor," and left behind a small stele marking the exact spot where Roosevelt had fallen.

The next party to decorate the grave consisted of Bill Preston, one of Quentin Roosevelt's classmates at Groton; Col. Frank Ross McCoy, once a White House aide to Theodore Roosevelt; and Father Francis P. Duffy of "Fighting 69th" fame. Presumably dispatched at the bequest of the former president, the three men arrived at Chamery four weeks after the flier's death and added yet another makeshift cross to the gravesite. At the same time, they probably secured the aircraft axle that became a keepsake for the Roosevelt family.[10] Several months later, as an expression of Franco-American unity, the French government provided a much more elaborate headstone, together with an oak railing designed to protect the grave from visitors. An American officer who happened to be in the vicinity witnessed the arrival of this "tribute from the French":

I was back of the lines . . . when down the road came a big open truck loaded with something which looked like a gigantic wooden

23. Quentin Roosevelt's grave near Chamery as it appeared in 1927.

bed—perhaps twelve feet long and eight feet wide [in actuality, the enclosure was five feet by six feet in size]. At the head of it there was a large shield, and above this a carved wooden cross. Did I not know the French idea of homage to the dead, I would not have recognized what it was. As we went by, I looked at the shield—in large carved letters I saw the words "Quentin Roosevelt."[11]

Fenced off like a shrine, Roosevelt's grave became one of the most visited—and most frequently photographed—spots on the Western Front. Indeed, it was perhaps the most famous grave of the First World War. Untold thousands of French and American troops, many on their way to or from battle, stopped to contemplate the flier's final resting place. Dignitaries visited in droves. And images of the gravesite, poignantly situated by itself amid a peaceful-looking tract of French earth, spread throughout popular culture (on both sides of the Atlantic) via commercial postcards and stereopticon slides. At the same time, a lurid image, an example of what one might call war porn, perpetuated Roosevelt's memory in a different and more disturbing way. Someone—whether French or German, no one could determine—had photographed the aviator's corpse while it rested next to his mangled aircraft. The resulting snapshot unsparingly records fatal gunshot wounds to the pilot's face. Produced commercially in Europe, this gruesome image became a popular souvenir postcard among American soldiers, presumably for its shock value, and was allegedly distributed in Germany as a piece of propaganda. Sadly, the photograph also fell into the hands of the Roosevelt family.

Whether translated into cultural currency through images of pastoral calm or violent grotesquery, Roosevelt's death was an iconic event that drew its power from a unique combination of cultural forces: the larger-than-life persona of Theodore Roosevelt; the romance and horrors of the world's first air war; and the sense of French-American kinship felt deeply by a significant portion of the population in both countries. And then there was Quentin Roosevelt himself, known as the "enlisted man's friend," who managed to live up to his father's standards of strenuous adventure-seeking while preserving his own unique and, by all accounts, captivating personality.[12]

Given these factors, one would have expected Roosevelt's memory, as constructed by both vernacular and official agents in 1918, to remain stable and secure during the decades that followed the war, his grave—again, perhaps the most famous grave of the entire conflict—a perpetual mecca for pilgrims, a destination as enduring in its meaning as the Pocket (the ravine in the Argonne Forest where the Lost Battalion made its stand) or Belleau Wood, sites of memory that continue to draw American visitors today. Such, however, would not be the case. By the end of the Great War, the story of Quentin Roosevelt and his resting place in France was only at its beginning. In the events that followed, the urgencies of family memory, enhanced by presidential prestige and political connections, took precedence over military and official agenda; American attitudes toward First World War commemoration, increasingly ambivalent and unsettled, clashed with those of the French, and the memory of one world war effectively effaced that of another. Ultimately, the twists and turns in the story of Roosevelt's memorialization reveal the fluid nature of war remembrance, as negotiated over time by multiple constituencies, and the impermanence of cultural memory (at least as that memory is originally formulated). Thus, this chapter will trace the strange destiny of the most celebrated casualty of World War I and then, in line with the theme of memory under revision, briefly examine how American culture from the 1940s through the early twenty-first century has remembered the First World War.

The Body of an American: The Postmortem Odyssey of Quentin Roosevelt, 1918–1959

During the closing months of the First World War, Quentin Roosevelt's grave near Chamery posed a dilemma for the U.S. Army Graves Registration Service, because it did not conform to official policy. All American war dead were supposed to be transferred to regional cemeteries, from which (it was thought at the time) they would eventually be returned to the United States. Yet officialdom, in this case, was outgunned: the request for an exception came straight from Theodore Roosevelt. In a letter to Charles C. Pierce, the head of the Graves Registration Service, dated November 2, 1918, Roosevelt expressed thanks for the service's recognition of his wishes and described the feelings behind them:

> My Dear Colonel Pierce:
> I thank you very much for your letter and the blue print of my son's grave, and I thank you even more for refusing to have the boy's body disinterred and transferred to one of our established cemeteries. His mother and I greatly prefer to have him lie where he fell and where the Germans buried him. When the war is over we will go to the place and have a little stone marked, but not have it interfere with the stone that is already there. We are very grateful to you for what you have done. We feel that where the tree falls there let it lie.
> With hearty thanks,
>   Faithfully yours,
>   Theodore Roosevelt[13]

As historian John Graham has noted, the former president's views on this most personal of matters soon became public and provided invaluable ammunition for mourning families who desired the option of leaving their fallen loved ones in France.[14] On November 18, 1918, the *New York Times* published in its entirety a letter written by Theodore Roosevelt to Army Chief of Staff Payton March several weeks before his communication with Pierce. Presenting a "respectful but most emphatic protest" against the notion of repatriating Quentin Roosevelt (and, by extension, any other deceased American soldier), the letter appeared under the eye-catching headline "Roosevelt Objects to Removal of Son."[15] From that moment on, the Roosevelt family's decision to leave the tree where it had fallen—an instantly famous metaphor—became a touchstone in the repatriation debate and probably had a direct impact on the War Department's decision in 1919 to allow families to decide whether their dead would be returned to the United States or not.

Although Roosevelt's published statement was, as Graham remarks, "greatly responsible for the thousands of Americans who left their sons' and husbands' bodies in Europe after World War I," he did not live to visit his son's grave.[16] Already ailing by the time of his correspondence with Payton March and Charles C. Pierce, Roosevelt succumbed to a heart embolism on January 6, 1919. However, the "stone" that he desired did become a reality even though its subsequent history was, as we will see, one that he could not have imagined and would not have sanctioned. Shortly after the former president's death, the Roosevelt family paid for a large marble slab that once sat beneath the wooden headstone provided by the French government and nearly filled the five-by-six-foot enclosure. On it were etched a pair of U.S. Army Air Service pilot's wings, the dates of Quentin Roosevelt's birth and death, a description of his Croix de Guerre (awarded posthumously), and a line from Percy Bysshe Shelley's "Adonais": "He has outsoared the shadow of our night." Nineteen-nineteen also saw the erection of two additional memorials intended to cement the pilot's memory within the corner of France where he had fallen. Mrs. Roosevelt commissioned the first of these, a functional memorial fountain, designed by the well-known architect Paul Philippe Cret (1876–1945), for the village of Chamery. Still standing today, the memorial features Lt. Quentin Roosevelt's name in large letters above an impressive lion's head, from which water falls into a stone trough. On each side of the lion's head appear the symbols of the French and American republics. A citizen of the United States, but French by birth and a veteran of the French army during the First World War, Cret was the perfect architect to capture the mythic dimensions of the flier's death: while the spigot in the center of the memorial suggests the masculine ferocity of the Roosevelt clan—Theodore Roosevelt, in fact, was nicknamed "the old lion"— the patriotic emblems on each flank establish Quentin as a member of two nations joined in sacrifice. The other memorial constructed in 1919, a bronze marker next to Roosevelt's grave, likewise emphasized French-American ties. Sent all the way from St. Louis, Missouri, the marker was a tribute from one of the very first American Legion posts established in the United States—a post named, appropriately enough, after Quentin Roosevelt, the most celebrated American casualty of the war.

The various commemorative fixtures presented so far in this chapter were all part of what American visitors to the Aisne-Marne region would have seen during the 1920s and 1930s, and it is perhaps useful to summarize them quickly. An inspector's report prepared by the ABMC in 1932 described a cluster of memorial apparatus at the Roosevelt gravesite: Above the marble slab with its pilot wings and quotation from Shelley, and enclosed by oak railings, stood the French headstone with its shield and cross. Next to the grave was the American Legion monument. And ten meters away to the northeast stood the stele, erected by the 302nd Engineers, marking the exact spot where Roosevelt's plane came down.[17] In Chamery, less than a kilometer away, visitors would have stopped at Paul Philippe Cret's elegant but practical memorial fountain before pressing on to the Hotel de l'Elephant in Château-Thierry, where the relics supposedly taken from Quentin Roosevelt's plane were displayed for the gullible.

Since there was no guest register at either the grave or the fountain, one cannot know for certain how many Americans made the pilgrimage to these sites during the interwar decades; however, the number must have run in the thousands, thanks in part to the involvement of remembrance organizations. A souvenir booklet for the American Legion's Second AEF convention includes Chamery among its list of memorable destinations for day trips from the French capital and features a full-page photograph of the gravesite.[18] Likewise, as John Graham has shown, Chamery was a regular stop on the Gold Star Mothers' pilgrimage itinerary. Indeed, a year before the first government-sponsored pilgrimage, Ethel Nock, Gold Star chairman of the American War Mothers, stressed the therapeutic value of visiting Chamery in a speech before Congress: "I hope that every mother who will be anywhere near Quentin's grave will be taken there. . . . The inscription on his grave [the line from "Adonais"] is the most comforting thing any woman can have said of her soldier son who has gone on."[19]

While the configuration of memorials at Roosevelt's gravesite remained intact between the wars—no monuments were added or taken away for more than two decades—the upkeep of the site was problematic. In 1927, Capt. E. J. Heller, a member of the American Legion Paris Post No. 1, found the oak enclosure "in bad shape" when he arrived to decorate the grave on Memorial Day.[20] Recorded in a newspaper article, his concern reached Mrs. Roosevelt at Sagamore Hill and produced assurance from Kermit Roosevelt, one of Quentin's brothers, that the fence would be "scraped and stained or repainted."[21] Within just five years, however, the effects of constant exposure to the elements were again apparent. The ABMC inspector's report from 1932 described the condition of the sepulcher as "fair" and noted that the French headstone was in need of painting.[22] Time had already begun its process of decay.

Adding to problems created by unsuitable building materials (a later report would recommend that the crumbling wood railing, now an eyesore, be replaced with cement) was the anomalous legal status of the gravesite, which belonged to neither the American nor the French government. Federal records reveal that the Roosevelt family maintained sole possession of Quentin's burial plot, having received the land as a gift from France, and that Theodore Roosevelt, perhaps unwisely, released the U.S. government from any responsibility for future maintenance of the site. As a result, in classic bureaucratic fashion, the ABMC painstakingly recorded the increasingly weathered condition of the grave but did nothing with the information. Thus, the 1932 inspector's report highlighted areas in need of repair or refinishing but concluded with the statement, "Recommend no further action be taken regarding this grave."[23]

Although the Roosevelt family employed "a French peasant" to maintain the site,[24] concerns about the deteriorating condition of Quentin Roosevelt's grave continued to reach U.S. Army officials in the 1940s. And the ABMC continued to wash its hands of the matter. In 1940, following the German invasion of France, the officer in charge of the ABMC's European office, Maj. Charles D. Holle, visited the grave as part of a general survey of American memorials. In particular, Holle wished to discover how many American memorials that had been hit by ordinance during the German blitzkrieg—or fallen prey to vandalism during the opening phase of the occupation. At Chamery, Holle found no "war damage." However, his report noted that the wooden railing, long identified as the least durable object at the gravesite, was in "bad condition": "The wood has rotted in a number of places, and the weathering has warped the wood and sprung some of the joints."[25] Suggesting that the enclosure be replaced, Holle even went so far as to obtain a price quote from a local carpenter, who calculated that a new railing would cost approximately thirty-six hundred francs. However, this recommendation never reached the Roosevelt family, thanks to a directive from none other than ABMC chairman John J. Pershing.[26]

Pershing's decision might seem puzzling. After all, he had no reason to do a disservice to the Roosevelts—far from it. In 1906 President Roosevelt had promoted Pershing from captain to brigadier general, "jumping him over 257 captains, 364 majors, 131 lieutenant colonels, and 110 colonels—in all, 862 officers senior to him."[27] In effect, Pershing owed his career to Roosevelt. Moreover, the former supreme commander had great affection for Quentin Roosevelt's older brother, Theodore Jr., a major in the First Division (Pershing's favorite unit in the AEF) and a member of the elite detachment of handpicked officers who accompanied the Iron Commander on his first trip to France in 1917. Inspired by neither personal animosity nor political calculation, Pershing's response to Holle's report was, if somewhat cold and inflexible, a matter of principle consistent with the foundational philosophy of the organization that he had chaired since 1923. From the beginning, the ABMC denied requests for individual memorials, no matter how heroic or distinguished the soldier in question, and, like its counterpart in Great Britain (the Imperial War Graves Commission), built permanent war cemeteries that stressed national unity and egalitarianism. Officers were buried among enlisted men. All soldiers received the same standardized headstone (a stone crucifix or Star of David). Personalized inscriptions on headstones were forbidden. Pershing and his fellow commissioners could not, of course, control the destiny of those remains that families opted to have returned to the United States. In fact, many soldiers among the repatriated dead received graveside memorials that were far more elaborate than anything permitted in France. However, with respect to the dead who remained overseas, the ABMC's position was clear: the ABMC would afford any fallen soldier a place of equal honor in one of the eight official war cemeteries; what it would not do was involve itself officially (or privately) with individual memorials that fell outside its scheme. For Pershing, this policy apparently applied even to the sharing of information with the Roosevelts.

In 1946 the question of just what role, if any, the federal government should play in the continued remembrance of Quentin Roosevelt came to a head when Archibald Roosevelt and his half sister, Edith Derby (the sole child of Theodore Roosevelt's first marriage), requested that the government assume responsibility for the upkeep of their brother's resting place. Their motives were perhaps partly financial. Although routine maintenance of the site had cost little—records show that the Roosevelts paid a woman from Chamery, one Madame Fourquest, ten dollars a year to clean the grave every Sunday and to plant flowers—more expensive repairs, such as the restoration of the wooden headstone and enclosure, had repeatedly been necessary. And given the millions spent by the ABMC on memorials and cemeteries in France, it would have been understandable if Quentin's siblings questioned the justice of their financial responsibility.

Yet their request most likely had less to do with money than with the tragically thin ranks of Theodore Roosevelt's family, now on the far side of its second world war. By 1946 only Archibald, Edith, and Ethel remained of the six Roosevelt children. Kermit Roosevelt, who had edited a memorial volume in honor of Quentin in 1922, slid into an alcoholic decline during the 1930s and committed suicide while serving with the U.S. Army Air Corps in 1943. One year later, Theodore Roosevelt Jr., who had rejoined his World War I unit to become one of the most decorated soldiers of World War II, died of a heart condition that he had carefully concealed from military doctors. Since both Kermit and Theodore Jr. rested in U.S. Army cemeteries, beneath standard headstones, Archibald and his sister may have felt that the continued enshrinement of Quentin, through a cluster of memorials whose upkeep they privately funded, had become inappropriate. Additional tragedies, in other words, had completely reshaped the context within which the Roosevelt family, what was left of it, viewed and understood Quentin's death. And then there was the slippage, obvious by 1946, in Chamery's status as a culturally resonant site of memory. Although the American Legion post in Paris continued to conduct a wreath-laying ceremony at the gravesite each Memorial Day, the stream of pilgrims that had once flowed into Chamery had now become a trickle.

Whatever its motives, the Roosevelts' request went nowhere. In a letter to Archibald dated October 16, 1946, Secretary of War Robert P. Patterson explained that the War Department could do nothing:

> This matter has been carefully looked into and you are advised that the records of this Department reveal the fact that "your parents released the United States Government from all future responsibility of Quentin's grave at Coulonges-en-Tardenois, Aisne, France, and assumed this responsibility in 1922. Therefore, the Army Graves

Registration Service has no connection with or jurisdiction over this grave whatsoever." Further, the records of the Department fail to show that the French Government has made a "Monument National" of the grave.

Patterson then passed the buck to another branch of the federal government: "If you desire to arrange for the future care and maintenance of your brother's grave it is suggested that you take the matter up with the State Department with a view to making such arrangements through the military Attaché in Paris."[28] In essence, then, Theodore Roosevelt's surviving children were trapped in a catch-22. Although they owned the land where Quentin was buried, apparently the land was not theirs to give away. Citing the Roosevelts' original waiver, the War Department would not go near Chamery. Nor, as the secretary of war's letter suggested, was the notoriously parsimonious French government a likely option.

The frustration that Archibald Roosevelt must have felt after receiving Patterson's letter would only have intensified had he known of the ABMC's latest display of bureaucratic inflexibility. Once again, the commission documented wear and tear at Chamery that it neither stepped forward to repair nor reported to the Roosevelt family. A new inspection of the gravesite, conducted shortly after Patterson received the Roosevelts' request, once again noted that the oak enclosure, long troublesome, needed replacement.[29] At the same time, architect John F. Harbeson, a member of the Philadelphia firm originally established by Paul Philippe Cret, happened to visit the memorial fountain in Chamery and expressed his concern about its upkeep in a letter to ABMC secretary Brigadier General Thomas North. At the close of his letter, Harbeson asked for clarification as to whether or not the commission could care for a memorial to an individual.[30] True to policy, North replied that the ABMC had "no official interest" in Cret's monument.[31] Harbeson subsequently wrote directly to Edith Derby, who apparently saw to it that the fountain was cleaned and repaired.[32]

Within months of the federal government's refusal to care for the grave, Quentin Roosevelt's surviving siblings made a new request of the War Department: they asked that Quentin's remains be disinterred and reburied in the American World War II cemetery at Saint-Laurent-Sur-Mer, next to those of their older brother, Theodore Roosevelt Jr. The path that had led the former president's eldest son to his own resting place in France would have made the "old lion" proud. After distinguishing himself in the

First World War, the twice-wounded Theodore Jr. had gone on to found the American Legion and to write a memoir, *Average Americans* (1919), of his service in the First Division.[33] In the 1930s he supported isolationism, but only halfheartedly. War brought out the best in him. In World War II he rejoined the "Big Red One" and commanded troops in North Africa, Sicily, and France—despite the fact that one of his First World War wounds had left him lame. Famous for leading from the front, Brig. Gen. Theodore Roosevelt Jr. bounced in and out of battle on a jeep nicknamed "Rough Rider," and for his fearless actions on Utah Beach he received the Congressional Medal of Honor. Henry Fonda would later play him in the 1962 Hollywood D-day epic, *The Longest Day*. But the strenuous life of service in two world wars came at a cost. Several weeks after the Normandy invasion, he collapsed in his command trailer and died of a heart attack at age fifty-seven. Although long aware of his diminished strength, the general had told no one of his coronary condition for fear that he would be discharged or confined to a desk.

Like their earlier request to the ABMC, Archibald and Edith's proposal for Quentin's exhumation and reburial probably reflected their discomfort with the inconsistent memorialization of their brothers, two of whom now rested in military cemeteries. In addition, the notion of reuniting Theodore Jr. and Quentin, heroic Roosevelts who died on French soil during two different wars, held an understandable sentimental appeal. Yet two additional motives came into play as well. In a letter to a family friend, Archibald explained that "it would be fine for us to have the two brothers together, especially since I am the only brother living of the four and when I die, none of Quentin's nephews and nieces would hardly know who he was. As they say, time marches on."[34] In other words, the transfer of Quentin's remains to Normandy, site of the epic D-day landings, would resituate his memory within a more vital context and thus ensure its survival. An icon of World War I would retain its meaning—or take on a different kind of meaning—once linked to the commemoration of World War II. And then, finally, there was the practical matter of upkeep. Since the maintenance of Quentin Roosevelt's private gravesite had already become problematic, just a few short decades after the armistice, what would happen as centuries passed?[35]

Despite these sound reasons, on March 25, 1948, Secretary of the Army Kenneth C. Royall wrote to Archibald with predictably bad news, maintaining that "neither existing law nor established policy of the Department of the Army permits the action you wish." Then, in an ironic twist that must have struck Archibald as a slap in the face, Royall went on to explain that he could not "break faith" with Theodore Roosevelt's "expressed desire" that his son forever remain at Chamery—a desire that had, since 1918, run directly contrary to War Department policy! Seeking to cut off any additional discussion of the matter, Royall closed his letter with a phrase that by now the Roosevelts had doubtless seen many times before in communications from the War Department—"no further action is contemplated."[36]

However, seven years later, federal resistance to the notion of burying the two Roosevelt brothers side by side finally began to evaporate, thanks primarily to the political influence of Eleanor Roosevelt, Theodore Jr.'s widow. In the mid-1950s Eleanor not only served as one of the eight commissioners on the head board of the ABMC, but she also enjoyed a friendly relationship with ABMC secretary Thomas North, the same officer who had earlier maintained that his organization had "no official interest" in Quentin Roosevelt's grave. In a letter to North dated June 4, 1954, Eleanor reintroduced the Roosevelt family's request as her own, suggesting that her brother-in-law's grave "be placed as close as possible" to her husband's at the American cemetery in Saint Laurent. In addition, she asked that the Roosevelts be allowed to transport the marble gravestone at Chamery back to Sagamore Hill.[37]

Although the ABMC officially approved the Roosevelts' proposal on April 6, 1955, several potential difficulties still stood in the way. First and foremost was the matter of the French. How would the citizens of Chamery respond to the loss of a cultural landmark (and tourist attraction) that had been part of their community since 1918? Ironically, Eleanor inadvertently raised this very issue in a different context. After receiving a lengthy letter from the former mayor of Saint-Mere-Eglise, who passionately argued against the removal of American "Unknowns" (casualties of the D-day campaign) from the local cemetery, she asked General North to "drop [the former mayor] a line and set his heart at rest."[38] Fearing a similar reaction in Chamery, North wisely counseled the Roosevelts to clear their plans with local French authorities. Thus, Archibald undertook the task of composing in French a torturously diplomatic letter outlining the family's plans to the chief official in the area, Monsieur Henri Bertin. "I hope," Archibald quipped afterward, "his honor does not have as hard a time reading this letter as I had writing it."[39] Engineering concerns also surfaced. In particular, ABMC officials wondered whether the thirty-six-year-old gravestone currently covering Quentin Roosevelt's tomb would go to pieces when removed. Would the stone, which weighed more than a ton, be in any condition to make the trip to Long Island? And, finally, there was the issue of precedence. What if other American families requested that their dead from the two world wars be allowed to rest side by side? And what of the many siblings interred in different military cemeteries, some on opposite sides of the world? How much additional work and expense would the Roosevelts' unorthodox request bring down on the Graves Registration Service (GRS)? (Here it should be noted that according to an often murky division of responsibilities, the GRS handled the exhumation, transport, and reburial of American war dead while the ABMC—not part of the War Department—oversaw the design, construction, and maintenance of permanent memorials and cemeteries. Relations between the two bureaucratic entities were typically less than good.)

Under North's personal supervision, each of these issues was quietly resolved. Apparently mollified by Archibald Roosevelt's letter, the townspeople of Chamery accepted the inevitable—at least publicly. As for the gravestone, an inspection revealed "a few hairline cracks," but nothing that would prohibit its removal and shipment to Oyster Bay, Long Island.[40] The biggest hurdle, as it turned out, was the GRS's fear that the transfer of Quentin Roosevelt's remains to Normandy would unleash an avalanche of similar requests. Indeed, this fear nearly derailed the entire project and created a serious conundrum for Thomas North. On July 12, 1955, North received word that the GRS would not participate in the proposed reburial. "[I]t would seem likely," North subsequently wrote to Archibald, "that they prefer to avoid creating a precedent which might be cited by tens of thousands of other families . . . So, I recommend that we abandon any thought of involving the Army."[41] But sidestepping the War Department was not easy. As North admitted, the ABMC had "no legal, or other, authority to disinter remains."[42] The only remaining recourse was that the Roosevelt family could hire a French undertaker to do what the U.S. Army would not—a sad and humiliating fate for the once-famous son of a former president.

North apparently found this final option so repugnant that three months later he openly defied the GRS: regardless of standing policy or procedures, the ABMC would handle the exhumation and transfer, and the Roosevelt family would cover all expenses. Thus, on September 22, 1955, a team of laborers led by Daniel Gibbs, chief of the ABMC's Burial Records Branch, removed the remains of Quentin Roosevelt from the tomb at Chamery where they had rested for thirty-seven years and loaded them into a truck bound for the American cemetery in Saint Laurent. In his detailed report, which held nothing back, Gibbs offered a description of the World War I flier that was both grisly and poignant:

> The sexton passed [the bones] up to Mr. Darois [a local offi-
> cial], who arranged them in their proper place on an O.D. [olive
> drab] sheet. There were no clothes except a few buttons and scraps
> of material; the leather aviator boots were in fair shape. Boots, but-
> tons, etc., were taken out of the grave and put with remains. A small
> metal cross that Lt. Roosevelt either had around his neck or in his
> breast pocket was found. I wrapped it in a piece of paper and asked
> Mr. Darois to take it to Paris for decision as to disposition. The dirt
> in the grave was sifted for small bones; the skeleton is, as far as I
> could judge, complete—lower jaw and one leg broken probably at
> time of death.
>
> The sheet was carefully folded over the remains and then an O.D.
> blanket was wrapped over the sheet and the remains were placed
> in the casket which had not been taken off the truck.[43]

The next day, Gibbs oversaw Quentin Roosevelt's reburial in Normandy, which was performed "without ceremony."[44]

No longer isolated, Roosevelt's grave was now like every other Ameri-can soldier's, its headstone bearing three matter-of-fact lines that stand in sharp contrast with the florid poetry inspired by the flier's death de-cades earlier: "Quentin Roosevelt / 1 LT 95 Aero Squadron / New York July 14 1918." Still, hints of Roosevelt's posthumous journey remain. As befitting its unorthodox history, the new grave created a slight irregularity in the row of white crosses. In order to place Quentin's remains next to Theodore Jr.'s, the gravediggers had to excavate at a spot slightly north of the existing graves.[45] And, as it turned out, Quentin Roosevelt's new resting place broke with conformity in another way: his is the only Ameri-can gravestone in Normandy that does not bear a military serial number. Serial numbers were not included on World War I gravestones, and, in any event, they were not issued to U.S. Army officers until 1921.

Once Roosevelt's remains were removed to Normandy, the various monu-ments concentrated at Chamery became unsettled, forming a diaspora, if you will, of increasingly tenuous remembrance. The marble stone that once covered the pilot's tomb proved sturdier than ABMC officials feared

(Gibbs found it cracked but still in one piece when he arrived at the grave-site in 1955), and eventually the slab made its way back to Sagamore Hill, where, set beneath the flagpole, it continues to confuse visitors in the early twenty-first century, many of whom conclude that Quentin Roose-velt is buried on the property. Over time, the American Legion marker disappeared (presumably removed by vandals), and the oak headstone and railing featured on so many postcards and stereopticon slides from 1918 through the early 1920s went to pieces. Despite its poor condition, however, the enclosure continued to serve as the focus of an annual wreath-laying ceremony organized by the American Overseas Memorial Day As-sociation. A faded snapshot of the 1958 Memorial Day ceremony, tucked inside the ABMC's Quentin Roosevelt file at the National Archives, shows a small group of American guests and French locals (including a grade-school choir) standing before the former gravesite, which is decorated with French and American flags.

With its juxtaposition of hollowness (an empty tomb) and patriotic dis-play, that poignant image would make a fit ending to the story of Quentin Roosevelt and his commemoration, suggesting both the mutability of collective memory and its sometimes surprising tenacity. However, the story is not quite complete. One of the Memorial Day Association mem-bers present at the ceremony in 1958, Karl S. Cate, subsequently wrote to Edith Derby with a suggestion: since the "little wooden fenced spot [was] likely to be forgotten with the passage of time," would the Roosevelt family consider marking the original gravesite with "a suitable and perma-nent stone memorial"? Noting that the gravesite was still "held sacred" by the local population, despite the removal of Quentin's body, Cate perhaps unknowingly outlined the perfect conciliatory gesture.[46] The erection of a new monument would reinforce the decades-old connection between Chamery and the Roosevelts, a connection that Quentin's exhumation in 1957 had threatened to sever. Thus, in 1959, after considering a variety of designs provided by General North, the Roosevelt family paid for a new monument, a modest, three-foot-tall marble block that today stands at the site of the original tomb and enclosure. Its inscription reads, "On This Spot Formerly Stood the Grave of Quentin Roosevelt."

Except for the stele left by the 302nd Engineers, now nearly hidden by weeds, nothing else remains to show that this lonely corner of rural France was once, for many Americans, the most hallowed ground of the First World War. Apart from an ever-smaller Memorial Day delegation that continues, nearly a century after the flier's death, to pay its respects, visitors are few—mostly military history buffs (and their reluctant spouses) and people with strong family memories of the War to End All Wars. Battlefield tour guide and World War I enthusiast Mike Hanlon regularly takes groups of Americans to Chamery. However, most of his clients are elderly, and the weather in northwest France is notoriously soggy. Usually his tour groups stop at the Quentin Roosevelt fountain and forgo the muddy trek to the original gravesite.[47] Two other Western Front tour operators, Tom Gudmestad and Frank Jordan, last visited the gravesite in 2004 when they "managed to drive a small passenger bus out along the dirt track, which leads there from the village." Each an expert on the Great War, the two men described for their party how the spot looked in its heyday. In Gudmestad's words, it was "at one time, a rather handsome affair."[48]

At first sight, the story of Quentin Roosevelt's memorialization seems to offer limited value as a case study in American war remembrance. The prestige of the Roosevelt name guaranteed from the start that the fallen airman would receive honors bestowed on few other casualties of the First World War. Afforded his own private burial plot, celebrated in multiple monuments, and visited by thousands, Roosevelt was revered as an *exceptional* American (from an exceptional family), not as an American everyman. Nor, as his tomb and monuments at Chamery slid into their inevitable decline, was the situation that resulted in any way commonplace. The vast majority of American war dead left in France became subject to federal policy, as drafted and implemented by the War Department (home to the GRS) and the ABMC. In Quentin Roosevelt's case, on the other hand, the government did what it could to avoid becoming responsible for his remains—and, by extension, his memory.

Nevertheless, the central issue in this deceptively anomalous narrative was not unique to Quentin Roosevelt or his legendary family. Like Curry's *The Return of Private Davis from the Argonne,* the story of Roosevelt's commemoration reflects a tension between two different visions of American participation in the First World War. Just as the distant horizon in Curry's painting, to which Davis's coffin literally points, invites the viewer to locate the meaning of the young soldier's death *over there,* in an international context, Roosevelt's monuments at Chamery emphasized that he had died for the sake of another nation. Indeed, Theodore Roosevelt Sr., a ferocious Francophile, would have wanted no less. Explicitly Gallic in appearance (thanks to its wooden headstone, crucifix, and gothic railing), Roosevelt's original gravesite commemorated a martyr from the

New World fallen in the defense of *La France*—an American cousin to Joan of Arc. In other words, the grave signified, in a powerful manner that for a time moved Americans and French citizens alike, America's virtues as a savior nation pledged to the selfless ideals of international progressivism. Once relocated to Normandy, Quentin's remains became open to a completely different interpretation. By placing the World War I flier next to his brother, and among American liberators of the Second World War, the Roosevelt family elevated the bonds of family and nation above Franco-American kinship, as idealistically celebrated in 1918. Thus, ironically enough, the family's action perhaps sprang from some of the same impulses that led to the mass repatriation of the dead in the early 1920s, an event that Theodore Roosevelt Sr. had tried his best to prevent.

Viewed with the twists and turns of its posthumous history in mind, the body of this once-famous American emerges as an exceptionally pliable signifier—an icon of World War I now wedded to the memory of World War II, a one-time symbol of internationalism redirected toward family and home. However, as we have seen throughout this study, most forms of American First World War remembrance produced similarly contradictory meanings. As a monument to ambiguity, Roosevelt's final resting place is situated in metaphorical proximity to Viquesney's *Spirit of the American Doughboy*, with its ambivalent blend of the modern and the traditional; the Tomb of the Unknown Soldier, a peace symbol morphed into a shrine to military duty; and, of course, Eby's equivocal *September 13, 1918: Saint Mihiel*, which simultaneously conveys the grandeur and futility of American intervention. At Chamery, Roosevelt's commemoration spoke clearly enough, but to fewer visitors each year and in a 1918-vintage idiom that grew irrelevant over time. By grafting Quentin's memory onto the Second World War, which thus produced a new version of that memory, the Roosevelts succeeded in rescuing the flier's name from oblivion (at least for now). At the same time, they provided a powerful lesson in the impermanence of *all* meaning carved in stone.

Remembered as Forgotten: The First World War and American Culture, 1942–2008

In many respects World War II vindicated Quentin Roosevelt's war. As the previously unimaginable scale and variety of Nazi atrocities came to light, many American veterans of the First World War concluded that they had indeed fought against the right enemy in 1917 and 1918. The fascist ideology of the Third Reich seemed but a vicious refinement of early twentieth-century German autocracy and expansionism. Meanwhile, among U.S. forces in Europe, the term "crusade," considered a dubious usage after more than two decades of disagreement over the meaning of American involvement in World War I, resurfaced with its original meaning intact. In early 1945, as weary American ground troops liberated concentration camps and saw with their own eyes what the Nazi agenda actually entailed, a new sense of purpose filled these soldiers. Suddenly the word "crusade" no longer seemed suspect.[49]

Many of the young men who fought against Nazi Germany and Imperial Japan were the sons of AEF veterans, and images of the Western Front loomed large in their childhood games and family life. Indeed, American personal narratives of World War II, the finest of which appeared in the late twentieth century, attest to the vibrancy of war memory, as passed from father to son, throughout the 1920s and 1930s. For example, in *Doing Battle,* Paul Fussell, who served as an infantry second lieutenant in France and Germany, recalls rooting through his father's World War I "Army Trunk" as a child and delighting in the memorabilia ("breeches, Sam Browne belt, jacket, and insignia") that he found there:

> As I examined and of course tried on these items, it was strikingly clear that they would be wonderful for play. Thus in one neighboring vacant lot my friends and I dug a system of three-foot-deep trenches, roofed with boards, old newspapers, and dirt, and lit by candles. Here we played trench warfare, bombarding one another's positions with dirt clods, blowing whistles to signal attacks, and coming as close as possible to miming the actualities of the Western Front as we'd seen them depicted in books. There, knitted out in Dad's uniform, with helmet and gas-mask carrier in place, I played boy officer, uncannily foreshadowing my destiny.[50]

Ironically, the trench dramatics enacted by Fussell and his playmates more closely resembled the experiences of the British war poets, which Fussell would later explore in *The Great War and Modern Memory,* than those of the former doughboy who provided the necessary paraphernalia.[51] Paul Fussell Sr. spent his war in an anticlimactic fashion worthy of the frustrated sad sacks in James Stevens's *Mattock*— "riding a horse daily around the perimeter" of an ammunition dump near Bordeaux.[52] However, this reality made little difference to the young boy who dressed up in iconic subaltern attire and, like thousands of other American children in the 1920s and 1930s, *played* World War I.

For William Manchester, who joined the marines and witnessed some of the most brutal campaigns of the Pacific, the Great War represented a more solemn inheritance. As related in *Goodbye, Darkness* (1980), Manchester's father, a "Devil Dog" of the First World War, survived a gangrenous shoulder wound so terrible that doctors confined him for five days in a "moribund ward" reserved for the dying.[53] The doughboy never forgave them. Unable to use his right arm for the rest of his life, William Manchester Sr. maintained an ambivalent attitude toward his service, resentful of the incompetent medical treatment that he had received but also "proud to have been a leatherneck." His son, who would fight at Peleliu and Okinawa, included among his "earliest memories" Memorial Day parades led by the disfigured marine in dress blues. Manchester also recalled standing at attention while his childhood bedroom underwent a "white-gloves inspection." Such experiences reinforced the future historian's "admiration for the military mystique."[54]

Fussell and Manchester entered armed forces that were prepared (as usual) to fight the previous war. Even the weaponry and equipment issued these young soldiers bore the mark of World War I. The World War II fragmentation grenade, employed against bunkers and pill boxes from North Africa to Iwo Jima, was essentially unchanged from the World War I model. The Model 1903 Springfield rifle, the same weapon carried by Viquesney's doughboy, stayed on as the standard bolt-action long arm, used (especially by snipers) alongside the more advanced semiautomatic M-1 Garand and M-1 Carbine. And the 1918-vintage Browning Automatic Rifle (or BAR) survived into World War II as well—much to the chagrin of its operators in Europe, who conceded the superiority of comparable German weapons. Gone were the doughboys' inexplicable wrap leggings, which always seemed to come unwound; however, the World War I "tin derby" (otherwise known as the Model 1917 shrapnel helmet) remained in service until 1942, visually linking the outnumbered defenders of Corregidor and Wake Island with the Lost Battalion. And it is an often forgotten fact that GIs carried gas masks right up to the end of the war in anticipation of a return to Western Front–style fighting conditions. Even the more advanced military machinery of World War II typically represented refinements of technology created decades earlier. Tanks and half-tracks owed their existence to the lumbering—and largely ineffectual—armored vehicles introduced to European battlefields in 1916. And World

War II airplanes, for all their speed and firepower, were propelled by engines that were little different, in terms of their basic engineering principles, from those developed during World War I (except, of course, for the Third Reich's jet aircraft).

Holdovers from World War I formed part of the Second World War's human materiel as well. Both in Europe and the Pacific, the American high command read like a who's who of notable AEF officers. While leading the Third Army, George S. Patton swept across ground he had first studied in 1918 while commanding a fledgling detachment of American tank troops outfitted with French vehicles (every one of which broke down or was blown up during the Argonne fighting). Students of World War II leadership should note that decades before he became notorious for slapping a shell-shocked soldier, Patton may have seriously injured an American infantryman—a panicked doughboy in the unfortunate 35th Division, whom the future general brained with a shovel.[55] Harry S. Truman's battery in the 35th Division was deployed perhaps a mile or two away at the time. Likewise, Douglas MacArthur first honed his theatrical style of command while serving as a brigade commander in the famous 42nd "Rainbow" Division, home to many of the First World War's most colorful personalities, including the poet Joyce Kilmer, the politician "Wild Bill" Donovan, and the fighting chaplain Father Francis Duffy. At one point during the Meuse-Argonne battle, a direct hit to a forward position held by the 42nd Division killed everyone in the vicinity except for MacArthur, who seemed to have a charmed life. Utterly fearless, the future commander of American forces in the Pacific dashed from one seemingly suicidal situation to another, always refusing to wear a gas mask (or an American steel helmet), his swagger stick tucked under his arm. And, finally, it was none other than George Marshall who at Pershing's command drew up the successful plan for shifting virtually the entire AEF from the Saint Mihiel battlefield to the Meuse-Argonne sector, a masterpiece of military logistics. Ten years after this remarkable feat, Marshall would tangle with Eisenhower over the best way for Pershing to write his war memoirs.

However, not every World War II participant with a direct connection to World War I was a general. Many of the individuals examined in this study returned to military service, regardless of their peacetime convictions or the version of war memory that they happened to uphold in the 1920s and 1930s. For example, in 1942 Laurence Stallings, whose novel *Plumes* (1924) had mocked the official symbolism of the Unknown Sol-

244 / *Memory's End?*

dier, rejoined the U.S. Marine Corps. Unable to serve in combat because of his artificial leg, a permanent reminder of his participation in the Battle of Belleau Wood, Stallings took a staff job in the Pentagon, where he apparently worked on military intelligence (under the guise of serving as a liaison between the U.S. Marine and Army Air Corps). Still suffering from chronic pain caused by his World War I wounds, the former doughboy probably pushed himself too hard. In 1943 he left the Corps for good, retiring at the rank of lieutenant colonel, and returned to writing, although without the automatic success that he had enjoyed in the 1920s. Stallings's World War II play, *The Streets Are Guarded* (1944), flopped, and his name did not resurface again in connection with war memory until 1963, when his nostalgic history of the AEF, *The Doughboys*, received widespread acclaim.

Perhaps the most poignant story to link the memory of both world wars is that of Kerr Eby, the accomplished New England etcher whose volume of protest art, *War* (1936), seemed to take aim at Harvey Dunn's *American Legion Monthly* covers and whose masterpiece, *September 13, 1918: Saint Mihiel*, brought together divergent constructions of memory within a single astonishing image. In 1941 Eby set out to witness at its full ferocity and horror the conflict whose arrival he had warned against, via his drawings and etchings of World War I, for more than two decades. His determination in this regard was characteristic. Now that the worst had happened, the artist felt compelled to face it directly and to record the truth of the war—as experienced by the U.S. military's lowliest and most expendable members—before it was whitewashed. Eby's deeply engrained sense of duty, inculcated by his missionary parents, demanded no less. Rejected by the U.S. Army because of his age, Eby found another path to the front line through a special artists program organized (with the full support of the War Department) by Abbott Laboratories, a leading supplier of blood plasma. Attached to the Marine Corps and charged with depicting doctors and medics in action, Eby went where plasma was needed in sickening abundance. In 1943, at age fifty-four, he violated orders and landed on Tarawa with one of the first waves of marines. The artist recorded the ensuing battle, one of the bloodiest in Marine Corps history, while under fire. Eby then bore witness to the fighting at Bougainville, where, as art historian Bernadette Passi Giardina points out, he "lived in a foxhole for weeks, observing and sketching the everyday life of troops in combat." Affectionately nicknamed "Pop" by the soldiers whose misery (amid the worst jungle conditions imaginable) he unsparingly recorded, the artist "kept up with marines who were half his age."[56]

However, in 1944, after hospitalization for a "tropical malady," Eby returned to the United States depressed and exhausted, his once robust health permanently shattered. And two years later, his Pacific War experience killed him. Although officially attributed to a "coronary occlusion," the artist's demise was hastened by tropical fever and other illnesses contracted on Bougainville.[57] In a very real sense, Eby died for his art—and for the sake of war memory, which he sought to shape only by meeting the most exacting personal standards of truth-telling. Others have given their lives in war for arguably far less.

Exhibited around the country in 1944 and now a permanent part of the U.S. Navy's Combat Art Collection, the drawings that Eby produced in the Pacific comprise one of the most powerful war-art series of the twentieth century, surpassing in composition and technique even the artist's protest works of the 1920s and 1930s. Sketched in dark, funereal tones, the images seem clinical and compassionate at the same time. As novelist James Jones later remarked in his classic *WWII* (1975), an analysis of war experience as presented in combat art, the marines in Eby's drawings appear as "faceless appendages of some greater organism that moves and manipulates them."[58] As with Eby's World War I etchings, the utter anonymity required by modern warfare—the reduction of the individual to a serial number on a dog tag—stands out in these pictures with a terrifying directness seldom captured by other war artists. However, as Jones realized when studying *Down the Net—Tarawa,* Eby's best-known World War II work, the artist never portrays his soldiers as anything less than human beings (see fig. 24). In Eby's most iconic image of the Pacific War, "Marines come flowing over the side [of the ship] in a stream of anonymous helmets and packs and legs, their backs to us, so alike as to be indistinguishable. And yet the viewer never forgets each is an individual, vulnerable man."[59] Elsewhere, Eby captured that vulnerability—just as Harvey Dunn had twenty-six years earlier in his best war paintings—with images of stark honesty: a marine matter-of-factly applying ointment to the buttocks of a comrade suffering from jungle rot; a shell-shocked soldier, with wild eyes, held down by two buddies; and the water-logged bodies of two marines snagged on barbed wire, post tide, atop the reef at Tarawa—a hellish spectacle later described by Eby as "the most frightful thing I have seen."

24. *Down the Net—Tarawa* (1944) by Kerr Eby. Courtesy of the
Navy Art Collection.

Appropriately enough, given what happened to the memory of World
War I after 1945, Eby's works for Abbott Laboratories largely eclipsed his
drawings and etchings of World War I—so much so that few Americans
today even know of the artist's connection to the earlier conflict. While
Eby's drawings of the Pacific theater have become fixtures in books and
Web sites devoted to the Second World War, his earlier war scenes remain (with the exception of *September 13, 1918: Saint Mihiel*) largely forgotten. Indeed, Yale University Press never even bothered to renew the

copyright on *War*, anyone wishing to reproduce the remarkable images in that volume may do so free of charge.

Eby's prominence as an artist of the Second World War rather than the First arguably reflects the superior quality of his final sequence of war pictures. At the same time, however, the obscurity of his work from the interwar decades mirrors a larger dynamic in collective memory— namely, the overshadowing of World War I by World War II. As historian Mark A. Snell observes, the greater scale and duration of America's war from 1941 to 1945 made this memory gap inevitable. The Second World War cost the nation far more "treasure and casualties [than the First], and it was even more global in scope."[60] Approximately sixteen million Americans served in the armed forces in World War II—as opposed to the roughly four and a half million inducted in 1917 or 1918—and as these men and women streamed home in 1945, they completely changed the complexion of the veterans organizations that had earlier focused on the memory of the First World War. Former doughboys became minorities in their own American Legion or VFW posts, surrounded by younger veterans who would transform the nation into a land of suburbs, shopping malls, and highway overpasses, a supersonic America whose ties to the quaint era of Woodrow Wilson, biplanes, and hand-cranked Victrolas seemed increasingly tenuous.

By the early 1950s, American World War I veterans already seemed sidelined by history—an irony given the crucial role of the American Legion, as led by former AEF officers, in the Servicemen's Readjustment Act of 1944 (or GI Bill), the benefits package that drove much of the postwar prosperity. However, during the 1960s, with the advent of the American war in Vietnam, World War I made a comeback in terms of collective memory. Indeed, the two conflicts seemed in many respects similar, an impression reinforced by both academia and Hollywood. For professors and filmmakers alike, World War I became a metaphor for military futility, a forerunner—because it supposedly achieved nothing—of the quagmire in Southeast Asia. In 1967 literary historian Stanley Cooperman published his landmark study, *World War I and the American Novel*, which concluded (based on a survey of works by Ernest Hemingway, John Dos Passos, Thomas Boyd, William March, and others) that disillusionment and revulsion defined the American literary response to the First World War.[61] Colored by Vietnam-era politics, Cooperman's book in effect aligned war writers of the 1920s and 1930s with war protesters of the 1960s and, in the process, largely ignored the ideological subtleties and contradictions that characterize many American World War I novels. Less explicitly tied to contemporary politics, historian Edward Coffman's important study of the AEF, published in 1968 (the year of the Tet offensive), nevertheless reflected the mood of the country through its ironic title: *The War to End All Wars: The American Military Experience in World War I*.[62] Three years later, Hollywood writer Dalton Trumbo, formerly blacklisted, directed a well-produced screen version of his 1939 novel, *Johnny Got His Gun*, the story of an idealistic doughboy who is horrifically wounded in battle.[63] As historian Michael E. Birdwell notes, the film's marketers stressed the cautionary relevance of the First World War, a proto-Vietnam, to the flower-power era: the movie's poster "featured a hand, forming a peace sign with a doughboy's image going over the top on its base."[64] Significantly, Trumbo's was the first major motion picture to focus on American troops in World War I since John Ford's remake of *What Price Glory?* in 1952. For a time, Hollywood seemed more captivated by foreign experiences of the Great War, as seen in Stanley Kubrick's *Paths of Glory* (1957), the story of a miscarriage of justice in the French army, and the aviation epic *The Blue Max* (1966), which focused on German fliers.

As the Vietnam War itself became a memory, America's doughboys faded from sight, their exploits commonly preserved and handed down in families (far more commonly, indeed, than most historians have perhaps realized), but now only rarely made the focus of public remembrance. Among the handful of popular writers and academics who continued to revisit World War I during the 1970s and 1980s, a mournful tone became somewhat standard, along with the venting of frustration over the First World War's ignominious neglect. In 1978 journalist Henry Berry subtitled *Make the Kaiser Dance*, his oral history of the AEF, *Living Memories of a Forgotten War*.[65] Now conceived of as utterly moribund, in terms of its once vital (if debate-ridden) presence in collective memory, the American experience of World War I became inseparable from adjectives like "lost," "invisible," or "forgotten."

With the arrival of the seventy-fifth anniversary of the armistice in 1993, American veterans of the Great War briefly reentered the public spotlight, and the federal government suddenly—some might say belatedly—awoke to the fact that very soon none of these eyewitnesses to history, most born before the end of the nineteenth century, would be left. Thus, the Defense Department struck a new decoration honoring World War I soldiers, a variation of the official Victory Medal issued in 1920, and awarded it to the few thousand veterans who still lingered, most of them in nursing homes. On its face the medal featured the same sword-bearing figure of Civilization as the original, only shrunken. The obverse read, "A Grateful Nation Remembers, 1918–1993, They Came on the Wings of Eagles." A grateful nation? After the passage of so much time, and with so many unanswered questions still surrounding their war, the ancient soldiers who fingered this medal perhaps wondered whether such gratitude still survived somewhere in the nation's memory—or even applied. After all, Americans had never agreed on the meaning of the war, not once since the guns along the Western Front fell silent on November 11, 1918. Considerably more pomp and circumstance attended France's tribute to these one-time crusaders. With Gallic panache, the French government commemorated the eightieth anniversary of the armistice in 1998 by awarding the Legion of Honor to all American veterans (roughly three thousand at the time), even dispatching officials to seek out each one and to confer the decoration with appropriate ceremony.

During the first decade of the twenty-first century, the total number of American World War I veterans dropped, with chilling suddenness, to less than a handful—and then to just one, a still-active Missourian named Frank Buckles (who at the time of this writing is 108), whose life, like so many mentioned in this study, intersects with the history of both world wars. In 1918, after enlisting at age sixteen, Buckles served with the U.S. Army Medical Corps in England and France. Twenty-four years later, while employed by an American steamship company, he was caught in Manila as the Japanese military invaded. Buckles subsequently spent three years diseased and malnourished as a prisoner of war—an experience that one would have expected to shave years, if not decades, off the veteran's life.[66]

In early 2008, as Buckles became the last doughboy standing, editorialists and historians indulged in the now-familiar trope of World War I as America's unknown or forgotten war. For example, in a piece inevitably titled "The War We Forgot," Tony Dokoupil of *Newsweek* called for "rebooting the memory of WWI" after decades of official neglect.[67] America, he observed, had no national memorial to the conflict, no set of "iconic images" to inspire public remembrance, and no plans to mark Buckles's passing with any official recognition.[68] Dokoupil presented a sad state of affairs, especially in comparison with the robust health of World War I commemoration in Great Britain, France, and Canada, nations committed to giving their last veterans lavish state funerals. In his overview of the Great Adventure's apparent slide into historical and cultural oblivion, Dokoupil struck many of the same notes as author Richard Rubin, who poignantly described the end of the doughboys' war as living memory several months earlier in an opinion piece for the *New York Times*. Rubin told the story of his initial quest, not long after 9/11, to locate America's last living World War I veterans. Remarkably, no one could help him—not "the Department of Veterans Affairs, or the Veterans of Foreign Wars, or the American Legion"—and "no one seemed to care either."[69] Rubin eventually found Buckles and several other veterans on his own. Meanwhile, among the most prominent academic voices to join in this mournful chorus was that of military historian Edward Lengel, whose brilliant history of the Meuse-Argonne offensive, *To Conquer Hell* (2008), opens with the lament that no one in America remembers the Great War: "Johnny Reb, Billy Yank, and the GI live forever in the American psyche. The Doughboy has been forgotten."[70] Also published in 2008, Mark A. Snell's *Unknown Soldiers: The American Expeditionary Forces in Memory and Remembrance* proceeds from the same assumption: "The problem with the American memory of World War I," Snell writes, "is that there seems to be none."[71] For all of these writers, present-day America's apparent lack of interest in World War I is symptomatic of a kind of cultural Alzheimer's disease, a condition whereby entire periods of history—those of little interest to moviemakers, reenactors, or video-gamers—simply no longer exist.

As we saw in the introduction to this study, the First World War indeed holds an odd and unsettled position in American culture—and for many reasons, some of which go back to the ambiguities of the event itself. However, there is something more than a little misleading about the oft-repeated assertion that World War I has become America's forgotten war. A truly forgotten conflict would not be described as such. It would not, in fact, be described at all.

And for academic authors to mourn the supposed death of the Great War in national memory is especially ironic, since the early twenty-first century has seen the largest explosion of new World War I books in eighty years. Important new firsthand accounts by AEF soldiers have become available—including Horace Baker's *Argonne Days in World War I* (2007) and William S. Triplet's *A Youth in the Meuse-Argonne: A Memoir, 1917–1918* (2000)—along with new works of military history such as Mark Ethan Grotelueschen's *The AEF Way of War: The American Army and Combat in World War I* (2006) and Mitchell A. Yockelson's *Borrowed Soldiers: Americans under British Command, 1918* (2008). And a slew of books, all published within the last five years, have revisited the Lost Battalion legend. Among them are Alan D. Gaff's *Blood in the Argonne: The "Lost Battalion" of World War I* (2005), Robert Ferrell's *Five Days in October: The Lost Battalion of World War I* (2005), and Robert Laplander's *Finding the Lost Battalion: Beyond the Rumors, Myths, and Legends of America's Famous WWI Epic* (2007). Meanwhile, literary critics and scholars of cultural history have rediscovered the war as well. Important recent studies in these areas include Jennifer Haytock's *At Home, At War: Domesticity and World War I in American Literature* (2003), Patrick Quinn's *The Conning of America: The Great War and American Popular Literature* (2001), and Mark Levitch's *Panthéon de la Guerre: Reconfiguring a Panorama of the Great War* (2006), which traces the history of a World War I mural from its conception in wartime Paris to its installation (and modification) at the Liberty Memorial in Kansas City.[72] Once relegated to six inches or less of shelf space in a typical Borders or Barnes and Noble bookstore (and often lumped together with books on the Napoleonic Wars), World War I titles now take up several feet—two to three full shelves in some locations. Silly as it may sound, bookstore inventory, shaped by demand and level of interest, is perhaps as reliable an indicator of what Americans still remember as any other.

As for public commemoration, the bleak picture painted by Dokoupil and others does not match up with the reality. True, some recent memorializing efforts have backfired, ironically signifying forgetfulness and mutability rather than enduring meaning. For example, in February 2006 the Kansas legislature honored Albert Wagner, the nation's oldest living Marine Corps veteran, by designating a section of State Highway 36, which ran past Wagner's home in the town of Smith Center, "The World War I Veterans Memorial Highway." Presumably intended to honor living veterans, the gesture proved grotesquely belated. Within two years, the total number of former doughboys dropped to just one; thus, the plural noun on the highway's signpost became obsolete almost from the moment of the memorial's creation. Such arguably bungled commemoration has not, however, been the norm. The designation of the Liberty Memorial in Kansas City, Missouri, as the National World War I Museum, together with the dramatic expansion and reopening of that facility in 2006, made headlines around the world. And on Memorial Day 2008, Frank Buckles, America's last doughboy, stood by as the guest of honor during a well-publicized ceremony held at this now-vibrant site of American memory. Indeed, even in the Meuse-Argonne region of France, a place with supposedly little meaning to most Americans today, signs of revitalized memory have begun to appear. Completed within the past few months, a privately funded monument to Alvin York now stands near Châtel-Chérey, together with an interpretive trail that enables visitors to "walk where York walked."[73]

Anything but absent in present-day American culture, the War to End All Wars is, in fact, undergoing a major revival of popular and academic interest that will, in all likelihood, only intensify as the one-hundredth anniversary of the armistice draws nearer. Several factors help to explain this renaissance in World War I study and commemoration. Now that the Second World War has begun to fade from our living history (more than half of the nation's World War II veterans have passed on), the conflict that the "Good War" once so thoroughly overshadowed no longer faces such a formidable disadvantage in terms of memory. In addition, the military and foreign-policy permutations that the United States has seen since 9/11 almost inevitably turn one's thoughts to America in the World War I era. While scholars reevaluate the AEF in combat, American troops in Iraq and Afghanistan face their own steep learning curve in conflicts that, like the Great Adventure, signal a reorientation (whether for good or ill) in America's relationship with the world. Moreover, war in the present almost inevitably inspires thoughts of heroism in the past— hence, perhaps, the wave of recent titles on the Lost Battalion.

Thus, it would appear that those who still bemoan the First World War's supposed invisibility and neglect have come to remember the conflict *as being* invisible and neglected—paradoxically, a construction of collective memory no less vital or meaningful than any other. The notion of a war that no one remembers raises uncomfortable questions about American exceptionalism, the desirability of crusader ideals (of any sort), and ultimately the legitimacy of war itself. For this reason, then, we can only hope that in the midst of its current revival World War I remains, at least on some level, America's "forgotten war."

Notes

Prologue

The prologue's opening epigraph comes from Citation for the "Disgusted Service Medal," undated, Box 1, Thomas North Collection, Eisenhower Library; hereafter, TNC/EL.

1. Review of *American Armies and Battlefields in Europe, Army Ordnance* (July–August 1939), press clipping, Correspondence File Developmental Materials, *American Armies and Battlefields in Europe*, Box 260, RG 117, Records of the American Battle Monuments Commission, National Archives, College Park, Maryland; hereafter, *AABE*.

2. See Dwight D. Eisenhower, "A Tank Discussion," *Infantry Journal* (November 1920): 453–58.

3. Stephen E. Ambrose, *Eisenhower*, vol. 1, *Soldier, General of the Army, President-Elect, 1890–1952* (New York: Simon and Schuster, 1983), 83.

4. Peter Lyon, *Eisenhower: Portrait of the Hero* (Boston: Little, Brown, 1974), 62.

5. Xenophon H. Price, memorandum, January 26, 1927, Eisenhower Library.

6. "Tentative Assignment of Work for the Guide Book," undated, TNC/EL.

7. Ambrose, *Eisenhower*, 1:82.

8. Lyon, *Eisenhower*, 62.

9. Press release for *A Guide to the American Battle Fields in Europe*, August 19, 1927, TNC/EL.

10. "Publication of 'American Armies and Battlefields in Europe' Announced by General Pershing," undated press release, *AABE*.

11. John J. Pershing to Robert H. Allen, August 15, 1927, John J. Pershing File, Box 92, Dwight D. Eisenhower Pre-Presidential Papers, Eisenhower Library.

12. Author's collection.

13. Dwight D. Eisenhower, *At Ease: Stories I Tell to Friends* (Garden City, NY: Doubleday, 1967), 204.

14. Frank E. Vandiver, *Black Jack: The Life and Times of John J. Pershing,* vol. 2 (College Station: Texas A&M Press, 1977), 1084. See John J. Pershing, *My Experiences in the World War* (New York: Frederick A. Stokes, 1931).

15. Eisenhower, *At Ease,* 208.

16. Ibid., 208–09.

17. Ibid., 209.

18. Ambrose, *Eisenhower,* 1:87.

19. Michael Korda's interpretation of Eisenhower's battlefield travels is a notable exception. Korda ties Eisenhower's "respect for his future allies" to the "silent reminders of a hecatomb" that the future general visited on the Western Front. See Michael Korda, *Ike: An American Hero* (New York: Harper Collins, 2007), 180–81.

20. Eisenhower, *At Ease,* 205.

21. "Publication of 'American Armies and Battlefields.'"

22. Dwight D. Eisenhower to Xenophon H. Price, October 28, 1929, TNC/EL.

23. Ibid.

24. American Battle Monuments Commission, *American Armies and Battlefields in Europe* (Washington, DC: U.S. Government Printing Office, 1938), 66.

25. Clifton B. Cates to Dwight D. Eisenhower, February 1, 1929, TNC/EL.

26. Ibid.

27. Copy of Clifton B. Cates to Dwight D. Eisenhower, February 1, 1929, with Eisenhower's handwritten comments, TNC/EL. Interestingly, in one of his less partisan suggestions, Cates pointed out that "the 1st Division has fifty per cent more labeled photographs in the Guide Book than any other division. The 29th, 36th, 79th, 82nd, 88th, and 91st have none at all." Pershing's partiality to the "Big Red One," his favorite unit in the AEF, is well known, and it is possible that his bias was passed on to his subordinates in the Historical Section.

28. Andrew T. Long to John J. Pershing, July 19, 1928, TNC/EL.

29. John J. Pershing to Andrew T. Long, July 21, 1928, TNC/EL.

30. Dwight D. Eisenhower to John J. Pershing, July 21, 1928, TNC/EL.

31. Dwight D. Eisenhower, "Gruber-Eisenhower Diary," in *Eisenhower: The Prewar Diaries and Selected Papers, 1905–1941,* eds. Daniel D. Holt and James W. Leyerzapf (Baltimore: Johns Hopkins University Press, 1998), 89.

32. Ibid., 91. Eisenhower's neo-Romantic response to the Black Forest and the Alps is perhaps one reason why he later refused to have his section of the "Gruber-Eisenhower Diary" reprinted. Perhaps he was embarrassed by his effusive prose. See Holt and Leyerzapf, *Eisenhower,* 96n1.

33. William R. Gruber, "Gruber-Eisenhower Diary," Box 1, William R. Gruber Papers, Eisenhower Library, 144.

34. Ibid., 144–45.

35. Ibid., 145.

36. Ibid.

37. Ibid., 146.

38. Ibid., 148.

39. Ibid., 149.

40. Ibid.

41. Xenophon H. Price, Memorandum for Major Dwight David Eisenhower, Infantry, U.S.A., TNC/EL.

42. Dwight D. Eisenhower to Xenophon H. Price, October 18, 1929, TNC/EL.

43. Ibid.

44. Citation for the "Disgusted Service Medal," undated, TNC/EL.

45. "Duty in Washington, September 26, 1929–December 25, 1931," in Holt and Leyerzapf, *Eisenhower,* 100.

46. Ibid.

47. The phrase "American Caesar" comes from William Manchester, *American Caesar: Douglas MacArthur, 1880–1964* (Boston: Little, Brown, 1978). For more on the Bonus Army, see Paul Dickson and Thomas B. Allen, *The Bonus Army: An American Epic* (New York: Walker, 2004), and Jennifer D. Keene, *Doughboys, the Great War, and the Remaking of America* (Baltimore: Johns Hopkins University Press, 2001), 179–204.

48. Dwight D. Eisenhower, "Report on the Bonus March Sent to the Secretary of War," in Holt and Leyerzapf, *Eisenhower,* 246.

49. Merle Miller, *Ike the Soldier: As They Knew Him* (New York: Putnam's, 1987), 265.

50. Ibid., 241–42.

51. Ibid., 267.

52. Erich Maria Remarque, *All Quiet on the Western Front* (Boston: Little, Brown, 1929).

53. Ernest Hemingway, *A Farewell to Arms* (New York: Collier, 1929), and William Faulkner, *Sartoris* (New York: Harcourt, Brace, 1929).

54. Steven Trout, "World War I in American Prose Works, Theater, and Cinema: A Chronology, 1919–1939," in *American Prose Writers of World War I: A Documentary Volume,* ed. Steven Trout, *Dictionary of Literary Biography,* vol. 316 (Detroit: Thomson Gale, 2005), 399.

55. Maxwell Anderson and Laurence Stallings, *What Price Glory?* in *Three American Plays* (New York: Harcourt, Brace, 1926), and R. C. Sherriff, *Journey's End: A Play in Three Acts* (New York: Brentano's, 1929).

56. "Two Million an Hour," *Roanoke World News,* May 6, 1939, press clipping, *AABE.*

57. Ibid.

58. Leslie E. Edmonds, "Just as It Seems to Me in War Times," *Topeka Capital Journal,* undated press clipping, *AABE.*

Introduction

This chapter's opening epigraph comes from Philip West, Steven I. Levine, and Jackie Hiltz, *America's Wars in Asia: A Cultural Approach to History and Memory* (Armonk, NY: M. E. Sharpe, 1998), 8.

1. Jay Winter, *Remembering War: The Great War between Memory and History in the Twentieth Century* (New Haven, CT: Yale University Press, 2006), 1.

2. Studies of American war remembrance that contain useful chapters or lengthy sections on the aftermath of the First World War include James M. Mayo,

War Memorials as Political Landscape: The American Experience and Beyond (New York: Praeger, 1988); G. Kurt Piehler, *Remembering War the American Way* (Washington, DC: Smithsonian Institution Press, 1995); and Michael Sledge, *Soldier Dead: How We Recover, Identify, Bury, and Honor Our Military Fallen* (New York: Columbia University Press, 2005). Though focused on the war years, David Kennedy, *Over Here: The First World War and American Society* (New York: Oxford University Press, 1980), and John S. D. Eisenhower, *Yanks: The Epic Story of the American Army in World War I* (New York: Free Press, 2001), offer atypical interpretations of the First World War's American legacy. Kennedy acknowledges widespread "disillusionment" during the 1920s, but stresses that positive interpretations of war experiences endured, within the American Legion and elsewhere, right up to the Second World War. Eisenhower concludes his study of American military operations in 1917–1918 by examining the often surprising links between the U.S. Army of World War I and that of World War II. Book-length treatments of American war remembrance in the 1920s and 1930s have finally begun to appear. They include John Graham, *The Gold Star Mother Pilgrimages of the 1930s* (Jefferson, NC: MacFarland, 2005); and Mark A. Snell, ed., *Unknown Soldiers: The American Expeditionary Forces in Memory and Remembrance* (Kent, OH: Kent State University Press, 2008). Although not focused on collective memory per se, Peter C. Rollins and John E. O'Conner, eds., *Hollywood's World War I: Motion Picture Images* (Bowling Green, OH: Bowling Green State University Popular Press, 1997), includes several essays that approach post-1918 American war films as cinematic examples of remembrance.

3. Exceptions include Edith Wharton's *A Son at the Front* (New York: Charles Scribner's Sons, 1923), and Willa Cather's *One of Ours* (New York: Knopf, 1922). Despite failing to conform to the high modernist version of the war, both novels command attention because of the canonical standing of their authors. Although filled with tragedy, Wharton's novel presents the Allied war effort as a sacred cause. Cather's novel offers a far more ambivalent picture of the war, inviting the reader to share her protagonist's sense of personal liberation in wartime while simultaneously undercutting his idealism. For an analysis of *One of Ours* as a work of contradictory remembrance and Conradian ambiguity, see Steven Trout, *Memorial Fictions: Willa Cather and the First World War* (Lincoln: University of Nebraska Press, 2002).

4. See Ernest Hemingway's *The Sun Also Rises* (1926; New York: Simon and Schuster, 1996); William Faulkner, *Soldiers' Pay* (New York: Boni and Liveright, 1926); E. E. Cummings, *The Enormous Room* (New York: Boni and Liveright, 1922); John Dos Passos, *Three Soldiers* (New York: Doran, 1921); and F. Scott Fitzgerald, *Tender Is the Night* (New York: Scribner's, 1934).

5. Historian Michael T. Isenberg puts forward essentially the same argument in his perceptive essay "The Great War Viewed from the Twenties: *The Big Parade*," in Rollins and O'Connor, *Hollywood's World War I*, 40. "Although many Americans doubtless took part in the war-induced climate of cynicism," Isenberg writes, "historians have tended to overlook the continuities of the period. The flaming passions of the jazz age probably held more smoke than fire, for family and church life continued as the hub of social activity for millions."

6. Keith Gandal, *The Gun and the Pen: Hemingway, Fitzgerald, Faulkner, and the Fiction of Mobilization* (New York: Oxford University Press, 2008), 33.

7. See review of *Three Soldiers* by John Dos Passos, *Nation* 113 (October 26, 1921): 480–81.

8. See Archibald MacLeish and Malcolm Cowley, "*The First World War:* Review and Rebuttle," *New Republic* 76 (September 20, 1933): 159–61, and "The Dead of the Next War," *New Republic* 76 (October 4, 1933): 214–16. See also Laurence Stallings, *The First World War: A Photographic History* (New York: Simon and Schuster, 1933).

9. Kennedy, *Over Here,* 230.

10. Samuel Hynes, *A War Imagined: The First World War and English Culture* (London: Bodley Head, 1990), 439.

11. Isenberg, "Great War," 53.

12. Robert Baird, "*Hell's Angels* above *The Western Front,*" in Rollins and O'Connor, *Hollywood's World War I,* 80.

13. Thomas Boyd, *Through the Wheat* (New York: Charles Scribner's Sons, 1923); and Stephen Crane, *The Red Badge of Courage,* in The Red Badge of Courage *and Other Stories,* Gary Scharnhorst, ed. (New York: Penguin, 2005).

14. Boyd, *Through the Wheat,* 266.

15. Steven Trout, "Thomas Boyd," in Trout, ed., *American Prose Writers of World War I,* 67.

16. John W. Crawford, "A Malicious Panorama," *Nation* 117 (July 18, 1923): 66.

17. Ibid.

18. Edmund Wilson, "The Anatomy of War," *Dial* 75 (July 1923): 93.

19. Crawford, "Malicious Panorama," 66.

20. A photograph of the original dust jacket appears in Trout, "Thomas Boyd," 77.

21. F. Scott Fitzgerald, review of *Through the Wheat* by Thomas Boyd, in *Through the Wheat* by Thomas Boyd, ed. Matthew J. Bruccoli (Carbondale: Southern Illinois University Press, 1978), 275.

22. See Brian Bruce, *Thomas Boyd: Lost Author of the "Lost Generation"* (Akron, OH: University of Akron Press, 2006).

23. See Thomas Boyd, *Points of Honor* (New York: Charles Scribner's Sons, 1925).

24. See, for instance, Thomas Boyd, "Johnny the Hard," *American Legion Monthly* (hereafter, *ALM*) 2, no. 3 (1927): 34–37, 87–88.

25. Willa Cather, preface to *Not Under Forty,* in *Willa Cather: Stories, Poems, and Other Writings* (New York: Library of America, 1992), 812.

26. "Never Again! But Wasn't It Great, Eh!" cartoon, *Outlook* 129 (November 23, 1921): 457.

27. Samuel Hynes, "Personal Narratives and Commemoration," in *War and Remembrance in the Twentieth Century,* eds. Jay Winter and Emmanuel Sivan (Cambridge: Cambridge University Press, 1999), 206–07.

28. Tony Horwitz, *Confederates in the Attic: Dispatches from the Unfinished Civil War* (New York: Random House, 1998), 7.

29. Ibid., 13.

30. See Hayden White, *Tropics of Discourse: Essays in Cultural Criticism* (Baltimore: Johns Hopkins University Press, 1978).

31. Horwitz, *Confederates in the Attic,* 7.

32. Hynes, "Personal Narratives," 207.

33. See Edward Tabor Linenthal and Tom Engelhardt, *History Wars: The* Enola Gay *and Other Battles for the American Past* (New York: Holt, 1996), and Edward Tabor Linenthal, *Sacred Ground: Americans and Their Battlefields* (Urbana: University of Illinois Press, 1993).

34. West, Levine, and Hiltz, *America's Wars in Asia,* 8.

35. For more on the Victory Highway, see Robert W. Richmond, "The Victory Highway: Transcontinental Memorial," *Shawnee County Historical Society Bulletin* 69 (November 1992): 204–10, and Steven Trout, "Forgotten Reminders: Kansas World War I Memorials," *Kansas History* 29, no. 3 (2006): 205–07.

36. Winter, *Remembering War,* 136.

37. John Bodnar, *Remaking America: Public Memory, Commemoration, and Patriotism in the Twentieth Century* (Princeton, NJ: Princeton University Press, 1992).

38. Exceptional readings of the Vietnam Veterans Memorial as a repository of memory include Kristin Ann Hass, *Carried to the Wall: American Memory and the Vietnam Veterans Memorial* (Berkeley: University of California Press, 1998); and Jenny Edkins, *Trauma and the Memory of Politics* (Cambridge: Cambridge University Press, 2003), 73–90.

39. Hemingway, *Farewell to Arms,* 196.

40. Silvina Fernandez-Duque, "First Division Monument," National Park Service, U.S. Department of the Interior, http://www.nps.gov/whho/historyculture/first-division-monument.htm#CP_JUMP_107374, accessed September 9, 2009. For more on this attractive memorial, see *The Spirit of the First Division: Addresses Given by President Calvin Coolidge and Major General C. P. Summerall at the Unveiling of the First Division Memorial, Washington, D.C., October 4, 1924* (N.p.: privately printed, 1924).

41. Rupert Hughes, "Memorial Temple Under Way in Washington," *New York Times,* February 23, 1919, 10, 14.

42. "$10,000,000 War Memorial," *New York Times,* June 1, 1919, 4.

43. Harlan Wood, "Unforgotten," *American Legion Magazine* 24, no. 5 (1938): 42.

44. Sledge, *Soldier Dead,* 212.

45. Derek Donovan, *Lest The Ages Forget: Kansas City's Liberty Memorial* (Kansas City, MO: Kansas City Star Books, 2001), 76.

46. See Robert H. Zieger, *America's Great War: World War I and the American Experience* (Lanham, MD: Rowman and Littlefield, 2000), 126–51.

47. Richard Slotkin, *Lost Battalions: The Great War and the Crisis of American Nationality* (New York: Henry Holt, 2005), 453–61.

48. Kennedy, *Over Here,* 202.

49. Robert H. Ferrell, *America's Deadliest Battle: Meuse-Argonne, 1918* (Lawrence: University Press of Kansas, 2007), 148.

50. See Thomas M. Johnson, *Without Censor: New Light on Our Greatest World War Battles* (Indianapolis: Bobbs-Merrill, 1928).

51. *The 88th Division in the World War of 1914–1918* (New York: Wynkoop Hallenbeck Crawford, 1919), 108.

52. Kennedy, *Over Here,* 208.

53. For a detailed description of the 35th Division's misadventures in the Meuse-Argonne and the congressional investigation that followed, see Robert H. Ferrell, *Collapse at Meuse-Argonne: The Failure of the Missouri-Kansas Division* (Columbia: University of Missouri Press, 2004). A more heroic version of the division's ordeal appears in Claire Kenamore, *From Vauquois Hill to Exermont: A History of the Thirty-fifth Division of the United States Army* (St. Louis, MO: Guard Publishing, 1919).

54. Laurence Stallings, *The Doughboys: The Story of the AEF, 1917–1918* (New York: Harper and Row, 1963), 375.

55. David McCullough, *Truman* (New York: Simon and Schuster, 1992), 142.

56. Ibid., 135.

57. Jay M. Lee, *The Artilleryman: The Experiences and Impressions of an American Artillery Regiment in the World War* (Kansas City, MO: Spencer Printing, 1920), 195.

58. Stallings, *Doughboys,* 377.

59. Ibid.

60. For an "anatomy" of chickenshit, see Paul Fussell, *Wartime: Understanding and Behavior in the Second World War* (New York: Oxford University Press, 1989), 79–95.

61. James Stevens, *Mattock* (New York: Alfred A. Knopf, 1927), 301.

62. Ernest Hemingway, "Soldier's Home," in *In Our Time* (New York: Simon and Schuster, 1996), 75.

63. For more on Hemingway's story as a critique of veterans' issues, see Steven Trout, "'Where Do We Go from Here?': Ernest Hemingway's 'Soldier's Home' and American Veterans of World War I," *Hemingway Review* 20, no. 1 (2000): 5–21.

64. Hemingway, "Soldier's Home," 69.

65. Carol R. Byerly, *Fever of War: The Influenza Epidemic in the U.S. Army during World War I* (New York: New York University Press, 2005), 187–89.

66. Bill Harris, *The Hellfighters of Harlem: African-American Soldiers Who Fought for the Right to Fight for Their Country* (New York: Carroll and Graf, 2002), 22.

67. Slotkin, *Lost Battalions,* 286–89.

68. See Ralph Ellison, *The Invisible Man* (1952; New York: Vintage, 1995), and Toni Morrison, *Sula* (1973; New York: Plume, 2002). Both of these novels contain compelling portraits of embittered African American veterans of World War I.

69. Mark Whalan, "'The Only Real White Democracy' and the Language of Liberation: The Great War, France, and African American Culture in the 1920s," *Modern Fiction Studies* 51, no. 4 (2005): 793.

70. Anthony Troncone, "Hamilton Fish Sr. and the Politics of American Nationalism, 1912–1945," PhD diss., Rutgers University, 1993, 81.

71. *Honor Roll of Livingston County, Missouri* (Chillicothe, MO: Chillicothe Constitution, 1919), 87.

72. Fred Henney, *Reno's Response: History of Reno County's War Work Activities during the World War, 1917–1918* (Hutchison, KS: n.p., 1920), 109.

73. *Honor Roll of Livingston County,* 87.

74. Leonard P. Ayres, *The War with Germany: A Statistical Summary* (Washington, DC: U.S. Government Printing Office, 1919), 122–23.

75. Niall Ferguson, *The Pity of War: Explaining World War I* (New York: Basic Books, 1999), 295.

76. Ibid.

77. Ibid.

78. Hemingway, *Sun Also Rises.*

79. Ayres, *War with Germany,* 122.

80. John R. Neff, *Honoring the Civil War Dead: Commemoration and the Problem of Reconciliation* (Lawrence: University Press of Kansas, 2005), 21.

81. Ibid.

82. Ibid.

83. For a thorough analysis of the theme of reconciliation and the memory of slavery that this theme came to displace, see David W. Blight, *Race and Reunion: The Civil War in American Memory* (Cambridge, MA: Belknap Press, 2002).

84. Neff, *Honoring the Civil War Dead,* 21.

85. Ibid.

86. Ayres, *War with Germany,* 120, 129.

87. Ibid., 23.

88. Charles H. Browne and J. W. McManigal, *Our Part in the Great War: What the Horton Community Did* (Horton, KS: Headlight-Commercial, 1919), 180.

89. Adjutant General of Kansas, *Kansas Casualties in the World War, 1917–1919* (Topeka: Kansas State Printing Plant, 1921), 11. See also Adjutant General of Kansas, *Supplement: Kansas Casualties in the World War, 1917–1919* (Topeka: Kansas State Printing Plant, 1921).

90. "The Legion's Care of the Home-Coming Dead," *American Legion Weekly* (hereafter, *ALW*) 4, no. 21 (May 26, 1922): 24–25.

91. "Impressive Military Funeral Conducted by Legion Boys in Honor of the Late Lieut. G. P. Cather Jr.," *Bladen Examiner,* May 6, 1921, 1. For a detailed discussion of Cather's reburial as a case study in World War I remembrance, see Trout, *Memorial Fictions,* 25–38.

92. "Impressive Military Funeral," 1.

93. Ibid.

94. For more on the policies and procedures followed by the Imperial War Graves Commission (later titled the Commonwealth War Graves Commission), see Philip Longworth, *The Unending Vigil: A History of the Commonwealth War Graves Commission, 1917–1967* (London: Constable, 1967). A history of the American counterpart to the Commonwealth War Graves Commission—the American Battle Monuments Commission—has yet to be written.

95. Piehler, *Remembering War,* 102.

96. John Dos Passos, *1919* (New York: Harcourt, Brace, 1932), 473.

97. Ibid., 471.

98. Billy Rose, "The Unknown Soldier," posted on Aftermath, original content by Mike Roden, 2002, http://www.aftermathww1.co.uk/billrose.asp, accessed August 19, 2009.

99. For more on *The Unknown Soldier Speaks,* see Jennifer Keene, "The Memory of the Great War in the African American Community," in Snell, *Unknown Soldiers,* 73.

100. E. O. Laughlin "The Unknown," in *Armistice Day*, ed. A. P. Sanford and Robert Haven Schauffler (New York: Dodd, Mead, 1928), 237–38, and Carl Sandburg, "And So To-Day," in *American Poetry 1922: A Miscellany*, ed. Louis Untermeyer (New York: Harcourt, Brace, 1922), 45.

101. See George H. Ralphson, *Over There with Pershing's Heroes at Cantigny* (Chicago: Donohue, 1919). In his series of boys' novels, Ralphson also took his young readers "Over There" with *The Marines at Chateau Thierry*, *The Canadians at Vimy Ridge*, and *The Doughboys at St. Mihiel*.

Chapter 1

This chapter's opening epigraph comes from Willard Waller, *The Veteran Comes Back* (New York: Dryden Press, 1944), 214.

1. Ibid.

2. Ibid., 215.

3. Marquis James, "Who Got the Money?: II. The Airplane Production Mess," *ALW* 4, no. 37 (1922): 5.

4. See John J. Pershing, "Our Plans for the National Defense," *ALW* 4, no. 19 (1922): 5–6, 28–29.

5. William Pencak, *For God and Country: The American Legion, 1919–1941* (Boston: Northeastern University Press, 1989), 50.

6. Ibid., 89.

7. Preston William Slosson, *The Great Crusade and After, 1914–1928* (New York: Macmillan, 1931), 287.

8. Dixon Wecter, *When Johnny Comes Marching Home* (Cambridge, MA: Riverside Press, 1944), 445.

9. Pencak, *For God and Country*, 94–95.

10. Notable studies written before the Second World War include Dorothy Culp, *The American Legion: A Study in Pressure Politics* (Chicago: University of Chicago Libraries, 1942), and William Gellermann, *The American Legion as Educator* (New York: Columbia University Teachers College, 1938). Culp's study originally appeared as a PhD dissertation in 1939.

11. See Roscoe Baker, *The American Legion and Foreign Policy* (New York: Bookman Associates, 1954); Justin Gray and Victor H. Bernstein, *The Inside Story of the Legion* (New York: Boni and Gaer, 1954); and Raymond Moley Jr., *The American Legion Story* (New York: Duell, Sloan and Pearce, 1966).

12. Thomas B. Littlewood, *Soldiers Back Home: The American Legion in Illinois, 1919–1939* (Carbondale: Southern Illinois University Press, 2004), xv.

13. See Thomas A. Rumer, *The American Legion: An Official History, 1919–1989* (New York: M. Evans, 1990).

14. Littlewood, *Soldiers Back Home*, 18.

15. See Charles Horne, ed., *Source Records of the Great War* (Indianapolis: American Legion, 1931).

16. Now known as the *American Legion Magazine*, this publication still exists today, in both print and online forms. For more information, see http://www.legion.org/national/divisions/magazine.

17. Waller, *Veteran Comes Back,* 214.

18. W. L. Roper, "Market for War Experiences," *Writer's Monthly* 33, no. 4 (1929): 304.

19. See Pencak, *For God and Country,* 25–47.

20. "Hun Helmets Boost Work," *Stars and Stripes,* February 28, 1919, 3.

21. "Bear Drive Hits Souvenir Market," *Stars and Stripes,* March 14, 1919, 7.

22. See "World War I Scrapbook of Sgt. Thomas Fletcher, AEF, Rouen, France," MS 262, Special Collections, University of Colorado Libraries, Boulder, Colorado.

23. World War I Photo Album of Clyde James, AEF, author's collection.

24. World War I Photo Album of Ray Wentworth, AEF, author's collection.

25. Paddy Griffith, *Battle Tactics of the Western Front: The British Army's Art of Attack, 1916–1918* (New Haven, CT: Yale University Press, 1994), 180.

26. "So Long," *Skirmisher* (April 1919): 3.

27. See "General Pershing Praises Review," *Jayhawkerinfrance* 1, no. 6 (1919): 1, 4; "Gen. Wright Decorates Regimental Colors," *Jayhawkerinfrance* 1, no. 8 (1919): 1, 4; and "General Bullard Reviews Regiment of Jayhawkers," *Jayhawkerinfrance* 1, no. 1 (1919): 1.

28. "Our Record," *Skirmisher* (May 1919): 8.

29. "Percivle Socrates Alonzo," *Skirmisher* (May 1919): 16.

30. "The guy that wears his service stripes before he earns them," *Skirmisher* (May 1919): 18.

31. "History of Some Places Where We Made History," *Jayhawkerinfrance* 1, no. 1 (1918): 2.

32. "The Fallen Have Not Been Forgotten," *Jayhawkerinfrance* 1, no. 2 (1919): 1, 4.

33. "Going Back," *Skirmisher* (April 1919): 21.

34. "Write that Farewell Letter Home Here!" *Jayhawkerinfrance* 1, no. 6 (1919): 3.

35. "The Old Ninth Infantry," in *The Ninth U.S. Infantry in the World War* (Neuwied am Rhein, Germany: Louis Heusersche, 1919), n.p.

36. Preface to *Ninth U.S. Infantry,* n.p.

37. *Company F Three Hundred and First Engineers* (Cologne, Germany: J. P. Bachem, 1919), 66.

38. Ibid., 64.

39. "Objective Obtained," in *Company F,* 147.

40. "1945 A.D.," in *Sapper* (April 1919): 5.

41. See Edward Bellamy, *Looking Backward: 200–1887,* ed. Cecelia Tishi (New York: Penguin, 1982).

42. Nick Nichols, *Memoirs of a Vet* (Chicago: Greenlee Co., 1939), 21.

43. Ibid., 25.

44. Ibid., 29.

45. Ibid.

46. Ibid., 37.

47. Ibid.

48. Ibid.

49. John H. Craige, "Would We Get In Again?" *ALM* 22, no. 4 (1937): 18–19, 58–61.

50. Frederick Palmer, "Known But to God," *ALM* 22, no. 4 (1937): 55.

51. Bernhard Ragner, "D.S.C.," *ALM* 22, no. 4 (1937): 12–13, 50–53.

52. Unfortunately, Jack Myron McLeod's "A Thematic Analysis of *The American Legion Magazine*, 1919–1951," MA thesis, University of Wisconsin, 1953, excludes all works of fiction and does not include heroism as a thematic category.

53. See Dan Edwards, "The Hero Stuff," *ALM* 5, no. 5 (1928): 6, 62–65.

54. See Dan Edwards, "Do War Stories Grow?" *ALM* 17, no. 4 (1934): 4, 55–57.

55. "A Source of Inspiration to Millions of Americans," advertisement for the *Chevrolet Chronicles, ALM* 9, no. 6 (1930): 39.

56. See "He carried a message through the enemy lines," advertisement for the *Chevrolet Chronicles, ALM* 10, no. 3 (1931): 35; "Hear Captain 'Eddie' Rickenbacker's personal story," advertisement for the *Chevrolet Chronicles, ALM* 10, no. 1 (1931): 4.

57. Ragner, "D.S.C.," 13.

58. Ibid., 52–53.

59. Ibid., 53.

60. See Leonard H. Nason, *Chevrons* (New York: Doran, 1926), and *Sergeant Eadie* (Garden City, NY: Doubleday, Doran, 1928).

61. Leonard H. Nason, *The Man in the White Slicker* (Garden City, NY: Doubleday, Doran, 1929).

62. Leonard H. Nason, "Lafayette, That Was Us!" *ALM* 22, no. 4 (1937): 6.

63. Ibid.

64. Ibid.

65. Ibid., 9.

66. Ibid.

67. Ibid., 44.

68. Newton D. Baker, "Why We Went to War," *ALM* 2, no. 4 (1927): 63.

69. Ibid., 64.

70. Quoted in Frederick C. Painton, "Why They Want to Go to France," *ALM* 2, no. 4 (1927): 40.

71. Ibid.

72. Ibid.

73. William Slaven McNutt, "A Pass to Paris," *ALM* 2, no. 4 (1927): 85.

74. Ibid., 86.

75. Ibid.

76. Ibid.

77. Ibid., 88.

78. Drew Hill, "Eggs," *ALM* 2, no. 4 (1927): 23.

79. Ibid., 69.

80. Ibid., 25.

81. Hemingway, *Farewell to Arms,* 196.

82. Ironically, Hemingway might have agreed, at least in private, with the legion's interpretation of war experience. Although frequently cited as evidence of the writer's personal disenchantment with the Great War, his so-called big statement (the passage that contrasts patriotic abstractions with concrete language) in *A Farewell to Arms* perhaps has more to do with changing fashions in war fiction at the end of the 1920s than with his personal views. Hemingway scholar Milton

Cohen recently presented this argument in "When Did Hemingway Turn against World War I?" a paper presented at War + Ink: The 13th International Hemingway Society Conference, Kansas City, Missouri, June 9–15, 2008.

83. Hill, "Eggs," 22.

84. Keene, *Doughboys*, 162.

85. Cyrus Leroy Baldridge, cover illustration, *ALW* 4, no. 11 (1922).

86. S. J. Woolf, cover illustration, *ALW* 4, no. 8 (1922).

87. Cyrus LeRoy Baldridge, cover illustration, *ALW* 4, no. 14 (1922).

88. Arthur Capper, "Practical Benefits of Compensation," *ALW* 4, no. 5 (1922): 5, 18–19; "The Great 'Bonus Raid' on the United States Treasury," cartoon, *ALW* 4, no. 8 (1922): 11.

89. Keene, *Doughboys*, 185.

90. Ibid., 187.

91. Paul Dickson and Thomas B. Allen, *The Bonus Army: An American Epic* (New York: Walker, 2004), 105.

92. Keene, *Doughboys*, 183.

93. "The American Legion," *Crisis* 19, no. 2 (1919): 66.

94. "Bursts and Duds," *ALW* 1, no. 11 (1919): 24.

95. Art Helfant, untitled cartoon, *ALW* 4, no. 9 (1922): 14.

96. "Unpublished Pictures of the War," cartoon, *ALW* 2, no. 47 (1920): 9.

97. "The Rhine 'Horror,'" *ALW* 3, no. 13 (1921): 16.

98. Ibid.

99. Ibid.

100. Wiley M. Pickens, "Be It Ever So Humble," *ALM* 22, no. 6 (1937): 18.

101. Ibid.

102. Ibid.

103. Ibid., 19.

104. Ibid.

105. Ibid., 56.

106. Hugh Wiley, "They Also Served," *ALW* 4, no. 12 (1922): 7.

107. See Hugh Wiley, "Four Leaved Wildcat," *Saturday Evening Post*, March 8, 1919, 18–23; *The Wildcat* (New York: Doran, 1920); and *The Prowler* (New York: Knopf, 1924).

108. Richard Slotkin, *Lost Battalions: The Great War and the Crisis of American Nationality* (New York: Holt, 2005), 517. See Charles E. Mack, *Two Black Crows in the A.E.F.* (Indianapolis: Bobbs-Merrill, 1928).

109. Hugh Wiley, "Private War," *ALM* 20, no. 5 (1936): 44.

110. Joseph Mills Hanson, "The 4th Comes to the Rosebud," *ALM* 5, no. 1 (1928): 12.

111. "The Open Door," cartoon, *ALW* 2, no. 32 (1920): 6.

112. Joanna W. Harting, "The Girl Who Took a Soldier's Job," *ALW* 1, no. 14 (1919): 18.

113. "For the Best New War Novel, $25,000," *ALM* (April 1928): 20.

114. "Results of the $25,000 War Novel Contest," *ALM* (August 1929): 5, 70–72.

115. Martha Gellhorn, "The Paths of Glory," *New Republic* 61, no. 306 (1930): 306.

116. "War at Length," review of *It's a Great War!* by Mary Lee, *New York Times Book Review*, November 17, 1929, 7.

117. Byron Darnton, "The Hard-Boiled Sergeant's and the Lady Idealist's War," review of *It's a Great War!* by Mary Lee and *God Have Mercy on Us!* by William Scanlon, *New York Evening Post*, November 2, 1929, 11.

118. Review of *It's a Great War!* by Mary Lee, *Times Literary Supplement*, February 13, 1930, 124.

119. "Results of the $25,000 War Novel Contest," 5.

120. "The Message Center," *ALM* (September 1929): 8.

121. "Author of 'It's a Great War' Says Publishers Are Too Materialistic," press clipping, *Boston Herald*, January 12, 1930, File 83-M262, Mary Lee Papers, Schlesinger Library, Radcliffe Institute, Harvard University; hereafter, Mary Lee Papers.

122. Darnton, "Hard-Boiled Sergeant's," 11.

123. "Results of the $25,000 War Novel Contest," 71.

124. Emily Williams to James F. Barton, July 29, 1929, File 82-M144, Mary Lee Papers.

125. Mary Lee to City Editor, Associated Press, January 31, 1930, File 83-M262, Mary Lee Papers.

126. "Newton Legion Ousts Mary Lee," press clipping, *Boston Herald*, File 83-M262, Mary Lee Papers.

127. Mary Lee to John T. Winterich, February 10, 1930, File 82-M144, Mary Lee Papers.

128. Mary Lee to Ferris Greenslet, February 18, 1930, File 82-M144, Mary Lee Papers.

129. Mary Lee to Ferris Greenslet, April 16, 1930, File 82-M144, Mary Lee Papers.

Chapter 2

This chapter's opening epigraph comes from George Carlin, *Brain Droppings* (New York: Comedy Concepts, 1997), 180.

1. X. E. Price to John J. Pershing, February 12, 1925, Pershing Correspondence File, Box 7, RG 117 Records of the American Battle Monuments Commission, National Archives, College Park, Maryland.

2. G. Kurt Piehler, *Remembering War the American Way* (Washington, DC: Smithsonian Institution Press, 1995), 105–11.

3. Earl D. Goldsmith, "Introduction," Earl D. Goldsmith's *Spirit of the American Doughboy* Database, http://members.tripod.com/doughboy_lamp/earlspages/id57.html, accessed September 23, 2007. (This Web site is no longer available; however, you can find Goldsmith's current Web site at http://doughboysearcher.weebly.com.)

4. Les Kopel, "The 12-Inch Doughboy Statuette," Grandma Quater's *Spirit of the American Doughboy* Lamp, http://doughboy_lamp.tripod.com/index.html, accessed September 23, 2007. (This Web site is no longer available; however, you can find Kopel's current site at http://doughboysearcher.weebly.com.)

5. Kopel, "E. M. Viquesney, Sculptor," Grandma Quater's *Spirit of the American Doughboy* Lamp.

6. Goldsmith, "E. M. Viquesney, Sculptor," Earl D. Goldsmith's *Spirit of the American Doughboy* Database.

7. Ibid.

8. Alan Anderson, "E. M. Viquesney: Portrait of *Doughboy*'s Sculptor," *Save Outdoor Sculpture! Update* 5, no. 1 (1994): 4.

9. Goldsmith, "The Spirit of the American Doughboy," Earl D. Goldsmith's *Spirit of the American Doughboy* Database.

10. Ibid.

11. Jennifer Wingate, "Over the Top: The Doughboy in World War I Memorials and Visual Culture," *American Art* 19, no. 2 (2005): 29.

12. Kopel, "Description and History," Grandma Quater's *Spirit of the American Doughboy* Lamp.

13. Goldsmith, "Appendix A: Dedication Dates," Earl D. Goldsmith's *Spirit of the American Doughboy* Database.

14. Goldsmith, "Spirit of the American Doughboy," Earl D. Goldsmith's *Spirit of the American Doughboy* Database.

15. Ibid.

16. Kopel, "Description and History."

17. Ibid.

18. Advertisement for *Spirit of the American Doughboy* statuette and lamp, *ALW* 4, no. 44 (1922): 27.

19. Advertisement for the "American Doughboy Art Lamp," *ALW* 4, no. 21 (1922): 17.

20. Advertisement for *Spirit of the American Doughboy*, *ALM* 2, no. 4 (1927): 64.

21. Kopel, "Viquesney Flier, C. 1928," Grandma Quater's *Spirit of the American Doughboy* Lamp.

22. Kopel, "An Ad for the 6-Inch Doughboy," Grandma Quater's *Spirit of the American Doughboy* Lamp.

23. Wingate, "Over the Top," 28.

24. Jennifer D. Keene, *World War I* (Westport, CT: Greenwood Press, 2006), 190.

25. Cather, *One of Ours*, 333.

26. "The Miniature Desktop Doughboys," E. M. Viquesney "Spirit of the American Doughboy" Database, http://doughboysearcher.tripod.com/id8.html.

27. George L. Mosse, *Fallen Soldiers: Reshaping the Memory of the World Wars* (New York: Oxford University Press, 1990), 80.

28. William A. Blair, *Cities of the Dead: Contesting the Memory of the Civil War in the South, 1865–1914* (Chapel Hill: University of North Carolina Press, 2004), 171–207.

29. Ibid., 174–75.

30. Ibid., 174.

31. Ibid., 176.

32. Ibid., 179–93.

33. Ibid., 204.

34. Ibid., 171–72.

35. Piehler, *Remembering War,* 118.

36. Neil Hanson, *Unknown Soldiers: The Story of the Missing of the First World War* (New York: Knopf, 2006), 344.

37. Piehler, *Remembering War,* 121.

38. Ibid.

39. Susan Meyer, "On the Front and at Home: Wharton, Cather, the Jews, and the First World War," in *Cather Studies 6: History, Memory, and War,* ed. Steven Trout (Lincoln: University of Nebraska Press, 2006), 210.

40. Mark Meigs, *Optimism at Armageddon: Voices of American Participants in the First World War* (New York: New York University Press, 1997), 147.

41. Piehler, *Remembering War,* 117.

42. Aviel Roshwald, *The Endurance of Nationalism: Ancient Roots and Modern Dilemmas* (Cambridge: Cambridge University Press, 2006), 64.

43. Michael Sledge, *Soldier Dead: How We Recover, Identify, Bury, and Honor Our Military Fallen* (New York: Columbia University Press, 2005), 67.

44. James Weldon Johnson, foreword to *Saint Peter Relates an Incident: Selected Poems by James Weldon Johnson* (New York: Penguin, 1993), xiii.

45. Johnson, "Saint Peter Relates an Incident," 15–17.

46. Ibid., 18.

47. Ibid., 21–22.

48. Laurence Stallings, *Plumes* (1924; Columbia: University of South Carolina Press, 2006), 5.

49. Ibid., 347.

50. Ibid., 347–48.

51. Harry Kemp, "The Unknown," in Sanford and Schauffler, *Armistice Day,* 240.

52. Elaine Scarry, *The Body in Pain: The Making and Unmaking of the World* (New York: Oxford University Press, 1985).

53. Dos Passos, *1919,* 472.

54. E. O. Laughlin, "The Unknown," in Sanford and Schauffler, *Armistice Day,* 237–38.

55. Ibid., 238.

56. For a discussion of Longstaff's work, see Jay Winter, *Sites of Memory, Sites of Mourning: The Great War in European Cultural History* (Cambridge: Cambridge University Press, 1995), 60–61.

57. Bruce Barton, "Unknown," in Sanford and Schauffler, *Armistice Day,* 230.

58. Ibid., 231.

59. Ibid., 232.

60. Ibid., 233

61. Ibid., 232.

62. *Congressional Record, Appendix and Index to Parts 1 to 9 of the Proceedings and Debates of the First Session of the Sixty-seventh Congress of the United States,* vol. 61, part 9 (Washington, DC: Government Printing Office, 1921), 8928.

63. Ibid., 88₅₅.

64. Quoted in Ernest Hamlin Abbott, "Simplicity, Honesty, Honor: Editorial Correspondence from Washington," *Outlook* 126 (November 23, 1921): 464.

65. Ibid., 465.

66. For an account of the 1921–1922 Naval Disarmament Conference and its problematic legacy, see *The Washington Conference, 1921–22: Naval Rivalry, East Asian Stability, and the Road to Pearl Harbor,* eds. Erik Goldstein and John H. Maurer (Newbury Park, Eng.: Frank Cass, 1994).

67. Barton, "Unknown," 233.

68. Dos Passos, *1919,* 473.

69. M. A. De Wolfe Howe, "The Known Soldier," in *The Red Harvest: A Cry for Peace,* ed. Vincent Godfrey Burns (1930; Miami: Granger Books, 1976), 350–51.

70. Margaret Stineback, "The Unknown Soldier," in Burns, *Red Harvest,* 340.

71. Arthur B. Rhinow, "The Unknown Soldier," in Burns, *Red Harvest,* 337.

72. Charles A. Wagner, "The Unknown Soldier," in Burns, *Red Harvest,* 344.

73. Ibid., 346.

74. Ibid., 346–47.

75. Harry Emerson Fosdick, "The Unknown Soldier," in *Riverside Sermons* (1933; New York: Harper and Brothers, 1958), 345.

76. Ibid.

77. Ibid., 351.

78. According to Saperstein's son, the rabbi's "personal library" contained John Haynes Holmes's *The Sensible Man's View of Religion* (New York: Harper Brothers, 1993), which included "The Unknown Soldier Speaks." See Harold I. Saperstein, "Must There Be War?" (1936) in *Witness from the Pulpit: Topical Sermons, 1933–1980,* ed. Marc Saperstein (Lanham, MD: Lexington Books, 2000), note on p. 51.

79. John Haynes Holmes, "The Unknown Soldier Speaks," in *A Summons Unto Men: An Anthology of the Writings of John Haynes Holmes,* ed. Carl Hermann Voss (New York: Simon and Schuster, 1971), 128.

80. Ibid.

81. Ibid., 137–38.

82. Ibid., 139.

83. Carl Sandburg, "And So To-Day," in *American Poetry 1922: A Miscellany,* ed. Louis Untermeyer (New York: Harcourt, Brace, 1922), 47.

84. Dos Passos, *1919,* 467.

85. Ibid., 468.

86. Holmes, "Unknown Soldier Speaks," 128.

87. Dos Passos, *1919,* 471.

88. Sandburg, "And So To-Day," 45.

89. See John W. Thomason Jr., *Fix Bayonets!* (New York: Charles Scribner's Sons, 1926).

90. Philip D. Beidler, introduction to *Company K* by William March (Tuscaloosa: University of Alabama Press, 1989), xv.

91. William March, *Company K* (New York: Harrison Smith and Robert Haas, 1933), 184.

92. Ibid.

93. Ibid., 178.

94. Ibid., 181.

95. Ibid., 181–82.

96. Piehler, *Remembering War,* 122.

97. Frederick Palmer, "Known But to God," *ALM* 22, no. 4 (1937): 10.

98. "Frequently Asked Questions," Society of the Honor Guard, Tomb of the Unknown Soldier, http://www.tombguard.org/FAQ.html, accessed September 2, 2009.

99. Goldsmith, "Appendix A: Dedication Dates," Earl D. Goldsmith's *Spirit of the American Doughboy* Database.

Chapter 3

This chapter's opening epigraph comes from J. André Smith, *In France with the American Expeditionary Forces* (New York: Arthur Halo, 1919), n.p.

1. See *Catalogue of Official A.E.F. Photographs Taken by the Signal Corps, U.S.A.* (Washington, DC: U.S. Government Printing Office, 1919).

2. "He Didn't Have to . . . but He Went Over the Top," *ALM* 21, no. 3 (1936): 45.

3. Ibid.

4. Ibid.

5. Ibid.

6. Quoted in Peter Krass, *Portrait of War: The U.S. Army's First Combat Artists and the Doughboys' Experience in WWI* (Hoboken, NJ: Wiley, 2007), 50.

7. Ibid., 194.

8. Reproduced in Robert F. Karolevitz, *Where Your Heart Is: The Story of Harvey Dunn, Artist* (Aberdeen, SD: North Plains Press, 1970), 54.

9. Edgar M. Howell, quoted in ibid., 55–59.

10. Quoted in Krass, *Portrait of War,* 170.

11. See William E. Moore and James C. Russell, *U.S. Official Pictures of the World War* (Washington, DC: Pictorial Bureau, 1920).

12. Robert F. Karolevitz, *Harvey Dunn War Works: Art from the American Expeditionary Forces,* exhibit brochure, South Dakota Art Museum, Brookings, SD, November 8, 2001–March 25, 2002, 4.

13. Ibid.

14. Krass, *Portrait of War,* 80.

15. Ibid., 231.

16. Ibid.

17. Alfred Emile Cornebise, *Art from the Trenches: America's Uniformed Artists in World War I* (College Station: Texas A&M University Press, 1991), 45.

18. Willa Cather, *The Professor's House* (New York: Knopf, 1925), 261. See Cather, *My Ántonia* (Boston: Houghton-Mifflin, 1918).

19. Karolevitz, *Where Your Heart Is,* 71.

20. See William E. Moore, "Painted at the Front," *ALW* 1, no. 10 (1919): 17–21.

21. Nina Molinaro, remark to author, March 17, 2007.

22. Krass, *Portrait of War,* 178.

23. Frederic Manning, *The Middle Parts of Fortune* (1929; New York: St. Martin's, 1977), n.p.

24. Karolevitz, *Where Your Heart Is,* 88.

25. Ibid., 85.

26. *ALM* 25, no. 2 (1938): 1.

27. Edward Lengel, *To Conquer Hell: The Meuse-Argonne, 1918* (New York: Henry Holt, 2008). Lengel includes three of Dunn's paintings in his section of well-chosen illustrations: *Prisoners and Wounded, In the Front Line at Early Morning,* and *Sunday Morning at Cunel.* No other works by AEF artists are reproduced. Additional evidence of Dunn's continued dominance of Americans' visual memory of World War I appears on the cover of Krass's *Portrait of War.* Although Krass's book tells the story of all eight official AEF artists, only Dunn's work appears on the dust wrapper—no fewer than three of his paintings, in fact!

28. Richard Slotkin, *Lost Battalions: The Great War and the Crisis of American Nationality* (New York: Henry Holt, 2005), 278–81.

29. See Alain Locke, ed., *The Negro in Art: A Pictorial Record of the Negro Artist and of the Negro Theme in Art* (Washington, D.C.: Associates in Negro Folk Education, 1940).

30. Judith E. Stein, "An American Original," in *I Tell My Heart: The Art of Horace Pippin,* Judith E. Stein, ed. (Philadelphia: Pennsylvania Academy of Fine Arts, 1993), 11.

31. Quoted in ibid.

32. Quoted in ibid.

33. Quoted in Slotkin, *Lost Battalions,* 141.

34. Slotkin, *Lost Battalions,* 142.

35. Ibid., 151.

36. Lengel, *To Conquer Hell,* 428.

37. "Ragtime by U.S. Band Gets Everyone 'Over There,'" *St. Louis Post Dispatch,* June 10, 1918, 40–41; Tim Gracyk, liner notes, *Lieut. Jim Europe's 369th U.S. Infantry "Hell Fighters" Band: The Complete Recordings,* Inside Sounds/Memphis Archives, 1996.

38. Gracyk, liner notes, 9.

39. Arthur W. Little, *From Harlem to the Rhine: The Story of New York's Colored Volunteers* (New York: Covici Friede, 1936), 201.

40. "Ragtime by U.S. Band," 40.

41. Slotkin, *Lost Battalions,* 45–46.

42. Quoted in Gracyk, liner notes, 14–15.

43. Quoted in Janis Stout, *Coming Out of War: Poetry, Grieving, and the Culture of the World Wars* (Tuscaloosa: University of Alabama Press, 2005), 100.

44. Ibid., 13.

45. Lynda Roscoe Hartigan, "Landscapes, Portraits, and Still Lifes," in Stein, *I Tell My Heart,* 96.

46. W. E. B. Du Bois, "Foreword," *Crisis* 20, no. 5 (1920): 213.

47. Ibid.

48. Kelly Miller, *Kelly Miller's History of the World War for Human Rights* (Washington, DC: Jenkins and Keller, 1919), 535.

49. Ibid.

50. Vincent Saunders, "The Horizon," *Crisis* 17, no. 1 (1918): 32.

51. Ibid., 33.

52. Ibid.

53. Vincent Saunders, "The Horizon," *Crisis* 17, no. 2 (1918): 82.

54. Ibid.

55. W. E. B. Du Bois, "An Essay toward a History of the Black Man in the Great War," *Crisis* 18, no. 2 (1919): 86.

56. Ibid., 87.

57. Judith Wilson, "Scenes of War," in Stein, *I Tell My Heart,* 62.

58. Richard J. Powell, "Biblical and Spiritual Motifs," in Stein, *I Tell My Heart,* 132.

59. "Paid Honor to Our Soldier Dead," *Winchester Star,* June 10, 1921, 3.

60. The only biography of the painter, Laurence Eli Schmeckebier, *John Steuart Curry's Pageant of America* (New York: American Artists Group, 1943), sheds little light on their friendship. Nor are any clues to be found in Patricia Junker, ed., *John Steuart Curry: Inventing the Middle West* (New York: Hudson Hills, 1998).

61. "Cudworth Post Gets Painting by Curry," *Milwaukee Sentinel,* June 1, 1940, press clipping, John Steuart Curry Papers, Correspondence File B, Archives of American Art, Smithsonian Institution; hereafter, Curry Papers.

62. Donald Davis, nephew of William L. Davis, interview with author, February 3, 2008.

63. John W. Davis, biography of William L. Davis, William L. Davis File, Collection 49: Gold Star Mother's Collection, Library and Archives Division, Kansas State Historical Society, Topeka, Kansas.

64. Ibid.

65. Homer F. Trapp, "Synopsis of the History of Company B," *Company B, 3rd Kansas N.G., 139th Infantry Memories of the Reunion, August 19–20, 1955* (N.p.: n.p., 1955), 8.

66. Ibid.

67. "Wm. L. Davis Dead," *Winchester Star,* September 27, 1918, 1.

68. "William Louis Davis," *Farmers' Vindicator,* June 10, 1921, 1.

69. Ibid.

70. Ibid.

71. Gold Star card, William L. Davis Collection, File 1, National World War I Museum, Kansas City, Missouri; hereafter, Davis Collection.

72. Card from the Military Sisterhood of Oskaloosa, Kansas, Davis Collection.

73. J. Davis, biography of William L. Davis.

74. Neil Hanson, *Unknown Soldiers: The Story of the Missing of the First World War* (New York: Knopf, 2006), 243.

75. Piehler, *Remembering War,* 96.

76. Ibid., 97.

77. Charles C. Pierce to "The Relatives of Our Dead," undated, Davis Collection.

78. R. E. Shannon, "Notice Regarding Reimbursement of Funeral Expenses," Davis Collection.

79. Telegram, Graves Registration Service to John W. Davis, June 1, 1921, Davis Collection.

80. Donald Davis, interview with author, February 3, 2008.

81. Interestingly, several variant titles of the painting made their way into newspaper coverage when the work was sold to the Alonzo Cudworth post of the American Legion (located in Milwaukee) in 1940. For example, the *Milwaukee Sentinel* ("Cudworth Post Gets Painting by Curry," June 1, 1940, Curry Papers) described the unveiling of *"Private Davis Returns."* The *Milwaukee Journal* ("New Curry Painting Is Accepted by Legion," May 31, 1940, Curry Papers) switched back and forth between *"The Return of Private Davis"* and *"Private Davis Returns from the Argonne."* It was Curry himself who established the painting's "proper title" (apparently for the first time) in a letter to Malcolm K. Whyte (May 13, 1940, Curry Papers), the representative of the Cudworth post. The title given in that letter is the title we know today, *The Return of Private Davis from the Argonne.* Since the painter indicated in a subsequent note to Whyte (June 22, 1939, Curry Papers) that "Davis was killed in the Forest of the Argonne," he may by this point (nearly twelve years after the funeral) have forgotten the location of his friend's death. But this seems unlikely. During the Meuse-Argonne battle the 35th Division did not fight in the Argonne Forest (the site of the Lost Battalion's famous struggle), but in the mostly open countryside located to the east. A desire to tie his painting to a familiar and mythologized battleground seems to have guided Curry as he selected his title.

82. Trapp includes William L. Davis in his list of eighteen total fatalities in "Synopsis of the History of Company B." Davis was apparently the only member of the company to die in Alsace. Davis's name appears incorrectly as "Lester M. Davis" in the roster of Company B included in Claire Kenamore, *The Story of the 139th Infantry* (St. Louis, MO: Guard Publishing, 1920), 70.

83. Schmeckebier, *John Steuart Curry's Pageant*, 59.

84. See Marjorie Swann and William M. Tsutsui, "John Steuart Curry: A Portrait of the Artist as a Kansan," in *John Brown to Bob Dole: Movers and Shakers in Kansas History*, Virgil W. Dean, ed. (Lawrence: University Press of Kansas, 2006), 241–52.

85. See Charles C. Eldredge, *John Steuart Curry's Hoover and the Flood: Painting Modern History* (Chapel Hill: University of North Carolina Press, 2007).

86. Henry Adams, "Space, Weather, Myth, and Abstraction in the Art of John Steuart Curry," in Junker, *John Steuart Curry*, 121.

87. Of course, as a veteran of the Western Front, Dunn may also have had a more indirect influence on Curry's painting. While studying under Dunn in Tenafly, Curry would have seen many of his mentor's war paintings—and the collection of World War I memorabilia that Dunn received as a gift from the U.S. Army.

88. Quoted in M. Sue Kendall, *Rethinking Regionalism: John Steuart Curry and the Kansas Mural Controversy* (Washington, DC: Smithsonian Institution Press, 1986), 83.

89. Schmeckebier, *John Steuart Curry's Pageant*, 254.

90. Kendall, "Alien Corn: An Artist on the Middle Border," in Junker, *John Steuart Curry*, 167.

91. Ibid.

92. Schmeckebier, *John Steuart Curry's Pageant*, 255.

93. Alfred Noyes, "The Victory Ball," in *Collected Poems* (Philadelphia: Lippincott, 1939), 339.

94. Ibid.

95. "Great Renaissance of Art Seen if United States Escapes War," *Cincinnati Times,* undated press clipping, 1939, no page number, Curry Papers, Correspondence File B, Archives of American Art, Smithsonian Institute.

96. Ibid.

97. Kendall, *Rethinking Regionalism,* 84.

98. Quoted in ibid.

99. Adams, "Space, Weather, Myth," 120.

100. "Statement of Account for Period June 16, 1939, to June 4, 1940," Curry Papers. The price discount may have reflected Curry's generosity and his desire to see his painting in an appropriate venue. However, Maynard Walker, head of the New York Gallery, where Curry's work was displayed and (on occasion) sold, felt that the artist overpriced his work. See Swann and Tsutsui, "John Steuart Curry," 252.

101. *Milwaukee Journal,* "New Curry Painting."

102. Quoted in *Milwaukee Sentinel,* "Cudworth Post Gets Painting."

103. Ibid.

104. See Sinclair Lewis, *Main Street* (New York: Harcourt, Brace, 1920).

105. Cather, *One of Ours,* 208.

106. James M. Dennis, *Renegade Regionalists: The Modern Independence of Grant Wood, Thomas Hart Benton, and John Steuart Curry* (Madison: University of Wisconsin Press, 1998), 8.

107. Scholarship on Eby is meager. A brief but useful biographical sketch can be found in Bernadette Passi Giardina, *Kerr Eby: The Complete Prints* (Bronxville, NY: M. Hausberg, 1997). For a contemporary assessment, see Dorothy Noyes Arms, *Kerr Eby, A.N.A., American Etchers,* vol. 8 (New York: Crafton Collection, P. and D. Colnaghi, 1930). Eby's pacifism and war art serve as the focus for Loramy Gerstbauer and Don Myers, "Peace Profile: Kerr Eby," *Peace Review: A Journal of Social Justice* 18, no. 2 (2006): 289–98. The question of why Eby remains a somewhat obscure figure, despite his powerful war art, receives attention in Gladys Engel Lang and Kurt Lang, "Recognition and Renown: The Survival of Artistic Reputation," *American Journal of Sociology* 94, no. 1 (1988): 79–109.

108. Kerr Eby, *War* (New Haven, CT: Yale University Press, 1936).

Chapter 4

This chapter's opening epigraph comes from Sanford Levinson, *Written in Stone: Public Monuments in Changing Societies* (Durham, NC: Duke University Press, 1998), 7.

1. Edward J. Renehan Jr., *The Lion's Pride: Theodore Roosevelt and His Family in Peace and War* (New York: Oxford University Press, 1998), 194.

2. Edward V. Rickenbacker, *Fighting the Flying Circus* (1919; Philadelphia: Lippincott, 1947), 196.

3. Kermit Roosevelt, *Quentin Roosevelt: A Sketch with Letters* (New York: Charles Scribner's Sons, 1922), 170–71.

4. John Graham, "Quentin Roosevelt and the Gold Star Mothers Pilgrimages," *Over the Front* 19, no. 3 (2004): 226. According to Graham, at least three

German pilots have been credited with shooting down Quentin Roosevelt: Christian Donhauser, Karl Thom, and (most recently) Carl Emil Gräper.

5. Rose E. B. Coombs, *Before Endeavors Fade: A Guide to the Battlefields of the First World War* (London: After the Battle, 1990), 147.

6. Roosevelt, *Quentin Roosevelt*, 237.

7. Quoted in Renehan Jr., *Lion's Pride*, 7.

8. Tonie Holt and Valmai Holt, *Major and Mrs. Holt's Concise Illustrated Battlefield Guide: The Western Front–South* (London: Pen and Sword, 2006), 27.

9. Roosevelt, *Quentin Roosevelt*, 175–76.

10. Renehan Jr., *Lion's Pride*, 206.

11. Roosevelt, *Quentin Roosevelt*, 178.

12. Ibid., 237.

13. Theodore Roosevelt to Charles C. Pierce, November 2, 1918, Quentin Roosevelt folder, Box 180, RG 117 Records of the American Battle Monuments Commission, National Archives, College Park, Maryland; hereafter, Quentin Roosevelt folder.

14. Graham, *Gold Star Mother Pilgrimages*, 92.

15. "Roosevelt Objects to Removal of Son," *New York Times*, November 18, 1918, 11.

16. Graham, *Gold Star Mother Pilgrimages*, 92.

17. "Inspector's Report," Quentin Roosevelt folder.

18. Chet Shafer, *The Second A.E.F: The Pilgrimage of the Army of Remembrance* (New York: Doty, 1927), 52.

19. Graham, *Gold Star Mother Pilgrimages*, 94.

20. Kermit Roosevelt to E. J. Heller, July 23, 1927, Quentin Roosevelt folder.

21. Ibid.

22. "Inspector's Report," Quentin Roosevelt folder.

23. Ibid.

24. Kermit Roosevelt to E. J. Heller, July 23, 1927, Quentin Roosevelt folder.

25. Charles D. Holle to James E. Mangum, September 9, 1940, Quentin Roosevelt folder.

26. James E. Mangum to Charles D. Holle, October 24, 1940, Quentin Roosevelt folder.

27. Renehan Jr., *Lion's Pride*, 132.

28. Robert P. Patterson to Archibald B. Roosevelt, October 16, 1946, Quentin Roosevelt folder.

29. Walter Krueger Jr. to Thomas North, January 6, 1947, Quentin Roosevelt folder.

30. John F. Harbeson to Thomas North, December 3, 1946, Quentin Roosevelt folder.

31. Thomas North to John F. Harbeson, December 4, 1946, Quentin Roosevelt folder.

32. John F. Harbeson to Edith Derby, February 3, 1947, Quentin Roosevelt folder.

33. Theodore Roosevelt Jr., *Average Americans, by Theodore Roosevelt, Lieutenant-Colonel, U.S.A.* (New York: G. P. Putnam's Sons, 1919).

34. Archibald B. Roosevelt to M. D. MacAlister, June 1, 1955, Quentin Roosevelt folder.

35. Thomas North to Officer in Charge, European Office, American Battle Monuments Commission, Paris, France, February 24, 1959, Quentin Roosevelt folder. In North's view, the issue of future maintenance was central to the Roosevelts' decision: "[T]he family of Quentin Roosevelt came to the conclusion a few years ago that the problem of finding in perpetuity someone (and his successor) who would properly maintain the grave was becoming impossible. They therefore reluctantly decided to ask that the body be removed to St. Laurent cemetery at the family's expense. This was done."

36. Kenneth C. Royall to Archibald B. Roosevelt, March 25, 1948, Quentin Roosevelt folder.

37. Eleanor B. Roosevelt to Thomas North, June 4, 1954, Quentin Roosevelt folder.

38. Ibid.

39. Archibald B. Roosevelt to Thomas North, April 5, 1955, Quentin Roosevelt folder.

40. Thomas North to Eleanor Roosevelt, June 22, 1954, Quentin Roosevelt folder.

41. Thomas North to Archibald B. Roosevelt, July 27, 1955, Quentin Roosevelt folder.

42. Thomas North to Jack D. Mage, April 12, 1955, Quentin Roosevelt folder.

43. Daniel Gibbs, "Report on Transfer of Body of Lt. Quentin Roosevelt from Coulonges-En-Tardenois (Aisne) to the Normandy Cemetery," Quentin Roosevelt folder.

44. Ibid.

45. Thomas North to Jack D. Mage, April 12, 1955, Quentin Roosevelt folder.

46. Karl S. Cate to Edith Derby, September 23, 1958, Quentin Roosevelt folder.

47. E-mail from Mike Hanlon to author, July 1, 2007.

48. E-mail from Tom Gudmestad to author, July 2, 2007.

49. Paul Fussell, *The Boys' Crusade: The American Infantryman in Northwestern Europe, 1944–1945* (New York: Modern Library, 2003), 157.

50. Paul Fussell, *Doing Battle: The Making of a Skeptic* (Boston: Little, Brown, 1996), 27–28.

51. See Paul Fussell, *The Great War and Modern Memory* (New York: Oxford University Press, 1975).

52. Fussell, *Doing Battle*, 27.

53. William Manchester, *Goodbye, Darkness: A Memoir of the Pacific War* (Boston: Little, Brown, 1980), 18.

54. Ibid., 21.

55. Lengel, *To Conquer Hell*, 111.

56. Bernadette Passi Giardina, *Kerr Eby: The Complete Prints* (Bronxville, NY: M. Hausberg, 1997), 9.

57. Ibid., 10.

58. James Jones, *WWII* (New York: Grosset and Dunlop, 1975), 118.

59. Ibid.

60. Mark A. Snell, "'The Price Was Made and the Price Was Paid': Grandpa's Scar and Other Memories of the AEF," in Snell, *Unknown Soldiers*, 23.

61. See Stanley Cooperman, *World War I and the American Novel* (Baltimore: Johns Hopkins University Press, 1967).

62. See Edward M. Coffman, *The War to End All Wars: The American Military Experience in World War I* (New York: Oxford University Press, 1968).

63. See Dalton Trumbo, *Johnny Got His Gun* (Philadelphia: J. B. Lippincott, 1939).

64. Michael Birdwell, "'After They've Seen Paree': The AEF in Film and Music," in Snell, *Unknown Soldiers*, 258.

65. Henry Berry, *Make the Kaiser Dance: Living Memories of a Forgotten War* (Garden City, NY: Doubleday, 1978).

66. For more information on America's last doughboy, see www.frankbuckles.org and the Library of Congress Veterans History Project (http://lcweb2.loc.gov/diglib/vhp-stories/loc.natlib.afc2001001.01070).

67. Tony Dokoupil, "The War We Forgot," *Newsweek*, February 18, 2008, available at http://www.newsweek.com/id/109681, accessed August 24, 2009.

68. Ibid.

69. Richard Rubin, "Over There—And Gone Forever," *New York Times*, November 12, 2007, A25.

70. Lengel, *To Conquer Hell*, 4.

71. Snell, preface to *Unknown Soldiers*, xv.

72. See Horace Baker's *Argonne Days in World War I*, Robert H. Ferrell, ed. (Columbia: University of Missouri Press, 2007); William S. Triplet, *A Youth in the Meuse-Argonne: A Memoir, 1917–1918,* Robert H. Ferrell, ed. (Columbia: University of Missouri Press, 2000); Mark Ethan Grotelueschen, *The AEF Way of War: The American Army and Combat in World War I* (New York: Cambridge University Press, 2006); Mitchell A. Yockelson, *Borrowed Soldiers: Americans under British Command, 1918* (Norman: University of Oklahoma Press, 2008); Alan D. Gaff, *Blood in the Argonne: The "Lost Battalion" of World War I* (Norman: University of Oklahoma Press, 2005); Robert H. Ferrell, *Five Days in October: The Lost Battalion of World War I* (Columbia: University of Missouri Press, 2005); Robert Laplander, *Finding the Lost Battalion: Beyond the Rumors, Myths, and Legends of America's Famous WWI Epic* (New York: Lulu, 2007); Jennifer Haytock, *At Home, At War: Domesticity and World War I in American Literature* (Columbus: Ohio State University Press, 2003); Patrick J. Quinn, *The Conning of America: The Great War and American Popular Literature* (Atlanta: Rodopi, 2001); and Mark Levitch, *Panthéon de la Guerre: Reconfiguring a Panorama of the Great War* (Columbia: University of Missouri Press, 2006).

73. Douglas Mastriano, "News from France," *Camaraderie: The Journal of the Western Front Association United States Branch* (August 2008): 9.

Bibliography

Archival Sources

Dwight D. Eisenhower Pre-Presidential Papers, Eisenhower Library, Abilene, Kansas.
John Steuart Curry Papers, Archives of American Art, Smithsonian Institution, Washington, DC.
Mary Lee Papers, Schlesinger Library, Radcliffe Institute for Advanced Study, Harvard University.
Records of the American Battle Monuments Commission, National Archives, College Park, Maryland.
Thomas North Collection, Eisenhower Library, Abilene, Kansas.
William L. Davis Collection, National World War I Museum, Kansas City, Missouri.
William R. Gruber Papers, Eisenhower Library, Abilene, Kansas.
World War I Kansas Soldiers Collection, Library and Archives Division, Kansas Historical Society, Topeka, Kansas.
World War I Photo Album of Clyde James, AEF, Author's Collection.
World War I Photo Album of Ray Wentworth, AEF, Author's Collection.
World War I Scrapbook of Thomas Fletcher, AEF, Department of Special Collections, University of Colorado Libraries.

Published Sources

Abbott, Ernest Hamlin. "Simplicity, Honesty, Honor: Editorial Correspondence from Washington." *Outlook* 126 (November 23, 1921): 462–65.
Adams, Henry. "Space, Weather, Myth, and Abstraction in the Art of John Steuart Curry." Junker, *John Steuart Curry*. 111–32.
Adjutant General of Kansas. *Kansas Casualties in the World War, 1917–1919.* Topeka: Kansas State Printing Plant, 1921.

———. *Supplement: Kansas Casualties in the World War, 1917–1919.* Topeka: Kansas State Printing Plant, 1921.

Ambrose, Stephen E. *Eisenhower. Vol. 1. Soldier, General of the Army, President Elect, 1890–1952.* New York: Simon and Schuster, 1983.

American Battle Monuments Commission. *American Armies and Battlefields in Europe.* Washington, DC: U.S. Government Printing Office, 1938.

———. *A Guide to the American Battle Fields in Europe.* Washington, DC: U.S. Government Printing Office, 1927.

"The American Legion." *Crisis* 19, no. 2 (1919): 66–67, 87.

Anderson, Alan. "E. M. Viquesney: Portrait of *Doughboy*'s Sculptor." *Save Outdoor Sculpture! Update* 5, no. 1 (1994): 4.

Anderson, Maxwell, and Laurence Stallings. *What Price Glory. Three American Plays.* New York: Harcourt, Brace, 1926.

Arms, Dorothy Noyes. *Kerr Eby, A.N.A. American Etchers.* Vol. 8. London: Crafton Collection, P. and D. Colnaghi, 1930.

Ayres, Leonard P. *The War with Germany: A Statistical Summary.* Washington, DC: U.S. Government Printing Office, 1919.

Baird, Robert. "*Hell's Angels* above *The Western Front.*" Rollins and O'Connor, *Hollywood's World War I.* 79–99.

Baker, Horace L. *Argonne Days in World War I.* Ed. Robert H. Ferrell. Columbia: University of Missouri Press, 2007.

Baker, Newton D. "Why We Went to War." *American Legion Monthly* 2, no. 4 (1927): 14–15, 62–64.

Baker, Roscoe. *The American Legion and Foreign Policy.* New York: Bookman Associates, 1954.

Barton, Bruce. "Unknown." Sanford and Schauffler, *Armistice Day.* 230–33.

"Bear Drive Hits Souvenir Market." *Stars and Stripes.* March 14, 1919, 7.

Beidler, Philip D. Introduction to *Company K* by William March. Tuscaloosa: University of Alabama Press, 1989.

Bellamy, Edward. *Looking Backward: 2000–1887.* 1887. Ed. Cecelia Tishi. New York: Penguin, 1982.

Berry, Henry. *Make the Kaiser Dance: Living Memories of a Forgotten War.* Garden City, NY: Doubleday, 1978.

Birdwell, Michael E. "'After They've Seen Paree': The AEF in Film and Music." Snell, *Unknown Soldiers.* 238–63.

Blair, William A. *Cities of the Dead: Contesting the Memory of the Civil War in the South, 1865–1914.* Chapel Hill: University of North Carolina Press, 2004.

Blight, David W. *Race and Reunion: The Civil War in American Memory.* Cambridge, MA: Belknap Press, 2002.

Bodnar, John. *Remaking America: Public Memory, Commemoration, and Patriotism in the Twentieth Century.* Princeton, NJ: Princeton University Press, 1992.

Boyd, Thomas. "Johnny the Hard." *American Legion Monthly* 2, no. 3 (1927): 34–37, 87–88.

———. *Points of Honor.* New York: Charles Scribner's Sons, 1925.

———. *Through the Wheat.* New York: Charles Scribner's Sons, 1923.

Browne, Charles H., and J. W. McManigal. *Our Part in the Great War: What the Horton Community Did.* Horton, KS: Headlight-Commercial, 1919.

Bruce, Brian. *Thomas Boyd: Lost Author of the "Lost Generation."* Akron, OH: University of Akron Press, 2006.

Burns, Vincent Godfrey, ed. *The Red Harvest: A Cry for Peace.* 1930. Miami: Granger Books, 1976.

"Bursts and Duds." *American Legion Weekly* 1, no. 11 (1919): 24.

Byerly, Carol R. *Fever of War: The Influenza Epidemic in the U.S. Army during World War I.* New York: New York University Press, 2005.

Capper, Arthur. "Practical Benefits of Compensation." *American Legion Weekly* 4, no. 5 (1922): 5, 18–19.

Carlin, George. *Brain Droppings* (New York: Comedy Concepts, 1997).

Catalogue of Official A.E.F. Photographs Taken by the Signal Corps, U.S.A. Washington, DC: U.S. Government Printing Office, 1919.

Cather, Willa. *My Ántonia.* Boston: Houghton-Mifflin, 1918.

———. *One of Ours.* New York: Knopf, 1922.

———. Preface to *Not Under Forty.* 1936. *Willa Cather: Stories, Poems, and Other Writings.* With notes by Sharon O'Brien. New York: Library of America, 1992. 812.

———. *The Professor's House.* New York: Knopf, 1925.

Coffman, Edward M. *The War to End All Wars: The American Military Experience in World War I.* New York: Oxford University Press, 1968.

Cohen, Milton. "When Did Hemingway Turn against World War I?" Paper presented at War + Ink: The 13th International Hemingway Society Conference. Kansas City, MO. June 9–15, 2008.

Company F, Three Hundred and First Engineers. Cologne: J. P. Bachem, 1919.

Congressional Record, Appendix and Index to Parts 1 to 9 of the Proceedings and Debates of the First Session of the Sixty-seventh Congress of the United States, Vol. 61, Part 9. Washington, DC: U.S. Government Printing Office, 1921.

Coombs, Rose E. B. *Before Endeavours Fade: A Guide to the Battlefields of the First World War.* London: After the Battle, 1990.

Cooperman, Stanley. *World War I and the American Novel.* Baltimore: Johns Hopkins University Press, 1967.

Cornebise, Alfred Emile. *Art from the Trenches: America's Uniformed Artists in World War I.* College Station: Texas A&M Press, 1991.

Craige, John H. "Would We Get In Again?" *American Legion Monthly* 22, no. 4 (1937): 18–19, 58–61.

Crane, Stephen. *The Red Badge of Courage.* 1895. The Red Badge of Courage *and Other Stories.* Ed. Gary Scharnhorst. New York: Penguin, 2005.

Crawford, John W. "A Malicious Panorama." *Nation* 117 (July 18, 1923): 66.

Culp, Dorothy. *The American Legion: A Study in Pressure Politics.* Chicago: University of Chicago Libraries, 1942.

Cummings, E. E. *The Enormous Room.* New York: Boni and Liveright, 1922.

Darnton, Byron. "The Hard-Boiled Sergeant's and the Lady Idealist's War." Review of *It's a Great War!* by Mary Lee and *God Have Mercy on Us!* by William Scanlon. *New York Evening Post.* November 2, 1929, 11.

Dennis, James M. *Renegade Regionalists: The Modern Independence of Grant Wood, Thomas Hart Benton, and John Steuart Curry.* Madison: University of Wisconsin Press, 1998.

Dickson, Paul, and Thomas B. Allen. *The Bonus Army: An American Epic.* New York: Walker, 2004.

Dokoupil, Tony. "The War We Forgot." *Newsweek.* February 18, 2008. http://www.newsweek.com/id/109681. Accessed August 27, 2009.

Donovan, Derek. *Lest the Ages Forget: Kansas City's Liberty Memorial.* Kansas City, MO: Kansas City Star, 2001.

Dos Passos, John. *1919.* New York: Harcourt, Brace, 1932.

———. *Three Soldiers.* New York: Doran, 1921.

Du Bois, W. E. B. "An Essay toward a History of the Black Man in the Great War." *Crisis* 18, no. 2 (1919): 63–87.

———. "Foreword." *Crisis* 20, no. 5 (1920): 213.

Eby, Kerr. *War.* New Haven, CT: Yale University Press, 1936.

Edkins, Jenny. *Trauma and the Memory of Politics.* Cambridge: Cambridge University Press, 2003.

Edwards, Dan. "Do War Stories Grow?" *American Legion Monthly* 17, no. 4 (1934): 4, 55–57.

———. "The Hero Stuff." *American Legion Monthly* 5, no. 5 (1928): 6, 62–65.

The 88th Division in the World War of 1914–1918. New York: Wynkoop Hallenbeck Crawford, 1919.

Eisenhower, Dwight D. *At Ease: Stories I Tell to Friends.* Garden City, NY: Doubleday, 1967.

———. "A Tank Discussion," *Infantry Journal* (November 1920): 453–58.

Eisenhower, John S. D. *Yanks: The Epic Story of the American Army in World War I.* New York: Free Press, 2001.

Eldredge, Charles C. *John Steuart Curry's* Hoover and the Flood*: Painting Modern History.* Chapel Hill: University of North Carolina Press, 2007.

Ellison, Ralph. *The Invisible Man.* 1952. New York: Vintage, 1995.

"The Fallen Have Not Been Forgotten." *Jayhawkerinfrance* 1, no. 2 (1919): 1.

Faulkner, William. *Sartoris.* New York: Harcourt, Brace, 1929.

———. *Soldiers' Pay.* New York: Boni and Liveright, 1926.

Ferguson, Niall. *The Pity of War: Explaining World War I.* New York: Basic Books, 1999.

Fernandez-Duque, Silvina. "First Division Monument." National Park Service. U.S. Department of the Interior. http://www.nps.gov/whho/historyculture/first-division-monument.htm#CP_JUMP_107374. Accessed August 27, 2009.

Ferrell, Robert H. *America's Deadliest Battle: Meuse-Argonne, 1918.* Lawrence: University Press of Kansas, 2007.

———. *Collapse at Meuse-Argonne: The Failure of the Missouri-Kansas Division.* Columbia: University of Missouri Press, 2004.

———. *Five Days in October: The Lost Battalion of World War I.* Columbia: University of Missouri Press, 2005.

Fitzgerald, F. Scott. Review of *Through the Wheat* by Thomas Boyd. Ed. Matthew J. Bruccoli. Carbondale: Southern Illinois University Press, 1978. 273–77.

———. *Tender Is the Night.* New York: Scribner's, 1934.
"For the Best New War Novel, $25,000." *American Legion Monthly* (April 1928): 20–21.
Fosdick, Harry Emerson. "The Unknown Soldier." 1933. *Riverside Sermons.* New York: Harper and Brothers, 1958. 343–52.
"Frequently Asked Questions." Society of the Honor Guard, Tomb of the Unknown Soldier. http://www.tombguard.org/FAQ.html. Accessed September 2, 2009.
Fussell, Paul. *The Boys' Crusade: The American Infantryman in Northwestern Europe, 1944–1945.* New York: Modern Library, 2003.
———. *Doing Battle: The Making of a Skeptic.* Boston: Little, Brown, 1996.
———. *The Great War and Modern Memory.* New York: Oxford University Press, 1975.
———. *Wartime: Understanding and Behavior in the Second World War.* New York: Oxford University Press, 1989.
Gaff, Alan D. *Blood in the Argonne: The "Lost Battalion" of World War I.* Norman: University of Oklahoma Press, 2005.
Gandal, Keith. *The Gun and the Pen: Hemingway, Fitzgerald, Faulkner, and the Fiction of Mobilization.* New York: Oxford University Press, 2008.
Gellermann, William. *The American Legion as Educator.* New York: Columbia University Teachers College, 1938.
Gellhorn, Martha. "The Paths of Glory." *New Republic* 61, no. 306 (1930): 306–07.
"General Bullard Reviews Regiment of Jayhawkers." *Jayhawkerinfrance* 1, no. 1 (January 29, 1919): 1.
"General Pershing Praises Review." *Jayhawkerinfrance* 1, no. 6 (March 5, 1919): 1, 4.
"Gen. Wright Decorates Regimental Colors." *Jayhawkerinfrance* 1, no. 8 (April 2, 1919): 1, 4.
Gerstbauer, Loramy, and Don Myers. "Peace Profile: Kerr Eby." *Peace Review: A Journal of Social Justice* 18, no. 2 (2006): 289–98.
Giardina, Bernadette Passi. *Kerr Eby: The Complete Prints.* Bronxville, NY: M. Hausberg, 1997.
"Going Back." *Skirmisher* (May 1919): 21.
Goldsmith, Earl D. "Earl D. Goldsmith's *Spirit of the American Doughboy* Database." http://members.tripod.com/doughboy_lamp/earlspages/id57.html. Accessed September 23, 2007.
Goldstein, Erik, and John H. Maurer, eds. *The Washington Conference, 1921–22: Naval Rivalry, East Asian Stability, and the Road to Pearl Harbor.* Newbury Park, Eng.: Frank Cass, 1994.
Gracyk, Tim. "James Reese Europe with his 369th U.S. Infantry 'Hellfighters' Band." Liner Notes. *Lieut. Jim Europe's 369th U.S. Infantry "Hell Fighters" Band: The Complete Recordings.* Inside Sounds/Memphis Archives, 1996.
Graham, John. *The Gold Star Mother Pilgrimages of the 1930s.* Jefferson, NC: McFarland, 2005.
———. "Quentin Roosevelt and the Gold Star Mother Pilgrimages." *Over the Front* 19, no. 3 (2004): 222–28.
Gray, Justin, and Victor H. Bernstein. *The Inside Story of the Legion.* 1948. New York: Bonie and Gaer, 1954.

"The Great 'Bonus Raid' on the United States Treasury." Cartoon. *American Legion Weekly* 4, no. 8 (1922): 11.

Griffith, Paddy. *Battle Tactics of the Western Front: The British Army's Art of Attack, 1916–1918.* New Haven, CT: Yale University Press, 1994.

Grotelueschen, Mark Ethan. *The AEF Way of War: The American Army and Combat in World War I.* New York: Cambridge University Press, 2006.

"The guy that wears his service stripes before he earns them." Cartoon. *Skirmisher* (May 1919): 18.

Hanson, Joseph Mills. "The 4th Comes to the Rosebud." *American Legion Monthly* 5, no. 1 (1928): 12–15, 60–63.

Hanson, Neil. *Unknown Soldiers: The Story of the Missing of the First World War.* New York: Knopf, 2006.

Harris, Bill. *The Hellfighters of Harlem: African-American Soldiers Who Fought for the Right to Fight for Their Country.* New York: Carroll and Graf, 2002.

Hartigan, Lynda Roscoe. "Landscapes, Portraits, and Still Lifes." Stein, *I Tell My Heart.* 82–123.

Harting, Joanna W. "The Girl Who Took a Soldier's Job." *American Legion Weekly* 1, no. 14 (1919): 18–19, 28.

Hass, Kristin Ann. *Carried to the Wall: American Memory and the Vietnam Veterans Memorial.* Berkeley: University of California Press, 1998.

Haytock, Jennifer. *At Home, At War: Domesticity and World War I in American Literature.* Columbus: Ohio State University Press, 2003.

"Hear Captain 'Eddie' Rickenbacker's personal story." Advertisement for the *Chevrolet Chronicles. American Legion Monthly* 10, no. 1 (1931): 4.

"He carried a message through the enemy lines." Advertisement for the *Chevrolet Chronicles. American Legion Monthly* 10, no. 3 (1931): 35.

"He Didn't Have to . . . but He Went Over the Top." *American Legion Monthly* 21, no. 3 (1936): 45.

Helfant, Art. Untitled Cartoon. *American Legion Weekly* 4, no. 9 (1922): 14.

Hemingway, Ernest. *A Farewell to Arms.* New York: Collier, 1929.

———. "Soldier's Home." *In Our Time.* 1925. New York: Simon and Schuster, 1996.

———. *The Sun Also Rises.* 1926. New York: Simon and Schuster, 1996.

Henney, Fred. *Reno's Response: History of Reno County's War Work Activities during the World War, 1917–1918.* Hutchison, KS: n.p., 1920.

Hill, Drew. "Eggs." *American Legion Monthly* 2, no. 4 (1927): 22–25, 64–69.

Holmes, John Haynes. "The Unknown Soldier Speaks." 1928. *A Summons Unto Men: An Anthology of the Writings of John Haynes Holmes.* Carl Hermann Voss, ed. New York: Simon and Schuster, 1971. 126–42.

Holt, Daniel D., and James W. Leyerzapf, eds. *Eisenhower: The Prewar Diaries and Selected Papers, 1905–1941.* Baltimore: Johns Hopkins University Press, 1998.

Holt, Tonie, and Valmai Holt. *Major and Mrs. Holt's Concise Illustrated Battlefield Guide: The Western Front–South.* London: Pen and Sword, 2006.

Honor Roll of Livingston County, Missouri. Chillicothe, MO: Chillicothe Constitution, 1919.

Horne, Charles, ed. *Source Records of the Great War.* 1923. Indianapolis: American Legion, 1931.

Horwitz, Tony. *Confederates in the Attic: Dispatches from the Unfinished Civil War.* New York: Random House, 1998.

Howe, M. A. De Wolfe. "The Known Soldier." Burns, *Red Harvest.* 350–51.

Hughes, Rupert. "Memorial Temple Under Way in Washington." *New York Times.* February 23, 1919, 10, 14.

"Hun Helmets Boost Work." *Stars and Stripes.* February 28, 1919, 3.

Hynes, Samuel. "Personal Narratives and Commemoration." *War and Remembrance in the Twentieth Century.* Jay Winter and Emmanuel Sivan, eds. Cambridge: Cambridge University Press, 1999.

———. *A War Imagined: The First World War and English Culture.* London: Bodley Head, 1990.

"Impressive Military Funeral Conducted by Legion Boys in Honor of the Late Lieut. G. P. Cather Jr." *Bladen Examiner.* May 6, 1921, 1.

Isenberg, Michael T. "The Great War Viewed from the Twenties: *The Big Parade.*" Rollins and O'Connor, *Hollywood's World War I.* 39–58.

James, Marquis. "Who Got the Money?: II. The Airplane Production Mess." *American Legion Weekly* 4, no. 37 (1922): 5–8, 28–30.

Johnson, James Weldon. "Saint Peter Relates an Incident of the Resurrection Day." *Saint Peter Relates an Incident: Selected Poems by James Weldon Johnson.* New York: Penguin, 1993.

Johnson, Thomas M. *Without Censor: New Light on Our Greatest World War Battles.* Indianapolis: Bobbs-Merrill, 1928.

Jones, James. *WWII.* New York: Grosset and Dunlop, 1975.

Junker, Patricia, ed. *John Steuart Curry: Inventing the Middle West.* New York: Hudson Hills, 1998.

Karolevitz, Robert F. *Harvey Dunn War Works: Art from the American Expeditionary Forces.* Exhibit Brochure. South Dakota Art Museum. Brookings, SD. November 8, 2001–March 25, 2002.

———. *Where Your Heart Is: The Story of Harvey Dunn, Artist.* Aberdeen, ND: North Plains Press, 1970.

Keene, Jennifer D. *Doughboys, the Great War, and the Remaking of America.* Baltimore: Johns Hopkins University Press, 2001.

———. "The Memory of the Great War in the African American Community." Snell, *Unknown Soldiers.*

———. *World War I.* Westport, CT: Greenwood Press, 2006.

Kemp, Harry. "The Unknown." Sanford and Schauffler, *Armistice Day.* 240.

Kenamore, Claire. *From Vauquois Hill to Exermont: A History of the Thirty-fifth Division of the United States Army.* St. Louis, MO: Guard Publishing, 1919.

———. *The Story of the 139th Infantry.* St. Louis, MO: Guard Publishing, 1920.

Kendall, M. Sue. "Alien Corn: An Artist on the Middle Border." Junker, *John Steuart Curry.* 165–82.

———. *Rethinking Regionalism: John Steuart Curry and the Kansas Mural Controversy.* Washington, DC: Smithsonian Institution Press, 1986.

Kennedy, David M. *Over Here: The First World War and American Society.* New York: Oxford University Press, 1980.

Kopel, Les. "Grandma Quater's *Spirit of the American Doughboy* Lamp." http://doughboy_lamp.tripod.com/index.html. Accessed September 23, 2007.

Korda, Michael. *Ike: An American Hero.* New York: Harper Collins, 2007.

Krass, Peter. *Portrait of War: The U.S. Army's First Combat Artists and the Doughboys' Experience in WWI.* Hoboken, NJ: Wiley, 2007.

Lang, Gladys Engel, and Kurt Lang. "Recognition and Renown: The Survival of Artistic Reputation." *American Journal of Sociology* 94, no. 1 (1988): 79–109.

Laplander, Robert. *Finding the Lost Battalion: Beyond the Rumors, Myths, and Legends of America's Famous WWI Epic.* New York: Lulu, 2007.

Laughlin, E. O. "The Unknown." Sanford and Schauffler, *Armistice Day.* 237–38.

Lee, Jay M. *The Artilleryman: The Experiences and Impressions of an American Artillery Regiment in the World War.* Kansas City, MO: Spencer Printing, 1920.

"The Legion's Care of the Home-Coming Dead." *American Legion Weekly* 4, no. 21 (May 26, 1922): 24–25.

Lengel, Edward. *To Conquer Hell: The Meuse-Argonne, 1918.* New York: Henry Holt, 2008.

Levinson, Sanford. *Written in Stone: Public Monuments in Changing Societies.* Durham, NC: Duke University Press, 1998.

Levitch, Mark. *Panthéon de la Guerre: Reconfiguring a Panorama of the Great War.* Columbia: University of Missouri Press, 2006.

Lewis, Sinclair. *Main Street.* New York: Harcourt, Brace, 1920.

Linenthal, Edward Tabor. *Sacred Ground: Americans and Their Battlefields.* Urbana: University of Illinois Press, 1993.

Linenthal, Edward Tabor, and Tom Engelhardt. *History Wars: The* Enola Gay *and Other Battles for the American Past.* New York: Holt, 1996.

Little, Arthur W. *From Harlem to the Rhine: The Story of New York's Colored Volunteers.* New York: Covici Friede, 1936.

Littlewood, Thomas B. *Soldiers Back Home: The American Legion in Illinois, 1919–1939.* Carbondale: Southern Illinois University Press, 2004.

Locke, Alain, ed. *The Negro in Art: A Pictorial Record of the Negro Artist and of the Negro Theme in Art.* Washington, D.C.: Associates in Negro Folk Education, 1940.

Longworth, Philip. *The Unending Vigil: A History of the Commonwealth War Graves Commission, 1917–1967.* London: Constable, 1967.

Lyon, Peter. *Eisenhower: Portrait of the Hero.* Boston: Little, Brown, 1974.

Mack, Charles E. *Two Black Crows in the A.E.F.* Indianapolis: Bobbs-Merrill, 1928.

MacLeish, Archibald, and Malcolm Cowley. "The Dead of the Next War." *New Republic* 76 (October 4, 1933): 214–16.

———. "*The First World War.* Review and Rebuttle." *New Republic* 76 (September 20, 1933): 159–61.

Manchester, William. *American Caesar: Douglas MacArthur, 1880–1964.* Boston: Little, Brown, 1978.

———. *Goodbye, Darkness: A Memoir of the Pacific War.* Boston: Little, Brown, 1980.

Manning, Frederic. *The Middle Parts of Fortune.* 1929. New York: St. Martin's, 1977.

March, William. *Company K.* New York: Harrison Smith and Robert Haas, 1933.

Mastriano, Douglas. "News from France." *Camaraderie: The Journal of the Western Front Association United States Branch* (August 2008): 9.

Mayo, James M. *War Memorials as Political Landscape: The American Experience and Beyond.* New York: Praeger, 1988.

McCullough, David. *Truman.* New York: Simon and Schuster, 1992.

McLeod, Jack Myron. "A Thematic Analysis of *The American Legion Magazine,* 1919–1951." MA Thesis. University of Wisconsin, 1953.

McNutt, William Slaven. "A Pass to Paris." *American Legion Monthly* 2, no. 4 (1927): 9–13, 86–88.

Meigs, Mark. *Optimism at Armageddon: Voices of American Participants in the First World War.* New York: New York University Press, 1997.

"The Message Center." *American Legion Monthly* (September 1929): 8.

Meyer, Susan. "On the Front and at Home: Wharton, Cather, the Jews, and the First World War." *Cather Studies 6: History, Memory, and War.* Steven Trout, ed. Lincoln: University of Nebraska Press, 2006. 205–27.

Miller, Kelly. *Kelly Miller's History of the World War for Human Rights.* Washington, DC: Jenkins and Keller, 1919.

Miller, Merle. *Ike the Soldier: As They Knew Him.* New York: Putnam's, 1987.

Moley, Raymond, Jr. *The American Legion Story.* New York: Duell, Sloan, and Pearce, 1966.

Moore, William E. "Painted at the Front." *American Legion Weekly* 1, no. 10 (September 5, 1919): 17–21.

Moore, William E., and James C. Russell. *U.S. Official Pictures of the World War.* Washington, DC: Pictorial Bureau, 1920.

Morrison, Toni. *Sula.* 1973. New York: Plume, 2002.

Mosse, George L. *Fallen Soldiers: Reshaping the Memory of the World Wars.* New York: Oxford University Press, 1990.

Nason, Leonard H. *Chevrons.* New York: Doran, 1926.

——. "Lafayette, That Was Us!" *American Legion Monthly* 22, no. 4 (April 1937): 6–9, 44–46.

——. *The Man in the White Slicker.* Garden City, NY: Doubleday, Doran, 1929.

——. *Sergeant Eadie.* Garden City, NY: Doubleday, Doran, 1928.

Neff, John R. *Honoring the Civil War Dead: Commemoration and the Problem of Reconciliation.* Lawrence: University Press of Kansas, 2005.

"Never Again! But Wasn't It Great, Eh!" Cartoon. *Outlook* 129 (November 23, 1921): 457.

Nichols, Nick. *Memoirs of a Vet.* Chicago: Greenlee Co., 1939.

"1945 A.D." Cartoon. *Sapper* (April 1919): 5.

The Ninth U.S. Infantry in the World War. Neuwied am Rhein, Germany: Louis Heusersche, 1919.

Noyes, Alfred. "The Victory Ball." *Collected Poems.* Philadelphia: Lippincott, 1939.

"The Open Door." Cartoon. *American Legion Weekly* 2, no. 32 (1920): 6.

"Our Record." *Skirmisher* (May 1919): 8.

"Paid Honor to Our Soldier Dead." *Winchester Star.* June 10, 1921, 3.

Painton, Frederick C. "Why They Want to Go to France." *American Legion Monthly* 2, no. 4 (1927): 40–42, 95.

Palmer, Frederick. "Known But to God." *American Legion Monthly* 22, no. 4 (1937): 10–11, 53–55.

Pencak, William. *For God and Country: The American Legion, 1919–1941.* Boston: Northeastern University Press, 1989.

"Percivle Socrates Alonzo." Cartoon. *Skirmisher* (May 1919): 16.

Pershing, John J. *My Experiences in the World War.* New York: Frederick A. Stokes, 1931.

———. "Our Plans for the National Defense." *American Legion Weekly* 4, no. 19 (1922): 5, 28–29.

Pickens, Wiley M. "Be It Ever So Humble." *American Legion Monthly* 22, no. 6 (1937): 18–19, 55–56.

Piehler, G. Kurt. *Remembering War the American Way.* Washington, DC: Smithsonian Institution Press, 1995.

Powell, Richard J. "Biblical and Spiritual Motifs." Stein, *I Tell My Heart.* 124–35.

Quinn, Patrick J. *The Conning of America: The Great War and American Popular Literature.* Atlanta: Rodopi, 2001.

Ragner, Bernhard. "D.S.C." *American Legion Monthly* 22, no. 4 (1937): 12–13, 50–53.

Ralphson, George H. *Over There with Pershing's Heroes at Cantigny.* Chicago: Donohue, 1919.

Remarque, Erich Maria. *All Quiet on the Western Front.* Boston: Little, Brown, 1929.

Renehan, Edward J., Jr. *The Lion's Pride: Theodore Roosevelt and His Family in Peace and War.* New York: Oxford University Press, 1998.

"Results of the $25,000 War Novel Contest," *American Legion Monthly* (August 1929): 5, 70–72.

Review of *It's a Great War!* by Mary Lee. *Times Literary Supplement.* February 13, 1930, 124.

Review of *Three Soldiers* by John Dos Passos. *Nation* 113 (October 26, 1921): 480–81.

"The Rhine 'Horror.'" *American Legion Weekly* 3, no. 13 (1921): 16.

Rhinow, Arthur B., "The Unknown Soldier." Burns, *Red Harvest.* 337.

Richmond, Robert W. "The Victory Highway: Transcontinental Memorial." *Shawnee County Historical Society Bulletin* 69 (November 1992): 204–10.

Rickenbacker, Edward V. *Fighting the Flying Circus.* 1919. Philadelphia: Lippincott, 1947.

Rollins, Peter C., and John E. O'Connor, eds. *Hollywood's World War I: Motion Picture Images.* Bowling Green, OH: Bowling Green State University Popular Press, 1997.

Roosevelt, Kermit, ed. *Quentin Roosevelt: A Sketch with Letters.* New York: Charles Scribner's Sons, 1922.

Roosevelt, Theodore, Jr. *Average Americans, by Theodore Roosevelt, Lieutenant-Colonel, U.S.A.* New York: G. P. Putnam's Sons, 1919.

Roper, W. L. "Market for War Experiences." *Writer's Monthly* 33, no. 4 (April 1929): 303–05.

Rose, Billy. "The Unknown Soldier." Aftermath. http://www.aftermathww1.co.uk/billrose.asp. Accessed August 27, 2009.

Roshwald, Aviel. *The Endurance of Nationalism: Ancient Roots and Modern Dilemmas.* Cambridge: Cambridge University Press, 2006.

Rubin, Richard. "Over There—and Gone Forever." *New York Times.* November 12, 2007, A25.

Rumer, Thomas A. *The American Legion: An Official History, 1919–1989.* New York: M. Evans, 1990.

Sandburg, Carl. "And So To-Day." *American Poetry 1922: A Miscellany.* Ed. Louis Untermeyer. New York: Harcourt, Brace, 1922. 41–48.

Sanford, A. P., and Robert Haven Schauffler, eds. *Armistice Day.* New York: Dodd, Mead, 1928.

Saperstein, Harold I. "Must There Be War?" 1936. *Witness from the Pulpit: Topical Sermons, 1933–1980.* Ed. Marc Saperstein. Lanham, MD: Lexington Books, 2000. 50–55.

Saunders, Vincent. "The Horizon." *Crisis* 17, no. 1 (1918): 32–37.

———. "The Horizon." *Crisis* 17, no. 2 (1918): 82–90.

Scarry, Elaine. *The Body in Pain: The Making and Unmaking of the World.* New York: Oxford University Press, 1985.

Schmeckebier, Laurence Eli. *John Steuart Curry's Pageant of America.* New York: American Artists Group, 1943.

Shafer, Chet. *The Second A.E.F.: The Pilgrimage of the Army of Remembrance.* New York: Doty, 1927.

Sherriff, R. C. *Journey's End: A Play in Three Acts.* New York: Brentano's, 1929.

Sledge, Michael. *Soldier Dead: How We Recover, Identify, Bury, and Honor Our Military Fallen.* New York: Columbia University Press, 2005.

Slosson, Preston William. *The Great Crusade and After, 1914–1928.* New York: Macmillan, 1931.

Slotkin, Richard. *Lost Battalions: The Great War and the Crisis of American Nationality.* New York: Henry Holt, 2005.

Smith, J. André. *In France with the American Expeditionary Forces.* New York: Arthur Halo, 1919.

Snell, Mark A. "'The Price Was Made and the Price Was Paid': Grandpa's Scar and Other Memories of the AEF." Snell, *Unknown Soldiers.* 3–27.

———. *Unknown Soldiers: The American Expeditionary Forces in Memory and Remembrance.* Mark A. Snell, ed. Kent, OH: Kent State University Press, 2008.

The Spirit of the First Division: Addresses Given by President Calvin Coolidge and Major General C. P. Summerall at the Unveiling of the First Division Memorial, Washington, D.C., October 4, 1924. N.p.: Privately printed, 1924.

Stallings, Laurence. *The Doughboys: The Story of the AEF, 1917–1918.* New York: Harper and Row, 1963.

———. *The First World War: A Photographic History.* New York: Simon and Schuster, 1933.

———. *Plumes.* 1924. Columbia: University of South Carolina Press, 2006.

Stein, Judith E. "An American Original." *I Tell My Heart: The Art of Horace Pippin.* Judith E. Stein, ed. Philadelphia: Pennsylvania Academy of the Fine Arts, 1993. 2–43.

Stevens, James. *Mattock*. New York: Alfred A. Knopf, 1927.

Stineback, Margaret. "The Unknown Soldier." Burns, *Red Harvest*, 339–40.

Stout, Janis. P. *Coming Out of War: Poetry, Grieving, and the Culture of the World Wars*. Tuscaloosa: University of Alabama Press, 2005.

Swann, Marjorie, and William M. Tsutsui. "John Steuart Curry: A Portrait of the Artist as a Kansan." In *John Brown to Bob Dole: Movers and Shakers in Kansas History*. Virgil W. Dean, ed. Lawrence: University Press of Kansas, 2006. 241–52.

"$10,000,000 War Memorial." *New York Times*. June 1, 1919, 4.

Thomason, John W., Jr. *Fix Bayonets!* New York: Charles Scribner's Sons, 1926.

Trapp, Homer F. "Synopsis of the History of Company B." *Company B, 3rd Kansas N. 6., 139th Infantry Memories of the Reunion, August 19–20, 1955*. N.p.: n.p., 1955.

Triplet, William S. *A Youth in the Meuse-Argonne: A Memoir, 1917–1918*. Ed. Robert H. Ferrell. Columbia: University of Missouri Press, 2000.

Troncone, Anthony. "Hamilton Fish Sr. and the Politics of American Nationalism, 1912–1945." PhD diss. Rutgers University. 1993.

Trout, Steven. "Forgotten Reminders: Kansas World War I Memorials." *Kansas History* 29, no. 3 (2006): 201–15.

———. *Memorial Fictions: Willa Cather and the First World War*. Lincoln: University of Nebraska Press, 2002.

———. "Thomas Boyd." *American Prose Writers*. 53–100.

———. "'Where Do We Go From Here?': Ernest Hemingway's 'Soldier's Home' and American Veterans of World War I." *Hemingway Review* 20, no. 1 (2000): 5–21.

———. "World War I in American Prose Works, Theater, and Cinema: A Chronology, 1919–1939." *American Prose Writers*. 397–401.

Trout, Steven, ed. *American Prose Writers of World War I: A Documentary Volume. Dictionary of Literary Biography*. Vol. 316. Detroit: Thomson-Gale, 2005.

Trumbo, Dalton. *Johnny Got His Gun*. Philadelphia: J. B. Lippincott, 1939.

"Unpublished Pictures of the War," Cartoon. *American Legion Weekly* 2, no. 47 (1920): 9.

Vandiver, Frank E. *Black Jack: The Life and Times of John J. Pershing*. Vol. 2. College Station: Texas A&M Press, 1977.

Wagner, Charles A. "The Unknown Soldier." Burns, *Red Harvest*. 344–47.

Waller, Willard. *The Veteran Comes Back*. New York: Dryden Press, 1944.

"War at Length." Review of *It's a Great War!* by Mary Lee. *New York Times Book Review*. November 17, 1929, 7.

Wecter, Dixon. *When Johnny Comes Marching Home*. Cambridge, MA: Riverside Press, 1944.

West, Philip, Steven I. Levine, and Jackie Hiltz. *America's Wars in Asia: A Cultural Approach to History and Memory*. Armonk, NY: M. E. Sharpe, 1998.

Whalan, Mark. "'The Only Real White Democracy' and the Language of Liberation: The Great War, France, and African American Culture in the 1920s." *Modern Fiction Studies* 51, no. 4 (2005): 775–800.

Wharton, Edith. *A Son at the Front*. New York: Charles Scribner's Sons, 1923.

White, Hayden. *Tropics of Discourse: Essays in Cultural Criticism.* Baltimore: Johns Hopkins University Press, 1978.

Wiley, Hugh. "Four Leaved Wildcat." *Saturday Evening Post.* March 8, 1919, 18–23.

———. "Private War." *American Legion Monthly* 20, no. 5 (1936): 8–11, 42, 44.

———. *The Prowler.* New York: Knopf, 1924.

———. "They Also Served." *American Legion Weekly* 4, no. 12 (1922): 7–8, 19.

———. *The Wildcat.* New York: Doran, 1920.

"William Louis Davis." *Farmers' Vindicator.* June 10, 1921, 1.

Wilson, Edmund. "The Anatomy of War." *Dial* 75 (July 1923): 93–95.

Wilson, Judith. "Scenes of War." Stein, *I Tell My Heart.* 56–69.

Wingate, Jennifer. "Over the Top: The Doughboy in World War I Memorials and Visual Culture." *American Art* 19, no. 2 (2005): 27–47.

Winter, Jay. *Remembering War: The Great War between Memory and History in the Twentieth Century.* New Haven, CT: Yale University Press, 2006.

———. *Sites of Memory, Sites of Mourning: The Great War in European Cultural History.* Cambridge: Cambridge University Press, 1995.

"Wm. L. Davis Dead." *Winchester Star.* September 27, 1918, 1.

Wood, Harlan. "Unforgotten." *American Legion Magazine* 24, no. 5 (May 1938): 5, 42–43.

Yockelson, Mitchell A. *Borrowed Soldiers: Americans under British Command, 1918.* Norman: University of Oklahoma Press, 2008.

Zieger, Robert H. *America's Great War: World War I and the American Experience.* Lanham, MD: Rowman and Littlefield, 2000.

Index